A I D S

A I D S

Readings on a Global Crisis

. . .

ELIZABETH RAUH BETHEL

LANDER UNIVERSITY

ALLYN AND BACON

BOSTON   LONDON   TORONTO   SYDNEY   TOKYO   SINGAPORE

Editors: Susan Rabinowitz and Karen Hanson
Production Supervisor: Jeff Chen
Production Managers: Alex Odulak and Kurt Scherwatzky
Text Designer: A Good Thing Inc.
Cover Designer: Hothouse Designs, Inc./Chris Migdol
Cover Photo: Richard Megna/Fundamental Photographs
Photo Researcher: Clare Maxwell

Copyright © 1995 by Allyn & Bacon
A Simon & Schuster Company
160 Gould Street
Needham Heights, Massachusetts 02194

Library of Congress Cataloging-in-Publication Data
Bethel, Elizabeth Rauh.
    AIDS : readings on a global crisis / Elizabeth Rauh Bethel.
      p. cm.
    Includes index.
    ISBN 0-02-309192-4
     1. AIDS (Disease)—Social aspects.   I. Title.
    RA644.A25B48 1995
    362.1'969792—dc20   94-13686
                                            CIP

PRINTED IN THE UNITED STATES OF AMERICA
10 9 8 7 6 5 4 3 2 1   99 98 97 96 95 94

Contents

Preface

Although I did not realize it at the time, this anthology began in the summer of 1991, when I challenged the students in my Social Problems and Social Change course to identify the five most pressing issues that Americans would confront in the 1990s. The students targeted a single issue—AIDS—and demanded that we focus the course on this health crisis. The selection of the readings in this anthology reflects the sociological imagination that my students and I have crafted as we read and discussed and distilled critical essays and monographic analyses, volumes of scholarly journals, pages of newspapers, and autobiographical accounts of life in the Age of AIDS. We could not have arrived at that understanding of how AIDS forms the intersection of personal troubles and public issues without incorporating many forms and styles of information. The diaries and memoirs of people who have lived and are living with HIV/AIDS have been as crucial as the social scientific research in constructing the perspective of this book. Journalists, who enjoy a latitude of interpretation not available to social and behavioral scientists, have raised early warnings and posed important questions that challenged and informed scientific inquiry. We have been enriched by blending these multiple perspectives.

At the same time, the very nature of the HIV/AIDS health crisis renders our understandings incomplete, always open to challenge and revision, for while in some respects HIV/AIDS certainly qualifies as an epidemic, it differs substantially from many previous infectious disease epidemics. Historical analogues have proved inadequate to predict the course of the HIV/AIDS epidemics or to illuminate the sociocultural forces that surround and envelop this health crisis. Likewise, public health strategies and policies forged to combat epidemics of other sexually transmitted diseases—and more broadly, epidemics of other infectious diseases such as influenza, tuberculosis, and polio—have been inadequate and inappropriate to the control of HIV transmission.

Taken as a whole, the selections in this anthology aim to reflect the conundrum of the HIV/AIDS health crisis: the diversity of meanings, perceptions and understandings about HIV/AIDS, and the ways in which that diversity has informed both human action and social policy. More specifically, the selections trace an evolving public awareness and understanding of the HIV/AIDS health crisis and examine the political and cultural forces that have fueled that evolution. I have also designed the book as a guide through the constantly expanding body of excellent HIV/AIDS scholarship, drawing whenever possible on multiple perspectives and points of view, with the hope that these readings will transcend the artificial boundaries of academic disciplines and foster a deeper understanding of the HIV/AIDS health crisis. While the book was designed in collaboration with undergraduate students and is certainly intended for that readership, it is also crafted for a more general audience. For those who seek deeper and more detailed information on particular aspects of the HIV/AIDS health crisis, I have included brief bibliographies of additional readings at the conclusion of each chapter.

At the personal level I was no stranger to AIDS in 1991. In the tenth year of the epidemic, a number of my friends had died, and others were, and are, HIV seropositive. Two of my middle-aged women friends were struggling with the newly disclosed seropositive status of their gay sons, and through them I was learning about and sharing the fear and sadness that HIV seropositivity brings to family systems. When the secretly bisexual father of a third friend died as the result of AIDS, I understood more fully the ways in which AIDS threatens public images and destroys family mythologies. One of my "safely" heterosexual sons had learned that he might have been infected with HIV through a casual sexual encounter. Through and with him I had experienced and then had come to understand the disabling psychological terror that is created by the mere threat of the HIV virus and the profound courage that is required to verify one's HIV status.

Despite these personal intersections with HIV/AIDS, I initially brought the issue, the epidemic, the HIV virus, and the diseases that are labeled Acquired Immune Deficiency Syndrome into my classroom with reluctance. I felt profoundly unprepared to offer a sociologically grounded course that addressed AIDS. How would my rural, Southern, predominantly heterosexual students respond to material that explicitly discussed homosexuality and AIDS? What did I have to offer in such a course other than personal concern and experience? Did such a course not more appropriately belong elsewhere in the university curriculum?

Despite these initial doubts and misgivings, my students have consistently demonstrated a capacity to transcend their own cultural backgrounds and personal experiences, and together we have confronted and probed the larger public issues that encompass the HIV/AIDS health crisis: the epidemiological dimension of a global health crisis; the metaphoric thinking that fuels public perceptions, understandings, and actions; the interconnections of homophobia and racism with this disease that have informed and distorted scientific thinking and public health policy; the very complex problems posed by educational programs aiming to change private and intimate behavior; the creation of an AIDS industry that is simultaneously driven by scientific, entrepreneurial, and survival motives.

Inevitably, these undertakings have led to an extension of both my labors and my intellectual debts. The section in the Social Problems and Social Change course became, with the support and encouragement of my friend, colleague, and Department Chair Professor Samrendra Singh, a course titled "The Sociology of AIDS." Singh provided the necessary support and administrative liaison for the development and implementation of a program of academic study, which in turn has been crucial to the development of this book. The students in the first Sociology of AIDS course designed, staffed, and implemented the first "AIDS Awareness Week" at Lander University. It is now an annual event that combines workshops, lectures, forums, panel presentations, and peer education about HIV/AIDS. Jeff May and Eleanor Teal, Lander's ad hoc AIDS angels, have provided the spiritual and the material support for this activity, and they have also provided me with the kind of personal support that makes hard work a pleasure. Over dinner one night in Washington, D.C., in March 1992, Richard Roughton peered through his smudged glasses and asked me what I was doing then that qualified as political action. The tone of his voice that night made me understand that there was more to do than work with the students on the AIDS Awareness Week. I began then to think about this anthology, understanding that effective AIDS education—confronting as it must the intersection of personal troubles and public issues—is a profoundly political act.

I have been fortunate to have been joined in this profoundly political act, this intellectual and pedagogical labor, by Susan Rabinowitz, whose editorial skills are a perfect blend of enthusiasm, criticism, and shrewd practical understanding of the textbook industry, and by the twenty-five undergraduate students who were enrolled in my fall 1993 Sociology of AIDS course. They have asked that they be mentioned by name, and I am happy to comply, for they willingly read this entire manuscript, maintaining good humor even in the roughest sections of the material, and they have provided me with the kind of critical feedback that is crucial in the preparation of an anthology intended for a collegiate readership. My thanks to all of you: Faith Barbour, Chris Bennett, Linda Beveridge, Tracy Boles, J. T. Brock, Ken Clarke, Marie Darnell, Leslie Doolittle, Paige Gillian, Darryl Hamilton, Rebecca Hardee, Jeff Harmon, Greta Johnson, Melissa Johnson, Mark Lewis, Alesia Lowe, David McAllister, James Parris, Tara Rice, Keith Rogers, Kerry Rushton, Kathy Slaton, Shannon Smith, Jeff Sorrow, and Robin Williams. Without the help and critical guidance of Rabinowitz and these students, and without the continuing support of Karen Hansen, my new editor, this anthology would not exist. Moreover, the suggestions, questions, and challenges that have been posed along the way by a series of anonymous reviewers have strengthened and sharpened the final book.

Projects such as this one have a technical dimension that is both invisible and critical to the final product. I have enjoyed and my work has benefitted from the skills of two good research assistants. Charlie Bethel, who has assisted me in previous work, and Ken Clarke, who is a relative newcomer to the chaos of my study, have checked endless sources, verified my notation system, located obscure and arcane references, and done so with dispatch. Lori McIntyre has provided invaluable assistance with the authors' and publishers' permissions to reprint material. The reference librarians at Lander, particularly Betty Williams and Dan Lee, have worked overtime to accommodate requests that have taxed the facilities and resources of an undergraduate library. I thank all of these people.

My friend Joan Scott reminded me at a crucial moment that books combine the product and the representation of the authors' hopes and dreams with an exercise of the intellect. I thank her for the reminder and for the solid friendship from which that reminder came. My friend and companion, Ann Crawley, has tolerated with extraordinary good humor all the vagaries of living in a house where a book is being produced. At various moments, the following people have been very important to the completion of this project: Judith Alexander, Linda Carson, Jeff Chen, Bet Coleman, Melvin Dixon, Patty Hill, Bettie Horne, Martha Jones, Tony Kahane, Linda Penland, Deborah Pickett, Carolyn Rhodes, Susan Shepherd, Meredith Uttley, Bette Waters, and John Michael Young. Each of them has made a special contribution to my work. Finally, I thank my good friend Amanda, who has been with me throughout, a constant source of wisdom and guidance.

Introduction

In 1981 the Centers for Disease Control, the government agency that monitors the nation's health and sicknesses, began to receive an unusually high number of physician and hospital reports of a rare type of pneumonia, *Pneumocystis carinii* pneumonia. (While most of us are exposed to the *Pneumocystis carinii* bacilli, our bodies' immune systems are able to fight the parasite off, and we do not become sick. Those who do are people whose immune systems have been suppressed—before the onset of the AIDS epidemics, typically people who had received organ transplants or intensive chemotherapy.) At the same time, the Centers for Disease Control was receiving an equally high number of reports of a rare type of cancer, Kaposi's sarcoma, a relatively rare and slow-growing skin cancer that—again, before AIDS—most often occurred among elderly men, usually of Mediterranean descent, who tended to die eventually of something else. In striking contrast to the prevailing known patterns of the two diseases, both *Pneumocystis carinii* pneumonia and Kaposi's sarcoma were reported in gay men between the ages of twenty-five and forty with no previous medical history of immune disorder or cancer. As the number of reported cases multiplied, the Centers for Disease Control initiated an epidemiological investigation that attempted to locate and identify the source of the illnesses and growing number of deaths that were resulting from those illnesses. Initially, the Centers for Disease Control focused on gay lifestyle "co-factors" to which the source of the epidemic might be traced, and, for want of a better label, the agency described the mysterious condition as Gay-Related Immune Disorder, or GRID. The syndrome was subsequently renamed Acquired Immune Deficiency Syndrome—AIDS—in response to accumulating reports of transfusion-related and pediatric cases in the United States and heterosexual transmission in sub-Saharan Africa. For more than two years case reports mounted and medical treatments failed while the culprit remained a mystery.

In 1984, a retrovirus was identified simultaneously by the French scientists at the Pasteur Institute, who labeled it LAV, and by the American scientists at the National Institutes of Health, who called it HTLV-III. It became known as HIV (human immunodeficiency virus) in 1986, and it is commonly believed to be the causal agent of the immune system breakdown and subsequent opportunistic infections and clinical conditions now called AIDS. At the biological level, after a relatively asymptomatic period of time that can range from a few months to as long as ten years (depending on how the virus was introduced into the body, the general health, and age of the infected person), HIV disables and then overwhelms the human body's natural immune system by attacking CD4+ T-lymphocyte, or T-helper cells. These crucial immune system regulators activate the body's biological defenses against disease. During this progressive destruction of the T-helper cells, the body becomes increasingly susceptible to serious opportunistic infections and cancers. AIDS is the clinically defined terminal stage of this progression.

Initial medical understandings of AIDS have been greatly modified and expanded, reflecting both a deepened biomedical knowledge about HIV disease and the contours of a global health crisis that is fueled by many hundreds of epidemics. In 1993 the Centers for Disease Control revised and expanded the surveillance case definition and divided AIDS into three clinical categories, based on a heightened understanding of the progressive nature of HIV infection and the diversity of clinical presentations of HIV disease. Despite the enormously expanded medical understanding of HIV infection and the progression of HIV disease, however, medical science alone cannot render an adequate understanding of HIV transmission or prevention of HIV transmission.

Throughout the text I have used the term *health crisis* inclusively to describe and to refer to the many and diverse HIV/AIDS epidemics around the globe, and I have used the term *HIV/AIDS* in the same inclusive fashion to refer to the disease in both its asymptomatic and symptomatic stages. HIV/AIDS follows a number of distinguishable transmission patterns, and the rate of transmission is varied. As a result, neither *epidemic* nor *pandemic* adequately describes the epidemiology of HIV/AIDS. A *health crisis* extends beyond the transitory nature of an epidemic, fueled by a disease that is chronic, persistent, resistant to treatment or cure, and costly in terms of human lives and social resources. As we have come to better understand the gradual and progressive nature of this disease, the distinction between HIV infection and AIDS has become increasingly artificial. I have chosen to combine the two, with the understanding that this is a slowly progressive, seemingly always fatal disease that begins at the moment of HIV infection.

HIV is transmitted through social networks and within the context of social relationships. As a result, the HIV/AIDS health crisis is utterly interwoven with the cultural, political, and economic fabrics of the human group, and the complexity of these interconnections is reflected in differentiated and shifting epidemiologies that describe the HIV/AIDS health crisis. This book is designed to examine the interconnections between infectious disease, the HIV/AIDS health crisis, and the sociocultural forces that have shaped perceptions and understandings of AIDS as well as public health and political responses to the HIV/AIDS health crisis.

Part I: The Ecology of HIV/AIDS describes the global contours of the health crisis and the cultural frameworks within which the physical illness has been perceived, understood, and acted upon. The HIV/AIDS health crisis has not proceeded in the typical pattern of an infectious disease epidemic, beginning at one population epicenter and radiating out from that epicenter. Instead, HIV/AIDS has had many epicenters, and the modes of HIV transmission that shape the epidemic profiles are linked directly to the details of social environments and cultural constructs: patterns of poverty, sexual practices and norms

governing private sexual behavior, the structure of the commercial sex industry, and injection drug use patterns and practices. The onset of the health crisis, gauged by AIDS cases reported to the World Health Organization Global
Programme on AIDS, has greatly varied, as have the primary modes of transmission; yet, there are discernible patterns of transmission within the health
crisis, and the sequence of their numbering traces the chronology as well as
the geography of the global HIV/AIDS health crisis. These patterns have provided the organizational framework for this book.

From the outset, in the United States, Western Europe, Australia, and New
Zealand, the vast majority of the reported AIDS cases have been gay men or
injection drug users. In these locations, commonly referred to as Pattern I epidemics, the prevalence of HIV infection in men remains considerably higher
than in women, although toward the end of the 1980s shifts in the ratio of
male-to-female HIV/AIDS cases reflect changes in the nature of the health crisis in these areas. Reported HIV/AIDS cases in Pattern I areas account for no
more than 15 percent of the global HIV/AIDS cases. At the same time, in part
because of their relatively early onset in the global health crisis—the early
1980s—and in part because they are located in the industrialized nations,
Pattern I epidemics have informed medical, scientific, and public health
responses to the global health crisis, and the global health crisis cannot be
fully understood without a close examination of the forces that shaped these
responses. Accordingly, **Part II: A Pattern I Epidemic** focuses on AIDS in the
United States during the early and mid-1980s.

Pattern II epidemics, in contrast to Pattern I epidemics, are marked by nearly equal male-to-female HIV prevalence rates. Pattern II epidemics were initially observed in sub-Saharan Africa and the Caribbean, although the epidemiological instability of the HIV/AIDS health crisis is reflected in the emergence of
a mixed transmission pattern, generally described as Pattern I/II, in geographical areas that had initially experienced HIV/AIDS as a Pattern I epidemic.
Typically, Pattern I/II epidemics are characterized by *increasing* HIV prevalence
rates among women, signaling a shift from homosexual to both homosexual
and heterosexual transmission vectors. **Part III: Pattern II and I/II Epidemics**
examines the sociocultural factors associated with these epidemic patterns by
focusing on AIDS in Africa, the quintessential Pattern II epidemic, where two-
thirds of the global HIV/AIDS cases are reported, as well as the transitional
Pattern I/II epidemics in Latin America, the United States, and Great Britain.

Part IV: Pattern III Epidemics and AIDS in the 1990s focuses on two inter-
related issues: the sociocultural profiles of Pattern III epidemics and the
HIV/AIDS dialogues of the 1990s. The profile of HIV/AIDS in Asian nations,
where case reports began in the late 1980s, mirrors patterns of the epidemic in
Eastern Europe, North Africa, and the Middle East. AIDS in Asia is regarded by
many as the "second wave" of the global health crisis. In these cases injection
drug use, blood transfusions, heterosexual and homosexual behavior all account
for significant numbers of reported AIDS cases. These Pattern III epidemics have

underscored the critical need to formulate public health policies, health care delivery systems, and medical research specifically tailored to the global health crisis. Dialogues concerning these issues are crucial to understanding the range of possible responses to the HIV/AIDS health crisis in the 1990s.

In the absence of effective medical therapies or an HIV vaccine, behavioral change remains today, as it was in 1981, the only protection against HIV transmission and the perpetuation of a global health crisis. **Part V: Designing Programs for Behavioral Change** examines the difficulties of promoting changes in private sexual behavior, changes that will not result from expanded knowledge and understanding alone. These changes can only be fostered through interventions designed with a sensitivity to cultural environments and with an empirical understanding of the populations who are at risk.

The glossary, which defines the medical terms and identifies the major players and organizations directly associated with the HIV/AIDS health crisis, can be found at the back of the book.

AIDS

The Ecology of AIDS

Perceptions of a Global Crisis

• • •

Understanding the ecology of HIV/AIDS must begin with an examination of the numbers of people around the world who are infected with the HIV virus, who are sick, or who have died as a result of AIDS. These numbers can be both confusing and overwhelming. The statistics used to describe HIV/AIDS are constantly changing, always subject to revision upward or downward. Nevertheless, there is an empirical dimension to the HIV/AIDS health crisis, and that dimension is most commonly expressed in numbers of people who are infected, sick, and dead. Prior to 1985, slightly more than 13,000 AIDS cases had been reported from nations around the globe to the World Health Organization. That year, the figure more than doubled, to 28,422 cases. Five years later, in 1990, the number of people with AIDS had increased thirteen-fold, to 390,206 reported cases worldwide. Between 1993 and 1995, an estimated 6.9 million women, men, and children around the world will become newly infected with the HIV virus, representing increases that range from a low of 28 percent in North America to a high of 95 percent in Northeast Asia.[1]

Figure 1 provides a global picture of *all* estimated HIV infections since the onset of the HIV/AIDS epidemics in the late 1970s, including those people who have died from the disease. These numbers of HIV infections are referred to as *incidence rates*. Figure 2 depicts the estimated numbers of people *living* with HIV in late 1993, the most recent statistics available when this book went to press. These are referred to as *prevalence rates*. The differences between incidence and prevalence rates account for the estimated number of deaths in a region directly related to HIV/AIDS and are also a general indicator of the

---

[1]Jonathan Mann, Daniel J. M. Tarantola, and Thomas W. Neeter, editors, *AIDS in the World* (Cambridge: Harvard University Press, 1991):101–105. *AIDS in the World* is an annually up-dated global summary of the HIV/AIDS pandemic and is an invaluable resource for monitoring and assessing the shape of the epidemics as well as policy and program responses to them.

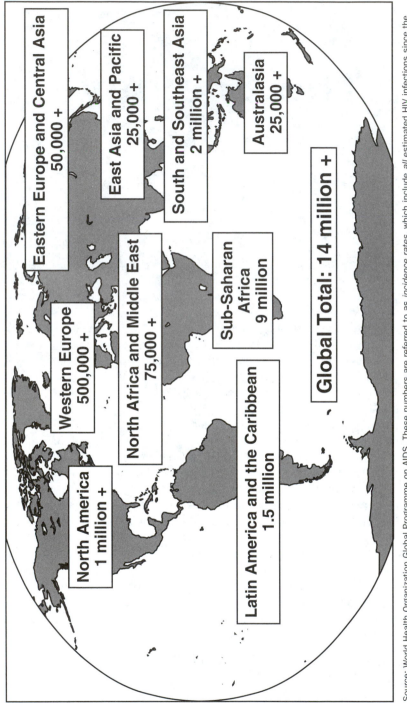

Source: World Health Organization Global Programme on AIDS. These numbers are referred to as *incidence rates*, which include *all* estimated HIV infections since the late 1970s, including those who have died.

Figure 1   Estimated Distribution of Cumulative Adult HIV Infections, Late 1993

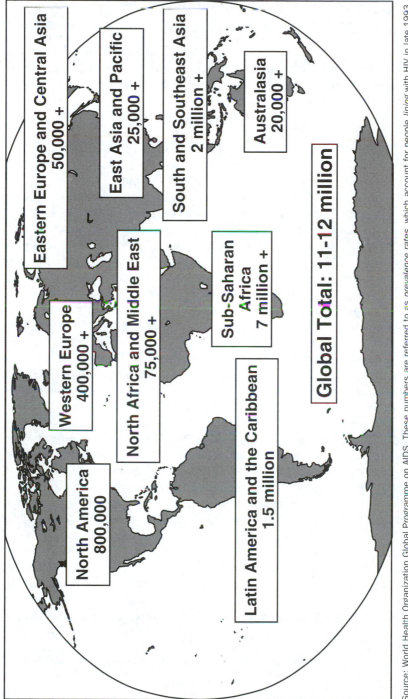

Eastern Europe and Central Asia
50,000 +

East Asia and Pacific
25,000 +

South and Southeast Asia
2 million +

Australasia
20,000 +

Western Europe
400,000 +

North Africa and Middle East
75,000 +

Sub-Saharan Africa
7 million +

North America
800,000

Latin America and the Caribbean
1.5 million

Global Total: 11-12 million

Source: World Health Organization Global Programme on AIDS. These numbers are referred to as *prevalence rates*, which account for people *living* with HIV in late 1993.

Figure 2   Estimated Distribution of HIV Prevalence in Adults, Late 1993.

progress of HIV/AIDS epidemic in specific regions. For example, in North America more than one million adults have been infected with HIV since the late 1970s, but only half that number—500,000 adults—are currently living with HIV/AIDS. Similarly, in sub-Saharan Africa a total of nine million adults have been infected with HIV, but there are only seven million adults in the region currently living with HIV/AIDS. Many people have died in the North American and sub-Saharan African epidemics. In contrast, in Latin America, the Caribbean, and South and Southeast Asia, there is little difference between cumulative adult HIV incidence and current adult HIV prevalence estimates because these are "young" epidemics. Many people are living with HIV infection. Few have died. Still, the most recent prevalence estimates project more than eleven million HIV/AIDS deaths over the next decade.

At all levels—local, regional, and national—and for many reasons, governments tend to underreport incidence and prevalence rates of HIV infection and AIDS cases. Like other aspects of the health crisis, the underreporting is, at least in part, culturally driven. Physicians and families and patients may seek to disguise HIV/AIDS as another, more "respectable" disease—cancer, tuberculosis, pneumonia, "a long illness"—in order to avoid the invasion of privacy; the loss of jobs, health insurance, friendships, freedom of movement, access to health care; and numerous similar obstacles that tend to follow an HIV/AIDS diagnosis. Because HIV/AIDS is a profoundly stigmatized disease, people may delay or forego medical treatment. In some places medical care is simply not available, epidemiological records are not maintained, or both. At the same time, because AIDS is not a single disease but rather a condition that has been constructed (and revised, updated, and expanded) by medical definition to include a number of diseases, HIV-infected people whose particular illnesses are not included in the currently accepted definition have been automatically ruled out of the statistics.[2]

Despite the inaccuracies, however, in any of the hundreds of ways of counting the epidemics (the present incidence rates of HIV infection, the number of AIDS-related deaths annually, the ratio of infections through homosexual behavior to those through heterosexual behavior, the projected number of pediatric AIDS cases five years into the future, the incidence and death rates locally, nationally, or internationally), the numbers describe a global health crisis of ever-increasing magnitude. The selections in Part I trace the outlines of that health crisis from its beginnings to the present. Costs once measured solely by the numbers of dead will be increasingly figured during the 1990s in broader terms: projected stresses on fragile and already overextended health care systems; the loss of productive workers in industry and agriculture; resulting food

---

[2]The 1993 revisions by the Centers for Disease Control employ a combination of T-cell counts and twenty-five diseases and infections to establish an AIDS classification. See "1993 Revised Classification System for HIV Infection and Expanded Surveillance Case Definition for AIDS Among Adolescents and Adults," in *Morbidity and Mortality Weekly Report*, vol. 41, No. RR-17 (December 18, 1992).

shortages, particularly in the urban areas of developing countries; labor short-ages, particularly in the service and agricultural sectors; the reallocation of resources at all levels of social life to care for the increasing numbers of peo-ple sick with AIDS.

To be sure, HIV/AIDS has had and will continue to have grave material impli-cations for the social and economic fabric of human communities. Yet there is another, more subtle dimension to HIV, for the biological and medical "facts" about the virus have often been blurred by cultural mythologies and artful defenses against a disease that does not recognize moral, economic, political, or religious boundaries. HIV has transformed the nearly universal metaphors for human life—blood, semen, and breast milk—into sources of contamination, pollution, and death. The sacred is profaned, and the biological facts sur-rounding this disease are distorted in culturally constructed vocabularies. The selections in Part I also explore the dynamic process by which the disease has been transformed into a culturally constructed "illness" in which the disease and the diseased share a moral blame designed to protect the sacred metaphors of life. As scientists have probed and prodded the virus in their test tubes and the health care industry has struggled to make old therapies and treatments extend the lives of people infected with HIV and sick with AIDS, as mothers and fathers, sisters and brothers, sons and daughters, spouses and lovers and friends have cared for the sick and buried the dead, fantastical thinking has guided public policy proposals. *Tattoo all people with AIDS. Quarantine them.* But in any event, *ban them from public places. Strip them of their civil rights, their health insurance, their access to schools and jobs. "They" must not contaminate "us."* The ecology of HIV/AIDS has both a physi-cal and a cultural dimension, and an understanding of the physical is simply not possible without an understanding of the cultural factors that have shaped the trajectory as well as the perceptions of the epidemic.

CHAPTER 1

Global Contours

• • •

In 1981, in New York and San Francisco, it was called the "Gay Plague." In Uganda and Tanzania, because of the extreme wasting seen in people suffering from it, the disease was called "Slim." The Haitian Revolutionary Internationalist Group claimed it was an "imperialist plot" designed to destroy the Third World. Because it was perceived as all of these, little action was taken. **Foreshadowings** sketches the subtle beginnings of the HIV/AIDS health crisis through the separate fatal illnesses that puzzled physicians in Copenhagen, Cologne, Paris, New York, San Francisco, and Los Angeles during the late 1970s and early 1980s.[1]

By 1983 the World Health Organization had recognized the disease, newly labeled the acquired immune deficiency syndrome, or AIDS, as an "unprecedented threat to global health" and initiated a surveillance program to monitor the spread of the worldwide health crisis. **The Sobering Geography of AIDS** describes the contours of this global pandemic. During the first five years of the epidemic, 1981 through 1986, the highest AIDS incidence rates were reported from the Americas, primarily the United States, and from Western Europe; the lowest incidence rates were reported from African, Asian, and Oceanic regions, in the world's developing nations. After 1986, however, in nations with initially low AIDS incidence rates, the epidemic curve began to increase suddenly and very dramatically. AIDS had become a "pandemic," a health crisis of global proportions. Initially understood in comparison to historical analogues—bubonic plague, cholera, yellow fever, influenza, and polio epidemics—the HIV/AIDS epidemic curve has not been uniform or stable. There are many smaller epidemics within the global health crisis, each raging at a different rate of incidence and prevalence within particular cultural milieux and political boundaries. **AIDS and Chronic Disease** argues that the long-term nature of the disease and the global dimensions of the health crisis require political, medical, and cultural responses to a chronic disease rather than to an epidemic.

[1]Shilts and other authors in this section make direct or indirect reference to an African origin for the HIV virus. A letter to the editor in the *Journal of the American Medical Association* [vol. 251 (1984):2657], however, reports a retrospective AIDS diagnosis of a 1968 St. Louis, Missouri, case, and suggests that at least a part of the current epidemic may be endemic to the United States. More recently, reanalysis of tissue samples from a 1959 death in Manchester, England, further backdates the origins of HIV, and simian research suggests that HIV-1 and HIV-2 may have different simian origins. See Margaret Cerullo and Evelynn Hammonds, "AIDS in Africa: The Western Imagination and Dark Continent," in Chapter 2 for a critique of the popularity of African origin stories in Western scientific thought.

Foreshadowings

Randy Shilts

September 1980
Copenhagen

Gasping, struggling for breath, the thirty-six-year-old fought against suffocation in his small, neat room in the *Rigshospitalet*. His palms were flushed light blue from lack of oxygen. The chart dangling from the foot of his bed had categorized the illness in a noncategory: unable to find specific diagnosis. By now, the young man's doctor, Jan Gerstoft, knew there was little he could do except watch his patient die.

Gerstoft knew why the agricultural engineer was left to so fiercely struggle for oxygen; that was not the mystery. Microscopic protozoa were filling the tiny air sacs of the man's lungs. A typical man has 300 million of these air pockets where the oxygen from inhaled breath eases into the bloodstream as part of the body's most basic fueling process. The air sacs, Gerstoft knew, also offer a warm, even tropical climate for the unseen *Pneumocystis carinii* organism.

This newly discovered protozoan had been found in guinea pigs back in 1910 by a Brazilian scientist, Dr. Carini. Three years later, doctors at the Pasteur Institute deduced that it lived quite comfortably in the lungs of ordinary Paris sewer rats. Not until 1942, however, was the tiny creature found to be living in people. A few years later, the first known outbreaks of pneumonia caused by the *Pneumocystis carinii* organism were reported in the orphanages of postwar Europe. Subsequent studies showed that the insidious protozoan, which traces its heritage directly to the most primitive one-celled animals from which all life evolved, can be found just about everywhere in the world's inhabited terrain. It is one of tens of thousands of creatures that are easily held in check by people's normally functioning immune systems.

Immune problems were what had always presaged the appearance of *Pneumocystis* pneumonia, whether among children subjected to overcrowding and poor nutrition or among people whose lymphatic systems were knocked out by cancer. When modern medicine learned how to intentionally suppress the immune system so the body would not reject transplanted kidneys and hearts, *Pneumocystis* flared sporadically, eager to take advantage of any opportunity to thrive in its preferred ecological niche, the lung. The disease, however, would disappear spontaneously once the immune system was restored. And the little creature would return to an obscure place in medical books where it was recorded as one of the thousands of malevolent microorganisms that always lurk on the fringes of human existence, lying dormant until infrequent opportunity allows it to burst forth and follow the biological dictate to grow and multiply. Humankind's evolution as a species that could survive diverse continents and climates was due in no small part to its ability to acquire immunity to such pests.

All this evolution, however, had been short-circuited for the man slowly suffocating in Copenhagen in the chilly days of autumn 1980. Something had created a deficiency in his immune system; this was the easy way to explain how the *Pneumocystis* microbe had taken such comfortable residence in his lungs.

Dr. Gerstoft had come from the State Serum Institute, Demark's governmental research agency, to study the less easily explained part of the man's diagnosis. What had happened to this man's immune system, and, of course, what might help? Intrigued, Gerstoft performed test after test, but nothing could explain why the protozoa had reproduced so prodigiously in the man's lungs, making him sweat and strain for wisps of oxygen. A review of his recent medical history revealed nothing remarkable. He was an agricultural engineer connected with Denmark's dairy industry, and in 1979, he had visited New York City to attend training courses in the proper use of milking machines. No clue there. He also was homosexual, but in Copenhagen, one of the world's most comfortable cities for gays, this was a matter that raised neither eyebrows nor medical suspicions.

Perhaps it should have, Gerstoft thought later, because just weeks before, he had seen another gay man who, for no apparent reason, was wasting away, suffering from unexplained weight loss and a frighteningly aggressive outbreak of anal herpes. The thirty-seven-year-old man, who was well known in the theater crowd of the Danish capital, had mentioned that his lover was also mysteriously ill.

Second thoughts, of course, would come much later, because even in our advanced times it is still not uncommon for people to fall sick and even die for unexplained reasons. In any event, the agricultural engineer was the first to die, passing away that September at the *Rigshospitalet*, not far from where a surgeon named Grethe Rask had succumbed to the same pneumonia a little less than three years before.

These deaths in Copenhagen presented their own salient clue to the identity of a killer that quietly stalked three continents in 1980. In Europe, the microbe's first victims were largely linked to Africa. Just weeks after Grethe Rask was rushed from South Africa to Copenhagen, a thirty-four-year-old airline secretary from Kinshasa took advantage of her employment travel benefits to fly her sickly daughter from Zaire to Belgium. The woman's three-year-old was suffering from oral candidiasis, a yeast infection of her mouth. One of the woman's children had already died of a respiratory ailment stemming from strange problems with her immune system, problems that started with a case of this candidiasis Within a few weeks of her arrival in Brussels, the mother was also suffering from the oral yeast infection. By mid-September, her lymph nodes were swollen, she was rapidly losing weight, and she was suffering from a severe infection of cytomegalovirus. The doctors could do nothing as waves of infection washed over the mother's body. By January 1978, as she withered away from severe diarrhea caused by an untreatable salmonella infection in her intestines, she flew back to Kinshasa, where she died a month later.

Weeks after this woman's death, baffled scientists in Cologne tried to understand why a successful young concert violinist should contract a case of Kaposi's sarcoma. The German musician was gay and had spent much of the decade traveling across Europe, but this provided no clue as to why he should fall victim to an old man's disease rarely seen in northern Europe. Nor did it explain why his lymph nodes seemed to explode three months later, as if they were fighting some unseen infection. Answers were no more forthcoming in the excruciating months ahead while doctors helplessly watched the forty-two-year-old's body be bombarded with disease after disease until finally, in January 1979, he died.

It was at about that time that Belgian doctors in Zaire began reporting an upsurge in cases of cryptococcosis at Kinshasa's Memo Yemo General Hospital. By 1980, physicians could document fifteen cases of this disease. The cysts that spread *Cryptococcus* are found in bird droppings the world over. The problem, therefore, was not the presence of new *Cryptococcus* germs but of some weakness in the patients' immunity that let the disease take root.

In Paris, the first case of the baffling pneumonia also had an African connection, appearing in 1978 when a Portuguese cab driver suddenly experienced difficulty breathing. The short, swarthy man had returned only a year or so before from Angola, where he had served in the Portuguese navy during the Angolan Civil War and, later, as a trucker, driving Angola–Mozambique routes that cut through the narrow coastal spit of western Zaire. Dr. Willy Rozenbaum of Claude-Bernard Hospital was called in to see the man in 1979 and easily diagnosed the parasite *Pneumocystis carinii*. Unable to fathom what immune problems might have engendered the pneumonia, Rozenbaum enlisted immunologist Jacques Leibowitch to try to solve the problem. Leibowitch was accustomed to seeing bizarre diseases among people who traveled to exotic parts of the world; it seemed he was always treating some airline pilot or steward for some obscure infection. The doctor first tested the man for lymph cancer, the condition that often proves to cause such rare bouts of immune deficiency. But the tests yielded nothing, as did further blood studies. Specialists from all over Paris were trooping to the man's bedside, drawn both to struggle for a cure and to explore an intriguing medical mystery. Meanwhile, colonies of thick white fungus bloomed in the patient's mouth and throat, while warts caused by ordinarily benign papovavirus swept over his body, covering his arms and legs.

The doctors were downright awestricken when the man's brain became infected with toxoplasmosis, another rare parasite. Nothing they could do yielded any help, however, and in 1980, the man returned to his wife and five children in Portugal to die. As he was nearing death in Iberia, two women were admitted to the intensive care unit of Claude-Bernard with *Pneumocystis*. One was a Zairian woman, who, like many in the elite of that French-speaking region of central Africa, had sought treatment in the more advanced hospitals of Paris after her African doctors could find no effective treatment for her. The second woman was French, but she, too, had lived recently in Zaire.

The European fall turned to winter. By the time winter was turning to spring, all of them—the cab driver in Portugal and the two women in Paris—had drowned in the primeval protozoa that had filled their lungs.

In the United States, unexplained maladies from a mysterious new syndrome would be traced back to 1979. It was on a balmy September day in 1979 that Rick Wellikoff had been sent to Dr. Linda Laubenstein for blood studies. She duly noted the generalized rash that resisted treatment, and the enlarged lymph nodes all over his body. Laubenstein surveyed the man and assumed he had lymph cancer. Later, a dermatologist told Linda that the man's rash was a skin cancer called Kaposi's sarcoma.

"What the hell is that?" asked Laubenstein.

It didn't take her long to find out all there was to know about it because the world's medical literature on the disease didn't take much time to read. The cancer was discovered originally among Mediterranean and Jewish men in 1871. Between 500 and 800 cases of this disease had been documented in medical books in the last century. It usually struck Jewish and Italian men in the fifth or sixth decade of their lives. In 1914, Kaposi's sarcoma, or KS, was first reported in Africa, where subsequent studies discovered that it was the most common tumor found among the Bantus, the disease generally remaining within distinct geographic boundaries in the open savannah of central Africa. There, KS patients represented one in ten cancer cases.

Typically, a victim would develop some flat, painless purple lesions and die much later, often of something else. As cancers went, Kaposi's sarcoma was fairly benign. In more recent years, reports circulated of a new, more aggressive form of the sarcoma in central Africa, but that did not appear to be what had stricken Rick Wellikoff. The lesions were not rapidly covering his body and internal organs, as had been reported among the Africans. Besides, he had never been to such exotic ports. The only characteristic that made Rick mildly different from the typical New York schoolteacher his age was that he was gay.

Given the rarity of the cancer—and the novelty of a case in such a young, non-Mediterranean man—Linda decided to follow Rick closely and mentioned him to several other doctors. She would have to write it up some day.

Two weeks after she first saw the schoolteacher, she got a phone call from a colleague at the Veteran's Administration Hospital, a few blocks south of New York University Medical Center on First Avenue.

"You're not going to believe it, but there's another one down here," he said.

Laubenstein quickly went to the VA Hospital to visit the other Kaposi's patient who seemed very similar to Rick. The man was much more handsome, to be sure; after all, he was a model. But he was thirty-seven years old, homosexual, and, in the strangest twist, the pair shared mutual friends. It was uncanny. Among their acquaintances, they said, was a dreamy blond flight attendant from Canada. He had an unusual name that stuck in Linda's mind.

"Gaetan. You should talk to Gaetan," the first two gay men to be diagnosed with Kaposi's sarcoma in New York City had told Linda Laubenstein in September 1979.

"You should talk to Gaetan because he's got this rash too."

October 1
Davies Medical Center,
San Francisco

Michael Maletta was curt and irritated as he was being admitted to Davies Medical Center, a major medical center on Castro Street, but he had been sick all year and he wanted to get to the bottom of it. His malaise was officially described as FUO—fever of unknown origin. His doctor, however, suspected much worse and ordered up biopsies of his liver, bone marrow, and lymph nodes. Perhaps it was Hodgkin's disease that hadn't surfaced, his internist thought. That would explain the lingering malaise that had bedeviled the hairstylist all year. To be sure, Michael had tried to proceed with his life as normal. He still gave the best parties in town and in June had taken over all four floors of the Market Street building above his hair salon to throw the year's ultimate bash. Boys cheerfully crammed the four-story outside stairwell, swigging beers, while hundreds more squeezed into the back patios, dancing to the disco deejay. Down in the basement, scores more groped and fondled each other in a large-scale recreation of a bathhouse orgy room. And in the middle of it was Michael, the perfect host, handing out tabs of the drug MDA to all comers. These were grand times to be gay in San Francisco, Michael thought, and he relished the life-style he had built for himself since moving from Greenwich Village after the glorious Bicentennial summer. He sometimes wondered what had happened to his friends there, people like Enno Poersch and his lover Nick who had been so close. Now he wasn't hearing much from any of the old gang that had spent such hot times together in those months when the tall ships came from all over the world to New York Harbor.

University of California Medical Center, San Francisco

"Too much is being transmitted here."

It was getting to be the standard finale to Dr. Selma Dritz's rote presentation on the problem of gastrointestinal diseases among gay men. She felt her analysis had particular gravity at this monthly meeting of the sexually transmitted disease experts at the University of California at San Francisco Medical Center. This was one of the most prestigious medical schools in the nation, she knew. These doctors needed to know that something new was unfolding in the bodies of gay men, and they needed to be alert, to see where it might lead.

This was not how Dr. Dritz, the infectious disease specialist for the San Francisco Department of Public Health, had planned to spend the later years of her career—being one of the nation's foremost authorities on organisms that were setting up residence in the bowels of homosexual men. Her expertise had started soon after 1967, when she became assistant director of the San Francisco Department of Public Health's Bureau of Communicable Disease Control.

Normally, five or perhaps ten cases of amebic dysentery a year crossed her desk, and they were usually from a day-care center or restaurant. Now doctors were reporting that many a week. She checked the figures again. Nearly all the cases involved young, single men, and an inordinate number were diagnosed at the Davies Medical Center on Castro Street. She mentioned to another health department staffer that it was odd because she hadn't heard any complaints about neighborhood restaurants. Her colleague took Dritz aside to explain that the cases were concentrated among gay men. Dritz didn't understand the relevance of the observation.

"It's oral–anal contact," he said.

"It's what?"

They didn't teach these things when Selma was in medical school in the 1940s, but she quickly learned the down-and-dirty realities about enteric diseases. Gay doctors had long recognized that parasitic diseases like amebiasis, giardiasis, and shigellosis were simply a health hazard of being gay. The problems grew with the new popularity of anal sex, in the late 1960s and early 1970s, because it was nearly impossible to avoid contact with fecal matter during that act. As sexual tastes grew more exotic and rimming became fashionable, the problem exploded. There wasn't a much more efficient way to get a dose of parasite spoor than by such direct ingestion.

Although all this was common knowledge among gay physicians, the awareness had evaded the public health profession. Earnest health officials at one point dispatched inspectors to Greenwich Village to test water after detecting unusual outbreaks of amoebas in the neighborhood.

The more expert Dritz became about the health problems of the gay community, however, the more concerned she grew. Gay men were being washed by tide after tide of increasingly serious infections. First, it was syphilis and gonorrhea. Gay men made up about 80 percent of the 70,000 annual patient visits to the city's VD clinic. Easy treatment had imbued them with such a cavalier attitude toward venereal diseases that many gay men saved their waiting-line numbers, like little tokens of desirability, and the clinic was considered an easy place to pick up both a shot and a date. Then came hepatitis A and the enteric parasites, followed by the proliferation of hepatitis B, a disease that had transformed itself, via the popularity of anal intercourse, from a blood-borne scourge into a venereal disease.

Dritz was nothing if not cool and businesslike. Being emotional got in the way of getting her message across, of making a difference. Her calm admonitions to gay men about the dangers of rimming and unprotected anal sex were well rehearsed by now, although they were out of beat with that era. The sheer weight of her professionalism, however, made Dritz immensely popular among gay doctors. Her children teased her that she was the "sex queen of San Francisco" and the "den mother of the gays." Gay health had become an area in which Dritz had an unparalleled expertise because she had spent much of the late 1970s meeting with gay doctors, penning medical journal articles, and traveling around northern California to issue her no-nonsense health warnings.

But here, in 1980, among these venereal disease specialists, Dritz found her message received cooly, at best. She recognized the response. Scientists had a hard time believing that the sexual revolution had turned Montezuma's revenge and hepatitis B, the junkies' malady, into a social disease. Dritz calmly repeated the statistics: Between 1976 and 1980, shigellosis had increased 700 percent among single men in their thirties. Only seventeen cases of amebiasis were reported in 1969; now the reported cases, which were only a small portion of the city's true caseload, were well past 1,000 a year. Cases of hepatitis B among men in their thirties had quadrupled in the past four years.

These diseases were particularly difficult to fight because they all had latent periods in which they showed no symptoms even while the carrier was infectious—gay men were spreading the disease to countless others long before they knew they themselves were sick. This was a scenario for catastrophe, Dritz thought, and the commercialization of promiscuity in bathhouses was making it worse.

Dritz looked down from her slide projector to the disbelieving faces in the conference room. These med-school types didn't believe anything unless they saw it in their microscopes or test tubes, she thought. This, they argued, was "anecdotal" information and they needed data. All this talk about buggery and oral–anal contact didn't make them any more comfortable either.

Dritz tried to broaden her point, so the doctors could see that she wasn't talking so much about this or that disease, or specific sexual gymnastics.

"Too much is being transmitted," she said. "We've got all these diseases going unchecked. There are so many opportunities for transmission that, if something new gets loose here, we're going to have hell to pay."

October 31
New York City

Ghosts swooshed their way through the winding streets of Greenwich Village, followed by double-jointed skeletons dancing behind misshapen spirits of darkness in the Halloween parade. All Hallows' Eve had for generations stood out as the singularly gay holiday. Sociologists noted that it made sense because it was the day for concealing identities behind masks, a penchant that social conventions had long made a homosexual norm. New York, however, is one of the only cities to mark this day with a parade, which is appropriately centered in its most famous gay enclave. That last night of October was filled with all approximations of grisly death. Larry Kramer didn't take much to costumes, but he joined in the parade with Calvin Trillin and a large group of writer friends, hooting and hollering at the flamboyantly freaky costumes along the route.

That night, the gay hot spots came alive with masquerades and special parties. At the Flamingo, one of the choicest private clubs where A-list gays discoed to dawn, Jack Nau enjoyed the revelry and tried to pick out friends behind the costumes. His boyfriend Paul Popham was out of town, which made it all the more tantalizing when Jack saw a familiar face. A blond smiled back in a particularly winning way, and before long Jack and Gaetan Dugas slipped away from the crowd and into the night.

"He's had some kind of seizure."

Uptown on Columbus Avenue, Enno Poersch frantically tried to revive Nick. A friend who had been staying with the ailing youth said tearfully that he had heard a shriek from Nick's room before Nick lapsed into unconsciousness. Enno had raced over and was kneeling beside the bed, trying to raise a flicker of awareness.

"We've got to get him to a hospital," Enno cried.

Even if he's unconscious, Enno thought to himself, I should explain it to him. Nick might be aware but just unable to talk.

"We're dressing you so we can take you to the hospital," he said.

Nick threw up a clear, yellowish liquid and had a bowel movement. Enno cleaned him, dressed him, and cradled him gently as he carried his lover down four flights of stairs.

"We're taking you downstairs, out the door," Enno shouted.

Cabs raced along the Upper West Side streets. None would stop for the tall man who was holding the wasted form in his arms. Enno realized that, because it was Halloween, the cabbies probably assumed they were drunks from some costume party.

The next morning, Dr. Michael Lange peered into Nick's room at St. Luke's-Roosevelt Hospital. A neurologist had found three massive lesions on the young man's brain during a CAT scan. Lange had been called in as an infectious disease specialist. Nick was slumped to one side of the bed. His gray eyes were covered with a milky white film and the left side of his face seemed to sag. His fever was escalating. Nick had been dying in slow motion for a year, the doctors told Lange, and nobody could say why.

The sight lingered with Lange for years, long after such deathly visages had become familiar and Lange became an international authority about such things. Lange would always recall that first moment, staring into the hospital room at Nick, as the event that separated his Before and After. Years later, Lange could instantly remember the date, the way he could recall the anniversary of his marriage or his kids' birthdays.

It was November 1, 1980, the beginning of a month in which single frames of tragedy in this and that corner of the world would begin to flicker fast enough to reveal the movement of something new and horrible rising slowly from the earth's biological landscape.

Study Questions

1. What factors might explain why the initial warnings of a global health crisis were so easily overlooked?
2. How did the details of the early cases combine to shape initial popular perceptions and understandings of HIV/AIDS, particularly in the United States?

The Sobering Geography of AIDS

Joseph Palca

Whenever molecular biologists are feeling cocky about the tremendous strides they have made in unraveling the mysteries of AIDS, Michael H. Merson has a way of bringing them down to earth. Merson is the director of the global program on AIDS for the World Health Organization

Reprinted with the permission of the American Association for the Advancement of Science from *Science,* vol. 252 (April 1991):372–373. © 1991 by the AAAS.

(WHO), and when he showed up last month at a scientific meeting[1] with his frequently updated slide show depicting the devastating spread of AIDS around the world, his audience of some of the top AIDS researchers in the United States listened with rapt attention. True, biologists have come a long way in a short time, but as Merson's slides show, they will have to pick up the pace if they are going to help alter the course of the AIDS pandemic.

The official numbers are horrifying, and they tell only part of the story. To date Merson's office at WHO headquarters in Geneva has recorded 340,000 cases of AIDS worldwide. But those are just the documented numbers: WHO officials know that some countries in the developing world are reporting only 5% to 10% of the actual number of AIDS cases. The true figure is closer to 1 million. And that's just for starters—another 8 to 10 million are estimated to have been infected by HIV. Until recently, it took scenes from sub-Saharan Africa, where WHO figures there are now more than 700,000 AIDS cases and another 6 million adults harboring the virus, to make front page news in the United States. Lately, though, health officials including Merson have begun to express alarm about new data from Asia and Latin America, where the population densities could quickly create an Africa-scale debacle. Indeed, if the virus takes hold in India, the experience in sub-Saharan Africa could pale by comparison. Which is why WHO officials, though bound by national sensitivities not to release infection rates for any individual country, are trumpeting the alarm to the nations most at risk.

Asia and Southeast Asia

Although the number of AIDS cases in India, Thailand, and southern China is extremely small for the present, James Curran, director of the Division of HIV/AIDS at the Centers for Disease Control in Atlanta, calls estimates of the number of people infected with HIV there "very frightening." According to James Chin, Merson's deputy who tracks the AIDS numbers, there are now approximately 500,000 people infected with HIV in Asia and Southeast Asia—mostly in India and Thailand. Making matters worse, these countries have historically high rates of sexually transmitted diseases, which can accelerate the spread of AIDS.

But even these WHO estimates may be conservative. Peter O. Way, chief of the health studies branch at the Center for International Research in the Bureau of the Census, has been collaborating with the Thai government on tracking the epidemic there. He says Thai health officials place the number of infections between 200,000 and 300,000 in their country alone. Despite difficulties getting comprehensive figures from India, there are clear warning signs that an epidemic is looming. In large cities such as Bombay and Madras, the virus is increasingly common among prostitutes, with some prevalence estimates as high as 20%. The fear, according to U.S. health officials who recently attended an AIDS meeting in Bombay, is that the virus will be transmitted to rural areas by migrant workers. Should this happen, it would completely overload Indian medical services.

Latin America and the Caribbean

Then there are the forgotten islands in the Western Hemisphere. Some of the highest rates of HIV infection in the world are now found in the Caribbean. In Haiti, one study found 1 in 10 pregnant women—not prostitutes, just ordinary citizens—infected with the AIDS virus. On a grander scale, the Pan American Health Organization, which gathers statistics for WHO in the Western Hemisphere, puts the number of people infected with the virus in all of Latin America at close to 1 million. Some may have felt relief that the rate of new infections in North America has slowed—a conclusion CDC reached more than a year ago (*Science*, 22 December 1989, p. 1560)—but the rate of infection in the southern part of the hemisphere has continued its steep rise.

William Blattner, chief of the viral epidemiology branch at the National Cancer Institute, finds it especially worrisome that, despite what Blattner calls "very informed and appropriate" approaches to education and intervention, infection rates in countries like Jamaica and Trinidad are showing signs of shooting up after having been well below the average for the region. "It's like any other intervention against a possible threat," he says, "it's not a threat that leads to sustained behavior change. One is faced with the reality to my mind that we can't hold this problem in check with just prevention campaigns. There's an urgent need for an effective vaccine, and we're not there yet."

Not everyone is as discouraged about the possibility of behavioral approaches slowing the epidemic's spread. Jeff Harris, AIDS coordinator for the U.S. Agency for International Development (AID), says the kind of behavioral interventions that could make a difference just haven't been tried, even in the Caribbean. Harris is encouraged by campaigns like the one in Kinshasa, Zaire, where condom use has now reached 8% to 10% of the adult male population—the kind of usage figures that models of the epidemic suggest will slow its spread. But he readily admits that the $80 million AID will spend on prevention campaigns this year is only a drop in the bucket compared to what would be needed to have a major impact on the way HIV infection is spreading.

Sub-Saharan Africa

In Africa, AIDS has reached tragic proportions. WHO's Merson says of the AIDS problem, "There is no other disease on the African continent with anywhere near this impact." In addition to the nearly 6 million infected adults there are an estimated 500,000 infected infants. The social and cultural impact of the disease is staggering. Merson reckons as much as 15% to 20% of the workforce in Africa could die from AIDS, and there could be as many as 10 million orphans in the next decade.

And even these estimates may be low because AIDS deaths may be masked by another disease that is paralleling HIV infection rates: tuberculosis. "We have seen in sub-Saharan Africa in general tuberculosis rates shooting up, starting around the mid-1980s," says Chin. Nearly half of AIDS patients in Africa also have active tuberculosis infections, which can be the direct cause of death. This has caused a morbid statistical question: "You can't kill a person twice," says Chin. "That's been the problem—whether to count this as a TB death or an HIV death with tuberculosis or a TB death with HIV. My recommendation is we keep double books."

Some of the most alarming numbers for Africa come from a computer model of the epidemic developed for the U.S. State Department's interagency working group (IWG) on AIDS. Designed by a team from the Census Bureau, Los Alamos National Laboratory, and the University of Illinois, the model uses demographic, behavioral, and epidemiologic data to project infection rates in the future. Using this model, overall infection rates in urban areas could be as high as 16% by the year 2015, and infection rates could be as high as 40% for adults in their 30s. Expected population for the whole of sub-Saharan Africa by 2015 could be reduced by as much as 50 million by the AIDS epidemic, compared with estimates without AIDS.

Like all AIDS models, IWG's rests on some risky assumptions. Population mobility, sexual activity, rates of sexually transmitted disease, prevalence of use of condoms, the prevalence of HIV infection in the population, and the likelihood of transmitting the infection from a single sexual contact are all variables that are often not well known but can affect the accuracy of the model. "It's a little bit like holding a fishing pole at the thin end," says Way. "If you have a very new epidemic, or no epidemic like China, it would be like holding the fishing pole at the tip and trying to tell where the handle is going." For Africa, Way says, researchers are still at the thin end of the pole, but now they have a better grip.

WHO makes no predictions about how infection rates will change. Chin says that with all the uncertainties about the way the virus is transmitted, predicting more than 5 years into the future is an extremely risky business. Still, the IWG AIDS model is serving a useful social function: it is providing a tool for countries that are interested in using it for making predictions about what intervention campaigns might work in slowing the epidemic. Last November, U.S. health officials and Ugandan scientists using the model created a scenario that convinced Ugandan President Yoweri Museveni to reverse his policy on condoms and start encouraging their use.

The Rest of the World

There are a few shreds of good news in WHO's numbers. So far the virus does not appear to have taken hold in any significant way in Eastern Europe, and the patterns of infection for North Africa and the Middle East also indicate that those areas should be relatively unaffected, for now. In Western Europe and the United States the epidemic seems to be spreading primarily in certain sub-populations. But even in developed countries the absolute numbers of AIDS cases will severely tax health care systems.

For the foreseeable future Merson will continue updating his slides and bringing his gloomy message to scientists and politicians. Today the critical problem is to alert health officials in Asia and Southeast Asia that a major epidemic is looming, but "it's important not just for the Indians and the Thais and the Chinese to know this," says CDC's Curran. "It's important for the whole world to know this."

Just 3 years ago, WHO asked epidemiologists studying AIDS to make predictions about where the epidemic would be by the year 2000. These expert guesstimates, which WHO dubbed the Delphi projections, indicated that there would be 15 million to 20 million infected individuals by the end of this century. "The Delphi projections may be too conservative," says Chin. "We think that the Delphi numbers may be reached by mid- to slightly after mid-1990s." Whether or not Chin is right, there's no arguing with Curran's conclusions: "Things are going to get much, much worse before they get better."

NOTES

1.   HIV Disease: Pathogenesis and Therapy. 13–17 March, Grenelefe Conference Center, Grenelefe, Florida.

STUDY QUESTIONS

1. Where are the greatest number of HIV-infected people located at the beginning of the second decade of the HIV/AIDS health crisis?
2. What areas of the world appear to be facing massive increases in HIV infection rates in the 1990s?
3. What factors might account for these anticipated increases?
4. What cultural and political forces might explain the relatively low rates of HIV infection and AIDS in Eastern Europe compared to the rates in Western European nations?
5. What factors explain the relatively recent appearance of HIV/AIDS in Asian nations such as India, Thailand, and China?

AIDS and Chronic Disease

Elizabeth Fee and Daniel M. Fox

In the early 1980s most accounts presented AIDS as a radical break from the historical trends of the twentieth century, at least in the industrialized nations: a sudden, unexpected, and disastrous return to a vanished world of epidemic disease. Historians and most other people who paid attention to AIDS addressed it as a startling discontinuity with the past. The new epidemic seemed to bear little relationship to the diseases that absorbed the most attention and resources—the chronic diseases of an aging population. Epidemic disease belonged to history, a history that most had comfortably forgotten. But faced with the new threat of AIDS, people felt a need to reach back into history to discover how previous epidemics had been handled: how had societies dealt with plague, cholera, and polio? We searched for analogues in the past.

We found some apparently significant parallels and some similar themes in past epidemics: themes that seemed useful. Most of the essays in *AIDS: The Burdens of History* followed this pattern, as did a set of conference papers published in *Social Research*.[1] The editor of the latter collection made explicit the analogy to past epidemics by choosing the title "In Time of Plague." Media accounts of the epidemic increasingly made use of historians' references to past plagues, and Susan Sontag drew on the work of historians for her influential *AIDS and Its Metaphors*.[2] Sontag, however, inverted the historians' argument that diseases must be understood in their social and cultural context; she wanted to strip disease of its social and cultural meanings, or metaphors, leaving behind only what she regarded as pure biology. Barbara Rosenkrantz's note of warning has largely gone unheeded: "The ordinary vices that tempt us to make simple sense of history are, not surprisingly, embedded in our culture. They offer the same temptations that we face in mounting resistance to the uncertainties of epidemic disease: the vice of 'whiggery' through which we celebrate linear progress and reassuringly demonstrate how evil is overwhelmed by good, and the vice of relativism, which separates the event from its context so we may conclude that nothing has really changed."[3]

Several aspects of the early years of the AIDS epidemic had made analogies with past epidemics seem relevant. AIDS was an infectious disease that defied cure and, for a few years, even the implication of a causal organism. More important, AIDS seemed to resonate to great historical themes—notably the victimizing and stigmatizing of helpless members of minority groups and the indifference of public officials callous to human suffering. The disease attacked gay men just a few years after they had, for the first time in mod-

Reprinted with the permission of the University of California Press from Elizabeth Fee and Daniel M. Fox, editors, *AIDS: The Making of a Chronic Disease* (Berkeley: University of California Press, 1992):1–5. © 1992 by The Regents of the University of California.

ern history, been freed from the most overt oppression and, at least in major cities, had asserted a visible political presence. The disease allowed some journalists and politicians a ready opportunity to express—more accurately, to resurrect—fear and resentment toward newly visible and assertive gay communties. Moreover, the disease struck at the time when containing health costs had become a major objective of goverments in the United States and Western Europe, and these governments were reluctant to recognize, let alone deal with, the potentially devastating costs of coping with a new epidemic. The battle between a beleaguered gay community and a government apparently indifferent to the epidemic provided the dramatic point and counterpoint for Randy Shilts's *And the Band Played On.*[4] Indeed, many of the themes of early AIDS historiography dealt with the insensitivity of governments, socially and morally repressive attitudes to sexual behavior, the tendency of those in power to blame the poor or other disenfranchised groups for harboring dread diseases, and the potential threat of quarantines or other attacks on individual rights—all themes that were complaints or fears of a gay community facing an unsympathetic, indeed hostile, administration in Washington (and, by some account, in the capital cities of Europe).

Debates about how to respond to the epidemic reinforced the belief that AIDS was discontinuous with the recent past. Oversimply, these were arguments between alarmists on the one hand and advocates of equanimity on the other. The alarmists found analogies to the present in the great epidemics of infectious disease—notably bubonic plague, cholera, yellow fever, influenza, and polio. They urged adoption of what had become the classic repertoire of public health responses to epidemics: enhanced surveillance, mobilization of medical resources, and increased research. Advocates of equanimity used different historical parallels. They recalled times in the past when exaggeration of the severity of an outbreak of infectious disease had led to the deflection of resources from areas of greater need, the exchange of individual rights for an illusory collective good, and diminished repute for the enterprise of public health. These advocates needed to go no further back than the flu nonepidemic of 1976, although historians soon supplied them with many earlier examples.

Both the alarmists and the advocates of equanimity agreed that AIDS was a contemporary plague. They shared the belief that history was pertinent to understanding the epidemic and that the events in the past that were most pertinent were those surrounding sudden, time-limited outbreaks of infection. This agreement was the result of the shock of discontinuity in the early 1980s. Many people were unwilling to believe that a disease that had emerged (it seemed) so suddenly, and appeared to be invariably fatal, was either deeply rooted in the past or likely to become part of the human condition for the foreseeable future.

Because the history of visitations of plagues was the only history that appeared relevant to the new epidemic, most people ignored the alternative historical models that were available. For example, most of those who used historical analogies avoided the most pertinent aspects of the histories of venereal disease and tuberculosis, emphasizing issues of surveillance and personal control policy and ignoring the problems of housing, long-term care, public education, and the financing of palliative care for people suffering from chronic infections. Tuberculosis and venereal disease had been, for many years, both endemic and intractable. For individuals, they were chronic, debilitating conditions; lifetime burdens. For the people who provided and paid for health services, these diseases were characterized by a few acute episodes and long periods when patients required no care or only supportive care. For public health officials, venereal disease and tuberculosis raised difficult problems about surveillance, public education, and the long-term control of noncompliant patients. Yet in the early years of the AIDS epidemic, people who sought historical analogies explored venereal disease and tuberculosis mainly for what they could learn about screening, contact tracing, and the restraint of patients who were dangerous to others. The history of the two leading chronic infectious diseases of modern times, that is, was used to understand a very different situation, a polity threatened by devastating plague.[5]

At the end of the first decade of what is now called the epidemic of HIV infection, the initial sense of discontinuity with the past seems ironic. For some people, especially those with the infection or close to people who have it, the psychological alternative to discontinuity is devastating. The alternative to discontinuity is admitting that the threat of disease is not transient, not a matter of a bad season or a terrible year; not, that is, like the Black Death or cholera or yellow fever. For public officials, health industry leaders, and physicians, the idea that AIDS would become another killer chronic disease, like heart disease, cancer, and stroke, has been unpalatable because it adds to the already overwhelming financial and organizational problems of health policy. Yet for all these people it is becoming increasingly plain that AIDS, like tuberculosis during most of the nineteenth century, may be, for particular populations, an endemic life-threatening condition.

By the mid-1980s concerned physicians, public officials, and gay leaders no longer had to demand attention to an unrecognized life-threatening epidemic. AIDS was institutionalized within academic medicine and the medical care establishment. The patterns of research, services, and financing of care in the 1990s have more to do with long-term strategies for responding to diseases such as cancer than with the epidemic diseases of the past. It may well be horrifying to realize that AIDS is fitting our patterns of dealing with chronic disease, since it puts the problem into a long-term perspective. But if we assume that the rate of HIV infection will continue for the 1990s much as it did for the 1980s; if we assume that, as with cancer, most treatments will prolong life rather than cure the disease; if we assume that scientific research will continue to expand our knowledge rather than soon provide a means of prevention or cure; and if we assume that we will continue to respond to AIDS through the provision of specialized hospital units, long-term care, and other institutional services, we must also conclude that we are dealing not with a brief, time-limited epidemic but with a long, slow process more analogous to cancer than to cholera.

NOTES

1. Arien Mack, ed., "In Time of Plague: The History and Social Consequences of Lethal Epidemic Disease," *Social Research* 55 (1988): special issue.
2. Susan Sontag, *AIDS and Its Metaphors* (New York: Farrar, Straus and Giroux, 1988).
3. Barbara Gutman Rosenkrantz, "Case Histories—An Introduction,"*Social Research* 55 (1988): 399.
4. Randy Shilts, *And the Band Played On: Politics, People, and the AIDS Epidemic* (New York: St. Martin's Press, 1987).
5. Most of the references to Allan Brandt's *No Magic Bullet* (New York: Oxford University Press, 1985, 1988) have addressed the analogies with plagues, what we call discontinuities, not the chronic disease aspects of venereal disease.

STUDY QUESTIONS

1. What, according to Barbara Rosenkrantz, is the "vice of 'whiggery'"?
2. How has that vice obscured our understanding of the HIV/AIDS health crisis?
3. What characteristics of AIDS made it relatively easy, during the early years of the health crisis, to compare it to other infectious disease epidemics?
4. What public health strategies from previous infectious disease epidemics informed early public health and medical responses to HIV/AIDS?
5. What events and circumstances have fostered a rethinking of the HIV/AIDS health crisis?
6. What distinguishes an epidemic from a chronic disease?

SUGGESTED ADDITIONAL READINGS

James Chin and S. K. Lwanga, "Estimation and Projection of Adult AIDS Cases: A Simple Epidemiological Model." *Bulletin of the World Health Organization,* vol. 69 (1991):399–406.

James Chin, P. A. Sato, and Jonathan Mann, "Projections of HIV Infection and AIDS Cases to the Year 2000." *Bulletin of the World Health Organization,* vol. 68 (1990):1–11.

Peter Radetsky, "The First Case."*Discover,* vol. 12 (January 1991): 74–75.

Edward O. Laumann et al., "Monitoring AIDS and Other Rare Population Events: A Network Approach."*The Journal of Health and Social Behavior,* vol. 34 (March 1993):7–22.

Ronald St. John, Maureen Clifford, Fernando Zacrias, and Jonathan Mann, "The Global Program on AIDS." *AIDS and Public Policy,* vol. 3 (1988):14–19.

Gary W. Shannon, "AIDS: A Search for Origins." Richard Ulack and William F. Skinner, editors. *AIDS and the Social Sciences* (Lexington, KY: University of Kentucky Press, 1991).

World Health Organization, "Update: AIDS Cases Reported to Surveillance, Forecasting and Impact Assessment Unit (SFI)" (Geneva, Switzerland: Global Programme on AIDS, 1992).

Culture, Metaphor, and AIDS

• • •

HIV infection is a medical condition with medical consequences. As such, it is a *disease* that presents clinically in specifiable ways, and to some degree those presentations are subject to medical therapies and treatments. At the same time, HIV infection is a culturally constructed *illness* that is perceived, understood, and acted upon (or not acted upon) within a framework of culturally derived meanings. Metaphors for guilt and innocence, morality and sin, and AIDS vary from culture to culture; as a result, there are also differences in the way AIDS is perceived, understood, and acted upon. The selections in Chapter 2 explore the connections between the medical condition, the *disease*, and the cultural meanings that have constructed the *illness*.

In the United States, typical of Pattern I epidemics,[1] the construction of a cultural framework for understanding and acting upon the illness began during the summer of 1981. On June 5, the Centers for Disease Control (CDC) described in its *Morbidity and Mortality Weekly Report (MMWR)*, a brief weekly newsletter that is circulated among physicians and public health practitioners, five cases on *Pneumocystis carinii* pneumonia.[2] All the patients were gay men in their twenties and thirties. Then, a month later, the CDC reported ten additional cases of *Pneumocystis carinii* pneumonia, and twenty-six diagnosed cases of Kaposi's sarcoma, a rare and slow-acting form of cancer most often seen in elderly men. Once again, all the patients were gay men who ranged in age from twenty-six to fifty-one. The initial connections between a medical condition and an already stigmatized status—homosexuality—had a profound and lasting impact on the way AIDS would be perceived, understood, and acted upon in the United States.

An Epidemic of Stigma: **Public Reaction to AIDS** describes the results of the AIDS-related metaphorical thinking that forged powerful associations between the disease, sin, guilt, and blame within the American cultural landscape of the mid-1980s. The demographic profile of the HIV/AIDS health crisis in the United States has changed considerably since Herek and Glunt published

---

[1]The Pattern I epidemics began in the mid- to late 1970s, initially transmitted among gay and bisexual men, then spread to injection drug users and blood transfusion recipients, with relatively few women infected during the initial stages of the epidemics.
[2]*Morbidity and Mortality Weekly Report*, Centers for Disease Control, vol. 30, no. 25 (July 3, 1981).

this research, yet an understanding of that metaphorical thinking—which evoked a parallel epidemic of fear and anxiety—is crucial to an understanding of the AIDS-related discrimination and the public debates that punctuated the early years of the AIDS epidemic in the United States.

AIDS and the Pathogenesis of Metaphor extends this analysis of metaphoric thinking into sub-Saharan Rwanda, a cultural environment that typifies Pattern II AIDS epidemics.[3] There, as in the United States, the value judgments a people makes about a disease are constructed by a socially and historically specific "metaphoric brush." With HIV/AIDS, as with other "great plagues," socially and historically specific metaphors have informed public policy and scientific research agendas as well as private perceptions while specific sociocultural and historical forces have fostered the climate of "moral opprobrium," within which HIV/AIDS is perceived and understood in Rwanda as well as in the West.

In the United States, discourse about HIV/AIDS in Africa has been grounded in partial and often inaccurate understanding of the varied African sociocultural environments. **AIDS and Africa: The Western Imagination and the Dark Continent** examines the impact of this flawed and stereotyped thinking on the construction of HIV origin stories, on the development of research agendas, on the imposition of HIV/AIDS-related health care programs, and on economic aid packages to African nations. Although in retrospect the gravity of the HIV/AIDS health crisis in Africa has not been exaggerated, the early-1980s mythologies that explicity linked HIV transmission in Africa to cultural practices often perceived by Westerners as exotic and arcane may well have obscured the medical realities behind a veil of misunderstanding.

[3]The Pattern II African epidemic began in the mid- to late 1970s, almost exclusively transmitted sexually among heterosexuals, with more or less equal numbers of adult women and men infected, then extending to include newborns infected through perinatal transmission.

An Epidemic of Stigma
Public Reaction to AIDS

Gregory M. Herek and Eric K. Glunt

A Massachusetts teacher was ordered to take a medical leave and then to resign when rumors circulated that he was being treated for AIDS. After demonstrating to school officials that his medical problems were associated with a blood disorder not related to AIDS, he was allowed to return to teaching. Threatening phone calls and harassment continued, however, and he felt compelled to take a leave of absence (Shipp, 1986).

Reprinted with permission from *American Psychologist*, vol. 43, no. 11 (November 1988):886–889. © 1988 by the American Psychological Association.

In White Plains, New York, a mail carrier refused to deliver mail to an AIDS Task Force office for two weeks because he feared catching the disease ("Mail Service Ordered to AIDS Center," 1987).

In Arcadia, Florida, three brothers tested positive for human immuno-deficiency virus (HIV). After word spread of their infection, their barber refused to cut the boys' hair, and the family's minister suggested that they stay away from Sunday church services. Eventually, the family's house was burned down (Robinson, 1987).

In the American Spectator, Christopher Monckton (1987) wrote: "Every member of the population should be blood tested every month to detect the presence of antibodies against [AIDS], and all those found to be infected with the virus, even if only as carriers, should be isolated compulsorily, immediately, and permanently" (p. 30).

In 1987, 1,042 incidents of harassment against gay people were reported to the National Gay and Lesbian Task Force (NGLTF) that involved references to AIDS; two thirds of the local groups who reported incidents to NGLTF expressed the belief that fear and hatred associated with AIDS have fostered antigay violence (NGLTF, 1988).

In a 1986 Op/Ed piece in the New York Times, *William F. Buckley, Jr., proposed that "everyone detected with AIDS should be tattooed in the upper forearm, to protect common-needle users, and on the buttocks, to prevent the victimization of other homosexuals" (p. A27).*

Understanding the AIDS epidemic in the United States requires understanding the phenomenon of widespread, intensely negative reactions to HIV-infected persons. These negative reactions have shaped the behavior of infected individuals and have limited the effectiveness of prevention efforts.

Persons infected with HIV must bear the burden of societal hostility at a time when they are most in need of social support. Attempts to avoid such hostility may compromise individuals' health: Fear of being harassed, of facing job discrimination, and of losing insurance coverage, for example, deters individuals from being tested for HIV infection and seeking early treatment for symptoms.

At a societal level, the opprobrium attached to AIDS directly interferes with research and public health efforts to monitor the epidemic by, for instance, discouraging physicians from reporting cases (King, 1986). Further, prevention efforts are hampered by social disapproval of behaviors that can transmit AIDS. The Centers for Disease Control, for example, withheld funding for educational programs that included explicit instructions for engaging in safe sex behavior (Panem, 1987), and the U.S. Senate has twice endorsed an amendment by Jesse Helms (R–NC) that would prohibit federal funds for AIDS education materials that "promote or encourage, directly or indirectly, homosexual activities" ("Limit Voted on AIDS Funds," 1987). By constricting the scope of risk-reduction education, such actions contribute to the epidemic's spread.

In the present article, we refer to these and similar phenomena as *AIDS-related stigma*. Under this rubric, we include all stigma directed at persons perceived to be infected with HIV, regardless of whether they actually are infected and of whether they manifest symptoms of AIDS or AIDS-related complex (ARC). We purposely avoid using terms that imply individual pathology, such as "AIDS phobia" or "AIDS hysteria." Instead, we base our analysis on the assumption that AIDS-related stigma is a socially constructed reaction to a lethal illness that has been most prevalent among groups that already were targets of prejudice.

A stigma is a mark of shame or discredit. The focus of social psychological research on stigma is not on the mark itself, however, so much as on the social relationships in which a particular mark is defined as shameful or discrediting (Goffman, 1963). In line with this approach we are concerned here with the social psychological processes through which people are discredited when they are perceived to be infected with HIV. We will briefly examine individual attitudes and behaviors that express fear or hostility toward persons with AIDS, as well as institutional policies that impose hardships on particular individuals or groups without slowing the spread of AIDS. We also will offer suggestions for combating stigma at both the individual and institutional levels.

Sources of Stigma

AIDS is now perceived as a lethal disease that can be transmitted by specific behaviors and is most prevalent among gay men and users of intravenous drugs. This definition of the syndrome results in a dual stigma: first, from identification of AIDS as a serious illness; second, from the identification of AIDS with persons and groups already stigmatized prior to the epidemic (Des Jarlais, Friedman, & Hopkins, 1985; Herek, 1984).

Illness and Stigma

As an illness, AIDS manifests the characteristics of stigma described by Jones et al. (1984). First, it is an incurable and progressive condition and, because it is transmissible, people infected with HIV are often perceived as placing others at risk; survey data show that almost all Americans have heard of AIDS and that most know it is transmitted through blood and sexual contact (Singer, Rogers, & Corcoran, 1987). Second, people with HIV infection often are blamed for causing their condition through riskful behavior; approximately half of Americans agree that "most people with AIDS have only themselves to blame" (Gallup poll, July 10, 1987)[1] and that "in general, it's people's own fault if they get AIDS" (Gallup poll, October 23, 1987). Finally, in face-to-face encounters, the symptoms of AIDS-related illnesses are frequently visible to others, often disfiguring, and likely to disrupt an individual's social interactions.

Like other life-threatening illnesses, AIDS confronts even the noninfected with the reality of death, provoking what Schutz (1962) described as the "fundamental anxiety." When people interact with a person with AIDS, hear AIDS discussed, or simply read about it in a newspaper, they are reminded of their own mortality; their day-to-day sense of reality is challenged in a profoundly disturbing way. According to Schutz, the pragmatic objective of daily life (the "natural attitude") is to construct experiences that avoid this fundamental anxiety. AIDS-related stigmatization represents such a construction: Healthy individuals distance themselves from death by defining the illness as an affliction of others. Early news reports about AIDS "risk groups," for example, permitted most Americans (those who were not gay men, intravenous (IV) drug users, Haitians, or hemophiliacs) to see themselves as removed from the epidemic and protected from it.

With some serious illnesses, such attempts to maintain the natural attitude lead to attributions of individual character flaws to diseased persons. Cancer patients, for example, are portrayed as repressing emotions or lacking the will to be well (Sontag, 1977). Although considerable victim-blaming on the basis of individual characteristics has also occurred with AIDS, blaming the social groups to which most Americans with AIDS belong has been much more common. We turn now to this second source of AIDS-related stigma.

AIDS and Preexisting Stigma

Because of the characteristics it displays as an illness, AIDS probably would have been stigmatized to some extent regardless of whom it infected. Through an accident of history, however, AIDS in the United States has been largely a disease of already stigmatized groups. Most adults diagnosed with AIDS in this country are men who were infected through homosexual behavior (63%). The second most common route of HIV transmission in the United States has been through sharing intravenous needles for illegal drug use (19%). Another 7% of cases fit both categories. Additionally, Blacks and Hispanics are disproportionately represented in all transmission categories except hemophilia (Centers for Disease Control, 1988).

In short, the American epidemic of AIDS has been socially defined as a disease of marginalized groups, especially gay men. Consequently, the stigma attached to AIDS as an illness is layered upon preexisting stigma. The result is that as public perceptions of AIDS become inextricably tied to perceptions of the groups among which it is most prevalent, the stigma of disease and death become attached to the groups themselves. AIDS has become a symbol: Reactions to AIDS are reactions to gay men, drug users, racial minorities, or outsiders in general.

This linkage of AIDS with stigmatized groups has been an integral part of the history of the epidemic. A name initially proposed for the syndrome was Gay-Related Immune Deficiency (GRID) (Shilts, 1987a), and press coverage has referred to AIDS as the "gay plague" (VerMeulen, 1982). Indeed, little press coverage of AIDS occurred until 1983, when it was discovered that individuals outside of the "risk groups" of homosexual and bisexual men and

IV drug users could be infected (Baker, 1986; Panem, 1987). Shilts (1987a) pointed out that the *New York Times* published only six stories about AIDS during 1981 and 1982, none of them on the front page. In contrast, the *Times* printed 54 stories in 1982 about the discovery of poisoned Tylenol capsules in Chicago in October of that year; four of those stories were on the front page. Seven people died from poisoned Tylenol; of the 634 Americans who had been diagnosed with AIDS by October 5, 1982, 260 had died. Shilts argued that the epidemic was virtually ignored by the nongay media because it was merely a "story of dead and dying homosexuals" (p. 191).

AIDS-related stigma interacts with preexisting stigma in complex ways. If a diagnosis of AIDS or ARC reveals a man's previously hidden homosexuality, for example, a double stigma immediately results. Using Goffman's (1963) terminology, being identified as a person with AIDS transforms a man from discreditable (secretly gay) to discredited (publicly gay). Such marking of individuals as outsiders (because they are gay or because they have AIDS) can increase a community's solidarity by clearly demarcating its boundaries (Durkheim, 1895/1982). The frequent use of the phrase "the general public" as a counterpart to "risk groups" conveys this distinction between in-group and out-group; gay men, IV drug users, and their sexual partners are not part of "the general public." Similarly, persons who did not contract AIDS through homosexual behavior or drug use have often been categorized as "innocent victims" (Albert, 1986). For example, a *Newsweek* caption early in the epidemic described a teenage hemophiliac and an infant with AIDS as "the most blameless victims" ("The Social Fallout From an Epidemic," 1985). The opposite, of course, is a "blameable victim," that is, one who was infected with HIV during stigmatized behavior.

Because of its prevalence among already stigmatized groups, AIDS can easily be exploited for ideological and political purposes. A Houston mayoral candidate (and former mayor), for example, publicly joked that his solution to the city's AIDS problem would be to "shoot the queers" (Shilts, 1987b). Such political uses of AIDS, in turn, heighten the stigma associated with the disease and the groups most affected by it.

The definition of AIDS as an ideological and political issue is exemplified in the following comments by Republican columnist Patrick Buchanan (1987):

> There is one, only one, cause of the AIDS crisis—the willful refusal of homosexuals to cease indulging in the immoral, unnatural, unsanitary, unhealthy, and suicidal practice of anal intercourse, which is the primary means by which the AIDS virus is being spread through the "gay" community, and thence, into the needles of IV drug abusers [and to others]. (p. 23)

Buchanan further suggested that the

> Democratic Party should be dragged into the court of public opinion as an unindicted coconspirator in America's AIDS epidemic [for] seeking to amend

state and federal civil rights laws to make sodomy a protected civil right, to put homosexual behavior, the sexual practice by which AIDS is spread, on the same moral plane with being female or being black. (p. 23)

In his attempt to link AIDS with the opposition political party and with homosexual behavior exclusively, Buchanan not only made illness a politicized issue, he also ignored the worldwide epidemic. AIDS is overwhelmingly an epidemic of heterosexual transmission (Institute of Medicine, 1986).

The federal government's initial slow response to AIDS can be understood in part as a response to this politicization of stigma. Although other organizational variables also were important (Panem, 1987), antigay sentiment appears to have played an important role in the Reagan administration's failure to confront the epidemic (Shilts, 1987a).

Other groups also have responded to AIDS on the basis of its association with stigmatized sexuality. The Catholic Church, for example, argued against civil rights protection for gay people in a statement that was widely interpreted as referring to AIDS: "Even when the practice of homosexuality may seriously threaten the lives and well-being of a large number of people, its advocates remain undeterred and refuse to consider the magnitude of the risks involved" (Congregation for the Doctrine of the Faith, 1986, p. 8). AIDS was equated with homosexual behavior and was used to justify antigay discrimination and hostility.

We have cited examples of AIDS-related stigma occurring at the level of groups and institutions. The construction of AIDS at this level helps to shape individual beliefs, attitudes, and behaviors related to the epidemic.

The Social Psychology of AIDS-Related Stigma

We have mentioned some of the social psychological processes related to stigma (e.g., Goffman, 1963; Schutz, 1962). In this section, we will explore these processes more extensively, with special attention to insights contributed by psychologists.

AIDS as Illness: Stigma, Anxiety, and Decision Making

AIDS evokes anxiety because of its association with death. Research on risk assessment (e.g., Slovic, 1987) further illuminates the characteristics of AIDS that evoke anxiety: It is a new illness that is uniformly fatal; it is caused by an unseen infectious agent that can remain latent in the body for an unknown period of time; the epidemic is perceived as both out of control and potentially catastrophic. Because of these characteristics, individual judgments and decisions associated with AIDS are often made under conditions of anxiety and are thus likely to be defective.

Anxiety evoked by AIDS, for example, may lead people to believe that not enough time remains to weigh carefully the strengths and weaknesses of various alternative solutions to an AIDS-related problem (e.g., whether to vote for a political candidate who advocates mandatory HIV testing, how to respond to a coworker with AIDS, whether to send one's child to a school where an HIV-infected child is enrolled). This belief is likely to foster a hypervigilant style of decision making in which the easiest or most readily available perceived solution is embraced precipitously without considering its consequences (Janis & Mann, 1977).

Because HIV is transmissible, for example, an individual might equate AIDS with other, previously encountered transmissible diseases, such as influenza. The consequence could be an overestimation of the danger of transmitting AIDS through media other than semen and blood. Those displaying this hypervigilant style of decision making might, then, endorse a policy of quarantine for persons infected with HIV. Because of the felt need to decide quickly, the individual would be unlikely to consider carefully the serious flaws (e.g., public health and civil liberties) of a quarantine policy. He or she may misuse cognitive heuristics, such as the representativeness heuristic, which involves assessing an event's probability by the ease with which various instances of it can be brought to mind (Tversky & Kahneman, 1974).

Even when public officials attempt to allay fears and counteract this process, their pronouncements on AIDS may be greeted with skepticism. This disbelief is fueled in part by another inappropriate use of the representativeness heuristic: Prominent examples of public officials' dishonesty in other situations (e.g., Watergate, Three Mile Island) can be easily recalled (see Morin, 1984); the fact that these earlier situations are not directly comparable to the AIDS epidemic is not recognized.

Public misunderstanding of scientists' use of probabilistic statements in describing the risks posed by AIDS further exacerbates the problem. A scientist, for example, might accurately say that the risk of HIV transmission through saliva is theoretically possible but extremely unlikely; as a person trained to know that the null hypothesis cannot be proved, however, the scientist will refrain from saying that such transmission is impossible. Lay people may misinterpret this phrasing, however, to mean that such transmission is possible or somewhat likely and may adopt a heuristic of "better safe than sorry" or "you can't be too careful" to guide their behavior.

AIDS and Stigmatized Minorities

As noted earlier, AIDS-related stigma is complicated by the epidemic's association with already marginalized groups. Consequently, most individuals do not respond to AIDS simply as a lethal and transmissible disease. Rather, they respond to it as a lethal and transmissible disease of gay men and other minorities. AIDS thus provides many people with a metaphor for prejudice—a convenient hook on which to hang their hostility toward out-groups. Approximately one fourth of the respondents to the *Los Angeles Times* polls, for example, consistently have agreed that "AIDS is a punishment God has given homosexuals for the way they live" (28% on December 5, 1985; 24% on July 9, 1986; and 27% on July 24, 1987). Several researchers have found that respondents who express negative attitudes toward gay people are more likely than others to be poorly informed about AIDS and are more likely to stigmatize people with AIDS (Gabay & Morrison, 1985; Herek, in press; Lennon & McDevitt, 1987; O'Donnell et al., 1987). These data suggest that understanding the social psychological processes underlying AIDS-related stigma will require examination of the dynamics of antigay attitudes.

The first author's research, for example, has demonstrated the utility of a functional approach to heterosexuals' attitudes toward lesbians and gay men (Herek, 1984, 1986, 1987). Within this perspective, attitudes are understood according to the psychological needs they meet. Antigay attitudes appear to fit into two broad functional categories. First, antigay attitudes can help a heterosexual person to fit experiences (past or anticipated) with lesbians and gay men into existing cognitive categories, thereby guiding future behavior with the goal of maximizing benefit to oneself. Second, expressing antigay attitudes can help an individual to increase self-esteem, reduce anxiety, or secure social support.

The psychological functions served by attitudes concerning AIDS may be closely related to those served by attitudes toward gay people. For example, people with AIDS may be assigned to a cognitive category already existing for gay people; the affect resulting from negative experiences with gay people may be transferred to people with AIDS. Negative stereotypes of gay people (e.g., as preying on young people) may be imputed to people with AIDS as well. Alternatively, a fundamentalist Christian might condemn homosexuality as a way of affirming her or his sense of self as a good Christian and thereby increasing self-esteem. AIDS might be interpreted as God's punishment for homosexuality, and expressing a similar condemnation for people with AIDS might bolster self-esteem. Or a person whose hostility toward gay people is based on unresolved intrapsychic conflicts may experience similar anxieties associated with AIDS; because AIDS links homosexuality with death, it may offer a focus for anxieties associated with both.

Strategies for Eradicating AIDS-Related Stigma

We have pointed to both individual and societal levels of AIDS-related stigma. Because of the dialectical relation between cultural ideologies and individual attitudes, any attempt to eradicate AIDS-related stigma must target both levels. AIDS-education programs must be designed not only to impart information to individuals but also to reduce the stigma attached to AIDS. Public policy not only must respond to the technical issues of treatment and prevention but also must help to establish clear social norms of respect and compassion for HIV-infected persons.

Changing Individual Attitudes

To the extent that individuals respond to AIDS primarily as a threat to personal well-being (their own or that of their loved ones), they will be most influenced by educational programs that clearly present factual information about AIDS in a context that reduces anxiety (e.g., by reassuring the audience that sufficient time is available in which to make careful decisions) while explicitly countering the misuse of cognitive heuristics.

Individuals whose responses to AIDS result primarily from its associations with stigmatized minorities, in contrast, are unlikely to be affected by educational campaigns that provide only facts about AIDS. Educational programs for them must also address the preexisting stigma. For example, an individual who advocates quarantine for persons with AIDS because of an underlying hostility toward gay men is not likely to be influenced by factual discussions about the ineffectiveness of quarantine; the individual's antigay prejudice also must be confronted.

Stigma and Public Policy

Eliminating AIDS-related stigma requires government action in at least three areas. First, an individual's HIV status must remain confidential; given the inevitably damaging effects of being identified as HIV-infected (Batchelor, 1987), stiff penalties should be attached to unauthorized disclosure of this information. Second, discrimination on the basis of HIV status should be prohibited; as noted by Admiral James D. Watkins, chair of the Presidential Commission on the Human Immunodeficiency Virus Epidemic, the fear of discrimination "will limit the public's willingness to comply with the collection of epidemiological data and other public health strategies, will undermine our efforts to contain the HIV epidemic, and will leave HIV infected individuals isolated and alone" ("Excerpts From Report," 1988, p. A16). Third, public education efforts must directly confront AIDS-related stigma. This means providing clear and explicit information about how AIDS is and is not transmitted to reduce fears of contact with HIV-infected persons, as well as to educate the public about safer personal practices.

Confronting stigma also means that AIDS-education programs must be designed to reduce the antigay prejudice that is so closely linked to AIDS-related stigma. Public policy that perpetuates antigay prejudice must be viewed as a major obstacle to stopping the epidemic. State sodomy statutes, for example, create the untenable situation in which safe-sex educational programs necessarily encourage criminal conduct; such laws should be overturned as part of an effective response to AIDS. The lack of legal sanctions against antigay discrimination in housing, employment, and services means that most HIV-infected individuals in the United States must legitimately fear discrimination based on presumptions about their sexual orientation even if AIDS-related discrimination is illegal; laws should be enacted prohibiting discrimination based on sexual orientation.

Although we have focused on the connection between AIDS-related stigma and antigay prejudice, other types of prejudice that fuel AIDS-related stigma should not be ignored. The stigmatization of IV drug users, for example, often leads to the assumption that behavior change is impossible in this group and consequently that AIDS-prevention efforts would be wasted. Increased street demand for sterile needles, however, indicates an awareness among drug users of how AIDS is transmitted and a desire to reduce personal risk (Des Jarlais et al., 1985). Public policy must encourage innovative approaches to AIDS education among drug users, while also expanding the availability of drug-treatment programs to assist users in overcoming their drug dependency.

As already noted, Blacks and Hispanics are overrepresented among people with AIDS in most categories of transmission. Because of preexisting racism, both individual and institutional, White policymakers have remained ignorant of the special needs of minority communities. Although increasing numbers of public officials, researchers, and educators realize that the content of risk-reduction programs must be tailored to the target communities, they often do not know how to accomplish this objective. Two issues of stigma thus must be confronted: (a) the stigma attached to AIDS, homosexual behavior, and intravenous drug use within minority communities, and (b) stigmatization of the minority communities by the prevailing White culture.

Psychologists have multiple roles to play in the effort to fight AIDS-related stigma. First, psychologists must educate themselves about the epidemic sufficiently so that they understand how their own reactions to AIDS may have inadvertently stigmatized persons who are HIV-infected. Second, psychologists should address problems resulting from AIDS-related stigma within their own area of expertise. Clinical psychologists, for example, should be sensitive to the concerns of persons with AIDS and persons such as gay men or Haitians who are likely to be stigmatized because of their membership in a suspect group. Health psychologists should assure that intervention programs directly address AIDS-related stigmatization and attempt to reduce it in their target populations. Social psychologists should utilize their knowledge of attitudes and prejudice to initiate research on how AIDS-related stigmatization can be eliminated. Finally, all psychologists should promote public policy that will deter stigmatization of persons with AIDS.

AIDS-related stigma is a problem for all of society. It imposes severe hardships on the people who are its targets, and it ultimately interferes with treating and preventing HIV infection. By attacking AIDS-related stigma, we create a social climate conducive to a rational, effective, and compassionate response to this epidemic.

NOTES

1. Unless otherwise indicated, data from public opinion polls were obtained through the Roper Center, University of Connecticut at Storrs. We thank Professor Bliss Siman of Baruch College, City University of New York, for her assistance in securing these data.

REFERENCES

Albert, E. (1986). Illness and deviance: The response of the press to AIDS. In D. A. Feldman & T. M. Johnson (Eds.), *The social dimension of AIDS* (pp. 163–178). New York: Praeger.

Baker, A. J. (1986). The portrayal of AIDS in the media: An analysis of articles in *The New York Times*. In D. A. Feldman & T. M. Johnson (Eds.), *The social dimension of AIDS* (pp. 179–194). New York: Praeger.

Batchelor, W. F. (1987). Real fears, false hopes: The human costs of AIDS antibody testing. *AIDS & Public Policy Journal, 2*(4), 25–30.

Buchanan, P. J. (1987, December 2). AIDS and moral bankruptcy. *New York Post,* p. 23.

Buckley, W. F., Jr. (1986, March 18). Crucial steps in combating the AIDS epidemic: Identify all the carriers. *New York Times,* p. A27.

Centers for Disease Control. (1988, June 6). *AIDS Weekly Surveillance Report.* Atlanta: Author.

Congregation for the Doctrine of the Faith. (1986). *Letter to the bishops of the Catholic Church on the pastoral care of homosexual persons.* Vatican City: Author.

Des Jarlais, D. C., Friedman, S. R., & Hopkins, W. (1985). Risk reduction for the acquired immunodeficiency syndrome among intravenous drug users. *Annals of Internal Medicine, 103,* 755–759.

Durkheim, E. (1982). *The rules of sociological method* (S. Lukes, Ed., & W. D. Halls, Trans.). New York: Free Press. (Original work published 1895).

Excerpts from report by AIDS panel chairman. (1988, June 3). *New York Times,* p. A16.

Gabay, E. D., & Morrison, A. (1985, August). *AIDS-phobia, homophobia, and locus of control.* Paper presented at the annual meeting of the American Psychological Association, Los Angeles.

Goffman, E. (1963). *Stigma: Notes on the management of spoiled identity.* Englewood Cliffs, NJ: Prentice-Hall.

Herek, G. M. (1984). Beyond "homophobia": A social psychological perspective on attitudes toward lesbians and gay men. *Journal of Homosexuality, 10*(1), 1–21.

Herek, G. M. (1986). The instrumentality of attitudes: Toward a neofunctional theory. *Journal of Social Issues, 42*(2), 99–114.

Herek, G. M. (1987). Can functions be measured? A new perspective on the functional approach to attitudes. *Social Psychology Quarterly, 50*(4), 285–303.

Herek, G. M. (in press). Heterosexuals' attitudes toward lesbians and gay men: Correlates and gender differences. *Journal of Sex Research.*

Institute of Medicine. (1986). *Confronting AIDS: Directions for public health, health care and research.* Washington, DC: National Academy Press.

Janis, I. L., & Mann, L. (1977). *Decision making: A psychological analysis of conflict, choice, and commitment.* New York: Free Press.

Jones, E. E., Farina, A., Hastorf, A. H., Markus, H., Miller, D. T., & Scott, R. A. (1984). *Social stigma: The psychology of marked relationships.* New York: W. H. Freeman.

King, W. (1986, May 27). Doctors cite stigma of AIDS in declining to report cases. *New York Times,* p. A1.

Lennon, R., & McDevitt, T. (1987, August). *Predictors of AIDS-phobic responses.* Paper presented at the annual meeting of the American Psychological Association, New York.

Limit voted on AIDS funds. (1987, October 15). *New York Times,* p. B12.

Mail service ordered to AIDS center. (1987, April 7). *New York Times,* p. B7.

Monckton, C. (1987, January). AIDS: A British view. *American Spectator,* pp. 29–32.

Morin, S. F. (1984). AIDS in one city: An interview with Mervyn Silverman. *American Psychologist, 39,* 1294–1296.

National Gay and Lesbian Task Force. (1988). *Anti-gay violence, victimization, and defamation in 1987.* Washington, DC: Author.

O'Donnell, L., O'Donnell, C. R., Pleck, J. H., Snarey, J., Snarey, R., & Richard, M. (1987). Psychosocial responses of hospital workers to acquired immunodeficiency syndrome. *Journal of Applied Social Psychology, 17*(3), 269–285.

Panem, S. (1987). *The AIDS bureaucracy.* Cambridge, MA: Harvard University Press.

Robinson, J. (1987, September 12). Senators told of family's plight with AIDS. *Boston Globe,* p. 1.

Schutz, A. (1962). Multiple realities. In M. Natanson (Ed.), *Collected papers, Vol. I. The problem of social reality* (pp. 207–259). The Hague: Nijhoff.

Shilts, R. (1987a). *And the band played on: Politics, people, and the AIDS epidemic.* New York: St. Martin's Press.

Shilts, R. (1987b, July 30). In Houston, "AIDS is spelled G-A-Y." *San Francisco Chronicle,* pp. 1, 4.

Shipp, E. R. (1986, February 17). Physical suffering is not the only pain that AIDS can inflict. *New York Times,* p. A8.

Singer, E., Rogers, T. F., & Corcoran, M. (1987). The polls, a report: AIDS. *Public Opinion Quarterly, 51,* 580–595.

Slovic, P. (1987). Perception of risk. *Science, 236,* 280–285.

The social fallout from an epidemic. (1985, August 12). *Newsweek,* pp. 28–29.

Sontag, S. (1977). *Illness as metaphor.* New York: Farrar, Straus, & Giroux.

Tversky, A., & Kahneman, D. (1974). Judgement under uncertainty: Heuristics and biases. *Science, 185,* 1124–1130.

VerMeulen, M. (1982, May 31). The gay plague. *New York Magazine.*

STUDY QUESTIONS

1. What are the psychosocial sources of AIDS-related anxiety?
2. How is such anxiety likely to affect private behavior and public policy?
3. What strategies do Herek and Glunt propose for reducing AIDS-related stigma?

AIDS and the Pathogenesis of Metaphor

Christopher C. Taylor

As AIDS continues to spread its way from one part of the world to another and from one sector of the U.S. population to another, it is becoming increasingly clear that societies are being forced to come to grips with two aspects of AIDS pathology, one which is directed toward AIDS the "disease" and another which is oriented toward AIDS the "illness." This disease/illness distinction (Kleinman, Eisenberg & Good, 1978: 251–52) differentiates between "disease," the biological and psychophysiological malfunctions occasioned by sickness,[1] and "illness," the manner in which a specific sickness is experienced by the sufferer (1978: 251–52) and culturally labeled, explained, and valued (Kleinman, 1980: 72). While biomedical practitioners generally concern themselves almost exclusively with the "disease" component of AIDS, it is apparent that for sufferers and society the "illness" component of AIDS is also important. AIDS as "illness" incorporates judgments about its meaning for sufferers and society, judgments that are culturally specific and receive expression through the medium of metaphor.

For example, we know that HIV suppresses the immune system, that in its later stages it invites "opportunistic infections," and that AIDS is almost always fatal; these are characteristics of the "disease," AIDS. However, many Americans fear and detest AIDS more for its perceived association with a "debauched" life-style, most notably, homosexuality and intravenous drug use, than for any direct health threat to themselves. The moral judgments leveled against gay men and IV drug users by certain segments of the American population have become part of AIDS as "illness," part of AIDS as a "social construct" (cf. Berger & Luckman, 1967). This construct, I maintain, has influenced the response that American health authorities have taken against AIDS as much as, if not more than, scientific thinking about the "disease" component of AIDS. Furthermore, the atmosphere of moral opprobrium evoked by AIDS has become as potentially harmful to society as the "disease" AIDS is to persons with AIDS. It is in this sense that AIDS has given rise to another pathogenic process, the production of socially destructive "illness" metaphors. Many people see AIDS as the sign of divine wrath directed against a society, in recapitulation of Sodom and Gomorrah, which has grown too permissive. From this perspective AIDS can only be cast out when the moral evils of society have been scourged and purified.

Although societies differ in the moral judgments they make about specific sicknesses and about the experience of sickness in general, all share a tendency to use sickness as a figure or metaphor. Susan Sontag (1977) laments this tendency and calls for a view of sickness that eliminates metaphoric thinking. Using a profusion of literary examples, Sontag shows that people afflicted with tuberculosis (TB) in the nineteenth century tended to be portrayed as persons who became ill because of their rarefied artistic and erotic sensibilities. In other instances, writers depicted TB sufferers as the victims of a poverty-stricken or otherwise harsh environment (Sontag, 1977: 15). In either case tuberculosis ennobled the sufferer, lifting him or her above the common plane of ordinary humanity to a semi-mystical locus between life and death. Placing TB sanitariums in the mountains was indicative perhaps of the nineteenth-century tendency to socially situate TB sufferers closer to heaven than to earth. Thomas Mann's *The Magic Mountain* (1924), for example, with its curious mixture of spiritual striving and social decadence seems to follow in this mode.

The twentieth-century person with cancer on the other hand, has received rather bad press, for he is portrayed as repressed, self-loathing, and emotionally inert (Sontag, 1977: 53). He is someone whose refusal to deal with his innermost feelings has left him prone to attack by destructive forces within his own body. Sontag cites the maverick psychoanalyst, Wilhelm Reich, as one of the chief proponents of this negative stereotype, for he attributed cancer to "emotional resignation" and "bio-energetic shrinking" (Sontag, 1977: 23). Since Sontag suffered from cancer herself, as well as from its characterization, she feels that the metaphors we create about disease are often as afflicting as the diseases themselves. One might think, therefore, that Sontag is advocating a "scientific," that is, value-free view of sickness, but many of the culprits in her story are medical scientists themselves. What seem like "facts" to these scientists, often turn out to be merely the value judgments about a disease which were in vogue at a particular social and historical juncture.

What Sontag advocates, however, is probably unrealizable; it is doubtful that there will ever be a completely metaphor-free view of all sicknesses, or in Kleinman's terms, "disease" without "illness." While certain sicknesses do not engender illness metaphors because of their innocuousness, sicknesses that are contagious, life-threatening, characterized by bizarre or debilitating symptoms, or associated with abnormal behavior are likely to give rise to imagery embodying positive or negative sociomoral judgments. Moreover, these judgments are further reinforced when the sickness manifests a propensity to afflict members of society who are already marginalized for reasons of ethnicity, life-style, or socioeconomic status.

Western culture abounds with historical examples of illness metaphors which, in my opinion, have served as models for those associated with AIDS today. Leprosy, for example, was clearly conceptualized according to notions of ritual purity. Biblical references to the "cleansing" of lepers illustrate this point, supporting Douglas's thesis (1966) that persons or things perceived to be "out of place" or classificatorily ambiguous tend to be treated as socially dangerous. In the Middle Ages, for example, many communities forced their lepers to live apart from the healthy. At the first symptoms of affliction, lepers underwent a "rite de passage"—a funeral mass—to mark their "death" (Gaignebet, 1974: 66–68). While lying in a coffin, the leper was read a list of the rules that would govern his future interaction with healthy people: prohibition against touching anything unless this was done with a stick, prohibition against approaching wells and springs, prohibition against speaking except when the wind was blowing in one's face (Gaignebet, 1974: 67). Once this mass was celebrated, the person left his home and family to live in a community with other lepers.

Once in this community, lepers could continue their lives unmolested only if they accepted the "liminal" existence (Turner, 1969) combining biological life and social death, which healthy society allotted them. Economically, leper communities were subjected to occupational marginalization.

They gained their livelihood by exercising ritually "dangerous" activities such as rope-making (Gaignebet, 1974: 65–86). Rope-making was "dangerous," because ropes were "liminal;" they traversed boundaries, they linked disparate realms of space, and in hanging condemned prisoners, they mediated the passage between life and death. Furthermore, medieval ropes were manufactured from hemp (*Cannabis sativa*). The discarded portions of the plant were burnt and undoubtedly the intoxicating fumes of the marijuana were inhaled (Gaignebet, 1974: 66). This conjunction of sickness, social marginality, and drug-induced pleasure was perhaps the first instance in Western epidemiologic history of themes foreshadowing our present imagery of AIDS.

Closer to AIDS because of its association with sexuality, syphilis has also been colorfully painted by the metaphoric brush. Fracastoro, the famed Italian Renaissance poet who wrote in Latin (cf. Eatough, 1984), gave the disease its name, attributing its origin to the hubris of a young shepherd named Syphilis, who dared to venerate his earthly king, Alcithous, above the Sun God, Apollo. Angered, Apollo afflicted the shepherd with the pestilence that came to bear his name. Cure came only after Syphilis expiated his fault through sacrifice (Eatough, 1984: 21). Fracastoro lived during a time of tremendous upheaval, the sixteenth century—an age of plagues, religious wars, voyages of discovery, and the expansion of mercantile capitalism (cf. Wallerstein, 1976). In explicitly comparing the contraction of syphilis to the breach of a ritual injunction, Fracastoro reflected an attitude that was quite widespread, for syphilis had begun to replace leprosy as a focus of religious concern (Eatough, 1984: 4). Furthermore, evidence from his time demonstrates that his Spanish contemporaries were using the specter of syphilis as a hegemonic tool to justify their conquest of the New World on the grounds that Native Americans were inferior beings, "pagans" and originators of the syphilitic plague (Eatough, 1984: 13). Syphilis was also used to reinforce xenophobic stereotypes. Italians called syphilis the "Spanish disease," French called it the "Neapolitan disease," English called it the "French disease," and Russians, the "Polish disease" (Barnouw & Clark, 1955: 4).

The most recent of the "great plagues," AIDS follows a pattern that is similar to those which preceded it. Perhaps this explains the hypothesis (Coulter, 1987) which places *Treponema pallidum*—the spirochete that causes syphilis—at the basis of the AIDS pandemic. Furthermore, this hypothesis relegates what is widely believed to be the virus that causes AIDS, HIV-1, to the status of a mere cofactor (Coulter, 1987: 66). This hypothesis has not, however, met with wide approval. One might further wonder if the resemblance between the "illness" of syphilis and the "illness" of AIDS has influenced this tendency of linking the two diseases. After all, scientists are not as free of metaphoric thinking as believers in science would like to have it.

Moreover, whether or not medical scientists intend this result, many of their research findings that receive attention in the press become input which contributes to the metaphoric elaboration of AIDS. Consider, for example, the question of geographical origin. In Rwanda, where I did field research on traditional medicine for 21 months, people believe that AIDS originated with gay men and IV drug users in the United States and Europe, and then spread to Rwanda with tourists. In the United States, on the other hand, we usually hear that AIDS has an African origin. Some theories trace the migration of the disease in this way: green monkeys transmitted the virus to Africans. Africans then gave the disease to Haitians working in Zaire and/or Cuban soldiers in Angola, who brought it back to the Caribbean. American gay men vacationing in Haiti brought the disease from the Caribbean to urban centers in the United States, where it was picked up by IV drug users. From there it began to spread to the white heterosexual population.

Although a great deal of research remains to be done to confirm or deny the validity of these hypotheses concerning the geographic trajectory of AIDS (though it is certain now that African green monkeys are not the source of AIDS), my point does not concern their truth value. Instead what interests me about these hypotheses is, first of all, their potential to be used metaphorically, and second, their capacity to justify xenophobic stereotypes in the popular imagination.

Let us take the idea that AIDS originated with monkeys, spread to sub-Saharan Africans, then moved on to gay men and IV drug users, before finding its way into heterosexual white society. There is an evolutionist cast to this scenario, something which resembles the eighteenth- and nineteenth-century belief in the "great chain of being" (cf. Lovejoy, 1936). This belief, it should be recalled, maintained that there was a gradual rise of beings from the least exalted to the most divine. Humankind, though beneath the angels, was superior to all other forms of biological life. In subsequent versions of the "great chain of being" idea, human races were arranged hierarchically according to their proximity or distance from divinity. It is not surprising that the originators of these ideas, who were white European males, believed that the highest rung of human evolution had been attained by male members of white European society. (Precursors to these notions, incidentally, can already be discerned in the sixteenth-century view of syphilis.) Added to this evolutionist idea, there was a diffusionist one: The absurd belief that everything progressive came from Europe and everything atavistic came from elsewhere.

One of the most deleterious results of these ideas was that they tended to become reified in nineteenth-century "science." The nascent study of anthropology, for example, reflected European lay society's prejudices and self-satisfaction (cf. Gould, 1981). Skulls from various races were measured and compared according to the theory that intercranial volume reflected intelligence. Not surprisingly, these researchers found in "objective reality" what they had already formulated in their own minds before the first skull was measured— Caucasians had the largest skull volume while Africans had the smallest

(Gould, 1981: 66). Although the work of these "scientists" has since been refuted, it must be noted that a similar theory has reemerged with the practice of testing for "intelligence quotient" or I.Q. As recently as 1979, Arthur Jensen has defended an hereditarian theory of I.Q. that essentially recapitulates the "great chain of being" idea (Gould, 1981: 317). Jensen claims that the "intelligence" of all animal life can be quantified and assigned a numerical value (Gould, 1981: 317). Not surprisingly, he situates black people on one of the lowest rungs of humankind. Africa has remained the "Dark Continent" in too many minds, a focus for fear, as well as for romantic projection.

My question then becomes: Is the origin story of AIDS, as it is construed in the United States, giving rise to metaphors that are inspired by and thus resemble the "great chain of being" idea? Is AIDS ontogeny recapitulating a false phylogeny? By placing lower primates at the beginning of the infectious chain, white male heterosexuals at the end of the chain, and black people, Hispanics, gay men, and IV drug users at intermediate points along it, aren't we running the risk of pointing the finger of responsibility for AIDS in the direction of people whom heterosexual white society perceives to be less highly evolved than itself? There is strong evidence that this is indeed the case, and that the "illness" perception of AIDS in the United States has contributed to the propagation of the "disease" through the failure to take it seriously.

Randy Shilts (1988) demonstrates that as long as white, middle-class, heterosexual Americans did not feel threatened by AIDS, there was little impetus on the part of politicians and public health authorities (with a few notable exceptions) to come to grips with the problem. To some observers, this indifference was conspicuous. In 1981, for example, commentator Frank Gifford wondered why, in the face of evidence that AIDS was spreading rapidly, no one was paying any attention to it (Shilts, 1988: 110). Later in April, 1982, Congressman Waxman made the cogent observation (1988: 143–44) that AIDS, unlike "Legionnaire's Disease," struck the socially unacceptable and was thus being ignored by the political establishment. The amounts of money spent on disease research in the United States during the first years of the AIDS epidemic are quite telling. While the National Institutes of Health spent an average of $34,841 in 1981 for each person who died of "Legionnaire's Disease," only $3,225 was spent by the same organization in 1981 for each person who died of AIDS, and only $8,991 in 1982 (Shilts, 1988: 186). Clearly the hierarchy of national health priorities during this time tended to reflect "illness" perceptions.

Furthermore, many of the most inflammatory statements concerning AIDS emanated from persons in the center of the public eye. On May 24, 1983, columnist Patrick Buchanan, formerly director of White House communications, commented: "The poor homosexuals—they have declared war upon nature, and now nature is exacting an awful retribution" (Shilts, 1988: 311). Two months later, "Moral Majority" leader Jerry Falwell echoed these sentiments with the observation that, "When you violate moral, health, and hygiene laws, you reap the whirlwind. You cannot shake your fist in God's face and get by with it" (Shilts, 1988: 347). The comments of these two men are not just noteworthy for their obvious insensitivity, what is also of interest is the direct relationship of these statements to illness metaphors employed in the Middle Ages and the sixteenth century. Although some elements of white heterosexual American society can still imagine themselves at the evolutionary pinnacle of the "great chain of being," the attitudes of its spokespersons with regard to sickness have not really advanced much in the past four centuries.

AIDS as "Illness" in Rwanda

It is interesting to compare our notions about AIDS with those prevalent in Rwanda. According to our ideas, Rwanda is situated very close to the geographical epicenter of the AIDS pandemic. But Rwandans, as I indicated earlier, see the disease as being of American and European origin and as having originated among gay men and IV drug users. While in Rwanda, I found a poster at the National University of Rwanda in Butare intended to warn students about AIDS. I was surprised, however, that the two figures in the poster, a man clad only in his underpants and a fully nude woman, did not have black features. While the artist may not have intended the poster to suggest this, the viewer might very well understand that AIDS is primarily a white disease. Another interesting aspect about this poster was that the woman was chasing the man and that it was the woman who was portrayed as infected. The poster was entitled, "Twilinde SIDA," meaning, "Let's guard against AIDS!" The woman in the drawing was depicted as saying, "Come, let me give it to you," while the man running away from her replies, "Oh, no! You won't infect me with AIDS!"

It would seem from this poster that the artist was attributing responsibility for the spread of AIDS in Rwanda first to Europeans and Americans, and second, to women. This second aspect, relating to women, is of interest for it reflects the ambivalence of Rwandan cultural attitudes toward female sexuality. While Rwandan culture has always promoted healthy female sexuality, females were also, in former times, very closely surveyed. The reason for this was that female sexuality, when left to its own devices, was perceived as uncontrollable. There were very stringent measures of repression. Young women who became pregnant out of wedlock could be hurled from cliffs, thrown into rivers, or brought to islands in the middle of Lake Kivu and abandoned there. In some regions of Rwanda, I was told, these measures persisted until the early 1950s.

. . . Many of the ambivalent attitudes associated with female sexuality, though, linger on. Women, especially in urban centers, enjoy greater freedom, but the belief persists that women should follow a stricter code of sexual conduct than men. In the spring and early summer of 1983, this attitude surfaced when hundreds of single, urban Rwandan women were rounded up, charged with "vagabondage," and placed in re-education camps. Although many of these women were indeed prostitutes, a much greater number were legally employed and guilty of nothing more than consorting with European men socially.

The French newspaper, *Libération,* commented sardonically upon this in an article entitled, "Touche pas à l'homme blanc" ("Don't touch the white man"). According to Rwandan men that I spoke with regarding these measures of repression, a few highly placed government ministers feared that the sexual mores of Rwandan women who had European fiancés or boyfriends could be corrupted. They might become prostitutes or take up European sexual practices such as fellatio, cunnilingus, and anal intercourse. Rwandan women thus continue to be regarded through the scrutinizing eyes of a male-centered society and this regard focuses particularly upon how women use their sexual capacity. Nevertheless, despite the greater severity applied to women, female sexual satisfaction remains valued as a necessary prerequisite to fertility, and fertility is probably the foremost value in Rwandan culture. There is thus a contradictory tendency inherent in the culture both to encourage, and to fear, healthy female sexuality.

While in the Rwandan capital of Kigali, I listened to a radio program concerning AIDS. The radio commentator, a man, seemed to place the entire responsibility for the spread of the disease upon females. Female prostitution and female conjugal infidelity were the primary reasons for the spread of AIDS, he maintained, and should be strictly discouraged. It did not seem to occur to him that men frequent female prostitutes, nor that more often Rwandan men are unfaithful to their wives than vice versa. My point is not so much that the commentator was wrong in laying the blame for AIDS upon women, as much as that he was relying upon an old cultural attitude concerning the nature of female sexuality to explain a new problem. Despite the newness of the "disease" of AIDS, the "illness" of AIDS has been, in part, culturally prefabricated. Hence, as in the poster described earlier in this chapter, an infected woman is chasing a reluctant man.

Conclusion

Societies around the world with a high HIV seroprevalence have tended to construct illness metaphors about the sickness in very specific ways. These metaphors often strike more at emotionality than at rationality, but they can be understood by looking closely at the society's history and culture. Illness metaphors draw social and moral boundaries between the imagined states of civility and disorder. They describe both the disruptive forces societies fear from outside their borders, as well as the subversive forces societies fear from within. Furthermore, these illness metaphors influence the course of action that social systems take to combat disease, for whether a society responds attentively or with indifference to a disease depends in large part upon its perception of the status of those who suffer from it. In some instances these metaphors become part of the problem, part of the pathogenic process associated with disease. Responsible health policy thus entails curing society of its "illnesses," as well as of its "diseases."

While it seems useful to denounce the process of constructing potentially harmful illness metaphors as Sontag (1977) has done, it is also naive. The process of attributing social and moral values to the largely fortuitous occurrence of contracting disease is probably an inevitable corollary to social existence. Instead, an attempt must be made to understand the specific cultural logic that underlies these metaphors. Even if metaphoric elaboration cannot be avoided with certain sicknesses, we should remember that metaphors can be changed, and that hopefully, we can discourage the tendency to blame our diseases on scapegoats. While no effort should be spared in attempting to understand AIDS as a "disease," we also need to comprehend AIDS as an "illness," and this means attempting to understand society and culture.

NOTE

1. The term "sickness" will be used throughout this chapter whenever it is unnecessary to rigorously distinguish between "disease" and "illness."

REFERENCES

Barnouw, E., and Clark, E. G., "Syphilis: The Invader," Public Affairs Pamphlet no. 24, Columbia University Press, New York, 1955.

Berger, P., and Luckman, T., *The Social Construction of Reality,* Anchor Books, New York, 1967.

Coulter, H., *AIDS and Syphilis: The Hidden Link,* Washington, D.C.: North Atlantic Books, 1987.

Douglas, M., *Purity and Danger,* Routledge and Kegan Paul, London, 1966.

Eatough, G., *Fracastoro's Syphilis.* Classical and Medieval Texts, Papers and Monographs 12, Francis Cairns, Liverpool, 1984.

Gaignebet, C., and Florentin, M. C., *Le Carnaval,* Payot, Paris, 1974.

Gould, S. J., *The Mismeasure of Man,* Norton & Co., New York, 1981.

Kleinman, A., *Patients and Healers in the Context of Culture.* University of California Press, Berkeley, 1980.

Kleinman, A., Eisenberg, L., and Good, B., "Culture, Illness, and Care: Clinical Lessons from Anthropologic and Cross-Cultural Research," *Annals of Internal Medicine,* vol. 88, 1978: 251–58.

Lovejoy, A., *The Great Chain of Being.* Harvard University Press, Cambridge, 1936.

Shilts, R., *And the Band Played On,* St. Martin's Press, New York, 1988.

Sontag, S., *Illness as Metaphor,* Farrar, Straus and Giroux, New York, 1977.

Turner, V., *The Ritual Process,* Cornell University Press, Ithaca, 1969.

Wallerstein, I., *The Modern World System,* Academic Press, New York, 1976.

STUDY QUESTIONS

1. What cultural patterns link perceptions and understandings of AIDS to syphilis and leprosy?
2. What is the "great chain of being" idea, and how has that idea found expression in the HIV/AIDS health crisis?

3. How does Taylor explain the very different responses of politicians and public health officials to Legionnaire's Disease and to AIDS?
4. How do the culturally specific Rwandan notions about female sexuality figure in government programs to combat HIV transmission and in the public understandings held by Rwandans about the origin of HIV?
5. In what ways does cultural climate distort scientific thinking and public health policy?[*]

[*] The "vulnerable rectum" versus "rugged vagina" hypothesis and the "toxic semen" hypothesis are quintessential examples of the overwhelming power of cultural constructions to shape scientific thinking. See especially John Langone, "AIDS: The Latest Scientific Facts," *Discover* (December 1985):27–52; and C. M. Mavligit et al., "Chronic immune stimulation by sperm alloantigens: Support for the hypothesis that spermatozoa induce dysregulation in homosexual males," *Journal of the American Medical Association,* vol. 251 (1984):237–241.

AIDS in Africa
The Western Imagination and the Dark Continent
Margaret Cerullo and Evelynn Hammonds

The Dark Continent

The word "plague" . . . conjured up in the doctor's mind not only what science chose to put into it, but a whole series of fantastic possibilities utterly out of keeping with the bourgeois town of Oran, where the plague struck. How could a disease so extraordinary as plague happen in a place so ordinary and dull?

—Paula A. Treichler, following Albert Camus, *The Plague*[1]

"AIDS," Paula Treichler points out in reference to gay men in the US, "in initially striking people perceived as alien and exotic by scientists, physicians, journalists and much of the US population, did not pose such a paradox." This is perhaps even more true of reports of AIDS in Central and East Africa, where the association with disease and "exotic" sexual practices comes naturally to the Western imagination. One of the troubling aspects one faces in trying to understand the AIDS pandemic is the Eurocentric and racist views that shape information about the prevalence of the virus in Africa.[2] First of all, the data from one city or country is routinely generalized across the continent as if "Africa" were a simple unity.[3] Imagine generalizing the AIDS picture in San Francisco to Boise, Idaho, as if the incidence or the risks were likely to be the same.

Reprinted with the permission of The Alternative Education Project (© 1987) from *Radical America,* vol. 21, nos. 2–3 (March–April 1987):17–23.

Second, researchers now recognize that early HIV surveillance in Africa (1983–85) produced significant numbers of false positive results, due to the fact that the presence of other diseases, in particular malaria which is quite common, produced a positive test result. Yet, as the Panos Institute points out, many researchers continue to quote the earlier incidence figures without noting the necessary revisions.[4]

Images of Africa as the dark, primitive continent persist. Because heterosexual transmission was identified early among HIV positive persons in many African countries, the US media continues to publish articles framing a debate on whether heterosexuals here (read "white middle class heterosexuals") are at risk for AIDS. *Cosmopolitan* author Robert Gould differentiates between the violent sex of African men "taking" their women and the gentle sex of white (civilized) heterosexuals in the West to account for the 1:1 ratio of men to women AIDS cases in Africa.[5] Fran Hosken repeats this fantasy with a feminist slant stemming from her concern with sexual violence against women perpetuated through "genital mutilation": "It is clear that traditional sexual practices by African men, as well as the widespread custom of genitally mutilating a large part of the female population, are responsible for the different pattern of AIDS transmission. The heterosexual transmission of AIDS in Africa is clearly [?] explained by violent sexual practices."[6]

The effort to separate "their" heterosexuality from "ours" has rested on three other main arguments. First is the emphasis on sexual "promiscuity" as a research focus. The risk factors that have been identified among heterosexuals include "number of sexual partners, sex with prostitutes, and being a prostitute" in part because these are the risk factors that have been looked for.[7] *Science* magazine recently reported approvingly the observation of a Belgian scientist that, among heterosexuals, individuals with a large number of sexual partners might be found more in African cities than in the West. *Science* was dismissive of the African health official who accused the Western scientist of "unscientific speculation."[8] Second is the speculation that heterosexual transmission in Africa results because anal intercourse is a common form of birth control.[9] The problem with such generalizations is not entirely whether they are true or false (though data do not seem to support this speculation), but that they are reported in such a way as to imply that such practices are so different from ours (which is questionable) and that it is such behavior that brought down this terrible scourge.

The third and probably the favorite argument about heterosexual transmission in Africa depends upon an abysmal lack of knowledge of the geography, let alone the cultural and political diversity of Africa. This is the argument associating the equal sex ratio of African AIDS cases with the "widespread" practice of female genital mutilation. In fact the areas where genital mutilation is practiced do not correlate with those countries in which AIDS is prevalent. That this point has not even been noticed indicates how little Americans know about Africa. The primary source for the accounts of female genital mutilation in Africa known to Western feminists is the writing of Fran Hosken, who is the source of the maps that are continually reproduced to represent the "widespread custom" of "genitally mutilating a large part of the female population in Africa."[10] Yet these maps are deceptive. By "coloring in" entire countries if the practice exists at all within them (and these practices vary considerably according to ethnic group, religion, and culture), the extent of female genital mutilation is exaggerated.[11] A second, and recently prominent source of the "genital mutilation" connection is Hannah Edemikpong, who writes from "the Women's Center in West Africa." (This is about as precise a designation as "the Women's Center in Western Europe," or "the Women's Center in the eastern US.") In a recent letter sent to a number of individuals and organizations in the US to appeal for funds for the grassroots campaign against genital mutilation she and her associates are waging, she claims they have dissuaded five million rural women from the practice.[12] She is also the source for Charles Hunt's assertion in *Monthly Review*'s article on AIDS in Africa of a likely connection between female genital mutilation and AIDS in Africa. He quotes Edemikpong as claiming to have authenticated a "research revelation: of the 98,000 reported cases of AIDS in Africa since 1984, three-quarters are women who are from the areas where female genital mutilation is widely practiced."[13] It is very difficult to know what to make of such numbers. According to the Panos Institute's most recent report (January 1988), compiled from WHO statistics, there are currently 8700 reported cases of AIDS in Africa.[14] And five million rural women dissuaded from genital mutilation would represent something of a cultural revolution in Africa which we might have heard of sooner. While we do not wish to make light of the possibility that genital mutilation could contribute to HIV transmission, at this historical moment, this connection does not seem to exist empirically.

Origin Stories

Paralleling the search for Patient "Zero". . . in the gay community, the scientific community intensified its efforts to find the place were the AIDS virus originated. By 1983, some evidence suggested that AIDS may have shown up first in Africa. As Western scientific and media attention focussed on this fact, health personnel from African countries found themselves on the defensive. Reports continue to highlight the "reluctance" of leaders from African countries to acknowledge the presence of AIDS in Africa while conversely not noticing the reluctance of our own country to confront the epidemic which has up until recently been dealt with by organizations in the gay community.[15] Few accounts (if any) have suggested that there might be legitimate reasons on the part of African medical personnel or politicians to question information about AIDS in their countries. The initial identification of AIDS as the gay plague clearly shaped their response as it has official response by countries around the world. But health workers in Africa also expressed resentment at the way in which the complexity of health and disease among their peoples was ignored by Western scientists and the press while "abnormal" sexual behavior was emphasized.

As Africa was identified as the place where the virus originated, response from other countries toward African travelers was predictable.[16] *African Concord* reported in October 1986 that the British government had proposed to screen all visitors from Uganda, Zambia and Tanzania for the HIV virus. As the article noted, ". . . though a number of African countries have experienced a number of deaths from AIDS, they are far outstripped by America, where figures have reached epidemic proportions. Yet the British government has no plans to screen the many Americans visiting the country."[17]

The popular press has seen no need to inform us that early reports of the prevalence of AIDS in Africa were invalid, as we have indicated, because of the high number of false positives among the results. As confirmatory tests and better equipment have become more widely available, many countries in Africa have acknowledged the presence of AIDS. In Uganda, Rwanda, and Zaire, research labs have been established, wider use of blood screening is occurring, and healthation programs are being implemented.

The fondness for African "origins" is illustrated by a recent research study and its reporting in the popular press. The study took place in Zaire where the availability of blood samples collected in 1976 made it possible to search retrospectively for HIV infection in rural Zaire. The study found a constant (low) presence of the HIV antibody in a similar population ten years later. This suggested to the researchers both that HIV infection has existed for at least ten years in some parts of Africa, and that "disruption of traditional lifestyles" due to urbanization may account for the stability of infection in "traditional, rural" Zaire compared to its sharp prevalence in the urban centers of Kinshasa and Kingali. By the time this research reached the Boston *Globe*, the headline read "Study in Zaire shows AIDS virus may have existed for 100 years," and the story began, "AIDS infections have *smoldered* in the *remote* villages of Zaire for the past twelve years—and possibly for as long as a century [*why not?*]—according to authors of a study published this week." (Italics ours)[18]

Modes of Transmission: Epidemiology of AIDS in Africa

As of 1987 most researchers agreed that AIDS first appeared in Africa in the late 1970s as it did in the US and Haiti. The countries with the highest number of reported cases are from East and Central Africa and include: Burundi, Kenya, Rwanda, Tanzania, Uganda and Zaire. Zambia also has a high caseload. Because the reporting of cases is still sketchy it is not possible to give an accurate number of the cases in Africa.

Since AIDS is a complex syndrome and not a single disease, it is not surprising that the picture of AIDS in Africa shows some marked differences from what we see in the US and Europe. In Africa the highest incidence of AIDS has been found among sexually active heterosexuals, twenty–forty years old, with equal numbers of men and women affected. The women tend to be younger than the men and a high percentage are thought to be prostitutes. [Researchers tend to use an expansive definition of "prostitute." For example, in research in Zaire, the term included "free women" (*femmes libres*), which it is recognized applies not only to prostitutes but to unattached, sexually active women.][19] Those who have the virus frequently also have a venereal disease. High rates of sexually transmitted diseases have been found in the general population and in HIV positive persons. Homosexuality and i.v. drug use are not considered factors in the transmission of the virus. However, that conclusion could be incorrect given that not much is known about homosexuality in African countries.[20] The opportunistic infections associated with AIDS in Africa are more often stomach or digestive infections, skin diseases, tuberculosis and meningitis rather than Kaposi's sarcoma and pneumonia reported in the US.

There is no clear answer as to why the HIV virus produces such different clinical results in East and Central Africa, though suppressed immune systems may be a key factor. Many Africans have diseases associated with poor nutrition and poverty that result in compromised immune systems. Protein-calorie malnutrition which is widespread in these countries is known to be the most common cause of T-cell immunodeficiency world-wide.[21]

The numbers of children with AIDS are also high in Central and East Africa and in Zambia. Many of them are believed to have been infected through blood transfusions. The children receive blood transfusions in African hospitals for malaria-related or sickle cell–related anemia. In Rwandan hospitals for example, about one child in three receives such transfusions. And nearly 20% of Rwanda's HIV positive children were infected in this way.[22]

As noted above, i.v. drug use is not considered a factor in the spread of AIDS in Africa but the use of needles for medical injections (often preferred by African patients who believe needle injections are more effective than oral medication) and ritual scarring may play some part in the spread of the virus. The re-use of needles is common because of the lack of adequate supplies of sterile ones.

What we know about the epidemiology of AIDS in Africa raises more questions than answers. The complex mesh of factors associated with the disease means that currently there is no way to ascertain the relative importance of the various methods of transmission.[23] For example, it is not known whether a prior history of sexually transmitted diseases is a risk factor because genital lesions facilitate the transmission of HIV or because of exposure to unsterilized needles for treatment of sexually transmitted diseases.[24]

Nor is it known how the number of sexual partners versus the frequency of sexual activity, or the presence or absence of genital lesions or compromised immune systems, act together to affect the course of the virus. In terms of morbidity and mortality, malaria, diarrheal disease and malnutrition may be more important than AIDS to people in Africa. And the way in which the HIV virus progresses in the presence of these factors could also lead to a rise in other endemic diseases like syphilis and tuberculosis in such a way that standard forms of treatment of these diseases would have to be modified in significant and probably more expensive ways.[25]

Implications: The Prospect of Testing

There has been increasing pressure from international aid agencies for African governments to institute programs of "routine" HIV-antibody testing among their populations, but this has been resisted by Africans as reflecting priorities of interest to Western aid agencies, not in tune with African realities. Mozambique, for example, is currently unable to test pregnant women (prime candidates for HIV-screening) for syphilis, which is treatable and known to be prevalent.[26] Testing is not only expensive, but there is concern that programs would be confounded by prejudice about who's "at risk."[27] There is also concern that publicity about AIDS would result in less blood donated. Evidence from the US, where more than half the population refuses to give blood because of confusion about AIDS transmission suggests that such concerns are well-grounded.

Screening the blood supply for the presence of HIV antibody would seem to be an urgent health priority in Africa. Tanzanians, for example, are currently advised to have blood transfusions only in cases of life or death emergency.[28] It is hard to imagine how people absorb this information and make decisions on the basis of it. Yet, many have pointed out that the cost of protecting the blood supply is prohibitive: a US House Select Committee on Hunger Report, e.g., estimates that blood bank screening in Africa would cost approximately thirty times the annual public health expenditures of the entire continent.[29] The idea that blood bank screening, because it is so expensive, is "out of the question"[30] is repeated by most analysts of AIDS in Africa, including radicals.[31] Yet, it is worth at least questioning the elements of the "cost" of the blood test.[32] As the test is currently performed, a single test kit set costs about $3–$5,[33] and repeated tests are often necessary to ensure valid results. All tests are subsequently sent to a laboratory for analysis by skilled technicians using special equipment (the electronic blood test machine is reported to cost $3000).[34] Clearly, as the Panos Institute Report points out, an inexpensive [test] beside blood test is urgently needed in Africa. But equally clearly, this is not likely to become a priority for pharmaceutical companies' research and development, any more than reduction of the "cost" of test kit sets. With the lucrative Japanese market about to open up as Japan moves to institute mandatory testing of their population (estimates put the Japanese market at $22.5 million),[35] the prospect of protecting the African blood supply cheaply does indeed begin to seem "out of the question." However, we must remember that how much it "costs" to test the African blood supply is not a natural fact. Like other costs, it involves a political determination.

AIDS and Maternal/Infant Health: A Development Crisis

AIDS "is no longer simply [sic] a medical emergency" in Africa, proclaims the House of Representatives Select Committee on Hunger report, it is a "development crisis." In addition to the people suffering from AIDS, and the enormous costs of treating them, which are already outrunning health budgets in some countries, there is concern that AIDS may reverse years of progress in promoting breast-feeding and childhood vaccination in Africa. Bottle-fed babies are twice as likely to die as breast-fed babies in poor communities in the Third World, due to unsterile bottles, contaminated water used in making formula, and/or malnutrition due to dilution of milk powder to save money. It is unclear whether HIV infection can be transferred from mother to child via breast milk; one case has been reported in the medical literature.[36] But, there are reports that African mothers have stopped breast-feeding their children for fear of passing the virus onto them.[37] And there is real concern that the multinationals, like Nestle, whose "dumping" of powdered milk on Third World countries has been challenged by campaigns for breast-feeding, will find a new selling point for their product in the age of AIDS.[38]

Vaccines for measles, whooping cough, polio, and tetanus have contributed significantly to decreasing childhood mortality and improving children's health in Africa, as elsewhere. However, it has apparently been common to reuse needles in vaccinating children, a potential source of HIV transmission. The fear of infected needles is apparently discouraging parents from having their children immunized.

You Have Been Chosen . . .

A recent report to the President's AIDS Commission that flashed in and out of the press[39] perhaps needs some closer attention by those concerned with the international politics of AIDS. The report by Dr. Anthony Fauci, director of the National Institute of Allergy and Infectious Diseases, concerned the (grim) prospects for developing an AIDS vaccine. If a vaccine does look promising in laboratory studies, however, large scale human trials "may have to be" conducted in Africa, according to Dr. Fauci, who directs the federal vaccine effort, because the spread of AIDS among gay men in the US has "slowed to an extremely low level." (I. V. drug users, among whom the disease is spreading rapidly, have already been ruled out by government scientists since they are not viewed as reliable subjects for experimental protocols. Their infected sexual partners, overwhelmingly women of color, are not even considered.) "Thousands and thousands" of volunteers would be required for a study to see whether a vaccine protects against AIDS, and American scientists are looking to Central Africa, "where the AIDS virus is still spreading explosively," to provide them. The precedents for testing unproven drugs and vaccines in the Third World should alert us to the potential significance of US health officials proposing to use Africans as guinea pigs for AIDS experiments.

Notes

1. Paula A. Treichler, "AIDS, Homophobia and Biomedical Discourse: An Epidemic of Signification," *Cultural Studies, Vol. 1, #3* (October 1987).
2. The usually quoted figures are 1.5 to 5 million. We have been unable to locate the statistical arguments that support these widely divergent estimates. They are continually being revised either dramatically upward or more recently, dramatically downward.
3. See e.g., T.C. Quinn, H.M. Mann, J.W. Curran, P. Piot, "AIDS in Africa: An Epidemiological Paradigm," *Science,* vol. #234, November 21, 1986, pp. 995–63, where incidence in Kinshasa, Zaire, one of the most heavily affected cities in Africa, is generalized to "Central Africa." It is common to read figures like 27 to 88% of female prostitutes or 1 to 18% of pregnant women infected, as if studies made with varying numbers of subjects in vastly different places can say something meaningful about the overall incidence of HIV infection in "Africa."
4. Panos Institute, *Panos Dossier I: AIDS In The Third World,* March 1987; update, Jan 1988. This is the best source we have found on AIDS in Africa.
5. Robert E. Gould, M.D., "Reassuring News About AIDS: A Doctor Tells Why You May Not Be At Risk," *Cosmopolitan,* January 1988, p. 147.
6. Fran P. Hosken, "Female Genital Mutilation and AIDS," *Sojourner,* February 1988, p. 7.
7. See Deb Whippen, "Science Fictions: The Making of a Medical Model for AIDS," *RA,* Vol. 20, No. 6 for a detailed argument about how the focus on promiscuity similarly blocked research into specific sexual *practices* associated with HIV infection among gay men in the US.
8. David Dickson, "African Begins to Face Up to AIDS," *Science,* Vol. 238, 30 October 1987.
9. Lawrence K. Altman, "Linking AIDS to Africa provokes bitter debate," *New York Times.* November 21, 1986, p. 8.
10. Hosken reproduces her famous map in *Sojourner,* February, 1988, p. 7. The same map appears in Joni Seager and Ann Olson, *Women in the World: An International Atlas* (New York: Pluto Press, 1986), Section 4. Seager and Olson's own map (also in Section 4) by emphasizing percentages of women affected, corrects the distortion. See also Hosken's letter to the *New York Times,* "Why AIDS Pattern Is Different in Africa," December 15, 1986.
11. We are grateful to Fran White for making this point to us, as well as for extensive discussion of the possible relationship between female genital mutilation and the heterosexual spread of AIDS in Africa.

12. Hannah Edemikpong, "Speaking Out on Female Genital Mutilation," *Gay Community News,* March 13–19, 1988.
13. Charles Hunt, "Africa and AIDS," *Monthly Review,* February 1988, quoting Edemikpong, p. 17.
14. Panos Institute, *op. cit.* Update on the worldwide incidence of AIDS. January 1988.
15. See e.g., David Dickson, *op. cit.*
16. Belgium is currently considering requiring an HIV test for visitors from some African countries, according to information presented at the International Summit on AIDS held in London. *The Economist,* January 30, 1988.
17. *African Concord,* October 23, 1986, p. 41.
18. Richard A. Knox, *Boston Globe,* February 6, 1988 reporting on N. Nzilambi et al., "The Prevalence of HIV Virus over a Ten-Year Period in Rural Zaire," *New England Journal of Medicine,* February 4, 1988.
19. N. Nzilambi, et al., *op. cit.,* p. 277. For a discussion of the concept of *femme libre,* see Janet MacGaffey, "Women and Class Formation in a Dependent Economy: Kisangani Entrepreneurs," in Claire Robertson and Iris Berger, *Women and Class in Africa* (New York: Holmes and Meier, 1986), pp. 174–75.
20. See, however, Gill Sheperd, "Rank, Gender and Homosexuality; Mombassa as a Key to Understanding Sexual Options," in Pat Caplan, ed., *The Cultural Construction of Sexuality* (Tavistock: London and New York, 1987). Nancy Krieger notes that only two studies in the literature have "indirectly implicated" homosexual transmission in Africa and the numbers are very small. "The Epidemiology of AIDS in Africa," *Science for the People,* January–February, 1987, pp. 18–19.
21. Paul Epstein and Randall Packard, "Ecology and Immunology," *Science for the People,* Jan/Feb 1987, p. 13.
22. Panos Institute p. 42. For Zaire, where 13% of the pediatric patients in a Kinshasa hospital were HIV positive and suspected to have been infected by blood transfusions used to treat malaria-related anemia, see A. Greenberg, et al., "The Association Between Malaria, Blood Transfusions, and HIV Seropositivity in Pediatric Population in Kinshasa, Zaire," *Journal of the American Medical Association,* January 22/29, 1986, vol. 259, No. 4.
23. Panos Institute p. 42.
24. T.C. Quinn et al., *op. cit.,* p. 959.
25. Piot, "AIDS: An International Perspective," *Science,* February 5, 1988, p. 57.
26. Julie Cliff, Najami Kanji, and Mike Muller, "Mozambique Health Holding the Line," *Review of African Political Economy,* No. 36 (September 1986), p. 18.
27. *Ibid.*
28. *African Concord,* September 25, 1986, p. 27.
29. *Africa News,* Vol. 28, No. 7, p. 12.
30. Cliff, Kanji, Muller, *op. cit.*
31. Besides Cliff, Kanji, and Muller, see Charles Hunt, "AIDS in Africa," *Monthly Review,* March 1988.
32. We are grateful to RA editor, Judy Housman, for raising this issue to us. For an enthusiastic analysis of the international AIDS testing market (currently estimated at $100 million annually, and expected to double over the next five years as calls for testing intensify), see Vicki Glaser, "AIDS Crisis Spurs Hunt for New Tests," *High Technology Business,* January 1988.
33. Panos Institute, *op. cit.,* p. 6.
34. *Ibid.,* "Sister Nellie in Kampala," p. 43.
35. *Ibid.,* p. 48.
36. *Ibid.,* p. 38.

37. *Africa News, op. cit.*
38. Panos Institute, *op. cit.,* p. 38.
39. "US Health Official Calls Africa Best Place to Test AIDS Vaccine," *New York Times,* February 19, 1988.

STUDY QUESTIONS

1. How have preexisting stereotypes of Africa shaped Western notions about HIV transmission in Africa?
2. How do Cerullo and Hammonds respond to the hypothesis that female genital mutilation fuels heterosexual HIV transmission in Africa?
3. According to the authors, how has the Western press distorted epidemiological evidence about HIV in Africa?
4. Why do Cerullo and Hammonds argue that malaria, diarrhea, and malnutrition might be more devastating to people in Africa than AIDS in 1987?
5. What forces and cultural perceptions inform the proposals of Western and international aid agencies to test drug therapies and HIV vaccines on people living in Africa?

Suggested Additional Readings

Dennis Altman, *AIDS in the Mind of America* (New York: Anchor Press/Doubleday, 1986).

Alan Brandt, *No Magic Bullet* (New York: Oxford University Press, 1985).

Elizabeth Fee, "Sin Versus Science: Venereal Disease in Twentieth-Century Baltimore." Elizabeth Fee and Daniel Fox. *AIDS: The Burden of History* (Berkeley: University of California Press, 1988):121–146.

Erving Goffman, *Stigma* (Englewood Cliffs, NJ: Prentice-Hall, 1963).

Dominique LaPierre, *Beyond Love* (New York: Time Warner, 1990).

Jeff O'Malley, "The Representation of AIDS in Third World Development Discourse." James Miller, editor. *Fluid Exchanges* (Toronto: University of Toronto Press, 1992):185–214.

Guenter B. Risse, "Epidemics Before AIDS: A New Research Program." Victoria A. Harden and Guenter B. Risse, editors. *AIDS and the Historian,* National Institutes of Health Publication No. 91-1584 (March 1991).

Susan Sontag, *AIDS and Its Metaphors* (New York: Farrar, Straus & Giroux, 1988).

Gordon Thomas and Max Morgan-Witts, *Anatomy of an Epidemic* (New York: Doubleday, 1982).

Paula Treichler, "AIDS, Homophobia and Biomedical Discourse: An Epidemic of Signification." *Cultural Studies,* vol. 1 (October 1987):31–70.

Simon Watney, *Policing Desire: Pornography, AIDS and the Media* (Minneapolis: University of Minnesota Press, 1987).

A Pattern I Epidemic

The United States Case

• • •

In those geographical areas that have been described as Pattern I epidemics—the United States, Western Europe, Australia, New Zealand, and some Latin American urban areas—AIDS was initially perceived and understood as a gay disease. From the late 1970s through the mid-1980s, Pattern I AIDS epidemics were characterized by (1) high rates of HIV sexual transmission among gay men, (2) low but persistent rates of HIV transmission through intravenous drug use and, prior to the development of the ELISA and Western Blot HIV antibody test in 1985, blood transfusions and the use of blood products for the treatment of hemophilia, (3) low HIV prevalence rates among women, and (4) low rates of perinatal HIV transmission. Yet, the contours of the HIV/AIDS health crisis in the geographical areas initially described as Pattern I epidemics have shifted over time: HIV prevalence rates have increased steadily among injection drug users, heterosexual women, infants, and children; and without effective behavioral interventions or medical therapies, prevalence rates among these groups will continue to rise.

In many respects the Pattern I AIDS epidemic is today an historical artifact. Nevertheless, the perceptions and understandings about AIDS that were forged during the Pattern I phase of the HIV/AIDS health crisis, and the social and cultural forces that informed those perceptions and understandings, are central to comprehending the current HIV/AIDS health crisis. The selections in Part II examine the psychosexual forces that shaped the initial public perceptions about AIDS and suggest the effects that those same psychosexual forces have had on public health policy, on medical therapies, on education and other behavioral intervention programs, and on the daily lives of people who are living with HIV and AIDS.

Sex

Politics and AIDS

Beginning with the Stonewall rebellion in June 1969 and continuing throughout the 1970s, urban gay communities shaped a liberation ideology that welded politics to sex. By 1981 and 1982, however, these communities, now epicenters of the U.S. AIDS epidemic, began to confront a tragic outcome of that well-crafted bond. Focusing on New York City and San Francisco, the selections in Chapter 3 trace the early responses to the epidemic within gay communities. While initial insights into and understandings about the mysterious plague that had emerged could have provided crucial clues about the nature of the disease, resistance to those insights and understandings ran high. The subtext of that resistance unmasked an intricate set of connections between sexual behavior, politics, public health policy, and epidemiology.

During 1982 and 1983, Dr. Joseph Sonnabend and Randy Shilts, both gay men, lived and worked within the vortex of a rapidly escalating gay health crisis. Both issued calls for sexual moderation that either went unheeded or initiated fierce public debate. The contours of those debates anticipated the battlegrounds—cultural, political, economic—that would limit efforts to disrupt and contain the epidemic throughout the 1980s.

A physician originally trained in infectious disease medical research, Joe Sonnabend maintained a Greenwich Village medical practice during the mid-1970s and 1980s. His patients were primarily gay men, and Sonnabend had noted a dramatic increase in both rates and types of sexually transmitted diseases among some of those patients. **The Clap Doctor** describes the research Sonnabend initiated in 1981 using his own patients as subjects.[1] As the scientists at the Centers for Disease Control and the National Institutes of Health searched in their laboratories for the elusive "AIDS agent," Sonnabend easily established laboratory documentation of diminishing T-4 helper cell counts among those patients who were sexually promiscuous and had a medical history of sexually transmitted diseases. In short, a Greenwich Village "clap doctor" first documented the principal route of trans-

---

[1]While Nussbaum refers to this research as an "experiment," it was not an experiment in the most technical sense. Nevertheless, Sonnabend's use of self-reported sexual behavior as a control variable—a common device in field-based behavioral research—certainly qualified his study as quasi-experimental.

mission for Pattern I AIDS epidemics. The rejection of Sonnabend's research by Dr. James Curran, the AIDS hero at the Centers for Disease Control, foreshadowed the strained relationships that would punctuate the epidemic in the coming years between people with AIDS and the scientists who searched in their laboratories for new and effective medical therapies for HIV/AIDS.

As Sonnabend discovered, calls for sexual moderation and for closing the bathhouses and foregoing the Fire Island summer orgies challenged one of the organizing principles of gay community life. By 1983, other gay men were also raising uncomfortable questions about the relationship between the sexual politics that had informed and anchored gay culture for a decade or more and the diseases that were striking down hundreds of gay men. Randy Shilts was one of them.[2]

Sex, Politics, and the Reporter traces the forces that transformed Shilts from a young, ambitious journalist to a critical observer and reporter of the AIDS epidemic. Shilts wrote about his own understandings and perceptions of the senseless sickness and dying that he witnessed and reported. Like Sonnabend's, Shilts's professional perspective set him apart from the "millions of men who have singled out promiscuity to be their principal political agenda, the one they'd die [for] before abandoning . . . a way of connecting—which becomes an addiction."[3] Yet, that sexually defined political agenda alone does not fully explain resistance within gay communities to the calls for sexual moderation. Particularly in the case of some gay businesspeople, financial incentives and concerns also fueled early 1980s resistance to the suggestion that AIDS was sexually transmitted.[4]

Sonnabend continues to be something of a maverick scientist today. He is the medical director of the Community Research Initiative on AIDS, which conducts speedy research of promising AIDS treatments. Sonnabend is also one of the first scientists to put forth the hypothesis that HIV may not be the only cause of AIDS. Shilts died of AIDS in February 1994 at the age of forty-two.

[2]Shilts lived and worked on the West Coast, and his journalistic voice during the early years of the epidemic was primarily regional. Larry Kramer, living and working in New York City during the same period, raised many similar questions about the relationship between gay male sexual behavior and the mysterious plague. See especially Kramer's editorial, "1,112 and Counting," in *New York Native,* March 5, 1983, which also critically questioned the low funding and action priority that local, state, and federal government agencies had assigned to AIDS.

[3]As explained by Larry Kramer's fictionalized self, Ned Weeks, in Kramer's *The Normal Heart,* Act 1, Scene 1, pp. 37–38.

[4]As the epidemic continued and the number of reported AIDS cases mounted, gay communities throughout the United States responded to the health crisis in efficient and effective ways, providing for many people with AIDS the only available primary health care and social services support they would receive. Within five years, the men and women who had voluntarily organized and staffed those health and social services organizations would initiate more explicitly political AIDS-related activities.

The Clap Doctor

Bruce Nussbaum

Joe Sonnabend grew increasingly convinced that sexually transmitted diseases were doing tremendous harm to his patients. He set out to prove it in one of the earliest AIDS experiments in the country. He turned to his practice for volunteers. Virtually every patient wanted to participate and help.

Sonnabend then turned to one of his old "interferon mafia" buddies for help in showing the relationship between STDs and body immunity. Dr. David Purtilo at the University of Nebraska was one of the first scientists to do work in human T-4 cell research. He pioneered in the technique of counting T cells and relating the count to immune function. Purtilo showed that as the T-4 count fell, so did the body's immunity.

Sonnabend drew blood from thirty gay patients: ten were in monogamous relationships with their male lovers; ten dated around; and ten were "sluts," according to Michael Callen, one of his patients who participated. "I was one of the sluts," he says. People in this group had many sexual partners, hundreds if not thousands of them. As a result they also had the highest number of sexually transmitted diseases.

Sonnabend sent the blood samples off to Purtilo at the University of Nebraska. Within a month he received the results. Sonnabend was astounded at the closeness of the correlation between STDs and immunity. The people with monogamous relationships had normal T-4 cell counts. All the "sluts" had extremely low counts; they had the most suppressed immune systems.

It was extraordinary research: clear, simple, and the first of its kind. Sonnabend showed that the immune system of an entire community, the gay community, was under severe stress because of constant attack by syphilis, gonorrhea, chlamydia, and other STDs. He showed that these diseases were wearing down an entire group's protection against infection.

Sonnabend published his results in the *Lancet* in early 1982. The last sentence in his piece said that promiscuity was suppressing the immune system. Just before the article came out, he turned to one of his patients and told him: "If you don't stop fucking around, you'll die." Sonnabend told him that he had almost no T-4 cells left. He was dangerously immunosuppressed. Sonnabend said that he had the same blood parameters as his patients who came down with *Pneumocystis carinii* pneumonia and Kaposi's sarcoma.

Then Sonnabend wrote the same warning in the *New York Native*. He said that the fast-lane gay lifestyle was killing people. He said they were going to have to stop being so promiscuous, that having hundreds if not thousands of sex partners was making them very sick and very vulnerable.

It was a message the gay community didn't want to hear at that time. After fighting for the freedom to be themselves, they didn't want to hear about restraint. Indeed, for a large part of the male gay community, freedom was not simply the ability to love other men without legal or social restraint; it was defined in terms of sexual promiscuity. For many, to be young and gay and liberated in New York City meant having anonymous sex with two, three, four partners a night, night after night, year after year, STD after STD.

Sonnabend began to preach to his practice. He told them to stop screwing dozens of men every week; to stop the crazy stuff, the fisting, the rimming, all the oral–anal sexual practices. He advocated condoms long before "safe sex" became fashionable. Condoms would reduce most of the venereal diseases afflicting his patients, both the old-fashioned ones and this new epidemic.

Sonnabend's *Native* article and his personal message to his patients provoked a tremendous storm of protest. He was perceived as agreeing with the most right-wing, religious moralizers of the new Reagan era in America, of blaming this new "gay disease," this "gay cancer," on the gays themselves. The victim was to blame, or at least the victim's lifestyle. In truth, Sonnabend *was* telling them they had some responsibility for this new epidemic.

For his efforts, Sonnabend was denounced by virtually all of the gay community's leaders. He was vilified in the community itself. It seemed that everyone, except perhaps the thirty patients who participated in the "sluts" research, was angry with Sonnabend. He couldn't quite understand it. It was simply logic. He had done an experiment and proved a point. He was trying to save their lives. Not only was the uproar baffling, it caused Sonnabend tremendous pain. His own community was turning on him. It was a betrayal.

Despite the barrage, Sonnabend was still happy about one thing. He was back in the lab doing important research, leading-edge research. This is where he was always the happiest. He showed his data to Mathilde Krim. She told him it was the most important work being done.

When Sonnabend heard that the Centers for Disease Control in Atlanta was sending someone to New York to check out the mysterious new wave of PCP and KS, he grew excited. He had all this new data to show the CDC, this important new information. Sonnabend thought they'd be incredibly impressed.

Jim Curran was in charge of the CDC's venereal disease prevention division. Cases of KS and PCP were appearing with increasing frequency in Los Angeles, San Francisco, and New York. An ad hoc group at the CDC had recently been put together to investigate this disturbing trend. In time it was formalized into the Kaposi's Sarcoma and Opportunistic Infections (KSOI) Task Force; its job was to hunt down any leads about these cases.

It wasn't easy. There were no succinct categories for what was happening around the country. Specialists in virology, venereal disease, immunology, cancer, and toxicology were in the KSOI. After publication of the June 5 article on PCP in the *MMWR* report, calls were coming in about the pneumonia. Interestingly enough, many of the doctors were also seeing several different infections in one patient. In addition to *Pneumocystis carinii,* KS was common, as was CMV, parasites, and often anemia.

Curran decided he had to see some of these patients. He flew to talk with Dr. Alvin Friedman-Kien and Dr. Linda Laubenstein at the cancer institute at New York University. Curran also wanted to talk with local doctors who were treating these patients. That led him to Sonnabend.

Sonnabend talked nonstop when Curran came to his office. He said that several patterns were beginning to emerge from his research, and he described them excitedly to Curran. So far, the only people coming down with KS and PCP were young gay men. But not all young gay men, he explained. It was the homosexuals with a long history of syphilis and gonorrhea, who usually also had had hepatitis B and various parasitic infections, who were getting KS and PCP. Both were usually accompanied by other infections. It was the combination of infections that was important; cumulatively they were weakening the immune system.

Sonnabend also told Curran that there appeared to be a social factor behind all the infections. Only those who lived in the gay fast lane seemed to be coming down with disease. Men who had many sex partners. Moreover, the sex was fairly kinky. Fisting, inserting the hand into another man's anus; and rimming, running the tongue around and into the anus, were common among people who came down with the most venereal diseases, including these new cases of KS and PCP.

Curran listened but seemed somewhat annoyed with Sonnabend. He didn't appear terribly interested, certainly not impressed. In fact, he left the strong impression that Sonnabend's research wasn't very good. After all, he had used patients in his practice, hardly a true scientific sampling of the population. The CDC, on the other hand, knew how to track down diseases.

"Leave it to us," Curran told Sonnabend. "You take care of your patients and we'll sort out this thing."

Curran's condescending attitude infuriated Sonnabend. He was, after all, a scientist by training. More important, Sonnabend felt that *he* was the one in the gay community actually treating these people. It was he who saw the trends. And it was he who did the research. Not the NIH. Not the FDA. Not the CDC. "Curran's comments really got me angry," Sonnabend says. It was a real put-down, and I've never forgotten that. Absolutely never forgotten that."

It was as if Curran had held Sonnabend and his work to be invisible. Curran's message—the CDC message—was clear. It was not Sonnabend's role to suggest theories about the growing epidemic. It was not Sonnabend's role to hypothesize about the origins of the infections or about the possible treatments. Leave that heavy-duty stuff to the professionals. Neither doctor nor patient was supposed to have the ability to figure out what was behind the epidemic killing the community. Certainly they were not supposed to know how to stop it.

When the National Institutes of Health finally got into the act several years later, America's top research scientists would also hold the community-based doctors and the community itself, the people with AIDS, to be invisible. They would ignore them for many years before a handful of AIDS activists and community doctors forced them to pay attention to the front lines of the epidemic. Unfortunately, in each year of the epidemic, thousands would die as a result of poor research protocols written by well-intentioned academic scientists in ivory tower labs cut off from what was really happening on the ground. These scientists just followed standard operating procedure. AIDS, however, turned out to be anything but a standard infectious disease.

In late July of 1982, the epidemic finally received its formal name. That happened at a meeting of hemophiliacs, blood industry officials, gay political leaders, and various big shots from the CDC, NIH, and FDA.

Several months earlier it had become clear that the new disease could be spread not only through sexual body fluids but through blood as well. The CDC hoped that from this meeting would come guidelines to prevent the contamination of the nation's blood supply. It wanted to ask people who fit into high-risk groups not to give blood. By this time, Haitians and IV drug users had joined gay men as being the most at risk for the new disease.

The meeting was a disaster. Hemophiliac groups didn't want their blood disorder to be associated with a gay disease. Gay community leaders were fearful that being prevented from donating blood was just the first step in quarantining all gay men. Indeed, right-wingers in Washington were already making noises about sending gays to "camps." The FDA and the CDC fought over turf. Regulation of the blood industry fell under traditional FDA authority. The involvement of the CDC was perceived as a threat. Many FDA doctors didn't even believe that a new disease existed. They thought the CDC was simply stitching together a number of unrelated diseases to boost their budget funding.

No one was willing to agree to anything except to wait and see. There was one accomplishment, however. Different groups on different coasts were calling the new disease by many different names. *Gay-Related Immune Deficiency* was the most popular, but it was clearly untrue since IV drug users and Haitians were shown to be vulnerable. *Gay cancer* was used mostly in New York, but it focused on only one of the many opportunistic infections associated with the disease.

Someone at the meeting suggested *AIDS*—Acquired Immune Deficiency Syndrome. It sounded good. It distinguished this disease from inherited or chemically induced immune deficiencies. It didn't mention the word *gay* or even suggest gender. AIDS. It stuck.

STUDY QUESTIONS

1. What first drew Dr. Joseph Sonnabend's attention to the possible relationship between AIDS and other sexually transmitted diseases?
2. What medium did Sonnabend choose to publicize his research findings?
3. Why did the gay community charge Sonnabend with "blaming the victim" when he began to advocate safer sexual practices, such as reducing the number of one's sexual partners?
4. How did Dr. James Curran of the Centers for Disease Control respond to Sonnabend's field research findings?
5. What forces explain Curran's cavalier rejection of Sonnabend's research efforts and findings?
6. What factors within the Pattern I epidemic fueled the change in designation of the immune breakdown from GRID (Gay-Related Immune Deficiency) to AIDS?

Sex, Politics, and the Reporter

James Kinsella

Reporter-cum-Politico

When Shilts returned to the *Chronicle* in October of 1982, he was in no shape to track the story as he claimed it should have been followed. He was drinking a lot, as well as snorting coke regularly. His romantic relationship with a local TV weatherman was on the skids. Finally, in late 1982, he moved out of his lover's apartment. As Shilts stepped out the door, his lover shouted, "Go out and be single and you'll be just another gay cancer statistic." The warning haunted him. Throughout that fall he would wake up startled in the middle of the night and begin searching for the telltale Kaposi's sarcoma lesions.

While Shilts floundered, the *Chronicle's* competition produced some important pieces. On October 24, 1982, the *Examiner* ran the first front-page story to appear in San Francisco's daily press. "New Worry about Gay Disease" outlined the threat of AIDS with a comprehensive analysis of the current medical knowledge. The *Chronicle's* Shilts was not covering the crisis then. Although he harshly criticized reports across the country for disregarding the epidemic, he was guilty of the same sin early on.

In early 1983, Shilts began to understand the scope of AIDS: not just its potential deadliness, but the political turmoil it was causing in the gay

Reprinted with the permission of Rutgers University Press from James Kinsella, *Covering the Plague* (New Brunswick, NJ: Rutgers University Press): 159–174 (edited). © 1989 by Rutgers, The State University of New Jersey.

community. For years, sexual liberation had been the cornerstone of the gay movement. Now, the Harvey Milk Democratic Club, which embraced the slain supervisor's pragmatic politics, was calling for gays to put a halt to promiscuous, unsafe sex. No one was better connected than Shilts to describe the new drive. The main forces behind it—the charismatic Bill Kraus; former street protestor-cum-political aide Cleve Jones; Supervisor Harry Britt, the political successor to Harvey Milk; and Britt's aide, Dick Pabich—had all been sources for Shilts in the past. He had also grown close to them while he wrote *The Mayor of Castro Street.* So intimate was he with that part of the gay political apparatus that, according to one Milk Club activist, though Shilts was never actually a member of the group, he nonetheless made his views known at the meetings.

These activists provoked Shilts into once again writing about the AIDS crisis. First, in March 1983, Bill Kraus had Shilts read Larry Kramer's "1,112 and Counting," which excoriated the government and gays for not taking the epidemic seriously. Then Shilts picked up the weekly gay newspaper, *Bay Area Reporter,* and happened upon a news story about a candlelight march being planned by a local therapist and AIDS patient named Gary Walsh. The protest was an attempt to push for more federal funds to fight the epidemic, the same thing Kraus and Kramer were calling for. Finally, when Kraus leaked to Shilts a study done by epidemiologists at the University of California at San Francisco, the reporter knew he had to take on the epidemic again.

Marked "CONFIDENTIAL," the report revealed the stunning statistic that one in every 350 single men in the city's gay neighborhoods had been diagnosed with AIDS. If the rate of increase continued, by the year's end one of every 175 single men in the gay neighborhoods would have AIDS. Not included in this bleak summary was the number of people who had been infected with the virus, but were not showing any signs of the illness. No one knew that total, which was the population most likely to be passing on the disease. Shilts thought back on his life and realized the odds of his having come in contact with the disease were frighteningly high.

When Shilts began doing the reporting on the study, he was hit with a strong chorus of opposition. Pat Norman, a gay activist in the Public Health Department, warned that the Shilts piece might cause hysteria: "We don't want people thinking they can't eat in Castro restaurants," she said. The president of the Alice B. Toklas Democratic Club claimed it would result in the authorities putting up barbed wire around the Castro. At the time, there was a bill in front of the Texas Legislature to repeal the state's prohibition against sodomy; Shilts got phone calls from Texans who said the law would not pass if he went ahead with the piece. Even the epidemiologists who did the study wanted to stop Shilts from publishing it. They said they had been warned that if they released the information, the gay community would no longer cooperate with their efforts to track the disease. Gays' assistance in the past had been crucial to understanding how the potentially deadly hepatitis B was spread and to developing a vaccine.

Shilts hesitated and then got angry. "I thought there was incredible denial in the gay community," a denial he had grappled with during those sleepless nights when he inspected his body for KS lesions. Shilts went to ask David Perlman's* advice. It was an important story, a good scoop. When he got the nod, Shilts produced the "Startling Finding on 'Gay Disease'," on March 23, 1983, which ran on page two of the newspaper. That breaking news marked a turning point: it was picked up by the wire services, published in a handful of papers across the country, and helped establish the national perception that San Francisco was the center of AIDS. It also represented Shilts's reentry into the story, which would take up increasingly more of his time.

The response from the gay community was quick and harsh. Shunned for his critical reporting in the late seventies, Shilts had received an award from gay community leaders for *The Mayor of Castro Street* in February of 1983. (That year, the same group honored David Perlman for his reporting on AIDS.) Now Shilts could not walk down Castro Street without being shouted at: "gay Uncle Tom," they'd holler, or "sexual fascist."

He was astounded. Shilts had been out of the closet for years, in fact had been a bathhouse regular. He had even worked in a Eugene bathhouse during college.

Sex, Politics, and the Reporter

The *Chronicle*'s coverage of the bathhouse issue was spurred in May 1983 with a lead item in the local column by Herb Caen. The pun-filled prose of this San Francisco media fixture draws many of the *Chronicle*'s 500,000 readers. During the more than half century that he has produced the daily column, he has established connections to almost every corner of the diverse city, and he has provided a wealth of tips to local reporters. From an unnamed source came the claim that an AIDS patient was frequenting the baths.

One of Shilts's editors saw the piece and wanted to know precisely what went on in the city's twenty or so bathhouses. So began the education of the *Chronicle*'s editors and readers about the realities of the city's sex establishments. The interest in San Francisco's bathhouses and backrooms was piqued in part by the fact that the annual Gay Freedom Day Parade, only weeks away, regularly attracted hundreds of thousands of out-of-town gay visitors to the city. The streets, bars, and baths would be filled with gays

---

* Editor's note: David Perlman was the science editor of the *San Francisco Chronicle* when Shilts began to treat AIDS as breaking news. Perlman was responsible for all the pre-Shilts coverage, insisting that the disease be treated as a medical rather than a social or political issue.

from across America, and from cities that might not yet be affected by the disease. Would some take the AIDS virus home after a tryst in the "tubs," as they were known?

That was the theme of Shilts's May 27, 1983, piece, "Gay Freedom Day Raises AIDS Worries": "'There's the potential that AIDS will be spread from here around the country,' said Dr. Mervyn Silverman, director of San Francisco's Department of Public Health. 'There has been some pressure on me to close the bathhouses . . . Certainly, promiscuous and anonymous sex appears to be linked with AIDS in the gay male community.'" But the most Silverman said he would do was bet on the better judgment of gay visitors: "I hope that people coming here will realize they can't do the kinds of things they might do at home."

To some gays, including the Milk crowd, Silverman was shirking his duty. Shilts quoted one vocal doctor involved in the AIDS effort: "I'd love to have a reason to close them [the bathhouses] down," but at the very least the bars and baths should be forced to post health warnings about the dangers of unsafe sex. Not surprisingly, Shilts was sure the Milk Club's battle plan was the right tack, and he hinted at this in a June 11 analysis titled "The Politics of AIDS."

"'They're going to destroy gay businesses,' snarled one Toklas leader," who was opposed to any actions taken against bathhouses or other sex establishments. A Milk leader got the last words in the article: "Business isn't the point. Gay people are dying and the Toklas people are only concerned about keeping their political power." In the piece Shilts speculated that the Toklas Club was having a far greater effect on city policy. The San Francisco Health Department had no plans to mail education pamphlets about AIDS. Could it be, Shilts suggested, that Mayor Dianne Feinstein was listening more closely to the Toklas Club because it had endorsed her in the last election, and the Milk Club had not? With this piece, many in the gay community thought Shilts had stepped over the line. Not only had he aired the gay debate in the straight press, but now he was editorializing in the news pages.

Political analysis often seems to cross the line into editorializing. The distinction is much more obscure when the writer is as closely involved in the organizations he or she is analyzing as Shilts was to the Milk Club and the gay community. The *Chronicle* editors might have recognized the problems this connection was raising had Shilts been covering almost any other brand of politics. Despite the paper's interest in reporting on gays, the editors did not pretend to understand, or to *want* to understand, gay politics. They kept hands off.

Shilts made his point of view clear in a bombastic article in *California* magazine. "Whitewash," the June 1983 cover screamed. Inside, two freelance journalists, Peter Collier and David Horowitz, detailed the trouble Shilts had run into in attempting to put together his "Startling Finding on 'Gay Disease'." The piece indicted Pat Norman, the gay Public Health

Department worker Shilts had quoted, along with some other gay leaders and the public health establishment. Nearly everyone, it seemed—at least everyone in power—was trying to downplay the epidemic for political reasons, according to Shilts.

To the supporters of Norman, who was challenging Milk's successor, Supervisor Harry Britt, for his seat on the Board and his place at the head of the gay community, the politics were being played by Shilts. After all, they said, it was clear Shilts supported Britt, the Milk Club candidate. The tempest drew the attention of a local TV station, which produced a documentary. The result was a TV story on a magazine story on a newspaper story, "media done with mirrors," Shilts said. He had chosen to be the most prominent image reflected in the glass. To defend himself, Shilts agreed to participate in a televised debate with Jerry Falwell, as well as with San Francisco's Public Health Director Dr. Silverman and psychotherapist Gary Walsh, who had become an AIDS activist. The broadcast devolved into a verbal wrestling match between Falwell and Walsh, with the preacher claiming AIDS was simply the wrath of God.

This was not the first time, nor would it be the last, that Shilts left himself open to accusations from politicos. That summer he was particularly vulnerable to criticism. On June 29, his mother was killed by a stroke. It was completely unexpected, and devastating for Shilts.

One night Shilts's lover, whom he had moved back in with, looked at a beleaguered reporter and asked, "Why do you continue writing this stuff?" Shilts thought about his reasons. His editors were not particularly thrilled about the broadsides he was taking. AIDS was an interesting beat, but there were many other aspects of the epidemic he could be covering besides San Francisco gay politics. At the bottom of it all was the fact that he had personalized the story. There were results he wanted, conclusions for which he was willing to weather some nasty storms. The desire to change things had directed him toward journalism in the first place. Now, he wanted to frighten his fellow gays into avoiding unsafe sexual behavior. He tried throughout 1983 and 1984 to get his stories on the dire consequences of promiscuous sex run on Friday, before men would hit the bars or baths. "I wanted everyone to have the fear of God in them."

One of the best examples of this was his reporting on AIDS just before the gay parade in late June of 1983. In one story Shilts reported the CDC's prediction that the current number of AIDS cases was a small fraction of the cases to come: "Because the incubation period gives victims a long time to transmit AIDS to sexual partners, . . . the 1,642 known AIDS victims in the country may be only 5 percent of the people who have been exposed to the still unknown element behind the illness." Embedded in the story was a sidebar announcing "Gay Parade, Celebration Tomorrow."

Shilts's articles, along with the work of other *Chronicle* and *Examiner* reporters and broadcast media like KPIX-TV, undoubtedly helped tame the voracious sexual appetites of many gay men in San Francisco. In mid-1983 three local psychotherapists found significant changes in sexual habits among six hundred gay men they polled. The Bay Area's media share much of the credit, with the San Francisco AIDS Foundation, for influencing behavioral change.

STUDY QUESTIONS

1. What kind of personal background did Randy Shilts bring to his AIDS reporting during 1982 and 1983?
2. What kinds of objections did the gay community in San Francisco raise to Shilts's AIDS reporting style? What were the motives for those objections?
3. What impact did Shilts's journalistic activities apparently have on gay male sexual behavior in San Francisco during the early 1980s?

Suggested Additional Readings

Ronald Bayer, "Sex and the Bathhouses," Chapter 2 in *Private Acts, Social Consequences* (New York: Free Press, 1989):20–71.

Margaret Cruikshank, *The Gay and Lesbian Liberation Movement* (London: Routledge, 1992).

T. A. Kellogg et al., "Prevalence of HIV-1 Among Homosexual and Bisexual Men in the San Francisco Bay Area: Evidence of Infection Among Young Gay Men." Presented at the Seventh International AIDS Conference, Florence, Italy (July 1991).

Arthur D. Kohn, *AIDS: The Winter War* (Philadelphia: Temple University Press, 1993).

Richard D. Mohr, *Gay Ideas: Outing and Other Controversies* (Boston: Beacon Press, 1992).

Larry Kramer, *The Normal Heart* (New York: Plume, 1985).

Tony Kushner, *Angles in America, Part One: Millennium Approaches* (New York: Theatre Communications Group, 1993) and *Part Two: Perestroika* (New York: Theatre Communications Group, 1994).

Randy Shilts, *The Mayor of Castro Street* (New York: St. Martin's Press, 1982).

Simon Watney, "The Politics of Gay Identity in the Age of AIDS." James Miller, editor. *Fluid Exchanges* (Toronto: University of Toronto Press, 1992):329–368.

Blood

Politics and AIDS

• • •

The principal HIV transmission vector in Pattern I AIDS epidemics has been gay male sexual behavior, followed by injection drug use and, before HIV was identified and an antibody test developed, HIV-contaminated blood transfusions and the use of blood products to treat for hemophilia. During the early 1980s, as the number of transfusion-related AIDS cases increased, so too did public pressure for solutions to the problem of HIV-contaminated blood. In July 1982—thirteen months after the first cases of *Pneumocystis carinii* pneumonia and Kaposi's sarcoma had been reported to the Centers for Disease Control—public health officials, administrators of the National Institutes of Health, the Food and Drug Administration, and the Centers for Disease Control, representatives of the blood industry and hemophiliac groups, and gay community leaders convened to consider what action should be taken to remedy the contamination of the nation's blood supply.[1]

The selections in Chapter 4 examine the forces that shaped public health officials' ability to assess independently the situation and then devise and implement appropriate policies to correct what had become a critical threat to the health of the American public. In the United States, widely differing economic and cultural special interest groups entered into this policy debate. The ideologically specific and often competing belief systems these groups brought into the debates tended to obscure the nature of the problem public health officials faced as well as the development of effective solutions to that problem. Within this climate, the American press provided very little coverage of a disease that was spreading rapidly and had claimed more lives than either Legionnaire's Disease or toxic shock syndrome. The *New York Times*'s first front-page coverage of the epidemic, **Health Chief Calls AIDS Battle "No. 1 Priority,"** appeared twenty-two months after the epidemic began, less than three weeks after James Oleske's study that was published in the *Journal of the American Medical Association* fueled public fears about transmission of AIDS through "routine household contact."[2]

---

[1]The number of reported AIDS cases had passed the 1,000 mark before the United States Public Health Service issued its first guidelines for blood donor self-deferral. PHS did not issue conditional recommendations for "safe sex" until March 3, 1983, twenty-one months after the epidemic began.

[2]James Oleske, "Immune Deficiency in Children." *Journal of the American Medical Association* (May 8, 1983):2345–2349.

People like Joe Sonnabend and Randy Shilts coped daily with the immediate and human consequences of AIDS. At the same time, research scientists, remote from the doctors' offices and the sick rooms, carried on their own war against the mysterious disease. In 1984, scientists at the National Institutes of Health in Bethesda, Maryland, and the Pasteur Institute in Paris, France, independently isolated the insidious "AIDS agent." The virus—called HTLV-III by the Americans and LAV by the French—would eventually be designated HIV. Within a year, the federal Food and Drug Administration had licensed the enzyme linked immunosorbent assay (the ELISA) and the more widely used, but also more difficult and more expensive, Western Blot test to detect the presence of HIV antibodies in human blood. **Screening Blood** traces the uncertainties of medical researchers, public health officials, and physicians about the medical meaning of a positive antibody test. Despite this uncertainty, however, all agreed that the availability of reliable HIV antibody tests raised a number of legal and ethical questions: Should blood donors be notified if their blood tested positive for HIV antibodies? If so, how should that notification be delivered? Would the results of the antibody tests be kept confidential, or should those results be reported to public health officials?[3]

Determinants of Public Opinion About AIDS examines public opinion data concerning the relationship between anti-gay attitudes and exaggerated beliefs about AIDS transmission. Prior survey research had established that by 1985, 95 percent of the American public had heard about HIV/AIDS, and the majority indicated that they understood that the disease could not be transmitted through "casual contact." These preexisting beliefs, attitudes, and values shaped public responses to AIDS in the United States during the early 1980s.

[3]The Department of Defense attempted to require blood donor agencies to report positive antibody tests of military personnel to appropriate military health agencies, thereby earning a dubious distinction as one of the earliest violators of the civil rights of people with AIDS. See Randy Shilts, *Conduct Unbecoming* (New York: St. Martin's Press, 1993):480–485, for an account of the DOD attempt to implement this policy.

Health Chief Calls AIDS Battle "No. 1 Priority"

Robert Pear

WASHINGTON, May 24—The Government's top health official said today that the investigation of acquired immune deficiency syndrome had become "the No. 1 priority" of the United States Public Health Service.

Dr. Edward N. Brandt Jr., and Assistant Secretary of Health and Human Services, said the Government was taking steps in an effort to identify the cause and find a cure for the mysterious illness, known as AIDS, which leads to a breakdown of the body's immune system against disease. Dr. Brandt announced six new research grants for study of the ailment and the approval of a new heat treatment for blood products, through which some scientists believe the infectious agent might be transmitted.

At a news conference, Dr. Brandt also said he was urging state and local health officers to report all cases of AIDS. He said the Federal Centers for Disease Control had stepped up surveillance of the disease. Since June 1981, the centers have received reports of 1,450 AIDS cases, of which 558, or 38.5 percent, resulted in death. Among the 78 cases diagnosed at least two years ago, the fatality rate was 82 percent.

In the last three weeks medical journals have carried reports suggesting that the disease could be sexually transmitted from men to women and could be transmitted to children through "routine close contact" with adults. But Dr. Brandt said there was "no cause for fear among the general public that individuals may develop AIDS through casual contact with an AIDS patient."

He confirmed that half the AIDS cases had occurred in New York City, but he said he did not know why. "If we knew the answer why," he said, "we would really begin to understand this disease much more effectively."

While expressing "a sense of great urgency" about the disease, Dr. Brandt said: "We have seen no evidence that it is breaking out from the originally defined high-risk groups. I personally do not think there is any reason for panic among the general population."

Dr. Jeffrey P. Koplan, an assistant director of the Centers for Disease Control, said 71 percent of the AIDS cases had occurred among homosexual or bisexual men. Seventeen percent of those who contracted the disease had taken drugs such as heroin through their veins. Haitian immigrants accounted for 5 percent of the cases, and people with hemophilia accounted for 1 percent. Six percent of the cases were not in any of these groups, but Dr. Koplan said they might have fit into one of the categories if doctors had done more complete investigations.

Dr. Brandt rejected the suggestions of some critics who said the Public Health Service had neglected the disease because it occurred mainly among homosexuals.

But after he spoke, Virginia M. Apuzzo, executive director of the National Gay Task Force, a homosexual rights organization, said: "The entire agency is conducting business as usual insofar as this particular health crisis is concerned. It is inexcusable that a supplemental budget request has not been submitted to Congress."

Shellie L. Lengel, a spokesman for Dr. Brandt, said the disease had been emerging as the top priority of the Public Health Service in the last 6 to 12 months. The priority, she said, was reflected in spending, in personnel devoted to work on the disease, in the number of investigations under way and in the time and attention given to the subject by Federal officials.

Dr. Brandt said the Government expected to spend $14.5 million for work on AIDS this year. That is almost as much as the $15.9 million the Government has spent combating legionnaires' disease since the first recognized outbreak in 1976, he said.

In another indication of growing concern in Washington, aides to Senator Lowell P. Weicker Jr. reported that he would seek $12 million in additional funds for research and other activities related to the immune deficiency syndrome. The money, to be proposed as part of a supplemental appropriation bill for the current fiscal year, would increase Federal spending on the disease by 83 percent. Mr. Weicker, a Connecticut Republican, is chairman of the Appropriations subcommittee that handles money bills for the Department of Health and Human Services.

Some police officers have expressed fears that they might contract the disease through first-aid work involving mouth-to- mouth resuscitation, and some laboratory technicians have worried about being infected when they handle blood samples.

But Dr. Brandt said: "There have been no cases of suspected transmission of AIDS from a patient to a health care provider, nor have there been any cases of suspected transmission of AIDS from laboratory specimens to laboratory workers. There is no evidence to date that indicates AIDS is spread by casual contact. On the contrary, our findings indicate that AIDS is spread almost entirely through sexual contact, through the sharing of needles by drug abusers and, less commonly, through blood or blood products."

Dr. Brandt emphasized that the disease posed a high risk to homosexual men only if they had many partners. The disease has reportedly led to significant changes in the "gay life style." Miss Apuzzo of the National Gay Task Force said homosexual men "had become a lot more reflective" in their relationships, and in some cases, there was a "reduction in the number of partners."

Study Questions

1. What kinds of editorial considerations might have been operating to place this piece on the front page?
2. How might its placement—below the fold and chopped—represent some kind of editorial compromise?*
3. In what ways did this and later similar media coverage of the epidemic foster a mass "moral panic" in the American public?
4. What were the manifestations of that moral panic?

---

* "Below the fold" refers to placement on the page. Toward the top reflects a greater level of newsworthiness than toward the bottom. "Chopped" refers to putting most of the copy on an inside page and thereby minimizing the visibility of the story. This piece, while indeed the first front-page coverage by the *New York Times,* was placed at bottom right on the front page, and the bulk of the copy was continued on A19.

Screening Blood

Ronald Bayer

A little more than a year after the Public Health Service announced its donor exclusion recommendations, Secretary of Health and Human Services Margaret Heckler announced at a national press conference that HTLV-III, a retrovirus, had been identified as the agent responsible for AIDS.[1] A scientific finding that built upon work of French and American researchers, the discovery would fundamentally affect all future efforts to understand AIDS. It also had immediate implications for protection of the blood supply. Government officials were quick to announce that a blood test for the antibody to the virus would be commercially available within six months. At last a test to protect the blood supply was on the horizon. Within a month of the announcement, the American Red Cross made public its plans to begin widescale trial testing of blood donations for antibody to HTLV-III.[2]

But no sooner had the prospect of the availability of such a long-awaited test been made public than concern about how it would be applied began to surface. Such anxieties were compounded by uncertainty about the clinical significance of the presence of antibody. In a letter to Edward Brandt, Jr. [an Assistant Secretary of Health and Human Services], Neil Schram of the American Association of Physicians for Human Rights posed questions about the ethics of the anticipated research and the course of future public policy. "Clearly," he wrote, "studies of gay males, health care workers, and transfusion recipients among others are needed. But what would a positive antibody result signify? Does that mean the individual is immune (if a state of immunity exists with this disease), is going to develop AIDS, or is a 'carrier' either infectious or noninfectious?"[3] With so many critical uncertainties, how would test results be used? Would health care workers with the antibody be permitted to stay in their jobs? Would research subjects want or have a right to examine the results of their antibody tests? Would physicians have an obligation to inform them? Given these critical questions, Schram proposed that the ethical and practical problems associated with giving informed consent to participation in the proposed research studies of HTLV-III antibody be considered by a special interagency panel that would include representation from those at risk for AIDS—gay men. His goal: the rapid development of knowledge "without causing undue concern."

Very quickly concerns within the gay community extended beyond the conditions under which research on the antibody to the AIDS virus would be conducted, to matters involving the ultimate uses of the test. What in mid-1984 might have appeared to be the alarmist response of those schooled in suspicion about the intentions of government would within two years seem prescient. Thus in early July, Jeff Levi of the National Gay Task Force asked a broad constituency of gay groups to consider a range of issues, including the responsibility of blood bankers to inform donors of test results and to maintain confidentiality. Levi was also concerned about how the test would be used more generally. He urged those to whom he wrote to consider the possibility that the antibody test would be used by insurers to make underwriting decisions, by employers to screen out workers and job applicants, by health care workers to identify those they would not treat, by the military to bar recruitment, and by the immigration and naturalization authorities as a barrier to entry into the United States.[4]

Such anxieties were fueled by every move that suggested that public health authorities might require lists of those who were positive. Lists were but a prelude to surveillance and a threatening breach of the privacy so critical to the protection of gay men from discrimination. Thus, for example, when James Curran of the CDC asked the chief epidemiologist of each state to consider the potential utility of an interstate blood donor deferral registry—a list of those found ineligible for donation—for those who tested positive, he provoked a sharp protest despite his explicit concern about whether such an effort would be compatible with the maintenance of the "right to privacy of persons with AIDS-related disorders or persons who are asymptomatic but antibody positive."[5] Neil Schram wrote to the director of the Centers for Disease Control of his "shock" and "outrage." "The risks," he wrote, "of a national list of people positive for antibody to HTLV-III/LAV are tremendous. If the list follows the same characteristics as the people with AIDS, then the list will be a national list of gay and bisexual men and IV drug users. Since homosexuality is still illegal in over 20 states and IV drug use presumably in all states, the potential of that list falling into police hands is tremendous."[6] In a letter to the members of the American Association of Physicians for Human Rights, Schram made clear the need to mobilize political opposition to proposals that even hinted at the prospect of creating a registry of those exposed to the AIDS virus. "I believe the Curran letter is the first attempt to develop a national list . . . of people positive for HTLV-III antibody. In order for that to be effective, the test would have to be a mandatory reported test in all states. This must be fought early and strongly."[7]

So alarmed had gay groups become about the imminent licensing of the antibody test that early opposition to donor exclusion on the basis of sexual orientation and practices virtually vanished. Thus, in mid-December 1984, when the Food and Drug Administration redefined the class of at-risk men to include "males who have had sex with more than one male since 1979, and males whose male partners have had more than one male partner since 1979"—an exclusionary classification that involved virtually every sexually active gay and bisexual male—there was no sign of protest.[8] That the FDA had demonstrated extraordinary sensitivity by stressing in its recommendations the importance of increasing the effectiveness of confidential "voluntary self-exclu-sion procedures" certainly contributed to the reception accorded these new exclusionary standards.

As part of the strategy designed to slow the rapid movement toward licensing of the antibody test, an effort was begun by gay political groups to argue that the test in preparation was inaccurate and might actually decrease the safety of the blood supply by inadvertently undercutting the force of vol-untary deferral guidelines. In a remarkable about-face, the long-sought objec-tive blood test was cast as the threat and exclusion on the basis of risk group membership was portrayed as the more appropriate strategy. "Few people," said Jeff Levi, "want to consider themselves to be at high risk to AIDS; with the government saying there is now a blood test that will screen out those who are truly at high risk, people will be more likely to donate—thinking the blood test will be their insurance against giving infected blood."[9]

But gay groups were not alone in their concern about how the imple-mentation of the new test would affect the safety and adequacy of the blood supply, especially if, as was anticipated, blood collection agencies would be required by federal officials to notify donors of their test results. Blood bankers were also disturbed about the burden—in time, resources, and pro-fessional staff requirements—that the anticipated requirement for notifica-tion would place on them. Indeed, there was considerable resistance to the very notion that blood bankers had an obligation to assume such a role.[10]

Finally, there was concern during the prelicensing period about the fact that the planned ELISA test (enzyme linked immunosorbent assay) would pro-duce an unacceptably high level of false positive findings in low-risk popula-tions. Designed to be especially sensitive, as a precaution against the possi-bility of contaminated blood passing through the screening procedure, the ELISA would, if used without a confirmatory test with a capacity for greater specificity, require the discarding of blood that was in fact untainted. False positive test findings would also result in the identification and potential stigmatization of donors never exposed to the AIDS virus. James Allen of the Centers for Disease Control was not even certain that the most widely used confirmatory test—the Western Blot—would preclude such untoward conse-quences for healthy donors. "Before I tell a person with no risk factors that he's positive, I'd want to know a lot more than I know now."[11]

But to the Food and Drug Administration, licensing of the blood test was a matter of the highest priority despite the uncertainties associated with its implementation. "All we know," said Dennis Donohue, special assistant to the FDA's director of the Division of Blood and Biologics, "at this moment is that an individual whose [blood result] is positive for antibody to HTLV-III has been exposed to the virus. . . . We also know that blood from such an individual should not be used for transfusion."[12] If there were to be errors, the dictates of public health required that they be on the side of safety.

On January 11, 1985, the Public Health Service issued its "provisional" recommendations for the screening of blood.[13] All blood donors were to be told that their blood would be tested for antibody to HTLV-III, that if positive, they would be notified in a confidential manner of the test results, and that their names would be placed on the blood collection agency's donor deferral list along with others deemed unacceptable as donors. Blood that was initially reactive to the antibody test was not to be used for transfusion or the manufacture of other blood products, even though it was admitted that the proportion of false positives among the general donor population on an initial ELISA would be high. It was therefore recommended that no notification occur before at least a second test was done—either a second ELISA or an alternative supplemental procedure. Finally, the FDA made clear that the antibody test was to serve in addition to, rather than as a replacement for, donor self-deferral. Such an approach was necessitated by the small possibility of false negative test results among those who had been infected by the AIDS virus, but had not yet developed sufficiently detectable levels of antibody.

Most remarkable in these recommendations was the insistence upon donor notification. Blood bankers could not avoid the responsibility; donors could not waive the right to such information. So forceful a stance went beyond the patient's "right to know" so central to medical ethics. Typically that right entailed the right not to know the result of medical examinations and tests. Autonomy included the right to shield oneself from the burden of a grim diagnosis. But here the calculus of public health and not clinical ethics was involved. Those who were antibody positive had to know that fact, even if they preferred otherwise, if others were to be protected from exposure through sexual relations or as a result of subsequent blood donations. Restraint and responsibility were predicated on such knowledge.

The insistence upon notification was all the more remarkable since the Public Health Service conceded that the "proportion of these seropositive donors who had been infected with HTLV-III is not known. It is therefore important to emphasize to the donor that a positive result is a preliminary finding that may not represent true infection."[14] Further evaluation by a physician was called for under such circumstances. But whatever the ultimate significance of the test results for any individual, the Public Health Service, having been pressed by representatives of the gay community, underscored the importance of conveying positive findings in a manner designed to protect confidentiality.

Three days after the publication of these recommendations, the Public Health Service's Executive Task Force on AIDS conducted a series of meetings with gay leaders, blood bankers, and public health officials to elicit their reactions.[15] At each session concern was voiced about the conditions under which blood testing would be undertaken, the potential impact on donors, and the consequences for the safety and adequacy of the blood supply. Though a broad coalition of gay organizations had at last acknowledged just days earlier that the testing of blood was an appropriate social intervention, concern about how the blood test might easily be misused in other settings—a long-standing fear—was reiterated. Blood bankers were worried primarily about how the onset of testing might negatively affect the blood supply and stressed the importance of developing a system of alternative test sites that could be used by those seeking to know their antibody status. Some went further and warned that the requirement of donor notification would have serious implications for the safety of the blood supply—even if alternative test sites were available. Inevitably, some high-risk individuals seeking to know their antibody status would use the blood banking system as a source for testing. Speaking for the Conference of Local Health Officials, Mervyn Silverman called on the federal government to fund alternative testing centers where free confidential screening could be done. He warned that a survey in his own city of San Francisco had found that 75 percent of high-risk individuals had stated that they would turn to blood centers for testing unless alternatives were available. Since false negatives could slip through the system, the results could be disastrous. Concerned, as well, about the capacity of local health departments to meet the needs of those who tested positive, Silverman called for a delay in the implementation of testing until an adequate local infrastructure to provide social, psychological, and medical supports was developed.

In the face of the impending licensure of a test designed to protect the blood supply, a broad consensus had thus developed around the need to provide individuals seeking knowledge of their antibody status—no matter how ambiguous the meaning of the test in early 1985—with a network of alternative sites to which they might turn. But at the very moment when this consensus was developing, it masked a profound disagreement that was to have important implications for the evolution of the debate over testing and public health policy in the next two years. Some advocates of testing outside of blood centers anticipated that the ELISA, when subject to adequate confirmation, could be a potentially valuable tool in the effort to meet the challenge posed by AIDS; others saw in the move toward alternative test sites an unfortunate compromise with the demands being made by anxious individuals who, in fact, would learn nothing from the test, whether the results were positive or negative. The January 11, 1985, "Public Health Service Provisional Recommendations" noted that "testing for HTLV-III antibody should be offered to persons who may have been infected as a result of their contact with seropositive individuals, e.g., sexual partners, persons with whom needles have been shared, infants of seropositive mothers."[16] In sharp contrast, Virginia Apuzzo of the National Gay Task Force stated, "[In the alternative test site] it will be essential to provide counseling before and after testing: before testing to *dissuade* the individual from taking the test, so he/she is aware of the potential risks and the fact that there is no clinical value to the test results; after, to try to explain the meaning of the test results—both positive and negative."[17] Even the Association of State and Territorial Health

Officials, which was ultimately to become a strong advocate of testing, warned in early February 1985 that it would be inadvisable, given the limitations of the ELISA test, to expand screening beyond blood centers and alternative test sites operated under research protocols.[18]

Though the concern of blood bankers, public health officials, and gay political leaders did not delay the commercial licensing of the ELISA test, the Food and Drug Administration did respond to the challenges raised during the preceding months of public and private negotiation. Most important, it recognized that donor notification had to be delayed pending the achievement of a level of testing proficiency—though even during the start-up period blood donations that tested positive would have to be discarded. In addition, the FDA recommended that the mandated blood testing be preceded by the development of alternative sites to which those seeking to know their antibody status could be referred.[19] Finally, in a "Dear Doctor" letter, Frank Young, commissioner of the FDA, underscored a point repeatedly made by those concerned about the prospects of the widespread misapplication of the ELISA, and the ensuing threat of stigmatization and discrimination. "The test," he wrote, was "not a test for AIDS."[20]

Blood bank testing began in April 1985. As blood collection agencies gained experience with the ELISA test, the importance of performing a Western Blot confirmatory analysis on repeatedly reactive ELISA's became ever more apparent. The American Red Cross reported that of 10,000 initially reactive blood donations, 1,700 were reactive on a second ELISA, and only 333 positive on the Western Blot test.[21] The Red Cross thus determined that no notification of donors would occur until the more expensive and more difficult Western Blot confirmatory test could be done on all repeatedly reactive donations.

In the wake of the implementation of blood bank testing, some states expressly forbade the notification of donors during the phase-in period. In New York David Axelrod, the commissioner of health, wrote to the state's physicians that "individual results will not be provided until a confirmation test has been carried out to avoid the added trauma of false positive results."[22] Furthermore, reflecting the influence of the political and scientific perspective of gay leaders, he actively sought to discourage the use of the test in settings other than blood banks. "The result can provide no definitive medical information and [can] lead to a false sense of security or anxiety. The available data on both the sensitivity and specificity of the test leave the potential for a wide margin of error in an individual test."

By July, three months after the initiation of screening, blood bankers felt prepared to undertake the task of notification. Some collection agencies merely informed donors of their test results and suggested that they seek appropriate medical follow-up. In New York, however, a decision was made by the New York Blood Center to undertake the initial task of counseling those who tested positive. A special task force was convened to review carefully the content of the educational material that was to accompany the process of informing those with confirmed antibody-positive results. Though both the written and video messages sought to avoid an alarmist tone by stressing that "the evidence . . . thus far seems to indicate that the majority of healthy people who are found to have this antibody will remain in good health," the warnings about the risks of transmission were uncompromising. "When you have sexual relations, use condoms. . . . It may be wise to avoid [the] transfer of saliva . . . in French kissing. . . . If you are a woman . . . don't become pregnant. . . . If you are a man . . . do not impregnate a woman."[23]

At a special July conference sponsored by the National Institutes of Health and the Food and Drug Administration, the first months of blood donor testing were evaluated. The conclusion: testing had been a success. The director of the Center for Drugs and Biologics of the FDA reported that "these tests are doing an extremely good job of screening potentially AIDS infectious blood units out of the blood supply."[24] But despite this sense of accomplishment, James Curran warned that there would be no immediate drop in transfusion-associated cases of AIDS. "Most of these will occur in those who received blood prior to the antibody test being introduced."[25]

Studies presented at the meeting dispelled whatever ambiguity remained about the significance of the presence of antibody in a donor's blood. Even given the technical limitations of viral recovery efforts, close to 60 percent of those with "strongly positive" antibody results were found to harbor the AIDS virus, a result that James Allen of the CDC termed "very high."[26] And so a test was now available that could, in fact, identify the asymptomatic carriers of the AIDS virus. The implications were clear for both those concerned with intercepting the spread of the virus and those fearful about how the desire to identify such individuals could lead to the enactment of compulsory broad-scale screening programs.

Seeking to reassure the American people about the safety of the blood supply achieved by virtue of both deferral recommendations and antibody screening, the Public Health Service was quick to respond to suggestions that there remained risks from contaminated blood that had nevertheless tested negative.[27] Indeed, repeated efforts were made to limit anxiety about the remaining statistical risk. It was, however, inevitable that transmission by blood transfusion, though essentially blocked, would still occur, and indeed within the year, the CDC reported the first such case.[28]

Notes

1. *New York Times* (April 24, 1984), C1.
2. *AMA News* (May 25, 1984), 1.
3. Neil Schram, Letter to Edward Brandt, April 23, 1984.
4. Jeff Levi, Memorandum to Interested Parties, July 3, 1984.
5. James Curran, Memorandum to State and Territorial Epidemiologists, July 20, 1984.

6. Neil Schram, Letter to James Mason, August 13, 1984.
7. Neil Schram, Dear AAPHR Member, September 1984.
8. Acting Director, Office of Biologics, Research and Review, Memorandum to All Establishments Collecting Blood, Blood Components and Source Plasma and All Licensed Manufacturers of Plasma Derivatives, December 14, 1984.
9. Jeff Levi, Memorandum to Ginny Apuzzo, December 19, 1984.
10. Conference on AIDS, Ethics and the Blood Supply, *Proceedings,* eds., Ronald Bayer, Nancy Holland, and Ernest Simon (American Blood Commission, 1985).
11. Marsha Goldsmith, "HTLV-III Testing on Donor Blood Imminent; Complex Issues Remain," *Journal of the American Medical Association* (January 11, 1985), 179.
12. *Ibid.,* 173.
13. "Provisional Public Health Service Inter-Agency Recommendations for Screening Donated Blood and Plasma for Antibody to the Virus Causing Acquired Immunodeficiency Syndrome," *MMWR* (January 11, 1985), 1–5.
14. *Ibid.,* 3.
15. Public Health Service, Executive Task Force on AIDS, Summaries of Meetings Held on January 14, 1985, Mimeo.
16. *MMWR* (January 11, 1985), 3.
17. Virginia Apuzzo, Letter to Lowell Harmenson, January 18, 1985.
18. Association of State and Territorial Health Officials, "Screening Position Paper," n.d., Mimeo.
19. Director, Office of Biologics, Research and Review, to All Registered Blood Establishments, February 19, 1985.
20. Frank Young, Dear Doctor, n.d.
21. Working Group on Medical, Social, and Health Policy Aspects of Screening Tests for AIDS, New York Blood Center, Minutes, July 17, 1985, Mimeo.
22. David Axelrod, Dear Colleague, March 22, 1985.
23. New York Blood Center, Information for Donors with HTLV-III Antibody, July 17, 1985.
24. Charles Marwick, "Blood Banks Give HTLV-III Test Positive Approval at Five Months," *Journal of the American Medical Association* (October 4, 1985), 1681.
25. *Ibid.,* 1683.
26. *Ibid.*
27. Public Health Service Executive Task Force on AIDS, Minutes, October 8, 1985.
28. *New York Times* (June 20, 1986).

Study Questions

1. What objections did the National Gay and Lesbian Task Force raise to applied research using the HIV antibody test as a screening tool?*

2. What objections and concerns did blood bank officials hold against the use of the ELISA to screen blood donations?

---

*"Basic" research is aimed at theory-testing. "Applied" research is aimed at problem-solving. While both are legitimate and commonly used in scientific inquiry, they begin from two very different points and are informed by different research agendas.

3. When did the Public Health Service mandate antibody testing of all blood donations in the United States? How did the screening recommendations handle notification of a positive result?
4. What were the implications of donor notification?
5. When did blood banks start testing for HIV antibodies?
6. In what ways did the availability of widespread HIV antibody testing sites heighten Americans' anxieties about the epidemic?

Determinants of Public Opinion About AIDS

Horst Stipp and Dennis Kerr

According to Singer, Rogers, and Corcoran (1987), the first U.S. poll on AIDS was conducted in June 1983. Since then, polls on AIDS and issues related to the epidemic have become increasingly frequent. Surveys have explored awareness, perceived importance of AIDS as a national issue, knowledge about transmission routes and affected groups, attitudes toward people with AIDS, opinions about policy issues such as spending, testing, and quarantine, and behavior in response to AIDS and its perceived risks, including precautions taken and changes in sexual practices.

Researchers have discussed these poll findings primarily in the context of agenda-setting models, looking at the media's impact on the public's perception of the issue. This is true of Singer, Rogers, and Corcoran (1987) and, as their title suggests, of Dearing, Rogers, and Fei's paper "The agenda-setting process for the issue of AIDS" (1988). However, the latter authors do not find that "traditional agenda-setting" models explain the processes they found in their analysis. Contrasting San Francisco—where AIDS was a major topic in most local media before 1983—with the rest of the U.S., Dearing, Rogers, and Fei think that the politically active gay community in San Francisco helped set the agenda for the media, whereas in the rest of the country the "traditional" media-to-public flow prevailed. Their analysis shows that the attitudes of those in the media toward the primary victims of the disease—homosexual men—were the main determinants of media attention during the early years of the epidemic.[1]

Findings from a survey by the Roper Organization that we are reporting here suggest that attitudes about homosexuals also play an important role in determining the public's reaction to media coverage. Even though the available data leave much to be desired—Roper's questions were not designed to address this topic, and only cross-sectional data are available—they raise the possibility that anti-gay attitudes constrain the ability of the media to effectively communicate information about risk factors and how the disease is transmitted. If true, this finding is important, for it suggests that AIDS education programs and the public debate about AIDS need to address anti-gay attitudes along with knowledge about transmission.

A July 1987 survey by the Roper Organization contained a number of questions about AIDS (nationwide representative sample, $N = 1,997$). As we were doing research on the influence of the media on the public's knowledge about AIDS, we were particularly interested in a question that was phrased as an attitude question but which seemed to be suitable as a substitute measure of beliefs about AIDS transmission (see Table 1).

Responses to these questions were quite similar to those from a set of straightforward transmission knowledge questions in a National Health Interview Survey conducted a few months after the Roper survey, which found, for example, that 30% thought it was "very likely," "somewhat likely," or "somewhat unlikely" that "a person will get the AIDS virus from . . . shaking hands with or touching someone who has AIDS"; 64% thought it "very unlikely" or "definitely not possible."[2]

The levels of risk perceived according to those findings are similar to those in the Roper data, even though they do not fully agree with the "would not do" responses to those questions—which is not surprising considering the differences in question wording. But both results fully agree that shaking hands with a person with AIDS is considered least risky; kissing such a person on the cheek or eating where a kitchen worker or cook has AIDS is considered most risky. The rank order of responses to the items common to both surveys is identical. Both findings also agree in that they indicate an enormous amount of misinformation.

Table 1   •   Attitudes Toward AIDS Transmission, July 1987

"People feel differently about having contact with a person who has AIDS. For each of the things on this list would you tell me whether it is or is not something you would be willing to do?" (Card)

	Would Not Do	Depends	Would Do
Shake hands with someone who has AIDS	36%	9%	50%
Work alongside someone with AIDS	44%	12%	38%
Send your children to school with a child who has AIDS	48%	11%	33%
Help take care of an AIDS patient	52%	18%	24%
Kiss someone on the cheek who has AIDS	71%	6%	17%
Eat in a restaurant where you knew a kitchen worker had AIDS	74%	6%	14%

Source: The Roper Organization.

AIDS researchers have been reporting for several years now that AIDS is spread through sexual intercourse, contact with contaminated blood (through dirty needles or, increasingly rarely, through blood transfusions), and birth to an infected mother. Transmission through other routes ("casual contact," health care work with protection, mosquitoes) or through unknown routes among specific kinds of people (Haitians) has been ruled out with increasing certainty.[3] This has apparently produced a slow trend toward better knowledge (Singer, Rogers, and Corcoran, 1987). Indeed, in polls, very few respondents profess ignorance about transmission of the virus and nearly everybody knows about the dangers of sexual and blood contact. However, almost half of respondents, all those who did not say "very unlikely" or "definitely not possible" to the items listed above, expressed clearly inaccurate beliefs about AIDS (or HIV virus) transmission.

Since AIDS is a complex disease and there are still conflicting reports about transmission routes, one might argue that it is difficult for many people to absorb the facts about AIDS. Further, less sexually active (e.g., older) people might not be particularly interested in this topic. (Singer, Rogers, and Corcoran, 1987, makes both these points.) One might, therefore, expect variables such as media exposure, educational attainment, and age to predict responses to poll questions about AIDS transmission.

In our analysis of the correlates of the responses to the Roper question we were able to look at education, sex, and age; data on media exposure were not available in this survey. However, since reading newspapers and newsmagazines is related to educational attainment, the education measure might be seen as a rough substitute measure for exposure to facts about AIDS. Because education might measure people's exposure to as well as ability to comprehend information about AIDS, we expected it to be the best predictor. We also included an attitude measure on discrimination against homosexuals that found 65% of the respondents in favor of equal treatment in employment and housing; 23% said they wanted discrimination to be legal, and 12% were classified "don't knows."[4] This question preceded the questions about AIDS in Roper's survey. We hypothesized that the responses might be related to opinions about AIDS and its transmission, since polls have shown that the public identifies homosexuals as the primary victims of the disease.

For the purposes of our analysis, we combined the six items measuring beliefs about AIDS transmission described above into a summative scale, where a higher score represents greater willingness to have contact with people with AIDS. (Responses to the individual items were coded as "would do" = 1, "depends" or "would not do" = 0.) A principal-components analysis confirmed that these items were unidimensional (eigenvalue = 3.5), and alpha for the scale was .85. The resulting index of "perceived risks" ranged from 0 to 6, with a mean of 1.9 and standard deviation 2.1. This index is the dependent variable for the analyses that follow.

Findings

Attitude toward gay rights, not education, was the best individual predictor of the index—those who believe discrimination against homosexuals should be legal would go to much greater lengths to avoid people with AIDS ($r = .33$). Less-educated respondents also scored lower on the perceived risks index ($r = .20$). Sex and age were weakly associated with the index. Thus, Roper's data provided little support for the hypothesis that older, less sexually active people would be less well informed about AIDS. As we expected, education was a significant predictor of knowledge about AIDS transmission, but it accounted for considerably less variance in the index than attitudes toward gay rights.

We considered several reasons why these two measures, attitudes toward gay rights and the index of perceived risks, might be related. It may be that the index is a measure of social distance rather than a measure of beliefs about AIDS transmission and we merely discovered that people who don't want to have anything to do with gays—not even work near them—are the same kinds of people who favor discriminating against gays in jobs and housing. We cannot rule out this possibility using Roper's data. However, if the index does measure perceived risks, this finding could mean that anti-gay sentiments limit people's acceptance of the facts about AIDS transmission. We conducted several analyses that are consistent with that hypothesis.

First, we considered the possibility that the perceptions measured by the Roper index affect attitudes toward gay rights, rather than the other way around. According to this model, many people believe it's easy to get AIDS—by shaking hands or working close to someone who has it—and since they are afraid of catching AIDS, they favor some extreme responses to those most likely to infect them. If this were true, we would expect anti-gay sentiment among the general public to be on the rise since the discovery of AIDS. This is not so; public opinion is now slightly more pro-gay, with 65% favoring equal treatment for homosexuals in July 1987, versus 57% when Roper asked the same question in July 1978. Other poll data show a similar trend.

A second possibility is that attitudes toward gay rights and perceived risks are related because they stem from a common cause, such as educational attainment. According to this model, better-educated people are both more likely to be tolerant toward gays and more likely to be exposed to and correctly grasp facts about AIDS transmission. If this were true, the observed association between gay rights attitude and perceived risks would attenuate when education was controlled. This did not occur; controlling for education yielded a partial correlation of .31 between gay rights attitude and the avoidance index, compared to .33 when education was uncontrolled.

Finally, we tested the possibility that people with prior prejudice against gays are indeed less responsive to media information about the low risks of casual contact than people without such prejudice. The best test of this causal model would be a field experiment in which people with different prior attitudes toward gays were exposed to AIDS information campaigns. Roper's data, however, are cross-sectional and contain no measure of media exposure, so a rigorous direct test of our hypothesis is not possible. We can only approximate such a test by allowing education, presumably an indicator of access to and comprehension of information, to serve as a rough proxy measure of media exposure. If anti-gay attitudes limit one's ability to assimilate information about AIDS transmission, we would expect media exposure to be less strongly related to perceived risks among people opposed to gay rights than among those who support gay rights. The same interaction, in attenuated form, should exist for the joint effects of education and anti-gay sentiment.

We tested this hypothesis by estimating the following interactive regression model:

$$I = .45 + .37b_1 + .03b_2 + .09b_3,$$

where I is the perceived risks index, b_1 is a dummy variable representing attitudes toward gay rights (0 = against, 1 = for gay rights), b_2 is years of education, and b_3 represents the product of gay rights opinion and education measures (the interaction term). As we expected, the interactive term is significant ($t = 2.7$, $p = .007$). Among those who support gay rights, each additional year of education adds an average of .12 to the index. Education makes considerably less difference among those who are opposed to gay rights, each additional year

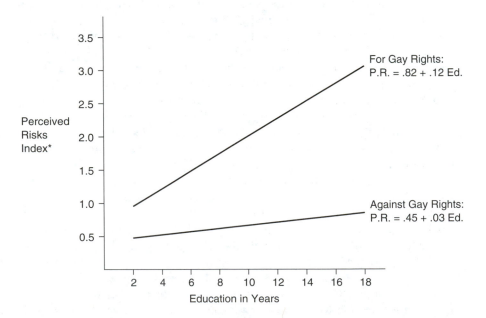

* High values represent greater willingness to have contact with people with AIDS.

Figure 1 Determinants of Perceived Risks: Interaction Between Gay Rights Attitude and Education (Best-Fitting Linear Regressions)

adding only .03 (see Figure 1). Thus, our data are consistent with the hypothesis that people with anti-gay attitudes are less responsive to information about AIDS.

Discussion

We have reported rather limited data on an aspect of the AIDS issue that previous investigations have not considered: the possibility that anti-gay attitudes foster exaggerated beliefs about AIDS transmission and prevent accurate information in the media from being accepted by substantial proportions of the population.

We hope this paper stirs researchers' interest in this issue and prompts them to undertake the kinds of investigation necessary to establish whether, or to what extent, the hypotheses presented here are accurate. Since our interpretation is based on the assumption that Roper's attitude items really measured perceived risks, the analysis first needs to be repeated with items which directly measure transmission beliefs. (One researcher recently told us that she has done that and replicated our findings.)[5] Comprehensive studies should look at awareness, beliefs about transmission, media exposure, and opinions about such issues as HIV testing and treatment of AIDS victims. They should also address possibly relevant attitudinal factors—feelings and assumptions about homosexuals, as well as the other major groups of AIDS victims, IV drug users and members of ethnic minorities.[6]

The knowledge to be gained from such efforts has some significant consequences. In the first place, we may find that AIDS education campaigns need to address prejudicial attitudes in order to effectively reach their audiences. The same is true of campaigns by business corporations that aim at educating their workers about AIDS in the workplace. We might find that the goals of such campaigns—accurately informing the public about protective measures and avoiding disruptions at the workplace—cannot be achieved without dispelling inaccurate assumptions about victim groups. Moreover, the processes we are talking about have important implications for policy issues such as quarantine, mandatory testing, policies regarding HIV-infected school children, and also the care of people with AIDS. The debate over these issues might become more rational, and policy decisions more effective, if justified concerns and unfounded fears are clearly separated. Public opinion and attitudinal research may be able to make significant contributions toward those goals.

Notes

1. According to Shilts (1987), the *San Francisco Chronicle* hired an openly gay reporter to cover issues of interest to their homosexual readers. In contrast, the *New York Times*—published in the city that had half of the nation's AIDS cases during the first couple of years—did not consider homosexual concerns "fit to print" at that time. Shilts's assertion is supported by content analyses of the *Times*'s coverage by Baker (1986) and Dearing, Rogers, and Fei (1988).

2. The survey, published by the National Center for Health Statistics (NCHS) in January 1988, was conducted in September 1987, $N = 3,098$ adults, personal interviews. Two more recent NCHS surveys both found small increases in accurate beliefs about casual transmission (Dawson, Cynamon, and Fitti, 1988; Dawson and Thornberry, 1988). A poll by Gallup in October 1987 produced comparable results (The Gallup Poll, November 26, 1987).

3. Most recently, the Centers for Disease Control reported that the number of cases with "unknown" risk factors was much smaller than previously reported and that cases that could be further investigated all pointed to the familiar risk factors, ruling out other transmission routes (*New York Times,* 4 March 1988). At the same time, a book by sex therapists W. Masters and V. Johnson (with R. Kolodny) discussed the "theoretical possibility" of "catching AIDS from a toilet seat." Press reports pointed out that the authors do not have any evidence that such infections occurred. Surgeon General Koop called their work "irresponsible" (*New York Times,* 6 and 8 March 1988; *Newsweek,* 14 March 1988; *USA Today,* 15 March 1988; *Time,* 21 March 1988).

4. "Some time ago, the citizens of Miami voted to repeal a county ordinance that banned discrimination in employment and housing based on a person's sexual preferences. The ordinance essentially meant that someone who is homosexual could not be kept from holding a particular job or living in any type of housing simply because he or she is homosexual. Which of these two statements best describes how you feel about the law and discrimination against homosexuals?" (Card) "a. Homosexuals should be guaranteed equal treatment under the law in jobs and housing. b. It should be *legal* to keep people out of jobs and housing if they are homosexuals."

5. At the 1988 meeting of the American Association for Public Opinion Research, discussant Laurie Bauman reported that she had replicated our finding with transmission knowledge questions among a sample of Bronx, New York, high school students. The data were obtained very recently, and additional analysis is planned (personal communication). At the same session, George Gallup, Jr., reported data from a new Gallup poll that found evangelicals are more likely to believe that AIDS is transmitted casually than other population groups— consistent with our hypothesis that preexisting attitudes limit the effects of AIDS information and education (Gallup Report nos. 268/269, 1988).

6. Such research should also look for explanations for a link between attitudes toward gays and beliefs about AIDS transmission. We found that there are no thorough empirical studies of prejudice against homosexuals in the literature. (A provocative analysis by British sociologist J. Weeks [1985] suggests a link between "catching AIDS" and "catching homosexuality" in the minds of those who express anti-gay feelings. However, his empirical data are limited.)

REFERENCES

Baker, A. J. (1986) "The portrayal of AIDS in the media: An analysis of articles in the *New York Times.*" In D. Feldman and T. Johnson (eds.), *The Social Dimensions of AIDS: Method and Theory.* New York: Praeger.

Dawson, D. A., M. Cynamon, and J. E. Fitti (1988) "AIDS knowledge and attitudes for September 1987: Provisional data from the National Health Interview Survey." Advance Data from Vital and Health Statistics, no. 148. Hyattsville, MD: Public Health Service.

Dawson, D. A., and O. T. Thornberry (1988) "AIDS knowledge and attitudes for November 1987: Provisional data from the National Health Interview Survey." Advance Data from Vital and Health Statistics, no. 151. Hyattsville, MD: Public Health Service.

Dearing, J. W., E. M. Rogers, and X. Fei (1988) "The agenda-setting process for the issue of AIDS." Paper presented at the annual meeting of the International Communication Association, New Orleans, May.

Shilts, R. (1987) *And the Band Played On: Politics, People, and the AIDS Epidemic.* New York: St. Martin's Press.

Singer, E., T. F. Rogers, and M. Corcoran (1987) "Poll Report: AIDS." *Public Opinion Quarterly* 51:580–595.

Weeks, J. (1985) *Sexuality and Its Discontents: Meanings, Myths, and Modern Sexualities.* London: Melbourne and Henley, Routledge & Kegan Paul.

Study Questions

1. What psychosocial forces explain public responses to AIDS in 1987?
2. In what ways, according to Stipp and Kerr, do preexisting attitudes about gay people or about people of color shape one's openness to accurate information about HIV/AIDS transmission?
3. What are the implications for mass-media educational programs? For the antidiscriminatory legislation and public policies recommended by Herek and Glunt in Chapter 2?

Suggested Additional Readings

Arthur Ashe and Arnold Rampersand, *Days of Grace* (New York: Knopf, 1993).

Joseph Bove, "Transfusion-Associated AIDS: A Cause of Concern?" *New England Journal of Medicine,* vol. 310 (January 12, 1984):115–116.

T. J. Coates, L. Temoshok, and J. Mandel, "AIDS Antibody Testing: Will It Stop the AIDS Epidemic? Will It Help People Infected with HIV?" *American Psychologist,* vol. 43 (1988):859–864.

Harlon L. Dalton, Scott Burris, and the Yale AIDS Law Project, editors, *AIDS and the Law* (New Haven: Yale University Press, 1987).

Marsha Goldsmith, "HTLV-III Testing on Donor Blood Imminent; Complex Issues Remain." *Journal of the American Medical Association,* vol. 253 (January 11, 1985):173–175, 179–181.

Janet Holland, Carolina Ramazanoglu, and Sue Scott, "AIDS: From Panic Stations to Power Relations, Sociological Perspectives and Problems." *Sociology,* vol. 25, no. 3 (August 1990):499–518.

Charles Marwick, "Blood Banks Give HTLV-III Test Positive Approval at Five Months." *Journal of the American Medical Association,* vol. 254 (October 4, 1985):1681–1683.

Thomas H. Murray, "The Poisoned Gift: AIDS and Blood." Dorothy Nelkin, David P. Willis, and Scott V. Parris, editors. *A Disease of Society:* Cultural and Institutional Responses to AIDS (New York: Cambridge University Press, 1991).

Jeffrey M. Siebert and Roberta A. Olson, editors, *Children, Adolescents, and AIDS* (Lincoln: University of Nebraska Press, 1990).

CHAPTER 5

Drugs, People, and Federal Regulations

A Matter of Life and Death

• • •

San Francisco General Hospital had opened the first AIDS ward in the United States, Patrick Buchanan had explained the AIDS epidemic as the wrath of God, and the World Health Organization had held its first meeting on the international implications of AIDS when Luc Montagnier at the Pasteur Institute and Robert Gallo at the National Institutes of Health separately announced the isolation of the HIV virus in April 1984. Setting aside the Franco–American scientific competition played out in the labs of the National Institute for Allergies and Infectious Disease in Bethesda, Maryland, and at the Pasteur Institute in Paris, the isolation of the virus advanced the possibility, at last, of a vaccine or, at the very least, effective medical therapies for HIV/AIDS. That was not to be the case. AZT, probably the most controversial drug to be developed during the epidemic to date, would not be approved formally for use until March 19, 1987. Even pentamidine isethionate, an established drug therapy for *Pneumocystis carinii* pneumonia, which was already approved by the Food and Drug Administration, was not commercially available until October 16, 1984.[1] Scientific research proceeds at its own pace and under its own rules. In the 1980s the pace was considerably slower than that set by the HIV virus, and both the "rules" of scientific inquiry and the FDA regulations that translated pharmaceutical developments into effective medical therapies seemed to contradict the needs of the sick and dying people the drugs were intended to serve. The selections in Chapter 5 describe the partnership between federal bureaucracies and private industry that moved AZT off the laboratory shelf and into the hands of people with AIDS. At the same time, tensions between scientists and bureaucrats, and between scientists and people desperate for drugs that might prolong their lives, compounded the process by which those drugs were developed, tested, and marketed. Mobilizing resources outside the medical community, many people with AIDS and the HIV virus crafted informal networks through which they exchanged knowledge, acquired and distributed various drugs and

---

[1]For a detailed discussion of the pentamidine isethionate saga, and the transfer of distribution rights from the Centers for Disease Control to LymphoMed, Inc., see Peter S. Arno and Karyn L. Feiden, *Against the Odds: The Story of AIDS, Drug Development, Politics and Profits* (New York: HarperCollins, 1988):83–88.

medical therapies, and initiated their own treatment programs. The social movement that followed rewrote the physician–patient canon, empowering the sick and fostering an egalitarian partnership between those who heal and those who seek healing.[2]

The laboratory search for the magic bullet against the HIV retrovirus required time, money, and a willingness on the part of biomedical bench (or laboratory-based) researchers—who rarely, if ever, directly interacted with sick and dying people—to undertake the dangerous task. Exposure to the deadly virus would be an ongoing risk that physicians faced routinely and which the researchers had to accept as a part of their work. Nevertheless, a set of loose connections between private enterprise and a cumbersome federal bureaucracy that included the Food and Drug Administration, the National Institutes of Health (NIH), and the National Institute of Allergies and Infectious Diseases (NIAID)—originally intended to insure that the American public would be protected from ineffective and even harmful pharmacological therapies—ultimately fostered that search. But by the early 1980s that partnership had evolved into a ponderous animal that initiated new research and processed new drug applications in an agonizingly slow and tedious fashion; and people who were living with AIDS, who felt the pressure of compressed lives, crafted various strategies to circumvent that animal. **The AZT Breakthrough** describes the professional networks within this partnership, the maneuvering and deal-making that produced the mythical AZT therapy and, ultimately, a $10,000-a-year drug with only a problematic track record for slowing the progression of the HIV virus.

While the scientists and bureaucrats negotiated and schemed and navigated through the maze of drug trials, time was running out for people with AIDS. The struggle for access to drugs—any drugs, even experimental, untested, potentially harmful drugs—intensified; and within gay communities, that struggle cohered into more or less organized action. Those who did not qualify for the NIH and NIAID medical trials of new drugs designed and implemented their own medical experiments. Those who could afford to do so made desperate medical pilgrimages to France and Israel, where experimental drugs and other medical therapies were more readily available than in the United States. Dextran sulfate, ribavirin, isoprinosine, suramin, and AZT were bootlegged, smuggled into the United States from the less regulated pharmaceutical markets in Mexico and Japan, and distributed at cost.

Paul Monette and his lover of fifteen years, Roger Horowitz, fought the metaphoric energy of AIDS as they lived together. **Networks**, the excerpts from Monette's chronicle of their fight, *Borrowed Time*, describes the texture of their struggle, their dependence on bootlegged drugs, and the nonmedical channels through which crucial medical information flowed. Monette's narrative of

---

[2]For an example of the broader impact of this movement, see Susan Ferraro, "The Anguished Politics of Breast Cancer." *New York Times Magazine,* August 15, 1993:23–27ff.

Roger's progressively debilitating illness describes as well the strategies gay men devised to counter and hold at bay not only the disease but its destructive metaphoric energy.

The belief systems that informed those strategies differed radically from the established canon of scientific medicine, and those strategies would provide the framework within which the established canon of scientific medicine and health care delivery would be revised and restructured.

The AZT Breakthrough

Peter S. Arno and Karyn L. Feiden

Sam Broder has been one of the central figures in the struggle to find effective treatments against AIDS. Driven by compassion, foresight, and ambition, he became a cheerleader, aggressive and enthusiastic in his efforts to lead the government's response and to boost private sector involvement in research.

A Special Task Force on AIDS was established at the National Cancer Institute in 1984. Bob Gallo was scientific director, Sam Broder the task force's clinical director. Broder needed help. He was going to need more than his small staff and an 800-square-foot laboratory to develop a treatment for AIDS. The pharmaceutical industry had to get involved.

Hat in hand, Broder began knocking on doors across the country, making a plea to drug company officials. Broder was flying solo in those days. There had not been much interest from the upper echelons of the federal government's public health bureaucracy. No one else bothered trying to jawbone the drug companies into pursuing AIDS research. On his sojourns into the pharmaceutical hinterlands, Broder pledged to test promising compounds in NCI laboratories to see if they were effective against HIV. But he wanted something in exchange—a firm commitment to develop and market drugs that showed potential.

One of the companies Broder approached was Burroughs Wellcome, the American subsidiary of Wellcome PLC, a British-based conglomerate. Broder knew BW had worked with nucleoside analogues, the broad category of antiviral therapies that his honed scientific instinct told him might combat HIV, and had a record of accomplishment in viral research. Its success in bringing acyclovir—the first drug to prove effective against the herpes virus—to market convinced Broder that Burroughs Wellcome was well positioned to get involved in AIDS research.

At the time he was excited about initiating a dialogue with BW and hopeful that its corporate largesse and technical know-how could be used to advantage. Broder didn't have any personal connections at Burroughs Wellcome, but his colleague Dani Bolognesi, who was equally committed to AIDS, did know a few people. Bolognesi was working at Duke University Medical Center. Bolognesi made a few telephone calls and the stage was set for Broder to meet with some of Burroughs Wellcome's top scientists.

The first meeting took place on October 5, 1984, at company headquarters in the Research Triangle of North Carolina, a booming tri-city area defined by the boundaries of Raleigh, Durham, and Chapel Hill, and anchored by computer firms and well-established universities. But if the region's economic prospects were good, early signals from Broder's autumn meeting with Burroughs Wellcome were not. At first the company turned its back on AIDS research.

One reason for this reluctance was the fear of working with live—and potentially fatal—AIDS viruses. Images of a haywire virus cutting a swath of death across the North Carolina laboratories haunted the dreams of BW scientists. One senior-ranking employee, in particular, knew from experience that such a vision was not confined to the pages of a science fiction thriller; he had watched helplessly as one of his colleagues died after being infected in the laboratory by a virulent virus he was studying. To be fully secure, HIV research had to take place in a highly controlled setting, termed a P-3 level of biosafety. Few labs in the research community were that safe, and the cost of readying one for HIV-related work was close to a quarter of a million dollars. Even for a company as large as Burroughs Wellcome, whose worldwide annual sales already exceeded a billion dollars, it was a sizable undertaking.

Such a commitment was especially formidable given the company's doubts that AIDS research could ever turn a profit. In one of the many ironies of the epidemic, Broder spent a lot of time that day convincing Burroughs Wellcome that an effective drug had commercial potential, that a reasonable return on investment could be secured. At first, corporate officials refused to budge. Broder finally flew off the handle at their indifference, insisting that AIDS was going to spread far beyond the 3,000 people who had already been diagnosed.

There is money to be made in AIDS, Broder said to Burroughs Wellcome. Perhaps big money.

Fear of working with the live AIDS virus was not restricted to drug companies. The NCI lab did not meet P-3 safety conditions either, but Broder felt he could not afford to wait until it was properly outfitted. Instead, he told his staff they were free to ask for a transfer. Many opted out. Hiroaki Mitsuya chose to stay.

Mitsuya, recruited by Broder from Japan because of his work on retroviruses, was a rising star who had already earned a medical degree and a doctorate in medical science from Kumamoto University. When Sam Broder first committed the National Cancer Institute to AIDS research, Mitsuya was earning less than $18,000 a year as a postdoctoral research fellow. Mitsuya turned his academic expertise on immune-system deficiencies to good use. He was the man who figured out an efficient, accurate, and safe way to screen compounds for their value against HIV. Mitsuya became, in Broder's words, "the best viral pharmacologist in the world, a one-person national resource."

Broder's persuasiveness, coupled with some coaxing from Bolognesi, eventually got Burroughs Wellcome to rethink its position on AIDS research. Along with fifty other drug companies, BW finally began shipping chemical compounds to NCI's lab to be tested for their effectiveness against HIV. Each sample was coded by letter to protect its identity—as well as the company's proprietary rights.

In February 1985, government researchers struck pay dirt. A drug shipped in by Burroughs Wellcome, and code-named Compound S, showed activity against HIV in the test tube. Apparently hoping to speed ultimate approval, Burroughs Wellcome also sent the compound to FDA laboratories for testing, but scientists there did not detect the same activity. Bolognesi and his colleagues at Duke University, however, did confirm the NCI finding.

Compound S was azidothymidine, also known as zidovudine, and soon to become known as AZT.

* * *

Within a few weeks, preliminary results from the Phase I trial were available—and they looked promising. Patients were able to absorb AZT, side effects were tolerable, and some clinical and immunological improvements were evident. But the trial still had months to run before researchers felt confident about the drug's safety.

Next came Phase II studies. Between February and June 1986, 282 people with AIDS or advanced symptoms of HIV infection were enrolled at twelve medical centers around the country. All but 13 were men. People with AIDS were required to have had a first episode of PCP (*Pneumocystis carinii* pneumonia) within the preceding four months, but to have had no other opportunistic infections. Those who had not been officially diagnosed with AIDS had to have unexplained weight losses, fungal infections, and at least one of a long list of other infections associated with the virus. Trial candidates were disqualified if they had recently used just about any other drug except aspirin, and even that required a researcher's permission.

Just six months into the trial, members of an independent monitoring board, who were privy to the data collected on all participants, were certain that patients on AZT were faring dramatically better than those on placebo—19 of the 137 patients on placebo had died, compared with just 1 of the 145 patients taking AZT.

On September 19, 1986, the blindfold was stripped from the trial, and all patients on placebo were offered the active drug.

Within a month, AZT was made available to some AIDS patients outside the trial on a compassionate-use basis while further testing continued. Between September 1986 and March 1987, BW gave away free AZT to some 4,500 people, or one-third of all those living with AIDS at the time. According to the company, the handouts cost $10 million.

The requirement for phase III studies was waived for AZT, a practice that is not uncommon when a life-threatening disease is involved. Instead of completing the last phase of the trials, BW buckled down to prepare its New Drug Application. Given the urgency of the need and the promise of the drug, the AZT application was submitted to the FDA in stages, beginning in October and ending on December 2, 1986.

Consistent with the rapid pace with which AZT had already rolled through the testing pipeline, FDA officials moved quickly to review the mountains of data in Burroughs Wellcome's application. There were grim reasons for the haste. As 1986 drew to a close, AIDS had claimed the lives of at least 23,000 Americans. Not one treatment had been approved. The FDA was under intense pressure to get a drug out.

Ellen Cooper was busy during that Christmas season. She had joined the FDA on a research fellowship in 1982. Her academic and medical credentials were impeccable—undergraduate work at Swarthmore, medical education at Yale and Case Western Reserve, a master's degree in public health from Johns Hopkins, and specialized training in pediatrics and infectious diseases. Everyone agreed that Cooper was a dedicated professional, a knowledgeable scientist, a top-flight researcher.

She also juggled more than an average share of family responsibilities, with four children—triplets and a youngster with Down's syndrome—to raise. Cooper's rise through the ranks of the FDA came swiftly. She was one of the first officials at the agency to become involved with AIDS drugs. When the FDA created the Division of Anti-Viral Drug Products to expedite its review of AIDS drugs, Cooper was chosen to head it. That position did not seem likely to place her solidly in the public eye. Ellen Cooper, after all, was a scientist, not a politician.

Circumstances, however, made her the point person for most of the FDA's early decisions about AIDS drugs. As a result, she found her judgments evaluated in a highly charged environment, and her reviews from FDA watchers were decidedly mixed. At times she became the target of rage and name-calling, bearing the brunt of some of the sharpest criticism levied against the FDA. But Cooper got high marks on AZT.

As others were drinking eggnog and making the rounds of tree-trimming parties, Cooper was performing yeoman's service. Day after day, night after night, she pored through Burroughs Wellcome's voluminous application. Her goal was to move AZT through the approval process as quickly as possible.

When Cooper had finished studying the AZT data, an FDA advisory committee was summoned to meet. The committee's job was to recommend to the FDA whether or not AZT should be approved. Usually, although not always, an advisory committee's recommendation on drug approval is followed to the letter.

The committee met just six weeks after Burroughs Wellcome had completed its application. The setting was the Parklawn Building in Rockville, Maryland, a bland glass box of a federal office building that is FDA headquarters. It is badly in need of a coat of paint and renovated elevators, and space is so cramped that the lounge in at least one women's rest room has been converted to an office. The building is an unmistakable symbol of the resource shortfalls that have long impeded the FDA's work.

One key question was on the table: Was AZT safe and effective enough to warrant the drug's approval? The answer would have far-reaching consequences.

Initially the debate suggested that data collected on the drug was insufficient. Over and over, committee members expressed grave concerns about the limitations of scientific knowledge about AZT and the fact that it had been tested during just one major trial lasting only six months. No one could say with certainty just who would benefit from AZT, or at what dose it should be administered. No one had determined whether the drug would remain effective over the long haul, or how toxic its side effects would prove to be.

Other doubts surfaced through the day. Committee members knew that even if the FDA approved the drug only for use by the narrow population in which it had been tested, physicians would make it much more widely available. Despite an absence of good data, Calvin Kunin, a committee member, observed that "once a drug is licensed, physicians do whatever they want to."

Ellen Cooper also expressed some reservations, warning, "Although we are all aware of the need for rapid clinical development of drugs to treat AIDS, the approval of a potentially toxic drug for marketing, particularly when it is anticipated that many less ill individuals will take it on a chronic basis, would represent a significant and potentially dangerous departure from our usual toxicology requirements."

There was talk about provisionally approving AZT and mandating further studies, but committee members agreed that it was hard to revoke a drug's license. "It is a fact of life that, once a drug is approved, it is almost impossible, as a practical matter, to withdraw that approval, unless there is a very serious safety consideration," said Edward Tabor, a high-level FDA manager.

At times the day-long meeting grew contentious, but in the end, the reservations that dominated the day's debate were set aside. By a ten-to-one vote, the committee gave thumbs-up to AZT.

Two months later, on March 19, 1987, the Food and Drug Administration accepted the committee's recommendation and approved the drug, clearing the way for any physician to write a prescription for its use by any patient. "For drug development," commented Sam Broder, "that is the speed of light."

Second Thoughts About AZT

Year after year, report after report, new drug after new drug, the AZT story has been touted as evidence that the testing and approval system can work. It was to be a model for the flood of therapeutic products expected to follow. And certainly there was much that was innovative about it.

Here was a public-private partnership in which the National Cancer Institute and a drug manufacturer worked in apparent harmony to test a promising compound quickly. Instead of passively awaiting Burroughs Wellcome's final application, the FDA followed the progress of the trials and reviewed available data at every step. The high-gear response to the drug allowed it to move from the IND [Investigational New Drug] stage to full marketing approval in less than two years, rather than the more typical eight years.

Anticipating approval, Burroughs Wellcome had disrupted production plans at several chemical plants and invested in new technology so that it could manufacture AZT in the necessary quantities. Right after the FDA okay, there were still shortages of the drug, largely because thymidine was hard to find—salmon and herring sperm weren't typically found on the shelves of most laboratories. Worldwide consumption of thymidine had long been stable at about twenty-five pounds a year, and the entire supply had been exhausted soon after AZT testing had begun. Fortunately, Pfizer developed a synthetic alternative to natural thymidine and began supplying it to Burroughs Wellcome. As a result, by the end of 1987, the drug was available in quantities sufficient to satisfy the explosive patient demand.

Despite these successes, fallout from the whole process was intense. AZT raised troubling issues that continued to surface as other promising drugs appeared on the horizon. Critics complained about the way the trial was designed and the fact that, in line with traditional scientific practice, the AZT Phase II study was conducted on a fairly homogeneous patient population—in this case, on gay white men. The goal was to limit variables that might distort the data.

That sounded reasonable—unless you were a drug user or a child with AIDS. Both groups were specifically excluded from access to the only drug that seemed to slow HIV. If you were a woman, getting on the Phase II AZT trial was extremely difficult—a total of thirteen women, less than 5 percent of the total number of participants, were enrolled. The exclusion of infected minorities and women, which began with AZT, continued for many years of AIDS drug research. As the demographics of the AIDS epidemic changed, that seemed steadily more discriminatory, spawned passionate complaint and even raised questions about the scientific validity of certain trials.

"The concept that good research, pure research, is color-blind begs the issue," said Janet Mitchell, a member of the board of directors of the National Minority AIDS Council. According to Dr. Mitchell, any study that failed to enroll population groups at risk for AIDS has not performed its job of assembling comprehensive data about a drug's value. "People are not specially bred laboratory specimens. Environment and culture can alter outcomes. . . . Research done in select populations cannot and should not be expected to produce results applicable to the general population."

Bitter questions were also asked about the astronomical price of AZT and eventually, about Burroughs Wellcome's right to its patent and to exclusive marketing rights. Some even questioned whether AZT worked at all.

*   *   *

AZT's critics, however, tend to forget that the drug was never intended as a magic bullet against AIDS. It was only a good start, a breakthrough as significant psychologically as it was scientifically because it shattered the myth that retroviruses could not be stopped. This historical context has too often been lost.

Sam Broder, the man some called "Mr. AZT," wanted more than anything else to prove wrong the assumption that retroviruses were untreatable, although he knew the drug was no miracle cure. Looking back to the landmark days when AZT stood at the brink of approval, Broder said, "There is nothing magical or anointed about AZT. The key issue in that era, really my obsession, was to find something practical that would be shown at a clinical level to work. I felt the fate of all future antiretroviral drug development programs would be linked to the success or failure of AZT. If AZT succeeded, then many other programs would be possible. If AZT failed, it would set the field back many years."

[Swiss-born cancer researcher turned AIDS activist] Mathilde Krim agreed, remembering how reports of AZT had stirred hope within the scientific community. It suddenly seemed that AIDS might be recast as a treatable disease, not an inevitably fatal one. "When AZT came around, it became believable that something could be done about the virus," said Krim.

Sam Broder and Mathilde Krim, like many pharmaceutical companies, laboratory researchers, and AIDS patients themselves, assumed that a long line of more effective drugs would follow on the heels of AZT. It has not happened. Until October 1991, AZT was the only FDA-approved drug targeted directly at the heart of the disease—the AIDS virus itself.

And its cost was stunningly high.

The Pricing Outrage

Shortly before the FDA announced the approval of AZT, Burroughs Wellcome dropped a bombshell: the drug would cost patients as much as $10,000 a year, making it one of the most expensive prescription drugs in the nation's history.

A few weeks later, California Congressman Henry Waxman, who chaired the Subcommittee on Health and the Environment, held hearings to scrutinize the cost and availability of AZT. Subcommittee members grilled T. E. Haigler, then president of BW, at length, trying to establish his justification for the $10,000 price tag.

Haigler refused to be pinned down about actual research and development costs, instead speaking vaguely about the factors that went into the pricing equation. He said relevant considerations included "the costs of developing, producing, and marketing the drug, the high costs of research, and the need to generate revenues to cover these continuing costs." Also, according to Haigler, the company had factored in the uncertain market for AZT, the expected introduction of better therapies, and a margin for profit—just how wide a margin was anyone's guess. Finally, on the defensive, Haigler declared that sound business principles had been used to price AZT, concluding, "We didn't pick a number out of the air."

Still, Haigler's imprecise statements exasperated Ron Wyden, a Democratic congressman from Oregon. When he could restrain himself no longer, Wyden exploded. "Why didn't you set the price at $100,000 per patient?" he asked.

Haigler was startled by Wyden's outburst, but he recovered quickly and shot back, "I think that would have been completely out of the realm of anything reasonable at all. We had to set the price at a reasonable level."

Wyden continued to press Haigler. "I'm still unclear about how you arrived at $10,000 rather than $30,000 or $25,000. I appreciate your feeling that $100,000 is unfair. But I must tell you that I think the pricing system is close to a random system."

Burroughs Wellcome's strongest defense was its expectation that other antiviral medications would follow closely on the heels of AZT. Researchers and patients shared that sentiment, which meant the company had a year, two at the most, to recoup its research and development costs.

Haigler also claimed that AZT was costly to produce, noting that ten separate chemical reactions were required to create a synthetic alternative to natural thymidine. An additional six steps converted thymidine to AZT.

To meet the soaring demand for the drug, BW further alleged to have poured $80 million into new technology and retooling so that it could shift production plans at several chemical plants. In fact, that $80-million figure was misleading, since a chunk of the money was actually spent on the raw materials needed for future production, rather than on the expenses of development. In any case, $80 million is still less than the cost of developing the average drug, estimated at between $90 and $231 million. Expenses were lower because drugs typically take eight to ten years to get to market and require clinical trials involving thousands of patients—but just two years had passed from the time AZT was sent to Broder's lab until it was licensed by the FDA. In the intervening time, only a few hundred patients were enrolled in trials.

Perhaps the most galling aspect of the pricing issue was that AZT was essentially a government drug. A reasonable principle of corporate investment is that the magnitude of profits should be related to the extent of risk. Typically, a drug company is fully responsible for the costs of preliminary research and drug development, with a lucrative payoff coming only if a compound is found to be safe and effective.

But AZT was financed very differently. In effect, the American taxpayer footed the bill for the development and use of the drug at least five times over. The first taxpayer dollars were funneled to Jerome Horwitz, who originally synthesized the drug, through a grant from the National Cancer Institute. Then more money came out of public coffers when the drug was tested at NCI labs in the mid-1980s. Next came government funding for Phase I clinical trials. The fourth public subsidy was the liberal tax credits and exclusive marketing rights given to BW for AZT under the terms of the Orphan Drug Act, federal legislation passed in 1983 to encourage drug development for rare diseases. Taken together, these breaks allowed the company to write off as much as 70 percent of its clinical trial costs. And finally—in the fifth use of government funds—Uncle Sam subsidized AZT for patients who could not otherwise afford the drug. That meant that, one way or another, Burroughs Wellcome could get its price and line its pockets with the proceeds.

Whatever the blend of justification and profiteering behind the price of AZT, it brought BW a firestorm of criticism. Although the company announced a 20 percent price cut by the end of 1987, citing a drop in production costs, the $8,000-a-year price tag remained a thorn in the side of both the patient community and the public health establishment. A later price cut, again in response to public outrage, brought it down further, to $6,500, and reductions in the recommended dosage also made the drug more affordable. But none of that let Burroughs Wellcome off the hook.

STUDY QUESTIONS

1. Who are Sam Broder and Bob Gallo?
2. Why did Broder and Gallo need help with their research?
3. Why were drug companies initially unwilling to engage in HIV/AIDS-related research?
4. What kind of deal did government scientists strike with Burroughs Wellcome to test Compound S?

5. What factors and considerations may have contributed to the exclusion of women, children, injection drug users, and minority groups from the AZT field trials? How might these exclusions have distorted the results of the original trials?
6. How did the Food and Drug Administration balance the requirements for scientific rigor against political pressure in processing the Burroughs Wellcome application for FDA approval of AZT? Did AZT undergo fair and adequate testing before it received FDA approval?

Networks

Paul Monette

There is such infinite variety about the way people tell you their negative status. Some are openly full of remorse and feel they have failed you. A man I've never met wrote me after an interview I gave about my antibody status:

> *When my test came back negative last month, I was overwhelmed with a sadness I hadn't expected. Coming back alive is a guilt, a terrible betrayal, a necessary starting point.*

Some hoot with excitement and forget you might not be as thrilled as they. I have friends who will not be tested at all because they know how shamefully glad they'll be. Their gut instinct is they're negative, so who are they trying to kid? They are always the first to tell you to stop being so AIDS-related. *Lighten up*, they say.

My own consistent opinion is selfish enough and sounds suspiciously Orange County. I want the two million—or the five million, depending on whose scenario piques your fancy—to have themselves tested and know, so I will have people to talk to. Because after midnight and during weekends I cannot talk to those who play at business as usual. I want to tap into the rage of the positives so we can throw buckets of sheep's blood on the White House lawn and spit in the faces of cops with yellow gloves.

How tired was Roger on Fridays? It's very difficult to assess, because that was the focus of our denial now. Appleton's weeks of diarrhea were something apart and ARC-related. The continuing cautions of Craig's researcher friend in Houston didn't somehow translate to the safe haven that looked out on the banyan tree. The sample was so minimal, after all, with only a hundred or so on suramin protocols throughout the country. Peter Wolfe

Reprinted with the permission of Harcourt Brace & Company from Paul Monette, *Borrowed Time: An AIDS Memoir* (New York: Harcourt Brace Jovanovich, 1988):164–166, 173–175, 205–209, 248–250, 306–308. © 1988 by Paul Monette.

was too busy now to be spending his mornings with the Friday club, and Suzette didn't seem to be privy to the latest data. Mostly we tried not to worry about the drug, because we had enough to worry about the disease.

The major drug reaction was rage anyway. It made us crazy to think the FDA or the NIH hadn't made funds available so that thousands could be on the drug. There was desultory talk in Washington of an HPA-23 study, when we all knew in the AIDS underground that the drug was useless. How could suramin still be the only game in town? We understood already, even as laymen, that what was needed was a new antiviral, especially one that would cross the dreaded blood–brain barrier. The gathering evidence during that summer indicated that a higher and higher percentage of AIDS patients were suffering from effects of the virus in the brain. The fear was that an antiviral that controlled HIV in the blood would somehow send it ravaging into the brain, where most drugs couldn't follow—including suramin.

By now I was fielding calls from all over, friends of friends saying they understood I knew someone on suramin. I would give the status report as hopefully as I could, sometimes referring them on to Bruce, the indefatigable spokesman. The burden of my own message was that everyone must start demanding these drugs, because the system wasn't out to cut the red tape. Indeed, red tape *was*—and largely still is—the system.

The rumors were appalling. It was said that everyone appointed by the Reagan administration in a major public health capacity was either a Morman or a fundamentalist. The chief spokesman for the administration now was the overripe and venomous Patrick Buchanan, one of whose major qualifications for the job was his widely quoted remark that nature was finally exacting her price on homosexuals for having spilled their seed against her. The right-wing firebrands are obsessed with sodomy, always forgetting that half of the gay world is women. This deterministic smugness, whereby we were only getting what we deserved, was so widespread in the upper chambers of the government that the AIDS issue probably never darkened the threshold of the Oval Office. Not to mention the fundamentalists: Though the press would not report anything about the antivirals and wouldn't assess the scope of the death of a gay generation, they reported with loving detail every ranting speech of the Falwell-Schlaflys and their money-changing brethren. "God's punishment" was the major level of public debate in 1985: hate, it appeared, was the only public health tool available.

*   *   *

It was right after that Bruce called, full of excitement. He was six doses into suramin and holding steady. This was the bulletin: One of his myriad sources had told him about a new antiviral just beginning human trials at the University of North Carolina. Compound S, it was called, and there were two AIDS patients on it. Bruce had been unable to track down anyone else who knew about it. Next day I mentioned it to Peter Wolfe, who'd heard of the drug that very morning but knew nothing more. We drew a blank with several other doctors, and Craig's sources in New York hadn't heard so much as a rumor.

Then, embarrassment of riches, Bruce called the next day to report new data about the Israeli drug—AL-721, an immune-boosting agent that had been used successfully on a child with an autoimmune dysfunction. The Israeli researcher had told Bruce that the FDA was throwing up roadblocks to prevent them from testing it in this country. So now we had our new underground agenda, and between us Bruce and I made hundreds of calls to find out more, though still we had no major sense of danger about suramin. We were just trying to keep ahead and be in the right place for the next phase.

On September 10, Craig arrived from New York for a week's visit, primarily so he could go to Mexico to get a supply of ribavirin. It was the one antiviral that was available over the counter, though the counter was across the border. Craig was impressed and delighted to find Roger looking so much better than four months before. By now Craig and I were accustomed to the two-tiered policy of talking nonstop about AIDS when together but not around Roger. Next morning the two of us got up early and headed south, taking the Datsun rather than the Jaguar so as not to be conspicuous at the border, where we would be bringing over a thousand dollars' worth of drugs. In theory one was allowed to carry back enough for "personal use," but the area was very gray. There was talk in the underground of detention and confiscation. The mind reeled at the challenge of avoiding germs in a Tijuana jail.

"The Treasure of the Sierra Madre" was our nickname for the drug that day. So many have gone over now to get it that the ribavirin buy has become a kind of reflex. Everyone knows which pharmacies can be trusted, which are rip-offs. There is such an elaborate system of mules that I can usually obtain the drug these days with a single phone call. A friend who keeps a fair stock on hand meets me on the corner of Western and Santa Monica, outside Fedco, to make the swap. But in the fall of '85 there was still a quality of the unexpected about the smuggler's journey. It only reinforced our sense of being outlaws, and for once there was a tinge of romance to it.

We had the names of four pharmacies, and decided to go to one outside the city center, which involved a rattlesnake drive along the Mexican side of the border. For a space of several miles we saw illegal immigrants pouring through holes in the chain-link fences, seven or eight in a family with trash bags full of their worldly goods. Taxis would screech to a stop at certain gaping holes, and the refugees would tumble out, wide-eyed at the port of entry as if Liberty herself had cut that fence.

The pharmacy was in a dusty town across from a bullring, in view of the green sluggish southern ocean, raw with the smell of kelp. We bought all the ribavirin and isoprinosine they had, chatting amiably with a couple from San Francisco who were buying cancer drugs. I realized then we weren't the only ones being driven underground by the FDA. We were part of the nether world of the sick, trying to get some control, taking risks the government wouldn't sanction, and all in the same boat.

We soaked up miles of atmosphere and were giddy as we waited in line at the border, trying to look proper and nonaddictive as we gestured toward a trunkful of drugs. We were waved on through and drove home into full gold sunset, exhilarated and in charge of fate. By the time we spun the story out to Rog it was already part of our history, something we had won.

*　　　　　*　　　　　*

Either the symptoms didn't seem to be getting worse, or they took second place to the drama of our parents' arrival on the moon. Saturday, November 17, was the Gay Community Center dinner at the Beverly Hilton, and I decided to go and host the table Roger had put together from his hospital bed the previous month. In the Hilton I ran into Rick Honeycutt, no longer impish and surferlike, looking tired and old as he told me he was off suramin. Eagerly I gushed about AZT, but he didn't want to hear about it. Several people came by the table and asked where Roger was, none of them having any idea that he had AIDS, and I said defiantly that he was doing fine and waiting for AZT. Nobody knew what the acronym meant, but they got the picture.

Charlie Milhaupt drove me home, and we went in to see Rog, who woke up in a smiling mood and said, "I just had a dream. There was this green liquid. And all I had to do was drink sixteen cups of it and I'd be fine."

The elixir dream. We laughed at the lovely fantasy of it and went to bed that night with nothing more on our minds for the week ahead than awaiting his parents' arrival and then the drug. We'd given both families a full measure of hope when we broke the news, for we had our pharmaceutical ace in the hole. But Sunday it was glaringly clear that we couldn't just sit and wait. The nausea was intensifying, the fevers were back and the fatigue had reached a stage where Roger could hardly get out of bed. We went over to UCLA for tests, and they admitted Roger, again just overnight, but by now we knew what a euphemism "overnight" could be.

And suddenly my memory is as blank as my calendar for almost the whole of the next two weeks. I remember only the bitter disappointment, to think that Al and Bernice would have to find us in the hospital. I know they arrived on Monday night, four days before Roger's forty-fourth birthday, by which point we knew he had hepatitis, of the type called NON-A/NON-B, noninfectious and probably drug-related. That would explain the nausea and lethargy, as well as the sunburned cast of Roger's face, which began to take on a dull gold flatness.

But the real point is that he nearly died that week—closer than he ever came in the whole nineteen months—and I don't even know when. You'd think the shadow of death would have your nerves screaming to imprint it. Richard Ide says he talked to Roger from Washington on Sunday night, soon after we checked in, and Roger was terrified and started to cry. "I love you, Richard," he said. And Richard knew in that instant that Roger was dying, that this was a call to say good-bye. Scrambling, Richard said he'd be on a plane and be in L.A. by Friday, so Roger had better hang on till then. Yet the fever point of the crisis had apparently passed by the time Richard landed on Friday night, so it must have been Tuesday or Wednesday Roger almost died.

But what exactly does "almost" mean? It wasn't until the next summer that I could even admit how bad it had been during the days of late November. At the time, anything anyone said about dying, however veiled, I simply didn't hear. Because he *couldn't* die, not with the drug just a week away. For this was precisely what was so tantalizing in the rumors of AZT, that it was turning people around even from the verge of nothingness. I recall wanting everyone to let us alone with the hepatitis—no treatment for that but time, the doctors said. We would take care of the time. Just get us the fucking elixir.

Not that our deep-throat sources weren't moving heaven and earth to acquire it. Word was that thirteen or fourteen patients were on it now, but every single one was back east and close to the National Institutes of Health. Superpower threats had to be made to coax the drug to California, and even so the manufacturer had all the time in the world. Meanwhile I had to deal with a pugnacious, cocky little intern called Runyon, barely five foot seven, who wouldn't stop running tests because he wasn't satisfied with hepatitis.

I grew maddened with all of Runyon's probing, but he managed to convince Dennis Cope that they ought to go one step further. Now came the first spinal tap, the first bone marrow biopsy, both tests as awful to contemplate—much less undergo—as medieval tortures. I remember Roger curling up in fear of the marrow test, holding my hand as Runyon, utterly lacking in bedside manner, explained the procedure in ghoulish detail. Yet where would we be without Runyon, bless him, who wouldn't stop brooding over certain ambiguous numbers, and who finally figured it out: Roger's adrenal glands were failing. I don't even remember why that is fatal; I only know it's treatable. When you live on the moon, *treatable* gets to be the holiest word in the language.

How Runyon crowed with triumph! He was easily five foot nine by the end of the week. And within an hour of his diagnosis Roger was on medication—Florinef, a terrific little lilac pill, one a day for the rest of his life—that would do all the adrenal functioning that needed doing. It wasn't until a week or two later that reports began to filter in through the AIDS underground that four suramin patients out of a hundred had lost adrenal function. So it was just an unlucky side effect, that grim companion of healing.

As for the suramin—water under the bridge, which seemed more lethal with every report that came in—of course I anguished to think how much we had wasted on snake oil. There's a moment in *Sunrise at Campobello* when the Roosevelts have been tirelessly giving some vigorous treatment to Franklin—rubbing his legs for hours for the circulation—and the doctor tells them they've been doing precisely the wrong thing. The sinking feeling is indescribable as you reach the dead end and realize you can't even go back to the fork in the road where you took the wrong turn. I felt ridiculous and ashamed, I who had pushed suramin all summer as practically a miracle cure.

But if I was gullible, there were others who knew exactly what they were doing. Though UCLA quickly moved to dismantle its suramin study as soon as it became clear the drug was too toxic, several other suramin programs were still going full force, with hundreds of patients clamoring to get in. Within a few weeks this moral blurring to protect the experimental data began to seem criminal to me. There was one doctor who kept his patients on suramin through the winter, even when we knew how lethal the side effects were, and even as the patients died off one by one.

*   *   *

After two ten-hour nights of sleeping in, Roger appeared to have proved me right, for he was much perkier Monday morning as we all sat at breakfast. Actually, as I remember now, Roger got up even later than I and was having breakfast himself, while the rest of us hovered and watched him eat. As he finished his cereal, he said almost offhandedly, "My eye feels funny." Immediately I was alert, but I casually asked him to elaborate, not wanting to alarm the family. "It's like there's a shadow in it," he said, blinking as he passed his hand back and forth in front of the right eye.

Though he shrugged it off, I said we'd call Kreiger when we got back to L.A., and the worry dissipated in the round-robin of family cheer as we made ready to leave. Michael, a rabid Cubs fan, gave Roger an umpire's cap from the National League for luck. Then all the way back to the city, I kept thinking of Leo on intravenous eye medication "for the rest of my life." A new drug that had come on line in recent months to battle cytomegalovirus was one of the few bright spots in treatment. Previously CMV had rendered a lot of AIDS patients blind in the early years of the calamity. Then I started obsessing about the cotton-wool patches that had floated benignly in Roger's retinal sky for a whole year now. Had one of those clouds begun to darken?

Beside me, Roger kept squinting, and I asked if it hurt or was getting worse. No, he said, but the squinting didn't stop. When we pulled into an off-ramp Denny's for a bite of lunch, I called Kreiger's office at UCLA in a panic, but he was away for the day and his service was picking up. As soon as we got back to the city we had to retrieve the dog at the kennel, and he was hysterical. So we had our hands full unpacking and settling in again, and Roger needed to rest from the trip, especially since his fever went up that night. We put off the eye till the next day.

I don't recall if Roger's vision was worse on Tuesday, but the fever was persistent, and now I was certain he'd picked up some kind of flu from Tony. Cope said that was entirely possible and told us to monitor the fever and check in by phone the next day. He knew how reluctant we were to come in for no reason at all, especially after the recent false alarm. As for the eye, since Kreiger would be out of town till Thursday, we made an SOS call to our ophthalmologist friend, Dell Steadman. He met us during his lunch hour at his office in Beverly Hills. As he gazed into Roger's eye with his scope, I held my breath the way I used to do as a child whenever we drove by a cemetery.

No, said Dell, there was no CMV in evidence. The cotton-wool patches were stable. And since he could see no other problems, he suggested the optic nerve might be temporarily damaged by a flu or cold virus. Roger's vision in that eye had dimmed some more, but not dramatically. We went home relieved and tried to forget it, tried to go back to waiting for AZT, but the fever wouldn't go away, so the next day Cope suggested we'd better come in.

The rest of the week is a blur of apprehension and horror. Kreiger and two other eye doctors examined Roger over and over, and though the business about the optic nerve made sense at first—by now Roger was *seeing* mostly shadows out of that eye—the retina began to show subtle signs of damage. Suddenly Kreiger wasn't satisfied. I could see he was puzzled and thoughtful, even as he concurred for a while that the vision would surely return—or perhaps he just neglected to contradict our own tense optimism. I don't know when he decided to put Roger on a high dose of acyclovir, the herpes drug. By then I was on the phone nonstop, trying to field all the info I could find about AIDS and the eyes. The problem was, there was no way to be sure it was a herpes infection, because you can't do a biopsy of the eye, except by autopsy. Yet Kreiger decided to treat it as if it were herpes, though he'd only know that he guessed right if the forward creep of infection stopped.

I don't know myself what I was trying to find out with all my phoning—any anecdote would do, it seemed, as I pieced together a nightmare collage. I remember talking to a man who didn't know who I was, whose number was given to me by one of the Tijuana mules. He had gone blind only a few weeks before and was still choked with sorrow about it, yet he bravely told me his whole story—the misdiagnosis, the prolonging of treatment till it was too late, the breaking of the news, the blackness.

I told him I was sorry and then about my friend. Yes, he said, he understood; his own friend had died just after Christmas. Among us warriors there is a duty to compose ourselves and pass on anything that might help, no matter how deep the grief. Two weeks after Roger died, a frantic acquaintance called to ask about the meningitis drug that hadn't worked for Roger, who died with it in his veins. Just the mention of the word took my breath away, as I answered questions about the convulsive side effects. But I thought of the blind man trying to help me save Roger's eyes, and so I stayed on the meningitis case till the crisis was past.

*   *   *

I scored my first batch of ribavirin that week from Jim Corty, an extraordinary hulk of a man whose passion for fighting fire with fire was as obsessive as mine. Jim was a nurse who cared exclusively for people with AIDS, and he personally drove a van over the border into Mexico every couple of weeks to haul back great quantities of ribavirin, supplying dozens on both coasts. His own lover, John, had been diagnosed in the spring, and Jim was constantly monitoring Roger's experience with AZT, eager to get it for John once the protocols were expanded. Jim always made me feel we would beat it, and never failed to rekindle my excitement about AZT. Ribavirin of course was a much less certain drug, but I went on it anyway, because there was no other game in town for me. I had been too vocal for too long that people ought to be getting tested so they could demand medication early, and it was time for me to put up or shut up.

I know I was growing increasingly desperate about Roger's cough, and if he suddenly had a jag I'd find myself getting irrationally angry, though I could usually swallow it. But I would have sworn there were no other ominous symptoms, no shortness of breath or overwhelming fatigue. This is not to say he didn't sleep a good deal, but between Scott and me we were very skilled at getting him up and going so he didn't sleep the day away. When he was up he was animated and alert, especially when anyone visited. The summer days were so lambent now, even as the summer waned—mornings in the garden while I read him the paper, evenings reading Plato, the smell of anise when we walked at night. These brief, immediate goals of the day-to-day we had come to cherish, no matter how constricted our movements.

It was Friday of Labor Day weekend when Scott asked me as he was leaving the house, "What does the doctor say the prognosis is?" I suppose I knew he was asking about the timetable of death, but that didn't seem to me the appropriate question at all. "The doctor says he's doing fine on the AZT," I replied, a bit defensively. Not that Cope had really said as much lately, but it was implicit in Roger's survival for nearly ten months now since he started the drug. He was the miracle man, period. He had to be, because thousands of our brothers were about to follow him on AZT.

A series had begun to run in the L.A. *Times*, a portrait by Marlene Cimons of an AIDS person in Boston. Jeff, his name was, and he'd been chosen to be in the AZT double-blind study being funded by NIH. It wasn't hard to get reanimated over AZT as news of its efficacy began to break in waves at last. We were thrilled by the *Times* story and very moved by the passion of the man's doctor, who reminded us in his patience and dogged persistence of Dennis Cope. So I tried not to overreact to the first bad news about AZT, which was Roy Cohn.

The press had uncovered the fact that Cohn was being treated at NIH in Washington, and the rumor was that it was AIDS, despite Cohn's drone of denial for the last two years. We had known through the grapevine for nearly a year that he was among the first AIDS people to go on AZT, after Nancy Reagan intervened in his behalf. The press was stumbling all over itself getting the story wrong about Cohn's demise, but I had a nearly day-by-day update from Craig, whose friend Donald was getting AZT intravenously on the same floor in Bethesda. "He's going to die in the next couple of days," said Craig, and I tried to keep the thought from racing in my mind: But no one's supposed to die on AZT.

CBS did a big report one evening that week about crack cocaine, the report we kept feeling they ought to be doing weekly about AIDS. Don't you understand? friends in New York would say, hoarse from screaming at the press for coverage. Cocaine wasn't a problem till it started turning up among the children of media dons and the Washington power elite. This at a time when I would hear at least every other week about the discreet death by AIDS of one or another rich man, the cause of death fudged on the certificate or otherwise unreported. Every gay man I know has stories of married bisexual men who died in the secret enclaves of family, town, church, and local GP, all without saying the "A" word. Even certain gay doctors, we heard, would blur a death certificate if the family was mortified enough.

STUDY QUESTIONS

1. What does Monette mean when he refers to the "AIDS underground"?
2. What is AL-721? What is suramin?
3. What strategies did Monette and Roger devise to obtain experimental drugs before they were readily available through normal medical channels?
4. What does Monette's willingness to share information about medical therapies with strangers suggest about the moral fabric of the gay "AIDS underground"?

Suggested Additional Readings

"Anatomy of a Disaster: Why Is Federal AIDS Research at a Standstill?" *The Village Voice* (March 13, 1990).

Martin Delaney, "The Case for Patient Access to Experimental Therapy." *Journal of Infectious Diseases,* vol. 159 (1989):416–419.

Harold Edgar and David J. Rothman, "New Rules for New Drugs: The Challenge of AIDS to the Regulatory Process." Dorothy Nelkin, David P. Willis and Scott V. Parriss, editors. *A Disease of Society: Cultural and Institutional Responses to AIDS* (New York: Cambridge University Press, 1991).

John Gamson, "Silence, Death, and the Invisible Enemy: AIDS Activism and Social Movement 'Newness.'" *Social Problems,* vol. 36 (1989):351–367.

David Handleman, "ACT UP in Anger." *Rolling Stone* (March 5, 1990):80–88.

Carol Levine, Nancy Dubler, and Robert Levine, "Building a New Consensus: Ethical Principles and Policies for Clinical Research on HIV/AIDS." *IRB: A Review of Human Subjects Research,* 13 (1991):1–17.

Paul Taylor, "AIDS Guerillas." *New York,* vol. 23 (November 2, 1990):62–63ff.

CHAPTER 6

Living with AIDS

Restructured Lives

• • •

More than 12,000 people in the United States had died of AIDS when the UPI broke the Rock Hudson story in July 1985. Five days after that announcement, the Western School Corporation of Kokomo, Indiana, barred thirteen-year-old Ryan White from school. Ryan, a hemophiliac, had been infected with HIV through contaminated Factor VIII (a blood product that enhances coagulation).[1] Measured against the level of knowledge and understanding about HIV/AIDS that had been revealed by the recent Gallup Poll, the Western School Corporation decision reflects in a most public fashion a new phase in the AIDS epidemic. Both public and private expressions of fears regarding casual transmission of the disease had heightened. Clinical physicians and epidemiologists had been documenting cases of pediatric and transfusion AIDS for five years when the Western School Corporation barred Ryan from school, yet those cases had been largely excluded from the public view. Ryan White's fate had been sealed by the public connections between HIV/AIDS and homosexuality.

An HIV/AIDS diagnosis brings with it a restructuring of social relationships. At the most immediate level of daily life, the responses of friends and families to the diagnosis are problematic, as are employment, personal safety, access to health care and to public facilities. All are jeopardized, and people who are physically weakened are often placed in positions of enormous psychosocial stress when they must confront and cope with a restructured public identity. Most Americans had heard something about AIDS by 1985, and the majority knew that the disease could be transmitted through blood transfusions, shared needles, and heterosexual intercourse, as well as through homosexual exchanges of semen. Most Americans also knew that AIDS could not be transmitted through casual contact such as shaking hands or being in a crowded place.[2] Yet objective knowledge proved an inadequate guide when Americans began to confront AIDS directly. The selections in Chapter 6 describe the daily struggles of people with HIV or AIDS who are living with the triple indemnity of declining physical vigor, public exposure of HIV status, and loss of support, acceptance, and the personal well-being that we assume are our inalienable

---

[1]Ryan White died of AIDS on April 8, 1990, at the age of eighteen. Ronald Reagan's op-ed piece in *The Washington Post* (April 10, 1990) called for an end to the "fear and ignorance that chased him from his home and school."

[2]*Morbidity and Mortality Weekly Report,* Centers for Disease Control [vol. 34 (August 23, 1985):513–514], summarizes the results of the poll.

rights as Americans. The final selection suggests the ways in which the religious beliefs that are embedded in the American value system have fueled rather than mediated that triple indemnity.

Hospitalman Third Class Byron Kinney, who joined the Navy in 1977 when he was twenty-one years old, lived out the scenario that the National Gay and Lesbian Task Force had feared when it voiced objections to the unrestricted use of the HIV antibody blood test. Shortly after his induction, Kinney had come to terms with his homosexuality. Acting against military regulations, he concealed his sexual orientation and continued his military service. In 1985, at about the same time that the Western School Corporation banned Ryan White from its classroom, the Navy initiated discharge proceedings against Kinney, who had been treated for AIDS in military medical facilities and was requesting a medical discharge. Using evidence obtained from his physicians and "confidential" medical records, the Navy obtained a general discharge on the ground that Kinney engaged in "false representations and deliberate concealment" of his homosexuality. The general discharge deprived Kinney of veterans' medical benefits.

In 1987, two years after Ryan White had been barred from public school in Kokomo, Indiana, three young boys in Arcadia, Florida, a small town fifty-five miles southeast of Tampa, Florida, who, like Ryan White, were hemophiliacs and infected with HIV but still asymptomatic, were also barred from public school by the DeSoto County School Board. The boys and their parents sued in civil court for readmission to school, and the school board countered with an offer to provide "separate but equal education" to them in an isolated classroom. **Nothing to Fear but Fear Itself** follows the community of Arcadia through the period of legal action, tracing the contours of the controversy through the press coverage, the parents' meetings, the rhetoric of a local Pentecostal minister, and the views of the Ray boys' classmates.

The experiences of Byron Kinney and the Ray family and the responses of institutions and communities to people with AIDS are shaped by a calculus of beliefs, attitudes, and values that bear little direct relationship to the medical realities of the *disease*. A Gallup public opinion poll conducted in 1988, the year after Arcadia, Florida, employed every possible means to ban the Ray boys from public school classrooms, found that evangelical Christians were more likely than other religious groups to believe that HIV/AIDS could be transmitted through casual contact. Drawing on data from the 1988 General Social Survey, **Religion and Attitudes Toward AIDS Policy** extends the analysis of this finding by examining the ways in which religious beliefs shape attitudes toward a variety of HIV/AIDS public policy issues. The conclusion of this analysis—that people who attended church regularly tended to oppose both government-funded and school-based AIDS-related sex education more often than those who were not regular churchgoers—helps to illuminate the connections between morality and public policy that form an ongoing subtext of the HIV/AIDS health crisis.

Hospitalman Third Class Byron Kinney

Randy Shilts

June 25, 1985
Courtroom 3, Building 1
Thirty-second Street Naval Station
San Diego, California

With his thick brown hair and chiseled features, Hospitalman Third Class Byron Kinney had been handsome once, but by that balmy morning in San Diego the purple lesions of Kaposi's sarcoma had stained his face and his Navy uniform hung loosely on his wasted body. Kinney was also terribly tired. He had been sick for fourteen months, always getting worse, never better. The doctors said perhaps he had four months to live—at most, ten months. But no matter how close to death he might be, the Navy appeared to have only one purpose: to punish Byron Kinney for being gay. That was why he was here that day, for the administrative board to separate him from the Navy.

This official posture came at a time when the armed forces could no longer procrastinate in deciding how they would cope with the growing numbers of AIDS sufferers. Three months earlier, the Food and Drug Administration had licensed the first blood tests for antibodies to the virus believed to cause AIDS. Scientists called it human T-cell lymphotropic virus—variant type III—HTLV-III for short. Since the HTLV-III antibody test kits were only now coming off the production line, the test's use was largely restricted to blood banks, but, once it became more widely available in a few months, its presence could have staggering social implications, not the least of which was for the Department of Defense.

Already there were calls for screening all 2 million active-duty service members. This proposal led to the next question: What would the services do with soldiers who tested positive for HTLV-III? Military doctors had already pressed their case: If medical testing revealed a soldier was stricken with cancer or heart disease, that soldier was medically retired and allowed a pension and use of military medical facilities. This tradition dated back generations and reflected a covenant between the military and its members. The military was a family, according to this covenant, and it took care of its own. It did not dump people when they needed help most.

But Acquired Immune Deficiency Syndrome would never be treated like just another disease in the United States, given the fact that its first cases were detected among gay men. Questions of how to handle AIDS would always merge with questions of how to handle homosexuals. Since this was not a nation that dealt with gay people kindly, it was not likely to deal with AIDS sufferers kindly, either. In the early years of the epidemic, this was certainly the case within the institution that had most formally codified society's attitudes against gays. Though the military's medical people called for compassion, some officers in the more conservative branches, especially in the personnel commands, would hear nothing of it. And as the civilian leadership of the Defense Department still floundered for official policies, individual commands began implementing their own. Which was why Byron Kinney stood, exhausted, before a separation hearing in San Diego that morning, and also why he was fighting his separation, so that other sick and tired people would not have to suffer as he was.

The crescendo had been building for the past year. Naturally, the service most dedicated to punishing homosexuals took the hardest line against service members with AIDS. In March, Hospitalman Second Class Bernard "Bud" Broyhill was diagnosed with Kaposi's sarcoma at his duty station in Puerto Rico. His Navy doctor insisted that it was essential for his diagnosis to know whether Broyhill had ever engaged in homosexual conduct. When the corpsman was reluctant to answer, the physician assured him that any answer would be held in the strictest confidence. Broyhill said he was gay. A few days later, the Naval Investigative Service informed Broyhill he was being charged with sodomy and homosexuality.

At about the same time, another San Diego–based sailor newly diagnosed with AIDS, Daniel Abeita, answered his doctors' inquiries about his sexuality by confiding that he, too, was gay. Rather than moving for a medical retirement, the Navy began processing Abeita for separation under the gay regulations. Without a medical retirement, Abeita's future would be seriously compromised. When Abeita said he would fight the discharge, the Navy put him on medical hold and refused even to give him leave to go home to Texas to see his parents. He would have to stay in San Diego until the Navy decided what to do with him, however long that took. Near death, Abeita gave in. "I have to go home to my family," he told military counselor Bridget Wilson, and she understood. He accepted his gay discharge and left.

The Navy had won, but one last affront remained. Navy regulations called for providing a separated sailor either a plane or bus ticket home. Though it was already mid-June and the weather was fiercely hot, the Navy would not buy Dan a seat on an airplane; he got a nonrefundable Greyhound ticket. In the end, Abeita's volunteer gay lawyer, Tom Homann, took money out of his own pocket to buy a plane ticket for the dying man.

For Byron Gary Kinney, his final skirmish with the Navy proved to be the last act of his short life. He had joined the Navy in 1977 at the age of twenty-one and trained as a medical corpsman. Not long after that, he came to grips with the fact that he was gay and made his first sorties to the gay scene of Washington, D.C., not far from his duty at Bethesda Naval Hospital. After his first enlistment ended in April 1981, he worked a few laboratory jobs around Bethesda, but the economy was weak and he was soon unemployed. In December 1981, Kinney joined the Navy again. Question 35f on his enlistment form asked: "Have you ever engaged in homosexual activity?" Byron did what everyone else he knew did and responded no.

He was assigned to the Oakland Naval Hospital, across the Bay from San Francisco. It was a very bad time to be a gay sailor on leave in San Francisco. Since neither the government nor the media talked much about "gay cancer," there was little warning of the deadly new disease. Byron took the virus with him to Okinawa in February 1984 when he was assigned as a senior corpsman with the First Marine Division. About two months later, he began having diarrhea.

By the time he reported to the base hospital in October, he had lost 10 percent of his weight, his mouth was spotted with lesions of oral candidiasis, and all his lymph nodes were swollen. His diarrhea was bloody now, and when doctors did a CT scan of his abdominal track they saw that his lower intestines and rectum were covered with lesions of Kaposi's sarcoma.

The first references to Kinney's sexuality were scrawled on his chart on October 23, 1984. "The patient became sexually active with men at age 21," the doctor wrote. Two weeks later when the AIDS diagnosis was made, another doctor noted, "The patient has a history of homosexuality and has had several partners." These notes did not prejudice the Navy captain and lieutenant commander who comprised the medical board that in December ruled Kinney qualified for medical retirement. They also deemed that Kinney was entitled to his base pay and continued medical treatment from the Navy. The entire matter might have ended there but for Rear Admiral David L. Harlow at the Naval Personnel Command. He insisted that Kinney not be medically retired but separated for homosexuality instead. Kinney's offense was not only that he was gay, but also that he had perpetrated an act of fraud against the Navy with his answer to question 35f. Because of the fraudulent enlistment charge, Harlow wanted Kinney to receive a general discharge rather than an honorable one.

By now, Kinney had been evacuated to San Diego. Though military personnel are not guaranteed confidentiality in their relationships with service physicians, the Navy doctors whose notes indicated that Kinney was gay were appalled at the Navy's moves against the dying man. Lieutenant Commander Fred Millard furnished a blistering memo for Byron's lawyers. "The information . . . was obtained from Byron with the understanding that it would be used purely for purposes of medical diagnosis and treatment," Millard wrote. "Any attempt to use this information for other purposes without Byron's permission represents an unconscionable breach of the principle of confidentiality between patient and caregiver."

Navy spokesman Lieutenant Stephan Pietropaoli countered: "Homosexuality is incompatible with military life. It is the Navy policy that all homosexuals be separated from the Navy. No punitive action is taken when someone has AIDS, that is a medical diagnosis. . . . There is only punitive action when a person is homosexual." For all their denials, admirals in the Pentagon were not reviewing the records of medical retirement boards for sailors with heart conditions or diabetes for evidence of homosexuality or fraudulent enlistment. They were doing so only for sailors with AIDS.

The Navy was signaling how it would treat sailors with HTLV-III by its treatment of sailors with AIDS, Bridget Wilson and other military counselors believed, which was what made Byron Kinney's case so crucial. Bridget and two key allies from the Military Law Task Force of the National Lawyers Guild, attorney Ted Bumer and counselor Kathy Gilberd, went to work on Kinney's case with every intention of pushing the matter into federal court if they lost the separation board hearing. It was not just Kinney's career but thousands of careers that were at stake that morning.

The Navy was aware of the stakes, as well. Lieutenant Nels Kelstrom was brought aboard to serve as the recorder, or prosecutor, for the hearing. A full commander, Joseph Vrbancic, served as legal adviser; they were not taking any chances.

At 9:12 A.M., with reporters and television cameras clustered outside, the hearing was called into session.

*   *   *

Kinney could sit up for only some of his separation hearing. For much of the procedure, he lay on a bench in the rear of the courtroom while the lawyers argued among themselves. In his opening argument, Lieutenant Nels Kelstrom, acting on behalf of the Navy, announced that he would present no witnesses, because he did not have to. Kinney's records spoke for themselves, he said. "I believe that the evidence presented today will firmly establish that Petty Officer Kinney absolutely has no place in the Navy and should be discharged and that should be the vote of this Board," Kelstrom said.

Kinney's attorney, Ted Bumer, attempted to present the objections of the physicians to the use of their records in the hearing. Kelstrom argued against it, saying, "In the military, the patient–physician privilege [of confidentiality] does not exist." When Bumer pressed further, the matter was taken out of earshot of the board to the legal adviser. "They obviously want members [of the board] to hear that their doctor is outraged by the fact of the use of those statements," Kelstrom complained. Such statements are "irrelevant and inflammatory," he argued. Commander Vrbancic, the Navy legal advisor, ruled against Bumer and for the Navy.

Bumer brought in AIDS experts from the University of California at San Diego to testify how long they thought Kinney could be expected to live. Bumer's intent was to show that the Navy had little to lose in the way of good order, discipline and morale by allowing Kinney to have a medical retirement. Kelstrom was angered by the line of questioning and asked it be halted. "That is irrelevant; it is nothing but a confusion tactic," he said. "We're here to decide whether or not he engaged in homosexual acts and a fraudulent enlistment, and that's all we're here to decide at this juncture." Again, the Navy legal adviser ruled for the Navy.

Back in the courtroom, Lieutenant Kelstrom delivered his final summation. The errant behavior, he argued, might continue if the board did not move immediately to kick Kinney out of the Navy. "I don't know; I can't tell you whether the likelihood of continued homosexual practices exists, but I know that it continued for a five- or six-year period," Kelstrom said. "It continued even after he had denied previous homosexual practices when he joined the Navy, and he knew good and well what the Navy's policy was regarding homosexuals or he wouldn't have lied when he signed the enlistment application and contract. So what is the likelihood for continuation? Well, I submit that under the circumstances of this case it is probably unlikely, but should we take a chance? . . . I think that we cannot speculate that it won't happen; if anything, I think we should speculate that it would perhaps continue. Will he be a disruptive or undesirable influence in present or future duty assignments? I submit he will be."

Though Navy regulations called for an honorable discharge for gay sailors, Kelstrom argued against mercy for Kinney, saying the "fraudulent enlistment" charge outweighed "the positive aspects of his performance" while a Navy corpsman.

In his closing argument, Bumer begged the board to consider the impact a separation would have on the military's ability to deal with AIDS. Sailors would be afraid to talk to their doctors; doctors would be afraid to talk to their patients. Before Bumer could get far into his closing argument, however, Kelstrom objected. AIDS was not the issue, he said, only homosexuality and fraudulent enlistment. None of this was relevant, he stated. And the Navy legal adviser ruled against Kinney and for the Navy.

Byron Kinney was allowed to make an unsworn statement before the board. "I feel I've given seven years of service," he barely whispered, "and this wouldn't be happening if I wasn't sick." And then he was too exhausted to speak any longer.

The board recessed to consider its decision at 4:45 P.M. Kinney shuffled down the hall and found an empty room where he shoved several chairs together and put his head on his backpack. It was not sleep he wanted so much as an escape from the voices, the noise.

At 5:14 P.M., the board's senior member, Lieutenant Commander Nancy Price, read the panel's unanimous decision: "By a vote of three to zero, the Board recommends that the Respondent be discharged from the naval service due to procurement of a fraudulent enlistment by knowing false representations and deliberate concealment of pre-service homosexual activity and homosexuality . . . and that the discharge be a general discharge.

"The Board will be adjourned," she said.

Byron's lawyers shielded him from reporters, but when one journalist shouted, "What's he going to do now?" Kinney turned and said simply, "I'll continue to fight."

The Kinney case did not generate much publicity outside the gay press and the immediate San Diego area, but the bad publicity made the Pentagon cringe, as did the mounting protests over the Defense Department plan to force blood banks to provide names of HTLV-III positive military donors. Inside the Pentagon, the conflict between line officers and military doctors continued.

A week after the Kinney hearing, Assistant Defense Secretary Mayer announced that the Defense Department would delay implementation of its order to civilian blood banks. Mayer wanted to "review concerns expressed by civilian blood collection agencies" centering on privacy issues, a spokesman said. After the Kinney hearing, it was no longer meaningful for the Pentagon to argue that it would never use medical tests to punish service personnel.

Before Kinney's separation became final—and before it could be legally challenged—the board's conclusion had to be accepted by the Naval Personnel Command. Bridget Wilson, who had been advising Kinney, hoped that Byron might win at that level, forgoing the need to drag him through a long court fight. Just how much longer Byron might live was a major concern for Wilson, Bumer, and Kathy Gilberd. When Wilson talked to Byron and heard the betrayal he felt, and his worry as well as his fear that the Navy would betray thousands more if he did not win, she realized that Byron was not about to expire. He was angry and was determined, and he was not going to die until this thing was won.

*   *   *

[Editor's note: One day before his scheduled discharge date, October 16, 1985, the Pentagon advised Kinney that he would be processed for medical retirement rather than discharged for homosexuality. On the following day, Kinney was admitted to Balboa Naval Hospital in San Diego, and died four days later, October 21, 1985. (paraphrasing of Shilts, p. 509)]

STUDY QUESTIONS

1. How in this case did AIDS serve as a proxy for homosexuality?
2. How does Kinney's case play out the ethical concerns that had informed the National Gay and Lesbian Task Force's objections to widespread HIV antibody testing?

Nothing to Fear but Fear Itself

Steven Petrow

Once the Rays went public, no one was without an opinion. A *DeSoto County Times* editorial titled, "Let's Apply the Basic Principles," stuck up for the Rays and for reason as the paper saw it:

> It's the kind of case that will suck your heart right out of your chest. Forget for a moment that Clifford and Louise Ray have been critical of our community. Forget for another moment that the DeSoto County School board and superintendent are scared to death on this one.
>
> Think about those three boys. From outward appearances, they're healthy as young horses. Look at those chubby faces. They like bubble gum and Nerds and Milky Ways and Mr. Pibb. Their shirts come out in the back, and their socks slip down in their shoes.
>
> Except for the fact that they are hemophiliacs who carry the AIDS virus antibodies, they are healthy as young horses.
>
> They don't have AIDS, but they are not allowed in a regular classroom situation with other children in DeSoto County. . . .
>
> Perhaps the most practical solution would be to put the three Ray boys back in the regular classroom next week. . . . Let them continue in a normal classroom setting through the summer. Publicity and attention would die down. Things could genuinely get back to normal in DeSoto County.
>
> The watch words here are realism, heart and guts. It would make us most proud to see the DeSoto County school board act with these things in mind.

Nevertheless, during the third week of May, the school board met in emergency session and voted unanimously to continue to exclude the Ray boys from the classroom despite the increased press coverage and the likelihood of a lawsuit. In a curious throwback to the days before Brown v. Board of Education (1954), the DeSoto County School Board offered to provide separate but equal instruction to the boys in an isolated portable classroom. In June, the Rays were notified that their boys could not attend summer school either.

The resulting flood of publicity infuriated many locals who felt that their side of the issue was not being heard. The letters column of the *DeSoto County Times* overflowed with mail from angry readers. Under the headline "Let's Hear It," the *Times* ran the following letter:

Reprinted with the permission of Lexington Books, an imprint of Macmillan, Inc., from Steven Petrow, *Dancing Against the Darkness: A Journey Through America in the Age of AIDS* (New York: Lexington Books):excerpts from 18–30. © 1990 by Steven Petrow.

Dear Editor:

Let's hear it for Arcadia . . . remember sticks and stones can break our bones, but names will never hurt us. It might smart a little to be unjustly accused, but if any of those pompous, finger-pointing, name-calling self-appointed judges think the people of Arcadia, Florida are going to roll over and play dead—they're wrong.

AIDS didn't start in Arcadia and it won't end here. This town has simply become the scapegoat for the bleeding hearts who refuse to admit what AIDS is and where it came from. . . .

There has been no fair, accurate or unbiased news coverage and the whole town of Arcadia has been judged and found guilty of it.

And now if the sniveling, mealymouthed letter writers and know-it-all editors will be patient the AIDS coverup will be exposed and Arcadia will be vindicated because like the old Chinese proverb, "Truth, like oil, will rise to the surface."

—Willie Duncan

The controversy also attracted the attention of Judy Kavanaugh, a prominent environmental lawyer in neighboring Sarasota. The soft-spoken but astute mother of five agreed to take the Ray case. Instead of continuing to work within the administrative procedures of the school district, Kavanaugh filed a suit in U.S. district court seeking a court order that the Ray boys be admitted to school without delay.

The legal action moved the conflict from the school board's meeting rooms to the federal courthouse in Tampa, some fifty-five miles northwest. During the court proceedings, the Rays' attorney and a plethora of medical experts presented materials to the court showing no documented cases of household or school transmission of the virus.

Although no school board had prevailed in excluding a child with AIDS or the AIDS virus from the classroom, Superintendent Browning hired a flamboyant civil action attorney, Harry Blair, from nearby Fort Myers, at a base cost of $50,000. Blair said he took the case "because it was offered to me." While the papers filed on behalf of the Rays stood five feet tall when stacked one on top of another, the defense materials barely covered a grown man's shoes.

After one month of testimony from local doctors, world-renowned AIDS specialists, mental health professionals, educators, and public health officials, U.S. district court judge Elizabeth A. Kovachevich issued a preliminary injunction allowing for the boys' return to school. In the opinion, she found no merit in the school board's argument, making explicit that the court would not be guided by "community fear, parental pressure, and the possibility [of subsequent] lawsuits."

The following day, August 6, the *Tampa Tribune* published an editorial that outraged many Arcadians and drew still others into the fray. The editorial, titled "Striking Down Ignorance in DeSoto County Schools," began this way:

> The ignorant and the stubborn were defeated yesterday when a federal judge ruled that three Florida brothers exposed to the virus that causes AIDS can no longer be banned from school.
>
> Educators are supposed to be an enlightened bunch. But DeSoto County school officials in west central Florida have acted like imbeciles in their dealing with these boys, who were exposed to the HIV virus in the process of receiving transfusions for their hemophilia.

It ended with the following admonition:

> We hope this ends the school system's despicable treatment of the Ray family. These children, and others like them, don't deserve to be blacklisted from school. Although AIDS is a deadly disease, there is no need to quarantine most individuals who have developed AIDS symptoms, much less those who show only signs of *exposure* to the HIV virus.

Four days before the start of school, the DeSoto County School Board sponsored its first AIDS information seminar as mandated by the court. In the year the Ray children had been out of school, neither the school board, the local doctors, the clergy, nor the county commissioners had organized any kind of educational program. When science was finally called in, it proved too weak a force against the earlier sensationalism and moralizing.

From My Journal:

Friday, August 21, 1987: Last night they held an assembly for parents at Memorial Elementary School to provide information about AIDS. It was so odd to see this little school cafeteria, the usual home of hungry and loud children, witness such a painful and somber event. Two sessions were held, but the combined audience wouldn't have filled the room once.

Everywhere I look I see ordinary people—with no pejorative intended in such a labeling—men and women with functional clothes, strong eyeglasses, worn faces, and sunburned arms. There is no evidence of the yuppie syndrome in Arcadia.

These parents are here, some with their children, because quite simply they are afraid. They are afraid for their children. They do not hate the Rays. They do not have an agenda. They are worried. Their faces show it as they listen intently to the presentation. Their tightly wrung hands evidence it. Their pointed questions reveal it.

There are no hysterics—not even when they are told, "Everyone diagnosed in 1980 is now dead." Not when they are told, "If there is no cure found, in twenty-two years everyone will have the AIDS virus." Not even when Superintendent Browning tells them that he is still fearful after two days of meetings with a panel of medical experts.

This is a terrible place to be. The court has ordered the Ray children into school, and these parents want a guarantee that their children will be safe. The medical profession can't give them that. This is about *their* children. This is no longer a story in *Time* or a segment on the network news.

*   *   *

The overriding concern of many parents was summed up in the sentence "The Rays are an accident waiting to happen." Most parents recognized—whether they articulated it or not—that in the ordinary course of events, their children would remain safe from the virus. Yet they envisioned an extraordinary set of circumstances that could lead to the infection of their children. The more often these scenarios were repeated around town, the more likely their occurrence seemed to be.

Robert Sanders talked about these scenarios whenever he could. At age forty, Sanders lived out-of-wedlock with the mother of their four-year-old boy. In a short time, he had become the most prominent opponent of allowing the Ray children to attend school with what he called "normal, healthy children." Before being pushed aside by more extreme voices, Sanders, the son of a Pentecostal preacher and, like Cliff Ray, an employee at the state prison, had come to represent Arcadia to the country, often appearing on television alongside the Rays.

ROBERT SANDERS: Basically, I have a responsibility for the safety and well-being of my child until he gets to be eighteen, nineteen, or twenty and decides to leave the nest and get out on his own. In every aspect of his life, I'm responsible. But this thing is so terribly deadly. An accident could happen.

What kind of accidents could happen in school? The list is long as my arm. You have guys out on the football field playing football; blood transfer could happen there. You have kids running up and down the halls, kids falling down stairs, kids tripping over each other, kids bumping their heads into their locker doors. I always had a locker on the bottom. Every time I raised my head, the person above me had their door open, and I always crowned my head on their door. The list is endless.

You can have a classroom of kids taking a test; everything seems calm and cool and serene, and, say, one child has to go to the bathroom badly. He's holding it and holding it and holding it. And all of a sudden, he just can't get hold of the teacher, so he jumps up, starts out of class, and trips over his desk or trips over somebody else's desk and falls down and busts his nose or whatever. It could cause a transfer in that respect. So it's an endless thing.

In Arcadia, the reactions of the young people mirrored those of their parents. As mothers and fathers congregated in the school lunchroom, a band of twelve-year-old boys sat out in the parking lot. The boys spoke softly, their faces glistening with sweat. Like any group of preteen boys, they talked mainly about sports and girls. But when the topic of the Ray boys arose—or the "R" word as they put it—their interest in it exceeded that in all previous talk about football or the girls in their class.

As I sat with them in the parking lot, I could tell these boys had thought a lot about the Ray situation. Clearly they had spoken with their parents and had even attended some of the late-night gatherings of concerned and angry citizens. Joey, who wore a baseball cap and snapped his gum, looked to be the leader of the pack. From the start, he dominated the conversation, appearing to influence the other boys' views.

"I went to one of those meetings that inform people about AIDS," Joey explained. "All our friends went just to see what the people up there had to say because they were letting people talk. And a lot of people were saying stuff like, 'We're going to meet them in the doors with shotguns or something.' And some people, they just stood up and said, 'You're not going to see my kids go to school with them!' You know, all that kind of stuff."

From the same meeting, Joey and some of the others learned what they know about AIDS. Chip, another seventh-grader, explained that "some people say you can't catch it easily, but I don't believe it unless you stay in a plastic bubble. Otherwise, I think if you stayed around long enough, you would catch it." Pausing for a moment, Chip concluded, "After you catch it, it'll finally kill you."

Asked for solutions to the Ray situation, each of the boys suggested some form of imposed or self-imposed segregation. According to Chip, "I think they ought to give them their own place to go to school—away from anyone else—and have a teacher trained to handle the situations and stuff. Just keep them out of the public school system!"

Joey appeared less strident. "I don't know what I'd do. I know if I had kids with the AIDS virus, I wouldn't want them to go to the same school." Then, as Chip was seconding his comment, Joey cut him off. "You know, there's no proof that this thing can spread without blood transfusions and stuff like that. They don't even have AIDS really. But everybody will probably make fun of them. When the Ray boys walk in the door, they will laugh and say, 'There's those AIDS kids; run away!'"

Finally, I asked them what they would do if one of their own circle of friends developed AIDS. Each boy was at a loss. "I don't know what I'd do if Chip had the virus," said Jeff, who had been silent to that point. "'Cause he's one of my best friends. I really wouldn't know."

Joey added, "It's not like we're friends with the Rays. They've never been friends of ours. But I would feel pretty bad if one of my friends got sick."

*   *   *

The rally was called to order by Reverend Donald Yates of the Calvary Baptist Church. After leading the crowd in the Pledge of Allegiance, he uttered a prayer that intertwined church, state, and morality as only a conservative pastor could.

Reverend Yates: I heard the other day that in New York City they offered a bribe to 106 folks who were doing business with the city. A hundred and five of them took the bribes. The hundred and sixth one didn't take the bribe because he said it was too small. That tells you something about where we are. Now I believe it's because we've let go some of the things that made us what we are: our commitment to the Lord and the Savior. We've turned away from those things.

Now I'm not trying to say AIDS is a direct result of all these things, but I'll tell you that you'd have to be blind to know that [the epidemic] wasn't a relationship to the moral condition of America. . . . Folks, the answer lies in searching the depths of our own souls, seeking God, and allowing Him to do work in our own lives. If we remain apathetic about those things we like to do—drugs, alcohol, and immorality—these other things that we see now are going to continue as they are. And I know that many of you probably think in your mind, "There goes that narrow-minded preacher again." Well, they haven't listened to us for the last two-hundred years, and look where we are.

The AIDS problem is not going to go away. And any man would have to be a fool to think it would go away. So I'm glad you came to do something about it, not just here tonight, and not just in your petitions. . . .

Father, I pray for a revival in America, that there would be a revival of old-fashioned, heartfelt, Holy Spirit caring for the things of the Lord, Jesus Christ. Lord, may You touch our hearts, may we come near to You. Father, help us to get our hearts back, and then as we serve You, these problems can be overcome. In Jesus' name I pray. Amen.

*   *   *

CAAIS [Citizens Against AIDS in the Schools] had been formed by a group of "concerned parents" in the wake of the federal order. With the courts now effectively closed to them, CAAIS leaders sought statewide legislation to eliminate the risk of AIDS to Arcadia's schoolchildren.

The testing and identification of all HIV-infected children became the group's primary goal. In this way, they argued, the danger could be removed. In the eyes of others, mandatory testing would raise even more issues. Who would be tested? If children are to be tested, what about individuals who come in contact with them: parents, grandparents, doctors, nurses, teachers, and babysitters? Who would pay for this extensive and expensive testing program? How would test results be used? What would happen to individuals who tested positive for the AIDS virus? These and other similar questions were not raised at the rally at the rodeo grounds.

CAAIS president Danny Tew followed Reverend Yates to the podium, speaking fervently to the crowd of nearly one thousand. Tew, a salesman of beauty products by day, captured his audience as he outlined the group's plans. Except for the whirr of the cameras, most everyone sat quietly inhaling Tew's message. Then, as if on cue, the crowd came roaring to life, giving Tew one ovation after another.

DANNY TEW: I'd like to outline at this time what this committee was organized for, what we stand for, and what we hope to accomplish in our endeavors. We have at this time two main goals that we're going to strive toward accomplishing. We're seeking legislation to implement mandatory testing within our school system to identify anyone who has been in contact with the AIDS virus. And we are also going to seek legislation to make it mandatory for the medical profession to make accessible to our school board information on anyone that has been tested positive to exposure to the AIDS virus. [vigorous clapping] Our second goal is to resurrect and find new and fresh evidence to go to the court system and have this federal injunction lifted. [applause]

I'd like to expound a little bit on some of these goals, and I'll go back to mandatory testing first. We feel as a committee that there is a sleeping giant within our school system that has not really been addressed in the public. We don't feel that the ones that have been identified as carrying an AIDS antibody or who have been exposed to the virus are as serious a problem as the ones that have not been identified. At least we can control some of the situations with ones that we know who have it. The dangerous situation is not knowing if the one sitting next to you has it, and that person may not know it either.

This is why we are seeking mandatory testing, mainly to identify the whole problem and not just a small part of it. We can probably thank the past events that have come upon us in the sense that it has awakened us to realize that there is a real problem within America, not just within the school system.

On our second goal of having the appeal lifted, our school board has really been out there working for us. It's just that their authority has been usurped by the federal government. We feel that it is our responsibility as citizens and parents, of the United States and of DeSoto County, to pick up that fight and continue it because our school board can't. Not that they don't want to, but they can't. So it is our responsibility to move in there and pick that fight back up and not let it die. And carry it on. Are we in agreement now? [extraordinary ovation of clapping and foot thumping]

The federal government can move in and tell our elected officials that they can't do something, but we are private citizens. We can do it if we want to! [again, a tremendous response]

This is just another example of how many things that have occurred in our past that we are losing control of, like our own local government. The school

system belongs to us. We elect people to manage it. We elect people to adminis-
ter our school system. We elect people to do our bidding in our school system.
But we did not elect an appointed judge. [applause]

STUDY QUESTIONS

1. Given the general level of public knowledge about HIV transmission and communicability, how can we make sense of the "moral panic" in Arcadia?
2. In this case, what role did Protestant fundamentalism play in Arcadia's treatment of the Ray boys?
3. What line of reasoning did Reverend Yates employ to morally distance Arcadia from HIV/AIDS?

Religion and Attitudes Toward AIDS Policy

Andrew M. Greeley

In the modern world there is relatively little connection in ordinary cir-
cumstances between religion and public policy with regard to contagious
diseases. The quarantine rules about leprosy (a much wider collection of
diseases than what is now called Hansen's Disease) in the Mosaic law—
rough and ready public health measures in retrospect—are now enforced
by governmental agencies and not by religion.

Acquired Immune Deficiency Syndrome, however, is a special case both because of the inevitable fatal outcome of the disease and because it is normally transmitted through sexual contact, is especially likely to spread under conditions of sexual promiscuity, and in the United States has in fact spread in great part through homosexual contact. Since the traditional religions have disapproved of promiscuity and homosexuality, AIDS has become or seems to have become an issue of morality as well as of public health. Indeed some religious leaders have pronounced it a punishment of God on immorality and especially homosexual immorality.[1]

Thus the question arises as to whether religious affiliation and devotion might have an impact on AIDS policy issues and decisions. Will the more devout have more repressive attitudes towards those who are victims of AIDS?

The 1988 General Social Survey (Davis and Smith 1988) contained two additional modules beyond the usual sets of GSS questions, the fortuitous

Reprinted with the permission of the author from *Sociology and Social Research,* vol. 75, no. 3 (April 1991):126–129. © 1991 by Andrew Greeley.

combination of which makes it possible to address this question.[2] The first module was a battery of questions about AIDS funded by NORC [National Opinion Research Center];[3] the second was an extensive series of items about religion.

The eight AIDS policy items[4] were as follows (the percentage in parenthesis indicates the proportion of respondents who took a position that indicated hostility towards AIDS victims):

Do you support or oppose the following measures to deal with AIDS:

A.   Prohibit students with AIDS virus from attending public schools. (26%)
B.   Develop a government information program to promote safe sex practices, such as the use of condoms. (14%)
C.   Permit Insurance companies to test applicants for the AIDS virus. (62%)
D.   Have the government pay all of the health care costs of AIDS patients. (67%)
E.   Conduct mandatory testing for the AIDS virus before marriage. (89%)
F.   Require the teaching of safe sex practices such as the use of condoms in sex education courses in public schools. (88%)
G.   Require people with the AIDS virus to wear identification tags that look like those carried by people with allergies or diabetes. (63%)
H.   Make victims with AIDS eligible for disability benefits. (40%)

The impact of denominational affiliation, frequent church attendance and religious imagery on responses to these items will be explored in the remainder of this note.

Denominational Affiliation

Statistically significant correlations were found between Protestant[5] affiliation and negative AIDS attitudes on three items—sex information (.10), sex education (.11), and identification tags (.16).

Seventy percent of the Protestants in the sample supported the imposition of identification tags on AIDS victims as opposed to .54% of the Catholics. Some of this difference was concentrated among members of Fundamentalist denominations (Smith 1986), of whose members 73% supported the identification tags, and Conservative denominations, of whose members 72% approved of the identity tags. However, 61% of Protestants in liberal denominations also supported identification tags for AIDS victims; the difference between them and Catholics is not statistically significant.

In an endeavor to explain the differences between Catholics and Protestants, this writer tried to reduce the .16 correlation (sixteen percentage points difference) to statistical insignificance through the use of multiple regression equations into which religious variables would be entered successively. My assumption was that variables associated with fundamentalist religious orientations would account for much of the differences between Protestants and Catholics.

When three items were inserted which measured attitudes towards the Bible,[6] the correlation (as measured by the beta in the regression equation) diminished to .11. Catholics, in other words, are less likely to support identification tags for AIDS victims than are conservative and fundamentalist Protestants because they are less likely to emphasize the Bible, as literally interpreted, than are Protestants.

The correlation was diminished to .09 when an attitude about formal church membership when growing up[7] is inserted in the equation and to .07 and statistical insignificance when the South as a region of the country is added.

Catholics are baptized into the Church and usually do not consciously reaffiliate in their adolescent years. However, members of the more conservative Protestant denominations are more likely to go through such a process of formal reaffiliation. It would appear that those who do are somewhat more likely to have a repressive attitude towards AIDS. Finally, Protestants, being disproportionately Southern in comparison with Catholics, may share a cultural attitude towards morality which has an impact above and beyond biblical fundamentalism.

Thus one can account for differences between Fundamentalist and Conservative Protestants and Catholics in their attitudes towards identification tags for AIDS victims by a model which takes into account explicit beliefs about the Bible, early formal relationship to a church, and region of origin.

It should be noted that 38% of all Americans believe in the strict literal interpretation of the Bible and 26% both believe in this interpretation and support prayer and bible reading in the public schools. 47% of Protestants believe in literal interpretation and 36% of Protestants believe in this interpretation and support prayer and bible reading in public schools. The "fundamentalist" strain in American religion is thus large. Moreover, it is not a new phenomenon. According to a Gallup index composed of the experience of being born again, belief in a literal interpretation of scripture, and an attempt to persuade others to "decide" for Christ, a fifth of the American population has been "fundamentalist" for the last several decades with neither increase nor decrease during that period of time (Greeley 1989). Fundamentalism is a major component of American religion which did not "emerge" during the nineteen eighties; rather the national elites and the national media discovered (again) what has existed in the United States since the First Great Awakening—in 1744. In attempting to understand the relationship between Fundamentalism and AIDS attitudes it is helpful to realize that half of the population of the south believe in the literal interpretation of the Bible as opposed to a quarter of the rest of the country.

There are also somewhat smaller relationships between Protestant affiliation and attitudes on AIDS education. 8% of Catholics oppose sex education about AIDS in public schools as opposed to 16% of Protestants. 10% of Catholics as opposed to 17% of Protestants oppose government information campaigns about "safe sex." Again there are no statistically significant differences between Catholics and liberal Protestants. Opposition among fundamentalist Protestants is higher—20% against sex education in the public schools and 25% oppose government information campaigns about "safe sex."

While there is, then, a correlation between Protestantism and especially fundamentalist Protestantism and opposition to information campaigns about AIDS, it is nonetheless true that at least three quarters of the fundamentalists do NOT oppose such campaigns.

Regression models based on the three biblical items used to account for differences between Protestants and Catholics on the issue of identification tags for AIDS victims reduce to statistical insignificance the differences between the two denominations in attitudes on information campaigns, both in the schools and outside the schools. It is precisely rigid biblical literalism which accounts for greater Protestant opposition to such campaigns.

Church Attendance

Church attendance does not correlate with attitudes towards identification tags for AIDS victims, but it does correlate negatively and powerfully with attitudes on sex education in the public schools and government information campaigns— -.32 and -.24. 38% of those who attend church weekly or more often oppose sex education about AIDS in public schools (as opposed to 6%) and 29% opposed government campaigns about "safe sex."

Again the differences between frequent attenders and others can be diminished substantially by use in multiple regression equations of models based on biblical and moral rigidity. The -.24 relationship with opposition to sex education in public schools is reduced to .13 by taking into account belief in biblical literalism and frequent reading of the Bible. It diminishes to -.08 (and statistical insignificance) when three attitudes on moral decision making are entered into the equation.[8] The difference in attitudes towards government informational campaigns is reduced by half by the same model: the correlation decreases from -.32 to -.16, though the difference remains statistically significant.

Those who attend church frequently are more likely to be opposed to AIDS education programs in substantial part because they accept a more literal interpretation of the Bible and because they see moral decisions in a more simplistic fashion than do those who do not attend church so frequently. Among those regular church-goers who do not have such rigid religious orientations there is less difference (or no statistically significant difference) from those who do not attend church weekly.

In one sense it is not such a striking series of findings that are reported here: The religious correlation with negative attitudes towards AIDS victims or AIDS education is the result of moral and religious narrowness among certain members of the more devout population. It is what one might have expected. Nonetheless this finding establishes that it is not religion as such but a certain highly specific type of religious orientation which tends to induce hostility on the subject of AIDS. While this religious orientation represents a strong component of American culture and society, it is not a majority orientation; and even among fundamentalists the majority support AIDS education programs.

The question remains, however, whether other kinds of religious orientation correlate positively with compassion on AIDS issues. Obviously more flexible attitudes on biblical inspiration and moral decision making produce greater tolerance and sympathy. But are there other indices of religious devotion which are likely to induce such positive attitudes?

Religious Images

Religion according to a theory developed elsewhere (Greeley 1982, 1988, 1990) finds its origins and its raw power in the imaginative dimension of the self. It begins with (1) *experiences* which renew hope, which experiences are encoded in (2) *images* (or symbols) stored in the imaginative memory, and shared in (3) *stories* with members of a (4) *community* with a common narrative and symbolic tradition, and often acted out in community (5) *rituals.* This paradigm is pictured not as a line but as a circle so that symbols, stories, community, and rituals in their turn shape the hope-renewing experiences of those who are part of a tradition. The symbols, stories, and rituals constitute a (pre-rational) system which purports to explain what creation and human life mean.

It is suggested that a quick and crude measure of the religious imagination can be obtained by measuring a person's image of God, since it is this image which summarizes in an abbreviated fashion the stories and symbols in a person's imagination. For several years NORC has been administering a battery of four items which attempt to measure a person's image and story of God and their relationship with Her/Him.[9]

A scale was constructed from these items in which one point was given for each response that pictures God as mother, spouse, lover, and friend.[10] The scale is referred to in the literature dealing with this theory as the GRACE scale because it purports to measure a more gracious story of what life means and to predict a more graceful response to problems and concerns of life. A person with a higher score on the GRACE scale, it is theorized, will have experienced a more benign relationship with the powers (or Powers) which govern the cosmos and hence will be more benign in his attitudes towards and relationships with other human beings.

There are modest but statistically significant positive relationships between the grace and tolerance on the AIDS questions—those who are more likely to have a gracious image of God are less likely to approve of identification tags for AIDS victims (-.13), of the exclusion of AIDS victims from public schools (-.14) and of premarital AIDS tests (-.09). They are also more likely to support education about "safe sex" in public schools (.11).

Thus religion measured not by affiliation nor by church attendance but by images of God correlates with tolerance and flexibility towards AIDS policy issues.

. . . For both groups tolerance increases with GRACE on all measures—save for attitudes towards premarital tests among Catholics. On two of the four measures—identification tags and attendance at public schools—the correlation is essentially the same for Protestants and Catholics, though on both Catholics are more tolerant than Protestants (only slightly more tolerant on the subject of public school attendance).

On the other two measures—premarital tests and AIDS education in the schools—there is essentially no difference between Catholics and Protestants at the higher end of the GRACE scale because the scale leads to an increase in tolerance for Protestants and no significant changes for Catholics.

Thus images of God's—codes which tell stories of a person's relationship with God and provide templates for relationships with other human beings—do correlate with AIDS policy attitudes. To understand the relationship between religion and AIDS policy attitudes, one needs to know not only about attitudes towards the Bible and moral decision making but also about the religious imagination which, according to the theory, underlies the formation and expression of such cognitive attitudes.[11]

Conclusion

Since 1988 Americans may have become more tolerant on such matters as identity tags for AIDS victims and premarital testing. Moreover, some religious denominations, especially liberal Protestant and Catholic, have insisted vigorously on the need for compassion for victims—though Catholic leaders have campaigned (with their usual success in such matters) against "safe sex" education campaigns. It would be useful to know whether these changes, should they have taken place, might also relate to religious convictions, practices, and images. One would predict that the greatest resistance to attitudinal change would come from those with rigid religious orientations and the highest likelihood of attitudinal change from those with the most gracious images of God.

It is to be hoped that a future research project would include both the religious measures and the policy attitudes discussed in this note.

Notes

1. It is perhaps appropriate that, as a cleric, at the beginning that I note that the God I know doesn't work that way. Are children born with AIDS guilty of anything? However, it is also true that in a non-promiscuous population, the disease would spread much less rapidly. This is a fact of epidemiology and not of divine justice.

2. The General Social Survey is funded by the National Science Foundation, which of course is not responsible for this analysis.

3. Unfortunately there was no funding available for subsequent replications of the questions so there are no data on changes in these policy attitudes since 1988. The first four items were asked of one half of the sample and the other four of the second half.

4. The size of the sample permitted only comparisons between Protestants and Catholics. For the total sample N=1381. Since the items on AIDS policy were administered to only half the sample, the number of cases on each of these questions does not exceed 700.

5. The size of the sample permitted only comparisons between Protestants and Catholics. For the total sample N=1381. Since the items on AIDS policy were administered to only half the sample, the number of cases on each of these questions does not exceed 700.

6. The wording of the three items:

   • Which of these statements comes closest to describing your feelings about the Bible: (a) The Bible is the actual word of God and is to be taken literally word for word; (b) The Bible is the inspired word of God but not everything in it should be taken literally, word for word; (c) the Bible is an ancient book of fables, legends, history and moral principles recorded by men.

   • The United States Supreme Court has ruled that no state or local government may require the reading of the Lord's Prayer or Bible verses in public schools. What are your views on this—do you approve or disapprove of the court ruling.

   • How important is each of the following in helping you to make decisions about life—the Bible.

7. Did you ever join a church when you were growing up, that is become a member by confirmation or such?

8. The items:

   • Morality is a personal matter and society should not force anyone to follow one standard.

   • Immoral actions by one person can corrupt society in general.

   • Right and wrong are not usually a simple matter of black and white; there are many shades of gray.

9. The question: There are many different ways of picturing God. We'd like to know the kinds of images you are most likely to associate with God. Here is a card with sets of contrasting images. On a scale of 1–7 where would you place your image of God between the two contrasting images: Mother, Father; Master, Spouse; Judge, Lover; Friend, King.

10. Or equally Mother and Father etc.

11. The scale correlates negatively will ALL the variables in the models discussed in previous sections of this paper Literalism -.22; Bible reading -.10; Bible in public schools -.11; Morality is personal not social .08; Morality is a matter of black and white not gray -.15; Immoral actions can corrupt society -.12.

REFERENCES

Davis, James A. and Tom Smith. 1988. General Social Surveys 1972–1988: Cumulative Codebook. Chicago: The National Opinion Research Center.

Greeley, Andrew. 1982. Religion: A Secular Theory. New York: The Free Press.

———— 1988. "Evidence That a Maternal Image of God Correlates with Liberal Politics." Sociology and Social Research. 73:3–8.

——— 1989. *Religious Change in America.* Cambridge Mass: Harvard University Press.
——— 1990. *The Catholic Myth.* New York: Charles Scribner.
Smith, Tom. 1986. "Classifying Protestant Denominations," GSS Technical Report No. 67, Chicago: NORC.

STUDY QUESTIONS

1. What kinds of religious orientations and religious images seem to be associated with more positive attitudes toward AIDS-related public policies and programs?
2. How does Greeley explain this finding?
3. Given the general opposition of the Catholic church to homosexuality and the use of prophylactic measures such as condoms, how can we understand the greater tolerance of Catholics, as compared to conservative Protestants, toward people with HIV/AIDS?

Suggested Additional Readings

Gary Albrecht, *The Disability Business: Rehabilitation in America* (Newbury Park, CA: Sage, 1992).

George J. Annas, "Legal Risks and Responsibilities of Physicians in the AIDS Epidemic." *Hastings Center Report,* vol. 18 (1988):S26–S32.

John D. Arras, "The Fragile Web of Responsibility: AIDS and the Duty to Treat." *Hastings Center Report,* vol. 18 (1988):S10–S20.

Peter Conrad, "The Social Meaning of AIDS." *Social Policy,* vol. 17 (1986):51–56.

Benjamin Freedman, "Health Professions, Codes, and the Right to Refuse to Treat HIV-Infectious Patients." *Hastings Center Report,* vol. 18 (1988):S20–S25.

Larry Gostin, "The AIDS Litigation Project: A National Review of Court and Human Rights Commission Decisions on Discrimination." Elizabeth Fee and Daniel M. Fox, editors. *AIDS: The Making of a Chronic Disease* (Berkeley: University of California Press, 1992):144–169.

David L. Kirp. *Learning by Heart* (New Brunswick, NJ: Rutgers University Press, 1989).

Marsha B. Liss, "The Schoolchildren with AIDS." Jeffrey M. Siebert and Roberta A. Oken, editors. *Children, Adolescents and AIDS* (Lincoln: University of Nebraska Press, 1990):93–118.

Barbara Peabody. *The Screaming Room* (San Diego, CA: Oak Tree Publications, 1986).

Mel Pohl, Deniston Kay, and Doug Toft. *The Caregiver's Journey: When You Love Someone with AIDS* (New York: HarperCollins, 1992).

Guenter B. Risse, "Epidemics Before AIDS: A New Research Program." Victoria A. Harden and Guenter B. Risse, editors. *AIDS and the Historian,* National Institutes of Health Publication No. 91-1584 (March 1991):2–13.

Eleanor Singer, Theresa F. Rogers, and Marc B. Glassman, "Public Opinion Before and After the 1988 U.S. Government Public Information Campaign." *Public Opinion Quarterly,* vol. 55 (1991):161–179.

Paula A. Treichler, "AIDS, Homophobia and Biomedical Discourse: An Epidemic of Signification." *Cultural Studies,* vol. 1 (October 1987):31–70.

Heather A. Turner, Robert B. Hayes, and Thomas J. Coates. "Determinants of Social Support Among Gay Men." *The Journal of Health and Social Behavior,* vol. 34 (March 1993):37–53.

Rose Weitz. *Life with AIDS* (New Brunswick, NJ: Rutgers University Press, 1991).

Pattern II and I/II Epidemics

Africa, Latin America, the United States, and Great Britain

• • •

In geographical areas that are characterized as Pattern II and I/II epidemics—sub-Saharan Africa in the early to mid-1980s and, increasingly, Latin America and the Caribbean in the late 1980s and some urban areas in the United States by the early 1990s—AIDS is a primarily heterosexual disease. HIV is transmitted between women and men and, inevitably and tragically, from pregnant women to their unborn babies. Particularly in the developing nations, where medical facilities and resources are limited, a smaller number of HIV/AIDS cases are accounted for through transfusion of HIV-contaminated blood, the use of unsterile medical instruments, and injection drug use.

Pattern I epidemics raised questions about how the psychosexual forces embedded in those cultures that initially experienced AIDS as a gay disease shaped societal perceptions, understandings, and actions directed at control of the AIDS epidemic during the 1980s. Similarly, Pattern II epidemics have raised questions about the complex equation that links gender and class, power and poverty, with HIV/AIDS. Like sexual orientation, gender and class inform personal identity, and they also mirror primary HIV transmission vectors. Across cultures, gendered inequality and structural poverty tend to define the subtexts of the HIV/AIDS health crisis.

Pattern I/II epidemics, or epidemics in transition from Pattern I to Pattern II, reflect the dynamic nature of the HIV/AIDS health crisis. The cases that fit the Pattern I/II model—particularly in Latin America, the Caribbean, and the urban United States—were marked during the early stages of the AIDS epidemic by high HIV prevalence rates among gay and bisexual men. By the late 1980s, however, there had been noticeable demographic shifts in the prevalence rates in many Pattern I areas. Greater numbers of women were showing symptoms of HIV infection and AIDS, and the incidence of perinatal transmission was also rising. Current epidemiological projections predict shifts away

133

from the Pattern I profile in all geographical areas where HIV/AIDS was labeled a gay disease in the early 1980s. Shaping the social networks that serve as HIV transmission vectors, two principal forces have fueled this transition—the gendered construction of interpersonal power that makes women particularly vulnerable to HIV infection, and the ways in which *core groups* of people who routinely engage in (primarily sexual) behaviors that involved a high risk of HIV transmission.

A Pattern II Epidemic

Africa

• • •

Gender and class are both crucial anchors of personal identity. They are also pivotal HIV transmission vectors in Pattern II AIDS epidemics, where prevalence rates among women are comparable to those among men. The selections in Chapter 7 explore the ways in which gendered power relationships and structural inequality and poverty shape the intimate interpersonal relationships between women and men and thereby craft the social context for Pattern II HIV transmission.

The macrosociological analysis in **Migrant Labor and Sexually Transmitted Disease: AIDS in Africa** examines the ways in which these culturally constructed vectors intersect with prevailing economic conditions, the structure of the labor market, and the particular male-to-female ratio of infection and disease that is associated with Pattern II AIDS.[1] The microsociological analysis of one urban epidemic, **AIDS-Related Knowledge, Sexual Behavior, and Condom Use in Kinshasa, Zaire,** examines gender differences in knowledge about AIDS and sexual behavior in the urban heart of the sub-Saharan African AIDS belt. In Kinshasa, as in the United States, awareness of HIV/AIDS is nearly universal. Sexually active adults have a relatively high level of understanding about modes of transmission, although about half of the Kinshasa respondents to a survey also tended to believe that HIV/AIDS could be transmitted by mosquito bites and that there is a vaccine or a "cure" for AIDS. Gender differences in knowledge about HIV/AIDS did not seem to exist. Younger people and those with greater amounts of education and higher socioeconomic status seemed to have a more accurate knowledge of HIV/AIDS than other respondents. Men in the Kinshasa survey indicated a reluctance to adopt condoms, and they also held incorrect beliefs about the reliability of condoms as a barrier to HIV transmission. The data that are summarized in **AIDS—The Leading Cause of Adult Death in the West African City of Abidjan, Ivory Coast** further illustrate that knowledge about HIV transmission and how to prevent HIV infection does not necessarily result in the adoption of condom use. In Abidjan, as in Kinshasa, AIDS is the leading cause of deaths among adult men and the second leading cause of deaths among adult women. These HIV infection and mortality rates reflect a Pattern II epidemic that continues to rage unabated.

---

[1]HIV-1 and HIV-2 are distinct genetic variations, and while there appear to be variations in the length of the asymptomatic period of HIV infection and the rate of immune system deterioration, current evidence suggests that both transmission vectors and risk factors are essentially the same for HIV-1 and HIV-2.

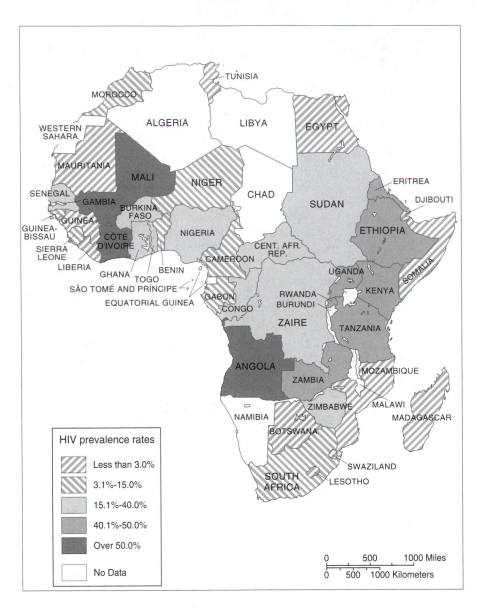

HIV Prevalence Rates* in Africa

*Based on data reported in the HIV/AIDS Surveillance Data Base, Center for International Research, U.S. Bureau of the Census, June 1993. The ranking categories represent a pooling of HIV-1 and (when available) HIV-2 prevalence rates for each country that is listed, but these rankings were not in the original data base. The ranges represent a wide fluctuation in prevalence rates and for the most part are based on urban, high-risk populations. With one or two exceptions, even within countries prevalence rates are not uniform.

Migrant Labor and Sexually Transmitted Disease

AIDS in Africa

Charles W. Hunt

The following paper integrates four areas of history, research, methodology, and theory. First, it incorporates a scientific understanding of the HIV-1 virus and the action of this virus in the creation of acquired immune deficiency syndrome (AIDS).

Second, in combination with an understanding of the biology of the HIV-I virus and of the AIDS that results, this paper uses an analysis of epidemiology known as "historical materialist epidemiology." Accordingly it assumes the primacy of economic life, economic patterns, and economic development. This economic foundation sets the basic parameters of health and illness in society. This method of approach is derived from work done by such early thinkers as Frederick Engels, Rudolf Virchow, and Salvador Allende (Waitzkin 1983, pp. 65–85). This approach may be described as a method that "relates patterns of death and disease to the political, economic, and social structures of society" (Waitzkin 1978, p. 272). Special applications have been made to Third World societies, relating underdevelopment, dependency theory, and health (Doyal 1981; Navarro 1974; Turshen 1977).

Third, this paper's assertions are based on a study of the historic, social, and economic development of eastern, central, and southern Africa, the Africa of migrant labor and the labor reserve. The structure of the household, its size, and its varying composition, as well as degree of proletarianization, wage and nonwage work, and migrancy, are integrated into the following analysis with considerations of health, well-being, and disease. These household structures are defined by their place in the world system; consequently, it is argued in the subsequent presentation, health and disease are defined by place—core or periphery—in that system.

Finally, an understanding of the medical and population geography of central, eastern, and southern Africa is integrated into the thesis advanced in this paper (see Hall and Langlands 1975; Kabera 1982; Langlands 1975; Mayer 1988; Prothero 1977, 1983; White 1978). The population's geographical movements in these regions of Africa, often termed oscillations rather than migrations, give rise to the characteristic concentrations of labor around

This selection has been edited and, based on the author's 1993 Uganda research, updated. Readers interested in the more detailed discussion of methodology and data analysis should refer to the original article.

Reprinted with the permission of the American Sociological Association and the author from *Journal of Health and Social Behavior,* vol. 30 (December 1989):353–373. © 1989 by the American Sociological Association.

plantations, mines, and other capital investments. These movements, interacting with historical development patterns, give rise to the labor reserve, the rural farming area which often is in decline because of the patterns established by dependency and migrant labor (P. Epstein and Packard 1987). This pattern of movement and labor market affects Africans' family and sexual patterns (see Murray 1977, 1980, 1981); as I argue here, it creates a population that is susceptible to sexually transmitted disease (STD), AIDS in particular. A study of past spatial patterns—the medical geography of STDs—will reveal the historical relationship of STDs to migrant labor. This pattern, it is argued, has been repeated in the AIDS epidemic of the 1970s and 1980s.

Africa and AIDS

It is extremely difficult to judge the exact extent of AIDS in Africa, either geographically or in the population. Rwanda, Burundi, Zimbabwe, Zaire, Malawi, Kenya, Tanzania, and Uganda seem to be particularly afflicted. Surveillance programs vary in quality throughout this region. It is not inconceivable that high estimates of AIDS in, for instance, Uganda are a result of an effective and very open surveillance program in that country, rather than a disproportionate number of AIDS cases. However, we can assert that AIDS cases do not occur on the African continent in a uniform fashion but rather form an "AIDS Belt" in central, southern, and eastern Africa.

Estimates have been made of the extent of AIDS in this region. Of an estimated total of 11,799,000 cases of AIDS in the world as of January 1, 1992, it is estimated that 7,803,000 occur on the African continent. This comprises approximately two-thirds of the world's cases of AIDS. In some areas of this region, the prevalence of infection with HIV is very high. It is estimated that 20 percent of the overall Ugandan population, and 40 percent of reproductive-age Ugandans, may be infected with HIV-1. If we look at a map of Uganda and the prevalence of AIDS cases reported by the Ugandan AIDs surveillance program, we can see that even within Uganda AIDS is not uniformly distributed (see Figure 1 on p. 146).

Aids was first discovered to be present in Africa when it was diagnosed in upper-class Africans seeking treatment in European hospitals. The first African cases were diagnosed in Europe shortly after the first diagnosis of AIDS occurred in the United States. African AIDS, however, has some distinctive aspects in relation to the AIDS epidemic in the United States.

First, the sex ratio of those who have AIDS in Africa is approximately 1:1, an equal number of females and males having AIDS. This ratio is in sharp contrast to the 16:1 ratio of males to females in the European and U.S. epidemic throughout much of the 1980s. This ratio in Europe and the U.S. has changed over time, with increased numbers of females contracting AIDS in the developed world, but it still remains at close to 8:1, males to females. This disparity in sex ratios between Africa and the developed world is related to the different risk patterns associated with AIDS cases. In Africa neither homosexual sexual relations nor IV drug use is associated with AIDS or found as a means of transmission for the AIDS virus.

When the illness is studied epidemiologically, primarily *sexually active heterosexuals* are seen to evidence the highest incidence of AIDS in Africa. Females who have AIDS in Africa tend to be younger than males, and are often single. There appears to be a higher incidence of AIDS among prostitutes than among African women generally. Because women contract AIDS in Africa much more often than in North America, and because it appears that AIDS can be transmitted across the placenta from the infected mother to the fetus, there are many more children with AIDS in Africa than in the United States; in fact, children constitute almost one-third of all AIDS cases in Africa. As in the United States, AIDS in Africa appears to occur much more frequently in large cities than in the rural areas, although this may also be a reporting bias.

As in Europe and the United States, those who are discovered to have the AIDS virus frequently have a medical history of previous venereal diseases and appear to be more sexually active than those without HIV infection or AIDS. Despite a few similarities, however, the patterns of AIDS infection in the industrialized countries of North America and Europe are so distinctive in relation to the patterns in Africa that the former is often termed Pattern I and the latter Pattern II AIDS.

A number of questions arise from this presentation of Africa and AIDS. The first questions simply address the geographical distribution of HIV infection and AIDS. Why is AIDS concentrated in the so-called AIDS belt in Africa? And, as a related question, why is there such non-uniformity not only in Africa generally, but even on a smaller scale, in the Ugandan cases, for instance? Why do we see the particular geographical patterns of high and low prevalence that we see in Africa?

The second set of questions concern the population epidemiology of AIDS and HIV infection in Africa. Why is there a different pattern of AIDS infection in Africa, when compared to Europe and the U.S.? Why are there at least two epidemiological patterns of AIDS? Further, why do we see such an explosive epidemic of AIDS in Africa, accounting for an estimated two-thirds of world-wide AIDS cases? As a related question, why is there such a high rate of infection in at least some areas in Africa? This rate of infection is much higher than in the developed world and there must be some explanation.

The biological agent, the HIV-1 virus, appears to be the same on both the African continent and in Europe and North America. Thus, it is not possible to argue that the biological agent of the infection and illness is the cause for these differences.

There are many other possible answers to these questions, however. Some assert that AIDS originated in Africa, and particularly came from the area around Lake Victoria in Uganda. Does this provide an answer for the geographical and population characteristics of AIDS in Africa?

In fact, the earliest cases of AIDS of which we are aware occurred in the United States in 1953. Early blood testing for HIV on African blood was not reliable and produced wildly inaccurate results. The first AIDS cases in Africa appear to have occurred in 1973. Further, medical practitioners and reliable informants assert that AIDS simply was not present in Africa before the late 1970s. A new disease in an area usually shows high rates of fatality. AIDS acts like a new disease in Africa, producing a fatal result even faster than in the U.S.

One of the common assertions made in the African origins theories is that Haiti provided the intermediary for the eventual transfer of AIDS from Africa to the U.S. This leg of the theory is also without support as the first cases of AIDS in Haiti do not occur among Haitians associated with Africans. In fact, research has established that the earliest cases of AIDS in Haiti were among sex trade workers who had been associated with U.S. tourists. None of the earliest cases of Haitian AIDS even knew an African or had met anyone from that continent! The Haitian epidemic of AIDS is more likely to have come from the U.S. than the reverse.

Theories concerning animal-to-human crossovers of monkey virus in the African context have been advanced but are totally unsupported by genetic research done on HIV and other viruses. It does not appear that HIV-1 virus descended from any of the monkey viruses in Africa. It is clearly NOT a genetic descendant of the African Equatorial Green Monkey retrovirus, as is so often asserted. In sum, there is no supporting evidence for an African origin of AIDS. The African origins theory does not provide the answers for which we are looking. It appears that biological explanations will not suffice.

When AIDS is viewed in this way, one can advance a strong thesis that the main historical fact of African social, political, and economic reality is the situation of underdevelopment and dependency in which most African countries find themselves with respect to the core capitalist countries. World System theory has advanced this relationship as the fundamental determinate of human history in the last 500 years. This relationship of underdevelopment and dependency, this core/periphery relationship, which affects African health, labor market organization, familial structure and rural agricultural development, has largely determined the pattern of HIV infection and AIDS in Africa. It is interesting to note, for instance, that the distinction between Pattern I and Pattern II AIDS corresponds to the division between the core and the periphery in World System theory.

This paper will argue, therefore, that the answers to the questions presented above—the key, in fact, to the understanding of the AIDS epidemic in Africa—can be found in social explanations, not biological ones.

Dependency and AIDS

The pattern of industrial development in southern, eastern, and central Africa, which was followed by colonization of this area by the European powers and has continued to the present, was based largely on a migrant labor system (Crush 1984; Davidson 1983; Doyal 1981, pp. 11–119; Freund 1984, 1988; Gugler 1968; Gutkind and Wallerstein 1976; Karugire 1980; C. Leys 1975; R. Leys 1974; Mamdani 1976; Parpart 1983; Roberts 1979; Sathyamurthy 1986; Stichter 1985; Turshen 1977, 1984; Wallerstein and Martin 1979). Mining, railroad work, plantation work, and primary production facilities absorbed capital investment and became enclaves of development in an immense, underdeveloped continent. Just as these industries absorbed capital, they absorbed large quantities of labor from the rural areas, concentrating great numbers of male workers. The effect on these men and on their families is described well by Lesley Doyal (1981) in *The Political Economy of Health:*

> The migrant labor system affected Africans' lives in many fundamental ways. Whatever the miseries of industrialization in Britain, it was usually possible for workers to keep their families together, but this has not been the case in third world countries. In Tanganyika, for example, male workers were typically recruited from designated labour supply areas great distances from the centres of economic activity. This entailed prolonged family separations which had serious physical and psychological repercussions for all concerned. The populations of African towns 'recruited by migration' were characterized by a heavy preponderance of men living in intolerably insecure and depressing conditions and lacking the benefits of family life or other customary supports (p. 114).

Through the migrant labor process and the enclave development system, the African workers, largely male, concentrated at the site of industry, agriculture, or extraction. In many cases the resulting depletion of males from the rural villages and farms caused a marked deterioration in women's ability to carry on alone and to provide for their families. A reduction in labor available to do farm work resulted from the men's employment-related migration (Stichter 1985). The dependency ratio (the number of very young and very old) increased in the rural areas and in the labor reserves (Murray 1981). In many cases, women began to change crops; although these crops were prolific and could feed many mouths, with the added benefit of requiring less labor input, they were largely carbohydrates rather than protein. Cassava is such a crop (Stichter 1985). This change in cropping patterns led to protein deficiencies and compromised the immune systems of persons living in the labor reserves (McCance and Rutishauser 1975). In fact, some studies show that simply the increased labor demand on women, with the reduction in time to attend to their children's nutritional concerns, leads to declines in children's nutritional status whether or not cropping patterns and crops have changed (Vaughn and Moore 1988).

Lack of labor to assist in land clearing produced overcropping of already-cleared areas, deterioration of the land, and loss of fertility. The loss of fertility also contributed to a reduction in yield, which further encouraged the growing of higher-yield crops on poorer soils, although these crops were less nutritious than in the past (Stichter 1985). A "bachelor wage" system usually produced little money income for migrant laborers to send back to a family on the labor reserve; thus the labor reserve subsidized other sectors of the economy to its own detriment (Stichter 1985). This cycle continues in a process of declining agriculture.

In addition, and particularly in recent decades, many unmarried rural women saw no means of adequate support for a family and thus emigrated to the city at a young age (see Murray 1981; Stichter 1985). Family conflict and separation also have caused many young women to migrate to the cities and to concentrations of male labor. Unfortunately, however, very few women have found wage labor or work of any kind (Doyal 1981, p. 116; Stichter 1985); there is little wage employment for women in the developing African economy (Stichter 1985, pp. 144–78). Some—perhaps many—of these women become prostitutes and enter the marginal or secondary labor market in the areas surrounding the large concentrations of men and development (Doyal 1981; Stichter 1985).

The combination of the migrant labor system with a heavy preponderance of male laboring jobs and long familial separations caused a breakdown in family and sexual patterns in central and southern Africa (Murray 1981). An explosion of both prostitution and sexually transmitted diseases (STDs) in these populations occurred well before the AIDS virus made an appearance (Bennett 1975; Brown et al. 1985; Rampen 1978; Sajiwandani and Babbo 1987; Sathyamurthy 1986).

In addition to the "pull" effect of industrialization and the migrant labor markets and the "push" effect of declining agriculture with reduced labor inputs, a "push" effect was produced by capital's takeover of African agriculture (Loewenson 1988; Sanders and Davies 1988). As in many Third World countries, the best and most fertile lands are used by capital to produce agricultural goods for export. Local food production is marginalized on poor land; rural labor needs become seasonal; as a result of large-scale monoculture and mechanization, rural "overpopulation" is "pushed" into urban slum areas. In these areas poor health, disease, and malnutrition abound. Employment is difficult, especially for women; family life may become difficult (Stichter 1985). The result, as with the "pull" effect of large capital developments, is the social creation of a population especially vulnerable to venereal disease and particularly to AIDS (P. Epstein and Packard 1987, pp. 10–17).

As a consequence of the migrant labor pattern and the capitalist takeover of rural African agriculture, AIDS had a ready population that suffered from an unusually high level of sexually transmitted diseases. Because of residual lesions and injury, the higher incidence of previous venereal disease (especially if untreated) increases the likelihood of contracting AIDS (Quinn et al. 1986, pp. 957–58; Stamm et al. 1988).

The manner in which labor is handled in migrant labor situations makes the resulting epidemics much worse. Such a labor system, in which migrants recruited from rural areas surround industrial and extractive developments, does not require care for the health or the safety of the working population. As long as labor power is in surplus in the rural and urban areas because of the expansion of capitalist agriculture and the existence of the labor reserve, injured or incapacitated workers can be replaced easily by subsequent migrants. Workers who no longer can work under such conditions simply return to their villages (Doyal 1981, p. 119). Further, workers' ability to combat poor working conditions and to demand health benefits from employment is severely compromised because migrant laborers are historically difficult to unionize or to organize for resistance to employers (Stichter 1985).

Urban slum dwellers, who lack medical care because of unemployment, also return home regularly when ill, carrying urban disease back to their rural villages (Doyal 1981). Thus a woman who is a prostitute and who becomes ill is very likely to return to her home village to be cared for by relatives.

In the case of sexually transmitted diseases and many other illnesses, this return home has tragic consequences. Tuberculosis and STDs are carried back to the village, infecting areas where they have not been seen before and striking populations that lack resistance or previous exposure. "Whether or not these migrants survived their diseases, the diseases invariably survived them, often spreading rapidly among an increasingly susceptible population" (Doyal 1981, p. 119).

Therefore there is little question that AIDS strikes a population which is not only susceptible to sexually transmitted diseases but which is also structured socially to hasten the transmission of the HIV-1 virus. Such structuring of a population to make it vulnerable to STDs is an integral part of the peripheral status of eastern, central, and southern Africa.

AIDS: The Pattern of an Epidemic in Africa

If the model that was presented above is valid for the AIDS epidemic in eastern and central Africa, the pattern in which the epidemic appears should show some evidence of the expected modes of transmission. In other words, if the epidemic occurs geographically in areas with high concentrations of male migrant labor, and particularly among males and females who have high levels of heterosexual activity, then high prevalence or incidence rates should appear first geographically in areas where labor is concentrated. Further, two population groups in these areas should be affected: the male migrant laborers themselves and their partners, usually female prostitutes living near the enclave of development. Thus a high rate of infection in these two groups would fit the model.

Further, if the spread of HIV-1 virus occurs through the return of male migrant laborers and female prostitutes to their villages due to illness, the second geographic sites that should begin to show high rates of infection are those areas in eastern and central Africa known as labor reserves. If we assume that the rural areas are infected with HIV-1 after the labor concentration areas are infected, these rural areas should show lower prevalence rates than the labor concentration areas. Yet the labor reserves—the migrant labor pool areas—should show higher rates of infection than surrounding rural areas which do not provide migrant labor. Thus prevalence of HIV-1 in the areas from which migrants are drawn by contract in order to provide the workers necessary for production should lag somewhat behind the areas where these workers labor. When the workers return home carrying HIV-1, it is assumed in this model that they will pass the infection on to their partners and to others after their return.

The prostitutes from these areas of male migrant labor concentration also tend to return home when illness prevents them from continuing their work. This trend may be less definite because prostitutes are not dismissed formally. They may continue prostitution activities and delay returning home, even though they are quite ill. They may be able to continue working and generating some income, although their capacity may be reduced considerably. Do the available data on seropositivity and AIDS prevalence fit the pattern that would result from the description presented above?

Data and Prevalence Surveys

The process of HIV-1 transmission, which was outlined above, is dynamic. Much of the data concerns prevalence, which can be examined spatially or geographically; incidence data are relatively scarce. Prevalence data are inherently static, not dynamic, and we can only infer the dynamic process from the static data. It is rare, however, to find truly adequate data in social science; therefore let us pursue the available data to see if they agree with the above model and with the hypotheses that the model has generated. In the discussion that follows, refer to Figure 2, which shows the labor concentration areas and the labor reserve areas in Uganda.

Spatial Distribution of HIV/AIDS

It is clear that AIDS cases and HIV infection generally have been most serious in cities in Uganda and in much of eastern Africa (Berkley et al. 1989; Biggar 1986; Economist 1987; Georges et al. 1987; Harden 1986, 1987; Mann, Francis, et al. 1986; Mugerwa and Giraldo 1987; Mugerwa et al. 1987; Van de Perre 1984). These are areas of labor concentration. This conclusion is also confirmed by cumulative prevalence data from Uganda (see Figure 1), which establish that the highest prevalence rate of AIDS in Uganda is contained in the half-moon area along the lakeshore of Lake Victoria, particularly in the Masaka and Kampala-Entebbe areas (Berkley et al. 1989, p. 83).

The problem with these data is that they reflect not only the possible reality of the epidemic but also the availability of medical facilities in these regions of Africa. Most medical facilities that are capable of recognizing and diagnosing AIDS in central and eastern Africa are concentrated almost exclusively in cities (Hall and Langlands 1975; Navarro 1974). Thus these areas will show a predominant number of diagnosed cases. Individuals from rural areas may not even be able to travel to the cities for diagnosis and may be either misdiagnosed or not treated at all. It has been noted frequently that AIDS patients in eastern Africa are more well-to-do than the average population (Georges et al., 1987; Harden 1987; Van de Perre 1984). This finding also may reflect the comparative ease with which the most affluent classes are able to enter the medical system in contrast to poorer or rural individuals.

In Uganda, however, it has been claimed that the prevalence of HIV-1 seropositivity does not seem as high in Kampala as elsewhere (Economist 1987), and that the southwest areas of the country have higher HIV-1 prevalence rates. This conclusion seems to be refuted by recent, more comprehensive studies and cumulative prevalence data (Carswell 1987; Berkley et al. 1989) (see Figure 1). In general, rural residents, particularly in the peasant farming areas of central Uganda, seem to have a rather low rate of HIV-1 seropositivity and AIDS (Berkley et al. 1989; Carswell 1987; Harden 1987; Van de Perre 1984). We can say, however, that rural southwestern Uganda appears to have very high prevalences of AIDS cases and HIV-1 infection (Berkley et al. 1989; Economist 1987; Serwadda et al. 1985). It has been estimated that one-third of this population is infected with HIV-1 (Economist 1987). It is clear from the cumulative prevalence data of AIDS cases that the southwest areas, particularly Anchole and Toro, have quite high rates of AIDS cases, in the 11–50/100,000 range. These two areas are labor reserves with high rates of circulating migration for work in the core developed areas in Uganda.

In studies of prostitutes in the town of Rakai, an area of major labor concentration south of Kampala, some 86 percent were HIV-1 positive (WHO 1988). Barmaids were 80 percent seropositive in this same area. It is easy to see the high cumulative rates of AIDS cases in this area on the map of Uganda (see Figure 1). In fact, this area south of Kampala has one of the highest rates of AIDS in Uganda, comparable to the Kampala-Entebbe area (see Figure 1).

The countries of Burundi and Rwanda have not established an AIDS surveillance system such as the one in place in Uganda. However, we know that both of these countries have high numbers of AIDS cases even without

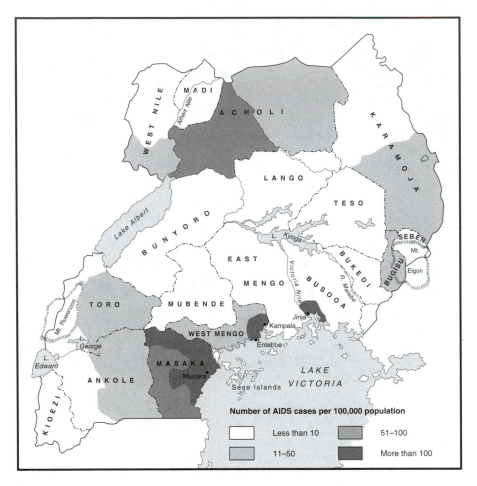

Figure 1 AIDS Cumulative Prevalence by DIstrict in Uganda

the presence of a surveillance system such as Uganda's. Burundi has, as of 1992, a cumulative total of over 3,300 cases of AIDS and Rwanda has over 6,500 cases. These two very small countries, about the size of a Ugandan district, have seroprevalence rates in the range of 5 to 10 percent of the urban population. In some areas of Rwanda the seroprevalence rate is as high as 30 percent and among male patients at STD clinics in Rwanda the seroprevalence rates in 1986–87 were almost 60 percent. The seroprevalence rate for commercial sex workers in Rwanda in 1983–84 was second on the continent only to the rate reached in Kenya in 1990 among commercial sex workers. These rates are quite high and are comparable to, and

Figure 2   Labor Concentrations and Labor Reserves in Uganda

sometimes exceed, the high rates found in Ugandan labor reserves and urban labor concentrations.

In the southern areas of West Nile District of Uganda, cumulative AIDs case prevalence figures establish that the rate is in the 11–50/100,000 range. In the northern areas, the rate is lower, 1–10/100,000 (see Figure 1). This, despite the fact that it has been claimed that there is a low rate of infection in the entire area of the West Nile (Carswell 1987). Why this variation and relatively low rate in the northern section of the West Nile?

There is some indication that the Tanzanian invasion and subsequent civil war, which started in 1978 and continued until 1985, impeded the movement of commerce and migrant labor from the West Nile district to the Kampala area, thus delaying the spread of HIV-1 (Avirgan and Honey 1982; Carswell 1987; Mamdani 1988). Further, the Nile River itself often forms a "formidable barrier to communication" and interchange (Carswell 1987). Unlike many previous wars and conflicts, the fighting in Uganda may have slowed down the spread of disease by slowing the flow of migrant laborers from the West Nile area into Kampala. Certainly the present prevalence of AIDS in the West Nile area is lower than in the Kampala area. There is some indication that the army may be spreading HIV-1 in its movements into the northwest to suppress the recent rebellion in this area of Uganda (Economist 1987).

Many cite Acholi in central-northern Uganda as the leading area of migratory labor (Kabera 1982; Mamdani 1976). Acholi's cumulative rate of AIDS cases is second only to that of the labor concentrations around Kampala-Entebbe and Masaka, with a 51–100/100,000 rate in the western sections of Acholi. The western section of Lango and the eastern section of Acholi also contain unusually high cumulative rates of AIDS at 11–50/100,000.

In eastern sections of Uganda, a high rate of cumulative AIDS case prevalence, 11–50/100,000, occurs in Bugisu area, also a major labor reserve and a source of migrant labor. This high rate extends northward into the Karamoja District which is not a major labor reserve area.

It is difficult to determine if the syndrome occurred earlier in the urban labor concentrations than in the labor reserves, but one can argue that the higher cumulative prevalence rates in the Kampala-Entebbe and Masaka labor concentrations are consistent with an earlier appearance. Certainly, it can be argued that AIDS seems to have had a longer time to reach high epidemic levels in these labor concentrations.

Migrant Laborers and HIV

Migrant laborers themselves should show higher rates of HIV-1 infection than others in the population; these data should correlate with family factors and with length of contracts.

In 1986, 74 truck drivers for a large freight company in Kampala (Uganda) were tested for HIV-1. Some 55.9 percent of the drivers were seropositive (Carswell 1987; Economist 1987). The overall HIV-1 infection rate for Kampala was estimated in 1986 to be approximately 10 percent (Harden 1986). Thus, we can say that in Uganda truck drivers have a much higher rate of infection than others in the population. These drivers and their mates, known as "turnboys," were either Ugandan or Kenyan nationals and had large numbers of sexual partners, particularly prostitutes (Carswell 1987).

In South Africa, the country with the most highly "developed" system of migrant labor, we might expect clearer findings in regard to HIV-1 seropositivity. South Africa has a very systematic labor reserve policy, termed a "homelands" policy; workers usually are banned from living with their families near where they contract to work. Thus the familial separation is enforced more strictly in South Africa, particularly in the mining regions.

In a study of South African migrant miners, 30,000 miners were selected randomly for HIV-1 testing. Some labor reserve areas and some countries showed a seropositive rate in the migrant labor group as high as four percent. In 1987, however, South Africa reported an overall infection rate of 0.1 percent, with only 46 cases of full-blown AIDS. Therefore it would appear that the AIDS epidemic is concentrated in the migrant labor population in South Africa.

Finally, with regard to migrant laborers, the countries of Rwanda and Burundi, particularly the former, seem to have a serious problem with AIDS infection (Biggar 1987; Brunet and Ancelle 1985; Harden 1987; Mann and Chin 1988; Mann, Chin et al. 1988; Quinn et al. 1986; WHO 1989). It is noteworthy that these two mountainous countries send massive numbers of migrant laborers to the labor concentration areas of Uganda. The high cumulative prevalence of AIDS cases in Burundi and the likelihood of high prevalences in Rwanda argue strongly for the hypothesis that AIDS prevalence will be high among these migrant laborers.

It is impossible to determine from these data whether the earliest cases of AIDS in South Africa or in central or eastern Africa occurred among migrant laborers. If we assume, however, that the AIDS epidemic is new in many of these areas (see Carswell et al. 1986), we may say that the prevalence data indicate where the epidemic began. Thus although cases may show up earlier in isolated groups in South Africa, the prevalence among migrant laborers argues for an early appearance in this group.

Prostitutes and HIV

One of the best-documented facts about the AIDS epidemic in Africa is its incredibly high prevalence rate among prostitutes in all countries. Prostitutes are at high risk for HIV-1 infection (Mann, Chin et al. 1988) and are recognized world-wide as transmitters of HIV-1 (Carael et al. 1988; Day 1988; Hudson et al. 1988).

The infection rate for women overall is consistently much lower than for prostitutes, as would be expected. The rate for sexually active persons of both sexes is approximately 20 percent (Mann, Chin et al. 1988, p. 85). In fact, women of childbearing age evidenced approximately a 10 to 15 percent infection rate in 1986 in Kampala, Uganda (Harden 1987). In one hospital in Kampala, 13 percent of 1,000 pregnant women were found to be HIV-1 seropositive in 1986. The same hospital showed a prevalence of 24 percent one year later among 170 pregnant women (Carswell 1987; Harden 1987).

In all of the countries of this region, the mean age of men with seropositivity was greater than the mean age of seropositive women (Quinn 1987; Quinn et al. 1986; Mann et al. 1986). Women account for most of the AIDS cases in the 20–29 age group in Kinshasa, Zaire. Most of the cases in the 40–49 and 50–59 age groups are male, although both of these groups generally contain smaller cohorts of AIDS cases than the 20–29 group (Mann et al. 1986). Among those suffering from AIDS, women are more likely to be unmarried than men (Mann et al. 1986; Quinn 1987; Quinn et al. 1986).

All of this evidence points to a sexually transmitted disease in which the number of partners increases the risk of exposure to the infection (Carswell 1987; Clumeck et al. 1985; Kreiss 1986; Serwadda et al. 1985; Van de Perre 1984). Prostitutes, having large numbers of partners, are particularly at risk, but the pattern also fits the larger social model which has been advanced. Young women migrating to concentrations of male migrant labor become prostitutes in order to earn a living in an environment in which women are rarely employed in wage labor or other "legitimate" jobs.

Labor Force Migration and HIV

There is little question of the complex nature of the AIDS epidemic in central, eastern, and southern Africa (Biggar 1987; Carswell 1987). This complexity may blind observers to the existing patterns and without geographic, historic, and economic information about the region observers cannot understand the map of cumulative prevalences of AIDS.

Yet on the basis of much of the data dealing with urban and rural prevalences of HIV-1 seropositivity and AIDS cases, it is quite clear that a rural-to-urban spread pattern is not present. Urban infection rates are considerably higher than rural (Berkley et al. 1989; Carswell 1987; Carswell et al. 1986; Clumeck et al. 1985; Nzilambi et al. 1988; Peterson et al. 1987; Recene et al. 1987; Van de Perre 1984; Wender et al. 1986). Therefore these data provide additional refutation of the argument that the HIV-1 virus was somehow endemic in rural Africa and then broke out into the broader community because of war and social disruption. Such an argument is not supported by the prevalence patterns we have seen here. It is much more logical to argue that this disease spread as a result of the complex migratory labor patterns in the eastern, central, and southern African economy. This would explain the complex pattern of cumulative AIDS prevalences seen in Uganda. The effects of these patterns on sexual practices and on the stability of the Africa family in these regions help to set up the pattern of AIDS epidemic, whose outline we can see from the scanty evidence available.

There seems to be substantial evidence, particularly in geographical cumulative prevalence data, as well as in HIV-1 seropositivity prevalence data among some specific population groups and geographical areas, that would support the model which we presented for the AIDS epidemic in eastern Africa. In a rather striking manner, this evidence supports the concept that the HIV-1 virus, and the resulting AIDS, first struck the labor con-centrations in Uganda and then moved outward to the labor reserves, car-ried by migrant laborers and prostitutes as they return to their birthplaces for care and assistance with illnesses consequent to infection with this virus.

Conclusion and Summary

The Western press and (to some extent) the Western scientific establishment have attempted to locate the origins of the HIV-1 virus, the biologically causative agent for AIDS, in Africa. In my opinion this attempt is based on a "victim-blaming" mentality and is fundamentally racist (Hunt 1988). The desire to see serious disease as coming from somewhere else, as an invasion, as a foreigner, is widespread (Sontag 1978, 1988; Brandt 1985). The "African origins" theory is based on many weak arguments; almost all have been dis-proved, including the genetic relationship of the HIV-1 virus to the simian variety of retrovirus found in the green monkey of equatorial Africa (see Gallo 1987; Mulder 1988). The "African origins" myth also arose because cases of AIDS were discovered earlier in Africa than in Europe or in North America. This argument, too, has been refuted decisively (see Carswell et al. 1986; Garry et al. 1988; Huminer, Rosenfeld, and Pitlik 1987; Hunt 1988).

One of the remaining props of the "African origins" myth is the pattern of spread of the disease in eastern, central, and southern Africa. The thesis of this paper provides an alternative explanation to the myth insofar as the myth is supported by the rapid or early spread of HIV-1 seropositivity in Africa. The historical pattern of sexually transmitted disease in eastern, central, and south-ern Africa is related intimately to dependency development and to migrant labor. It provides a much more adequate explanation for the rapidity and the complexities of the spread of HIV-1 seropositivity in Africa than do any assumptions about the origins of HIV-1. "African origins" theories contradict the evidence not only genetically and clinically, but also epidemiologically.

In conclusion, we can tentatively answer some of the questions which were presented at the beginning of this work. The AIDS belt in central, east-ern, and southern Africa, the area of highest prevalence of AIDS cases on the continent, is also the area where a system of migrant labor was histori-cally developed in Africa. This system has, in a sense, "over-determined" this population for an epidemic of AIDS. First, the migrant labor system socially structures this population for such an epidemic and, second, previ-ous untreated epidemics of STDs set favorable conditions for the present epidemic of AIDS. Finally, the migrant labor system provides a transmission belt for infectious spread.

Thus the geographic pattern of AIDS prevalences on a macro level can be correlated with the existence of a migrant labor system. On a micro level and a much smaller scale, in Uganda, Rwanda, and Burundi the particular distribution of AIDS geographically can be correlated with the presence of labor reserves and labor concentrations which result from the migrant labor system. We can answer, therefore, the question concerning the distribution of AIDS cases in terms of uniformity. The pattern is not uniform because the migrant labor system is not uniform throughout a country or the continent. The lack of uniformity can be correlated to the particular place which a country, or the districts within a country, take in the migrant labor system.

This same system also provides an explanation for the explosive nature of the epidemic in Africa. As mentioned above, the migrant labor system provides routes of infection and transmission which radiate out from the labor concentration to the labor reserve areas throughout the country. The migrant labor system provides not only a vulnerable population but also an efficient and effective mode of spread and transmission.

Finally, why are there different epidemiological patterns of AIDS in the world? Why are there Pattern One and Pattern Two AIDS? The populations at risk in the core countries and the peripheral countries are fundamentally different. In the peripheral countries the nature of the economic system creates a large population of active heterosexuals who are at risk for HIV infection and AIDS. It is this population-at-risk that forms the bulk of the AIDS cases in Africa. Perhaps we may agree with a medical sociologist who wrote in the 1970s, before the AIDS epidemic had occurred, and stated that epidemics are social not biological events.

REFERENCES

Avirgan, Tony, and Martha Honey. 1982. *War in Uganda: The Legacy of Idi Amin.* Westport, CT: Lawrence Hill.
Bennett, F.J. 1975. "Venereal Disease and Other Spirochaetal Diseases." Pp. 64–65 in *Uganda Atlas of Disease Distribution,* edited by S.A. Hall and B.W. Langlands. Nairobi: East African Publishing House.
Berkley, Seth, Samuel Okware, and Warren Naamara. 1989. "Surveillance for AIDS in Uganda." *AIDS.* 3:79–85.
Biggar, Robert J. 1986. "The AIDS Problem in Africa." *Lancet,* January 11:79–83.
———. 1987. "AIDS in Subsaharan Africa." *Cancer Detection and Prevention* Supplement 1:487–91.
Brandt, Allan M. 1985. *No Magic Bullet: A Social History of Venereal Disease in the United States since 1880.* New York: Oxford University Press.
Brown, Stuart T., Fernando R.K. Zacarias, and Sevgi O Aral. 1985. "STD Control in Less Developed Countries: The Time Is Now." *International Journal of Epidemiology* 14(4): 505–509.
Brunet, J.B., and R.A. Ancelle. 1985. "The International Occurrence of the Acquired Immunodeficiency Syndrome." *Annals of Internal Medicine* 103(5):670–74.
Carael, Michel, Philippe H. Van de Perre, Philippe H. Lepage, Susan Allen, Francois Nsenquimuremyi, Christian Van Goethem, Melanie Ntahorutaba, Didace Nzaramba and Nathan Clumeck. 1988. "Human Immunodeficiency Virus Transmission Among Heterosexual Couples in Central Africa." *AIDS.* 2:201–205.
Carswell, J. Wilson, 1987. "HIV Infection in Healthy Persons in Uganda." *AIDS* 1(4):223–27.
Carswell, J. Wilson, N. Sewankambo, G. Lloyd, and R.G. Downing. 1986. "How Long Has the AIDS Virus Been in Uganda?" *Lancet,* May 24:1217.

Clumeck, Nathan, Marjorie Robert-Guroff, Philippe Van de Perre, Andrea Jennings, Jean Sibomana, Patrick Demol, Sophie Cran, and Robert C. Gallo. 1985. "Sero-epidemiological Studies of HTLV-III Antibody Prevalence Among Selected Groups of Heterosexual Africans." *Journal of the American Medical Association* 254(18):2599–2602.

Crush, Jonathan. 1984. "Uneven Labour Migration in Southern Africa: Conceptions and Misconceptions." *South African Geographical Journal* 66(2):115–32.

Davidson, Basil. 1983. *Modern Africa*. New York: Longmans.

Day, Sophie. 1988. "Prostitute Women and AIDS: Anthropology." *AIDS*. 2:421–28.

Doyal, Lesley, with Immogen Pennell. 1981. *The Political Economy of Health*. Boston: South End Press.

Economist. 1987. "In the Heart of the Plague." *The Economist,* March 21–27:45.

Epstein, Paul, and Randall Packard. 1987. "Ecology & Immunity." *Science for the People,* Jan/Feb:10–17.

Farmer, Paul. 1992. *AIDS and Accusation: Haiti and the Geography of Blame*. Berkeley: University of California Press.

Freund, William. 1984. *The Making of Contemporary Africa: The Development of African Society since 1800*. Bloomington: University of Indiana Press.

———. 1988. *The African Worker*. New York: Cambridge University Press.

Gallo, Robert C. 1987. "The AIDS Virus." *Scientific American* 256(1):46–56.

Garry, Robert F., Marlys H. Witte, A. Arthur Gottlieb, Memory Elvin-Lewis, Marise S. Gottlieb, Charles L. Witte, Steve S. Alexander, William R. Cole, and William L. Drake. 1988. "Documentation of an AIDS Virus Infection in the United States in 1968." *Journal of the American Medical Association* 260(14):2085–87.

Georges, Alain J., Paul M.V. Martin, Jean-Paul Gonzalez, Daniele Salaun, Christian C. Mathiot, Gerard Grezenguet, and Marie-Claude Georges-Courbot. 1987. "HIV-1 Seroprevalence and AIDS Diagnostic Criteria in Central African Republic." *Lancet,* December 5:1732–33.

Gugler, Josef. 1968. "The Impact of Labor Migration on Society and Economy in Sub-Saharan Africa: Empirical Findings and Theoretical Considerations." *African Social Research,* December 6:463–86.

Gutkind, Peter C.W., and Immanuel Wallerstein. 1976. *The Political Economy of Contemporary Africa*. Beverly Hills: Sage.

Hall, S.A., and B.W. Langlands. 1975. *Uganda Atlas of Disease Distribution*. Nairobi: East African Publishing House.

Harden, Blaine. 1986. "Uganda Battles AIDS Epidemic." *Washington Post,* June 2:A1, A18.

———. 1987. "AIDS Seen as Threat to Africa's Future." *Washington Post,* May 31:A1, A18.

Hudson, Christopher P., Anselm J.M. Hennis, Peter Kataaha, Graham Lloyd, A. Timothy Moore, Gordon M. Sutehall, Rod Whetstone, Tim Wreghitt and Abraham Karpas. 1988. "Risk Factors for the Spread of AIDS in Rural Africa: Evidence from a Comparative Seroepidemiological Survey of AIDS, Hepatitis B and Syphilis in Southwestern Uganda." *AIDS*. 2:255–60.

Huminer, David, Joseph B. Rosenfeld, and Silvio D. Pitlik. 1987. "AIDS in the Pre-AIDS Era." *Reviews of Infectious Diseases*. 9(6):1102–1108.

Hunt, Charles W. 1988. "Africa and AIDS: Dependent Development, Sexism and Racism." *Monthly Review* 39(9):10–22.

Kabera, John B. 1982. "Rural Population Redistribution in Uganda since 1900." Pp. 192–201 in *Redistribution of Population in Africa,* edited by John I. Clarke and Leszek A. Kosinski. London: Heinemann.

Karugire, S.R. 1980. *A Political History of Uganda*. Nairobi: Heinemann.

Kreiss, Joan K. 1986. "AIDS Virus Infection in Nairobi Prostitutes: Spread of the Epidemic to East Africa." *New England Journal of Medicine* 314(7):414–18.

Langlands, B.W. 1975. "Introduction: The Geographic Basis to the Pattern of Disease in Uganda." Pp. 1–10 in *Uganda Atlas of Disease Distribution,* edited by S.A. Hall and B.W. Langlands. Nairobi: East African Publishing House.

Leys, Colin. 1975. *Underdevelopment in Kenya: The Political Economy of Neo-Colonialism.* Los Angeles: University of California Press.

Leys, R. 1974. "South African Gold Mining in 1974: 'The Gold of Migrant Labour.'" *African Affairs* 74 (295):196–208.

Loewenson, Rene. 1988. "Labour Insecurity and Health: An Epidemiological Study in Zimbabwe." *Social Science and Medicine* 27(7):733–41.

Mamdani, Mahmood. 1976. *Politics and Class Formation in Uganda.* New York: Monthly Review Press.

———. 1988. "Uganda in Transition: Two Years of the NRA/NRM." *Third World Quarterly* 10(3):1155–81.

Mann, Jonathan, Daniel J.M. Tarantola, and Thomas Netter (eds.). 1992. *AIDS in the World.* Cambridge: Harvard University Press.

Mann, Jonathan, and James Chin. 1988. "AIDS: A Global Perspective." *New England Journal of Medicine* 319(5):302–303.

Mann, Jonathan M., James Chin, Peter Piot, and Thomas Quinn. 1988. "The International Epidemiology of AIDS." *Scientific American* 259(4):82–89.

Mann, Jonathan M., Henry Francis, Thomas Quinn, Pangu Kaza Asila, Ngaly Bosenge, Nzila Nzilambi, Kapita Bila, Muyembe Tamfum, Kalisa Ruti, Peter Piot, Joseph McCormick and James W. Curran. 1986. "Surveillance for AIDS in a Central African City." *Journal of the American Medical Association* 255(23): 3255–59.

Mayer, Jonathan D. 1988. "Migrant Studies and Medical Geography: Conceptual Problems and Methodological Issues." Pp. 136–54 in *Conceptual and Methodological Issues in Medical Geography,* edited by Melinda S. Meade. Chapel Hill: University of North Carolina, Department of Geography.

McCance, R.A., and I.H.E. Rutishauser. 1975. "Childhood Malnutrition." Pp. 89–92 in *Uganda Atlas of Disease Distribution,* edited by S.A. Hall and B.W. Langlands. Nairobi: East African Publishing House.

Mugerwa, R., and G. Giraldo. 1987. "Some Clinical Aspects of AIDS in Uganda." Paper presented at Second International Symposium on AIDS and Associated Cancers in Africa, Naples. Abstract S.3.2.

Mugerwa, R., R. Widy-Wirski, and S. Okwake. 1987. "Assessment of a Provisional WHO Clinical Case—Definition of HIV Related Illness in the Referral Hospital of Uganda." Paper presented at Second International Symposium on AIDS and Associated Cancers in Africa, Naples. Abstract TH-89.

Mulder, Carel. 1988. "Human AIDS Virus Not from Monkeys." *Nature* (333):396.

Murray, Colin. 1977. "High Bridewealth, Migrant Labour and the Position of Women in Lesotho." *Journal of African Law* 21 (1):79–96.

———. 1980. "Migrant Labour and the Changing Family Structure in the Rural Periphery of South Africa." *Journal of Southern African Studies* 6(2):139–56.

———. 1981. *Families Divided: The Impact of Migrant Labour in Lesotho.* Cambridge: Cambridge University Press.

Navarro, Vincente. 1974. "The Underdevelopment of Health or the Health of Underdevelopment." *Politics and Society,* Winter:267–93.

Nzilambi, Nzila, Kevin M. DeCock, Donald N. Forthal, Henry Francis, Robert W. Ryder, Ismey Malebe, Jane Getchell, Marie Laga, Peter Piot, and Joseph B. McCormick. 1988. "The Prevalence of Infection with Human Immunodeficiency Virus over a 10-year Period in Rural Zaire." *New England Journal of Medicine* 318(5):276–79.

Parpart, Janc L. 1983. *Labor and Capital on the African Copperbelt*. Philadelphia: Temple University Press.

Peterson, Hans D., Bjarne O. Lindhardt, Peter M. Nyarango, Tula R. Bowry, Alex K. Chemtal, Kim Krogsgaard, and Albert Bunyasi. 1987. "A Prevalence Study of HIV Antibodies in Rural Kenya." *Scandinavian Journal of Infectious Diseases* 19:395–401.

Prothero, R. Mansell. 1977. "Disease and Mobility: A Neglected Factor in Epidemiology." *International Journal of Epidemiology* 3(6):259–67.

———. 1983. "Medical Geography of Tropical Africa." Pp. 137–53 in *Geographical Aspects of Health,* edited by N.D. McGlashan and J.R. Blunden. San Francisco: Academic Press.

Quinn, Thomas C. 1987. "AIDS in Africa: Evidence for Heterosexual Transmission of the Human Immunodeficiency Virus." *New York State Journal of Medicine* (May):286–89.

Quinn, Thomas C., Jonathan M. Mann, James W. Curran, and Peter Piot. 1986. "AIDS in Africa: An Epidemiological Paradigm." *Science* 234:955–63.

Rampen, F., 1978. "Venereal Syphilis in Tropical Africa." *British Journal of Venereal Disease* (54):364–68.

Recene, U., S. Orach, and A. Petti. 1987. "HTLV III-TB Association in Northern Uganda (Gulu District)." Paper presented at Second International Conference on AIDS and Assoicated Cancers in Africa, Naples. Abstract TH-80.

Roberts, A. 1979. *A History of Zambia*. New York: Africana.

Sajiwandani, Jonathan, and K.S. Babbo. "Sexually Transmitted Diseases in Zambia." 1987. *Journal of the Royal Society of Health* 5:183–86.

Sanders, David, and Rob Davies. 1988. "The Economy, the Health Sector and Child Health in Zimbabwe since Independence." *Social Science and Medicine* 27(7): 723–31.

Sathyamurthy, T.V. 1986. *The Political Development of Uganda, 1900–1986*. Brookfield, VT: Gower.

Serwadda, D., N.K. Sewankambo, J.W. Carswell, A.C. Bayley, R.S. Tedder, R.A. Weiss, R.D. Mugerwa, A. Lwegaba, G.B. Kirya, R.G. Downing, S.A. Clayden, and A.G. Dalgleish. 1985. "Slim Disease: A New Disease in Uganda and Its Association with HTLV-III Infection." *Lancet,* October 19:849–52.

Sontag, Susan. 1978. *Illness as Metaphor*. New York. Farrar, Straus and Giroux.

———. 1988. *AIDS and Its Metaphors*. New York: Farrar, Straus and Giroux.

Stamm, Walter E., H. Hunter Handsfield, Anne M. Rompalo, Rhoda L. Ashley, Pacita L. Roberts, and Lawrence Corey. 1988. "The Association Between Genital Ulcer Disease and Acquisition of HIV Infection in Homosexual Men." *Journal of the American Medical Association* 260(10):1429–33.

Stichter, Sharon. 1985. *Migrant Laborers*. New York: Cambridge University Press.

Turshen, Meredith. 1977. "The Impact of Colonialism on Health and Health Services in Tanzania." *International Journal of Health Services* 7:7–35.

———. 1984. *The Political Ecology of Disease in Tanzania*. New Brunswick: Rutgers University Press.

Van de Perre, Philippe. 1984. "Acquired Immunodeficiency Syndrome in Rwanda." *Lancet,* July 14:62–69.

Vaughn, Megan, and Henrietta Moore. 1988. "Health, Nutrition and Agricultural Development in Northern Zambia." *Social Science and Medicine* 27(7): 743–45.

Waitzkin, Howard. 1978. "A Marxist View of Medical Care." *Annals of Internal Medicine* (89):264–78.

———. 1983. *The Second Sickness: Contradictions of Capitalist Health Care*. New York: Free Press.

Wallerstein, Immanuel, and William G. Martin. 1979. "Peripheralization of Southern Africa: Changes in Household Structure and Labor-Force Formation." *Review* III(2):325–71.

Wender, I., J. Schneider, B. Gras, A.F. Fleming, G. Hunsmann, and H. Schmitz. 1986. "Seroepidemiology of Human Immunodeficiency Virus in Africa." *British Medical Journal* 293:782–85.

White, Richard. 1978. *Africa: Geographic Studies.* London: Heinemann.

World Health Organization (WHO). 1988. "A Global Response to AIDS." *Africa Report,* November–December:13–16.

———. 1989. "Statistics from the World Health Organization and the Centers for Disease Control." *AIDS.* 3:113–17.

STUDY QUESTIONS

1. In what ways does Hunt anticipate the direction of HIV/AIDS epidemics during the next ten years?
2. If Hunt is correct, what kinds of economic and political conditions will fuel the spread of Pattern II AIDS?
3. Why does Hunt argue that the "African origins" hypothesis is a fundamentally racist (rather than scientific) explanation of the geographical origins of HIV?

AIDS-Related Knowledge, Sexual Behavior, and Condom Use Among Men and Women in Kinshasa, Zaire

Jane T. Bertrand et al.[*]

Acquired immunodeficiency syndrome (AIDS) constitutes a major public health problem in Zaire. It is estimated that 6–8 percent of the adult population of Kinshasa, the capital city of Zaire, are seropositive, based on serosurveys of selected populations.[1] Six percent of babies delivered in the two major hospitals in Kinshasa in 1987 were born to seropositive mothers.[2] In 1988, 50 percent of the admissions to the internal medicine ward of the major public hospital, Mama Yemo, were HIV (human immunodeficiency virus) seropositive.[3] It is estimated that 80–90 percent of AIDS in Kinshasa is transmitted through sexual contact.[1] Since homosexuality is rare in Kinshasa, heterosexual relations constitute the major means of AIDS transmission among this population.

*The other authors of this article are Makani Bakutuvwidi, Susan E. Hassig, Lewu Niwembo Kinavwidi, Djunghu Balowa, Muanda Mbadu, and Chirhamolekwa Chirwisa.

Reprinted with permission from *American Journal of Public Health,* vol. 81, no. 1 (January 1991):53–58. © 1991 by American Journal of Public Health.

Until a vaccine or cure is found, public information and education remain an important weapon against AIDS. Since 1987, AIDS messages have been broadcast frequently on radio and television. Luambo, a popular singer in Zaire, further publicized the dangers of AIDS through a widely diffused song.

The current study was conducted city-wide in 1988 among the adult population to measure awareness of AIDS, its modes of transmission and means of prevention; coital frequency and extramarital sexual relations; knowledge and use of condoms; perceived risk of getting AIDS; and attitudes toward HIV testing. This module on AIDS formed part of a larger survey on contraceptive prevalence in Kinshasa, conducted by the Projet des Services des Naissances Désirables, the national family planning services project.

Methods

The projected sample for this survey consisted of 1,500 men (ages 20–59 years) and 1,500 women (ages 15–49 years), randomly selected from the 24 administrative zones of Kinshasa. The age criterion differed by sex, in an effort to obtain the population at greatest risk of AIDS. Four zones were intentionally oversampled for other research purposes (a field study to test the impact of an AIDS prevention program, not reported herein), bringing the projected sample size to 2,500 per sex.

Two-staged sampling was involved: first, 72 of 251 *quartiers* (the largest administrative unit within an administrative zone) were randomly selected and subsequently mapped; second, *parcelles* (a compound containing one or more households) were systematically selected. Men and women were interviewed in alternate *parcelles;* thus, the male/female data constitute independent samples, not husbands and wives.

Because the average number of eligible respondents per *parcelle* was higher than expected, the total number of respondents (6,625) exceeded the projected sample. In the accompanying tables, the results have been weighted to adjust for oversampling. The n in each case is based on the unweighted sample (actual number of people who were asked the question), whereas the percentages are based on the weighted sample.

Data collection for this survey took place from January to September 1988. All interviewers underwent a 20-day training course on sampling and data collection procedures prior to the fieldwork. All interviews were conducted in Lingala, the local language, by an interviewer of the same sex, using a pretested, structured questionnaire. Each interview lasted an average of 30–40 minutes.

All questionnaires were verified for completeness and logical consistency; where necessary, interviewers were sent back to the field to verify or complete responses. SPSS/PC+ and BMDP/PC were used for the analysis.

Results

The total sample included 3,140 men and 3,485 women (Table 1). Over half of all respondents had at least some level of secondary education; however,

Table 1 • Sociodemographic Characteristics of
the Study Population.*

	Men N = 3140	Women N = 3485
Age (years)	%	%
15–19	-	23.0
20–24	23.5	23.2
25–29	36.2	20.0
30–34	12.8	14.6
35–39	9.8	10.2
40–44	9.6	5.6
45 and over	8.1	3.2
Mean age (years)	33.4	26.6
Highest education level attained		
None or primary	19.1	36.4
Secondary	61.0	60.5
Beyond secondary	19.5	2.7
Marital status		
Married (1 wife)	53.1	44.1
Married (2+ wives)	4.3	8.3
Consensual union	2.0	9.5
Separated, divorced, or widowed	3.6	8.5
Single, never married	37.0	29.5
Household amenities		
Has electricity	33.6	35.3
Has running water in house	9.2	7.8
Has toilet inside house	11.5	8.6
Has a working radio	51.8	49.3
Has a car or truck	9.4	7.0

* The "N" given in this and all subsequent tables is based on the unweighted sample (i.e.
actual number of people who answered the question); the percentages are based on the
weighted sample.

significantly more men (20 percent) than women (3 percent) had gone
beyond secondary school. The majority of men (59 percent) and women (62
percent) were married or living in consensual union.

Knowledge of AIDS

Awareness of AIDS is almost universal in Kinshasa (99 percent of men and 96
percent of women). Details of specific AIDS knowledge items are presented
in Table 2. Of note, only half the study population knew that mosquitoes do
not transmit AIDS and only 70 percent had correct information regarding
casual contact. Ninety-four percent of men and 88 percent of women believed
that AIDS could be prevented through behavioral changes.

Table 2 • AIDS Knowledge Items and Perceived Risk of HIV Infection Among Those Who Have Heard of AIDS (percent with correct response)

	Men N = 3099	Women N = 3351
The AIDS virus is transmitted by:		
• eating unclean food	82.6	76.6
• transfusion with infected blood[*]	96.8	92.7
• mosquitoes	50.5	55.3
• sexual relations with an infected person[*]	98.7	96.4
• living in the same house with AIDS patient	66.5	56.6
• injection with unsterile needle[*]	95.7	91.3
• wearing used clothing	71.0	63.7
• working beside an AIDS victim	71.3	62.4
• (infected) mother to fetus[*]	94.0	89.2
The following are symptoms of AIDS:		
• frequent vomiting	63.5	63.5
• prolonged diarrhea[*]	81.6	81.7
• heavy bleeding for women	63.3	63.9
• recurrent fever[*]	45.2	43.2
• extreme weight loss[*]	78.2	68.7
• loss of hearing	75.2	73.6
• pain in the joints	57.1	56.1
• general, prolonged fatigue[*]	43.4	28.8
Transmission beliefs:		
• person can be infected without knowing[*]	87.9	77.5
• person can be infected without feeling sick[*]	84.5	73.1
• person who feels healthy could transmit the AIDS virus to another person[*]	84.2	72.1
• person with multiple partners has more risk than person with one partner[*]	78.9	72.6
• it is advisable for a woman infected with AIDS virus to get pregnant	97.4	95.7
• person infected with the AIDS virus will eventually get the disease[*]	76.0	71.2
There is a vaccine against AIDS	58.6	43.1
AIDS can be cured	52.0	68.0
AIDS can be prevented[*]	93.7	88.0
AIDS can be prevented by:		
• taking antibiotics before sex	81.5	65.4
• using condoms for extramarital sex[*]	70.1	41.6
• going to a traditional healer	90.3	79.1
• avoiding sex with multiple partners[*]	93.7	85.4

(continued)

Table 2 continued

	Men N = 3099	Women N = 3351
Perceived risk of contacting AIDS:		
• Very high	10.6	10.2
• Moderate	6.8	5.9
• Low	21.0	9.3
• None	46.8	62.9
• Don't know	13.8	11.3

*The asterisks indicate which items are correct as stated.

Thirty-six percent of men and 45 percent of women at the time of this survey believed that there was a vaccine against HIV. Moreover, 40 percent of men and 21 percent of women believed that a person with AIDS can be cured. An additional 5–12 percent were unsure regarding both of these points.

Seventeen percent of men and 31 percent of women knew someone with AIDS at the time of the interview. Half of all respondents knew at least one person who had died of AIDS.

All respondents who had heard of AIDS were asked whether they had seen or heard something about AIDS via different communication channels. More adults in Kinshasa have been reached via radio than any other medium: 96 percent of men and 83 percent of women. Almost identical percentages of each group reported having heard the Luambo song on AIDS. A slightly lower percentage (86 percent of men, 70 percent of women) had seen something about AIDS on television. The percentages who had seen brochures, newspaper articles, or posters on AIDS were lower, ranging from 38–60 percent for men and 22–34 percent for women.

The vast majority of respondents, 95 percent of men and 89 percent of women, wanted to learn more about AIDS.

Multivariate Predictors of Knowledge of AIDS

In a multiple regression of the summed knowledge score by demographic and descriptive variables, males and females both had similar results (Table 3). Higher knowledge scores in both groups were associated with higher socioeconomic status (SES), higher educational attainment, length of time and number of messages they had heard about AIDS, personally knowing someone who has AIDS or had died of AIDS, and professing to a non-Christian religion. Being raised in a rural environment was negatively associated with knowledge for women, but not for men. Being older was negatively associated with knowledge for men but not for women. (In both males and females, age was negatively correlated with level of education.) Despite the number of significantly

Table 3 • Multiple Regression of Summed Knowledge Score by Demographic Variables[*]

	Male		Female	
	Coeff	SE of Coeff	Coeff	SE of Coeff
Socioeconomic status	0.4488	0.0706	0.3709	0.0798
Age	-0.0295	0.0116	-0.0025	0.0136
Non-Christian religion	-0.2165	0.1008	-0.4542	0.1157
Multiple partners or extramarital partners	-0.0503	0.0680	0.6069	0.5444
Time source heard of AIDS/HIV	0.3650	0.0608	0.2405	0.0636
Number of information channels	0.4384	0.1027	0.8820	0.1240
Know someone with/ died of AIDS	0.5844	0.1859	0.6707	0.2181
Rural residence	0.0384	0.1062	-0.3273	0.1245
Level of education	0.7765	0.1284	1.0612	0.2135
Marital status	0.2859	0.2275	0.1092	0.2193
	Adjusted R^2 = 0.18		Adjusted R^2 = 0.18	

[*]The knowledge score is based on one point for each correct answer to the items listed in Table 2 (except for "perceived risk").

associated variables, the adjusted r square for both the male and female models was only 0.18. Thus, it is apparent that the variability seen in the knowledge scores in this population cannot be truly defined by the available variables.

Sexual Behavior, Knowledge, and Use of Condoms in Marriage

The median age at first sex (among those who had initiated sexual relations) was 17 years for men and 16 years for women. One percent of men and 14 percent women had not had sex, while 9 percent men and 4 percent women did not respond to the question.

All married respondents (N = 4,008) were asked whether they had had sexual relations in the previous month; 66 percent of 1,885 men and 60 percent of 2,123 women reported having had relations during this period. Abstinence was associated with the postpartum period or having an absent partner. Among those married respondents who had had relations, the mean number of days of sex during the previous week was 1.3.

Over 90 percent of married and single men, 77 percent of married women, and 61 percent of single women had heard of condoms. Despite the high recognition level, relatively few of the respondents in this survey had ever used condoms, with 12 percent of married men reporting ever using them with their spouse.

Eight percent of married men and 7 percent of married women reported current condom use with their spouse, although less than 2 percent of either sex reportedly used them "always" or "most of the time." The predominant reason for using condoms with one's spouse was to prevent pregnancy; the second, to prevent sexually transmitted diseases (STDs) in general, and the third to prevent AIDS. Mention of pregnancy prevention was higher among married than single respondents (reporting on condom use with their current partner), whereas singles cited prevention of other STDs and AIDS more often than married respondents.

Extramarital Relations and Use of Condoms

Twenty-three percent of married men and 1 percent of married women reported having had an extramarital partner or partners in the past six months; 12 percent of men and 1 percent of women reported such relations in the four weeks preceding the interview. Of men having had extramarital activity in the past six months, half reported having only one such partner (Table 4). Among

Table 4 • Frequency of Extramarital Relations and Condom Use Among Married Respondents Who Have Heard about AIDS

	Men N = 1885	Women N = 2123
Number of extramarital partners in past 6 months		
0	77.4	98.6
1	11.7	1.3
2	5.6	0.1
3	2.9	-
4 or more	2.3	-
Percentage reporting extramarital relations in past four weeks	12.1	1.2
Among those with extramarital partners in past 6 months	(N=401)	(N=22)
Percentage who use condoms with extramarital partners	24.0	11.8
The frequency of use among these condom users	(N=90)	(N=4)
Always	35.4	(N too small
Most of the time	14.5	to report %)
Sometimes	27.4	
Never	22.7	

the relatively few women who admitted to extramarital sexual activity, almost all claimed that it was with a single partner.

Factors associated with extramarital activity in men included younger age (<35 years), moderately higher education and SES levels, increased belief in the existence of a vaccine against HIV, and residence in a major urban area since adolescence. Men acknowledging extramarital activity also had slightly more misconceptions regarding false modes of HIV transmission, had heard more messages regarding AIDS than those denying extramarital activity, were more likely to cite condoms as a prevention method for AIDS, to perceive themselves to be at "very high" or "high" risk of AIDS, and to have known someone who had died of AIDS.

In women, the factors linked with such activity were more difficult to define, given the small numbers of women who acknowledged the behavior, but a few basic factors were similar to the men: younger age and urban residence since adolescence were associated with extramarital activity.

While the numbers are admittedly small, condom use was higher with extramarital partners (24 percent among men, 12 percent among women) than with one's spouse. In addition, the frequency of use was more consistent with extramarital partners than with spouses; half of the male users did so "always" or "most of the time." Among unmarried men, 27 percent reported having used condoms with their current partner, with a frequency of use similar to married men in their extramarital relations.

Attitudes Toward Condoms

Over 52 percent of all male respondents believed that condoms tear easily during sexual relations, that they can stay in the vagina after sex, and that they diminish sexual pleasure. An additional 12–28 percent had no opinion on these questions. Single men were slightly more favorable toward condoms than married men.

Among women, 30–50 percent believed that condoms have the above-mentioned disadvantages. However, well over 30 percent of both married and single women answered "don't know" to these questions, which could reflect their ignorance of the method, lack of experience with condoms, or embarrassment over the questions. Married women were slightly more knowledgeable or favorable than single women (data not shown).

Factors associated with condom use and with relatively positive attitudes toward condoms for men were younger age (<35), having had extramarital activity or multiple partners in the last six months, and not having a steady partner. Men with positive attitudes toward condoms were more likely to have used condoms and to cite condoms as a means of HIV prevention. Neither SES, education, religion, nor urban residence showed any association with condom attitudes (data not shown).

Perceived Risk of Getting AIDS

Table 5 shows the distribution of perceived risk in the male and female study populations. What is most striking is that 47 percent of men and 63 percent of women believed that they were at no risk of getting AIDS. For men, factors associated with an increased perception of risk include younger age, higher education and SES levels, knowing someone who died of AIDS, having less accurate knowledge regarding false modes of HIV transmission, having heard more messages regarding AIDS, being either Catholic or Protestant, and having had multiple sexual partners or engaged in extramarital activity in the last six months.

An increased perceived risk in women was associated with higher education and SES levels, engaging in extramarital activity or having multiple sexual partners, having heard more messages regarding AIDS and knowing

Table 5 • Perceived Risk of AIDS and Correlates
of High Perceived Risk

	Men N = 3099	Women N = 3351
Perceived risk of contacting AIDS:	%	%
High	10.6	10.2
Moderate	6.8	5.9
Low	21.0	9.3
None	46.8	62.9
Don't know	13.8	11.3

Selected correlates of increased
    risk of AIDS (percentage with high
    or moderate response)		

Know person who has died of AIDS		
Yes	22.6	23.5
No	17.9	10.9
(p-value)	(0.03)	(<0.00000)
Multiple sexual partners in last 6 months		
Yes	26.3	32.6
No	16.4	19.9
(p-value)	(0.00001)	(0.05)
Number of AIDS messages heard		
1–3	10.7	16.5
4 or more	22.3	24.5
(p-value)	(<0.00000)	(0.0002)
In relationship with a stable partner		
Yes	19.7	21.2
No	21.0	14.4
(p-value)	(NS)	(0.0005)

of AIDS for a longer period of time, receiving their AIDS information from informal sources such as friends and neighbors, and knowing someone who died of AIDS. Women with high perceived risk also had less knowledge regarding common means of AIDS prevention and were slightly more likely to recognize that there is no available vaccine. Surprisingly, women who had a stable or regular partner also perceived themselves to be at increased risk versus those women without such a partner. This may be a reflection of female awareness of or concern over male infidelity.

The association of perceived high risk with misconceptions regarding modes of AIDS transmission and means of prevention suggests that at least a part of this perception may not be based on fact. However, considerable denial regarding AIDS risks is also playing a role in this population. Although having multiple sexual partners is a well-recognized risk behavior for AIDS, 74 percent of men actually engaging in extramarital relationships perceive themselves to be at little or no risk of AIDS.

Attitudes Toward Testing for the AIDS Virus

Thirty-nine percent of men and 16 percent of the women had heard of the term "seropositive"; two-thirds of those who claimed to know the word defined it correctly. The majority of respondents, 78 percent of men and 57 percent of women, reported that they would accept being tested for HIV. Over 90 percent of respondents would want to be informed if either they or their spouse or child were diagnosed with AIDS or HIV infection.

Discussion

The results of this study provide the first available data on levels of knowledge and attitudes with regard to AIDS among a probabilistic sample of the adult population of Kinshasa. While awareness and knowledge may have increased since the study ended in September 1988, the results nonetheless constitute a useful basis for the planning and evaluation of future information-education-communication (IEC) activities for AIDS.

Awareness regarding transmission of HIV via sexual contact is very high, but misconceptions persist over transmission by casual contact and mosquitoes. The fact that only a relatively low percentage could identify symptoms of AIDS may be explained by the fact that health officials have not stressed these aspects in their educational messages.

The misconceptions among a significant portion of the population regarding a vaccine and cure for AIDS are reason for concern, since they may create a sense of false security. The belief regarding the vaccine may result from periodic news stories about vaccine research ongoing in Zaire. The belief that AIDS can be cured may also be attributable to the widespread publicity about a new drug "MM1," which was presented to the Zairian public in November 1987 as a treatment for AIDS. Two recent surveys in different populations have shown a drop over the past year in the percentage that believe in a vaccine and/or cure.[4,5]

Comparisons between the Kinshasa population and a May–June 1988 nation-wide survey of the adult population in the United States[6] reveal that both populations were highly knowledgeable on modes of transmission and reported a high level of exposure to AIDS messages via the mass media; in Zaire the most far-reaching channel was radio, whereas in the US it was television.

However, the two populations differed markedly in several other respects: belief in a vaccine or cure for AIDS was far more common in Zaire, while belief that condoms were effective prevention measures was less common in Zaire. These differences also underscore the areas in which campaigns in Zaire will need to be more explicit.

This study is the first to provide data on two key variables related to HIV transmission—extramarital relations and condom use—from a large, probabilistic sample of both men and women in Zaire. The responses to the questions on sexual behavior should be interpreted with some caution, however, as such items are highly sensitive.[7] Based upon anecdotal evidence from Kinshasa residents, it was initially believed that the current data underestimated both coital frequency (median number of days of sex per week: 1.3 for married respondents) and extramarital relations (23 percent of married men and 1 percent of married women in the past six months).

However, our findings are similar to results obtained from a study of over 12,000 workers and their spouses in two businesses in Kinshasa.[8] Among 4,487 married couples, the mean number of days during the past year in which the couples had sex was 84; this yields a mean of 1.6 days per week. Regarding extramarital sex, 29 percent of married men reported at least one extramarital partner in the past 12 months. This percentage is slightly higher than that found in our study but covers a 12-month rather than six-month period. The question of extramarital relations was posed to females at only the smaller of the two study sites and yielded a prevalence similar to ours (<2 percent).

By contrast, in a study of health personnel (ranging from doctors to traditional practitioners) from all regions of Zaire except Kinshasa, the percentage of men reporting a history of extramarital relations in the past was 58 percent in 1987, dropping to 43 percent in 1988; among women, these percentages were 29 percent in 1987, decreasing to 18 percent in 1988.[9] These percentages are substantially higher than those found for the Kinshasa population in general. Possible explanations for these differences could be that the time period for the activity was not clearly specified, the health workers had greater economic means with which to engage in such activities, or they felt more comfortable with the circumstances in which the information was obtained.

We believe that the data from the current study underestimate the extent of extramarital relations, especially among women. In a subsequent study of sexual behavior in Kinshasa based in part on focus groups, both male and female participants were asked whether married men and married women would be likely to answer truthfully to questions regarding extramarital relations on a survey. The general consensus was that it depended on the interviewer's skill at putting the respondent at ease. However, there was strong consensus that a married woman could not risk revealing anything about extramarital affairs, lest this get back to her husband.[10]

The findings with regard to knowledge and use of condoms among married women concur with previous studies in Zaire.[11-13] In addition, the data from the current study confirm the widespread supposition that condoms are used much more frequently for extramarital sex than for relations with one's spouse. Despite the fact that relatively few men report having used condoms, the majority claim that they tear, stay inside the women's vagina, and decrease sexual pleasure. These negative attitudes must be based on conjecture rather than experience. Unsubstantiated rumors have apparently discouraged the use of condoms to such a degree that the Zairian public does not perceive their importance in the fight against AIDS. The percentage of married men and married women reporting current condom use yielded very similar results from two independent samples. This refutes the hypothesis that women tend to underreport condom use (at least for relations with one's spouse), an issue which has been raised in connection with female-only contraceptive prevalence surveys.

Regarding perceived risk, most of the individuals engaging in extramarital and multiple partner sexual activity did not acknowledge any perception of risk, even though the majority of these same people intellectually "know" that sexual activity with multiple partners provides an elevated risk of HIV exposure. In addition, many persons with high perceived risk believed in the possibility of mosquito-born and/or casual transmission. An unfounded perception of risk, such as this, may be counterproductive in the course of HIV infection and AIDS. If people persist in fearing casual contact with infected individuals, the subsequent ostracism of such persons will place an unmanageable burden upon limited governmental resources. It may also limit the population's response to efforts to promote behavioral change.

To conclude, the findings from this survey have several important implications for ongoing and future efforts to prevent the spread of AIDS in Kinshasa:

- Greater efforts are needed to combat the still prevalent misconceptions that AIDS can be transmitted by casual contact and by mosquitoes.
- IEC efforts should reinforce the idea that the two main means of protection from sexually transmitted HIV infection or AIDS are total mutual fidelity within monogamous couples and where that is not considered possible, use of condoms.
- Condom promotion should include messages directed at changing the negative attitudes toward condoms reflected in this study.
- Information campaigns should emphasize the fact that there is no effective vaccine against AIDS and that the disease is fatal.
- Education campaigns should be directed at teens as well as adults; by the age of 17, half of males and females have engaged in sexual relations.

REFERENCES

1. N'Galy B, Ryder RW: Epidemiology of HIV infection in Africa. J Acquir Immune Defic Syndr 1988; 1:551–558.
2. Ryder RW, Nsa W, Hassig SE, *et al:* Perinatal transmission of the human immunodeficiency virus type 1 to infants of seropositive women in Zaire. N Eng J Med 1989; 320:1637–1642.
3. Hassig SE, Perriens J, Baende E, Bishagara K, Kapita B: The economic impact of HIV infection in adult admissions to internal medicine (IM) at Mama Yemo Hospital. Vth International Conference on AIDS, Montreal, Canada, June 1989, Abstract No. THO 9.
4. Moore M, Lusakulira N, Hassig SE, *et al:* Knowledge and behavior related to AIDS: A study of 3,500 Zairian health workers. Vth International Conference on AIDS, Montreal, Canada, June 1989, Abstract #MGO 16.
5. Bertrand J, Bakutuvwidi M, Balowa D, Kinavwidi N: Knowldege of AIDS, sexual behavior and condom use in ten sites in Zaire. American Public Health Association annual meeting, Chicago, October 1989.
6. Dawson D: AIDS knowledge and attitudes for May and June 1988. NCHS Advance-data, from Vital and Health Statistics of the National Center for Health Statistics. No. 160, September 26, 1988.
7. Pickering H: Asking questions on sexual behavior . . . testing methods from the social sciences. Health Policy Plann 1988; 3(3):237–244.
8. Ryder RW, Hassig SE, Ndilu M, Behets F, Nanlele K, Malele M: Extramarital/prostitute sex and genital ulcer disease (GUD) are important risk factors in 7,068 male Kinshasa factory workers and their 4,548 wives. Vth International Conference on AIDS, Montreal, Canada, June 1989, Abstract #MAO 35.
9. Moore M, Hassig SE, Lusakulira N, Bertrand WE, Kashala T-D: Sexual behavior and perceived AIDS risk among 3,500 Zairian health workers. Vth International Conference on AIDS, Montreal, Canada, June 1989, Abstract #MDO 17.
10. Bertrand JT, Bakutuvwidi M, Balowa D, Kinavwidi LN: Connaissances du SIDA et Comportement Sexuel dans 10 Sites au Zaire. New Orleans, LA: Tulane University, working paper (unpublished). July 1989.
11. Bertrand JT, Bertrand WE, Miatudila M: The use of traditional and modern methods of fertility control in Kinshasa, Zaire. Popul Stud 1983; 37:129–136.
12. Bakutuvwidi M, Kinavwidi LN, Way A: Planification famialle, fecondité et santé familiale au Zaire 1982–84. Kinshasa, Zaire: Institut National de la Statistique, and Columbia, MD: Westinghouse Public Applied Systems, 1985.
13. Betrand JT, Nlandu M, Matondo M, McBride M, Tharp J: Strategies for the delivery of family planning services in Bas Zaire. Int Fam Plann Perspect 1986; 12(4):108–115.

STUDY QUESTIONS

1. What factors are associated with higher levels of knowledge about HIV/AIDS in the Kinshasa sample?
2. What considerations and circumstances are associated with favorable attitudes toward the use of condoms?
3. How do men's and women's beliefs and attitudes about condoms differ?
4. What effects do mass media educational messages seem to have had on the Kinshasa repondents?

5. What differences about beliefs and attitudes toward condoms exist between the Kinshasa sample and the U.S. public opinion poll conducted at about the same time?
6. What cultural factors may be operating to shape the reluctance of Kinshasa men to adopt condoms? How do those factors differ from reluctance among American men to adopt condoms?
7. How are prevailing attitudes about condoms and willingness to use them shaped by factors other than knowledge about HIV transmission?
8. What are the implications of this research for organized AIDS prevention programs?

AIDS—The Leading Cause of Adult Death in the West African City of Abidjan, Ivory Coast

Kevin M. De Cock et al.[*]

In 1988 to 1989, 698 adult cadavers in Abidjan's two largest morgues were studied, representing 38 to 43% of all adult deaths in the city over the study period, and 6 to 7% of annual deaths. Forty-one percent of male and 32% of female cadavers were infected with human immunodeficiency virus (HIV). Fifteen percent of adult male and 13% of adult female annual deaths are due to acquired immunodeficiency syndrome (AIDS). In Abidjan, AIDS is the leading cause of death and years of potential life lost in adult men, followed by unintentional injuries and tuberculosis. In women, AIDS is the second leading cause of death and premature mortality, after deaths related to pregnancy and abortion. AIDS-specific and AIDS-proportional mortality rates may be higher in other African cities where AIDS has been found for a longer time than in Abidjan.

Although the prevalence of infection with HIV, the causative agent of AIDS, is high in many countries of sub-Saharan Africa *(1)*, data concerning mortality due to AIDS are scarce. In Kinshasa, Zaire, the annual incidence of AIDS in adults was reported to be 500 to 1000 cases per million in 1985 *(2)*, with an annual AIDS-specific adult mortality rate of at least 1 per 1000 *(1)*. In

*The other authors of this article are Bernard Barrere, Lacina Diaby, Marie-France Lafontaine, Emmanuel Gnaore, Anne Porter, Daniel Pantobe, Georges C. Lafontant, Augustin Dago-Akribi, Marcel Ette, Koudou Odehouri, and William L. Heyward.

Reprinted with the permission of the American Association for the Advancement of Science and Kevin M. De Cock from *Science,* vol. 249 (August 17, 1990):793–796.

Abidjan, Ivory Coast, where infection with both HIV-1 and HIV-2 occurs *(3)*, the epidemic of AIDS has developed rapidly since recognition of the first AIDS cases in 1985. A recent study in this West African city documented a minimum annual incidence of AIDS of 1447 cases per million in adult men and 340 per million in adult women *(4)*.

In African cities that have high rates of HIV infection, AIDS is having important, but little assessed, effects on patterns of mortality. We undertook the present study to determine the proportion of adult deaths due to AIDS, to estimate minimum rates of population-based AIDS-specific mortality, and, by estimating cause-specific years of potential life lost (YPLL), to assess the importance of AIDS as a cause of premature mortality.

Our study was based on examination and HIV testing of adult (aged >14 years) cadavers admitted consecutively to the morgues associated with Abidjan's two largest hospitals, in December to January 1988–1989 and April to May 1989 for periods of 62 days (Mortuary A) and 43 days (Mortuary B), respectively. Together, these mortuaries receive about 60% of all deaths officially reported in the city. All patients dying in the two hospitals and all fatalities outside of hospital that require an autopsy for forensic reasons are brought to these mortuaries.

Demographic data were recorded on all cadavers studied, and all corpses were examined within 24 hours of admission to the morgue for the physical signs listed in the World Health Organization (WHO) clinical case definition for AIDS *(5)*. Hospital charts and death certificates were reviewed to assess the cause of death in each case, and to see whether features of the WHO AIDS case definition had been recorded.

Blood was drawn from each cadaver by intracardiac or central venous puncture. Serum specimens were tested for antibodies to HIV-1 and HIV-2 by whole virus enzyme-linked immunosorbent assay (ELISA) (Genetic Systems). Repeatedly reactive specimens were further tested by the appropriate virus-specific immunoblot (Du Pont de Nemours for HIV-1; Diagnostics Pasteur for HIV-2) and by synthetic peptide ELISA tests (Diagnostics Pasteur) recognizing antibodies to the transmembrane glycoproteins of HIV-1 and HIV-2, as previously described *(6)*.

Deaths were considered due to AIDS if all the following criteria were met: (i) the cadaver was HIV antibody-positive; (ii) no other specific, non-AIDS-related cause of death (for example, hypertension) was listed; and (iii) at least two major WHO clinical case definition criteria, or one major and one minor criteria, or Kaposi's sarcoma were present, or one of the following was listed as the cause of death: AIDS, retroviral disease, wasting, pneumonia, chronic diarrhea, extrapulmonary tuberculosis. For adult cadavers with pulmonary tuberculosis as the listed cause of death, cough and fever were not counted as criteria for the diagnosis of AIDS *(7)*. For other specific diseases, the cause of death was taken from the death certificate or from the clinical records.

To determine the minimum annual number of cause-specific as well as total deaths, we adjusted the numbers of observed cause-specific and total deaths during the study period in each mortuary to deaths expected over 1 year, corrected for seasonal variations observed for total mortality in Abidjan. Adult AIDS-proportional mortality (proportion of adult deaths due to AIDS) was calculated by dividing the estimate of minimum annual adult deaths due to AIDS by the total number of adult cadavers expected in the mortuaries over 1 year.

Minimum adult AIDS-specific mortality rates (number of adult deaths due to AIDS per 100,000 population per year) were calculated by dividing the annual number of AIDS deaths, derived from the observed cases, by the estimated total population of Abidjan on 1 January 1989 (8).

To assess the impact of specific diseases on adult premature mortality, we made calculations of disease-specific YPLL for persons aged 15 years and older (9). Calculation of annual YPLL for a specific disease was performed by multiplying expected annual numbers of cases of that disease by the difference between the ages at death of cases and an arbitrary expected age of 55 years (10).

To assess the representativeness of deaths studied, and to assess the extent to which deaths are reported, we compared official city death registers in each of Abidjan's ten districts, where by law all deaths should be reported, with a sample of deaths studied in the mortuaries. In addition, we analyzed deaths reported to the official city registers over the past year by age and sex, so as to know official mortality statistics. We also compared our number of studied deaths with an independent estimate by a demographer (B.B.) of the true number of deaths (reported to the city death registers and unreported) expected over a year in Abidjan.

We studied 698 adult cadavers: 181 (26%) represented deaths in the community (almost all received in Mortuary A) and 517 (74%) represented deaths in the hospitals. Overall rates of reactivity to HIV (HIV-1 and HIV-2 combined) were 43 and 34% in men and women, respectively, in Mortuary A, and 35 and 27%, respectively, in Mortuary B. Table 1 shows the age-specific rates for HIV infection in all cadavers studied. The highest rates were found in men and women aged 30 to 39 years. Serologic reactivity to HIV-1 alone (24% in males, 21% in females) was more frequent than reactivity to both viruses (11% in males, 7% in females), which in turn exceeded reactivity to HIV-2 alone (6% in males, 4% in females) (6).

Overall HIV reactivity rates in cadavers brought to the mortuaries from the community, 50/134 (37%) in males and 13/47 (28%) in females, were not significantly different from rates in cadavers derived from in-hospital deaths studied in Mortuary A, 116/257 (45%) for males and 40/111 (36%) for females.

Inadequate information existed to determine the cause of death in 69 (10%) of the 698 adult deaths studied, and these were excluded from further analysis. Table 1 also shows the distribution by age and sex of observed AIDS

Table 1 • Prevalence of HIV Infection in Cadavers and AIDS-Specific and AIDS-Proportional Mortality in Abidjan, 1988 to 1989.

Age (years)	Observed HIV-positive cadavers/total cadavers tested	Percentage	Observed AIDS death/total deaths of known cause	Percentage	Expected annual AIDS deaths/total deaths of known cause	Percentage	Population*	Expected annual minimum AIDS-specific deaths per 100,000 population per year
				Males				
15–19	1/10	10%	0/10		0/56		103,425	
20–29	46/110	42%	18/95	19%	97/542	18%	227,535	43
30–39	88/165	53%	32/150	21%	182/886	21%	147,553	123
40–49	35/93	38%	12/84	14%	62/502	12%	71,314	87
50+	27/102	26%	8/97	8%	46/590	8%	37,627	122
Total	197/480	41%	70/436	16%	388/2,576	15%	587,454	66
				Females				
15–19	4/18	22%	2/12	17%	10/75	13%	123,125	8
20–29	22/57	39%	6/51	12%	35/335	10%	205,865	17
30–39	25/63	40%	10/58	17%	52/363	14%	108,547	48
40–49	10/34	29%	3/28	11%	16/162	10%	46,886	34
50+	8/46	17%	7/44	16%	45/270	17%	31,323	144
Total	69/218	32%	28/193	15%	158/1,204	13%	515,746	31

*Population is estimated for 1 January 1989.

deaths and total deaths; the minimum AIDS deaths and total deaths expected over the course of 1 year, weighted to correct for the different time periods worked in the two mortuaries and for seasonal variations; and minimum annual AIDS-specific mortality rates. These annual rates are considered minimum estimates in the sense that they are based on observed cases only.

Sixty-four (65%) cadavers with AIDS were reactive to HIV-1 and 10 (10%) to HIV-2, and 24 (24%) showed reactivity to both HIV-1 and HIV-2. AIDS was the cause of death in 16% of the male adult cadavers that we studied, and in 15% of female adult cadavers. The weighted data suggest that 15% of the annual male deaths in Abidjan and 13% of the annual female deaths are due to AIDS. The minimum AIDS-specific mortality rate (AIDS-specific deaths per 100,000 population per year) was 66/100,000 for men, 31/100,000 for women, and 49/100,000 for both sexes combined. The high mortality rate from AIDS in women aged 50 years and older reflects the fact that seven of the eight seropositive cadavers examined met the AIDS case definition, as well as the small population denominator in this group.

Table 2 shows minimum cause-specific annual deaths, cause-specific proportional mortality (proportions of annual deaths expected from specific causes), and annual cause-specific and proportional YPLL. AIDS is the leading cause of death in men, and the leading cause of YPLL, accounting for 17% of premature mortality measured in this way. In women, AIDS is the second most common cause of death and YPLL, after conditions related to pregnancy, including deaths from induced abortion. Pregnancy-related deaths are responsible for 15% of female mortality and 22% of YPLL. When data for male and female adults are combined, AIDS accounts for 14% of deaths and 16% of YPLL, more than any other specific disease. Compared with AIDS, maternal mortality accounts for a disproportionate number of YPLL in women because pregnancy-related deaths tend to occur at a younger age than deaths from AIDS.

Official city death registers were examined to see what proportion of 498 mortuary cadavers, 71% of all those studied, that were identifiable by name had been reported as deaths to the authorities. Seventy percent of these adult cadavers were registered in the official city death registers.

The number of officially reported adult deaths in Abidjan in 1988 was 6,192 (4,700 men and 1,492 women), corresponding to a crude mortality rate of 448/100,000 per year in persons aged 15 years and older *(11)*. Assuming that 70% of all 629 studied cadavers were officially reported, the study captured 7% of all deaths officially reported in Abidjan in 1988, or approximately 43% of deaths reported over the study period.

A demographer (B.B.) estimated the true mortality rate in adults in Abidjan in 1988 to be 879/100,000 per year, giving a total of 9,826 deaths *(12)*. Total adult deaths studied in the morgues (reported and unreported) represented 629/9,826 (6%) of the estimated true deaths in Abidjan during 1988, or approximately 38% of true deaths citywide over the study period.

Table 2 • Cause-Specific and Proportional Mortality, and Cause-Specific and Proportional YPLL in Abidjan, 1988 to 1989. (Percentages in parentheses indicate percent or annual deaths of YPLL due to a specific cause. NA, not applicable.)

Condition (n)	Males		Females	
	Cause-specific annual deaths (%)	Cause-specific YPLL (%)	Cause-specific annual deaths (%)	Cause-specific YPLL (%)
AIDS (98)	388 (15%)	7,532 (17%)	158 (13%)	2,793 (12%)
Maternal mortality (25)	NA	NA	180 (15%)	5,015 (22%)
Unintentional injury (74)	351 (14%)	7,181 (17%)	87 (7%)	2,000 (9%)
Tuberculosis* (64)	290 (11%)	3,695 (9%)	66 (6%)	1,129 (5%)
Gastrointestinal diseases† (41)	183 (7%)	2,511 (6%)	97 (8%)	1,750 (8%)
Cancer (41)	142 (6%)	1,689 (4%)	124 (10%)	1,544 (7%)
Cardiovascular disease (28)	142 (6%)	1,694 (4%)	20 (2%)	418 (2%)
Chronic liver disease‡ (26)	125 (5%)	1,883 (4%)	30 (3%)	565 (3%)
Cerebrovascular disease (28)	121 (5%)	922 (2%)	74 (6%)	1,221 (5%)
Meningitis (32)	119 (5%)	2,279 (5%)	47 (4%)	1,062 (5%)
Diarrheal disease (non-AIDS) (26)	103 (4%)	1,786 (4%)	40 (3%)	451 (2%)
Homicide and suicide (15)	67 (4%)	1,694 (4%)	10 (1%)	181 (1%)
Viral hepatitis (11)	40 (2%)	985 (2%)	21 (2%)	249 (1%)
Malaria (3)	20 (1%)	586 (1%)	0	0
Infectious diseases, misc.§ (58)	233 (9%)	4,626 (11%)	113 (9%)	2,222 (10%)
Other, noninfectious ‖(59)	251 (10%)	4,227 (10%)	138 (12%)	2,213 (10%)
Total (629)	2,575 (100%)	43,290 (100%)	1,204 (100%)	22,813 (100%)

* Excludes HIV-positive extraprapulmonary tuberculosis, which has been classified as AIDS; includes HIV-positive pulmonary tuberculosis without other evidence of AIDS (see text).
† Noninfectious causes only.
‡ Hepatocellular carcinoma is included under cancer.
§ Includes all other infectious diseases not listed and not meeting AIDS case definition.
‖ Includes all other noninfectious diseases not listed.

Caution is needed in interpreting hospital and autopsy data, since hospital deaths may differ substantially from deaths in the community. The present study assessed 6 to 7% of all officially reported or estimated true deaths in Abidjan in 1988. Twenty-six percent of the cadavers we studied were from outside the hospital, and no significant difference in levels of HIV infection was found between hospital and community-derived cadavers. Therefore, despite the potential for selection bias, we believe the data are representative.

AIDS is now the leading cause of death in Abidjan for adult men and the second most common cause of death for women. Fifteen percent of adult male deaths and 17% of male YPLL resulted from AIDS. In women, AIDS accounted for 13% of deaths and 12% of YPLL, second only to deaths and YPLL from maternal mortality. The higher incidence (and hence associated mortality) of AIDS in men than women in Abidjan has been previously discussed (4). The observed deaths in women related to pregnancy indicate a minimum maternal mortality rate of the order of 200 per 100,000 live births, a serious cause for concern.

These figures probably underestimate the true mortality due to HIV infection. Factors leading to underassessment of AIDS-related deaths include exclusion of pediatric patients from the estimates, the rigidity of the case definition used, lack of clinical information concerning a number of deaths, the unknown proportion of AIDS deaths not brought to the study mortuaries, and the cultural practice of seriously ill persons leaving Abidjan to die in their home area. Deaths due to pulmonary tuberculosis, the third-ranking cause of male adult death, were specifically not counted as AIDS cases, although with 50% of such cadavers testing HIV-positive, an important fraction of such deaths were probably attributable to HIV infection. Since our study assessed less than half of all Abidjan deaths over the study period, but used the whole population as denominator, true AIDS-specific mortality rates must be considerably higher than the minimum estimates quoted.

The disparity between rates of AIDS-specific mortality in Abidjan and in the industrialized world is extreme. Minimum AIDS-specific mortality rates in both men and women in Abidjan are higher than those in New York City (13). Maternal mortality is also strikingly more frequent than in the developed world. Twenty-eight percent of adult female deaths, and 34% of adult female YPLL, were due to AIDS, pregnancy-related conditions, or induced abortions, illustrating how reproductive health dominates the lives and deaths of women in this city (14).

Calculation of YPLL offers a useful way of estimating premature mortality (9) and of assessing the broader social impact of specific diseases. A number of other cities in Africa have been affected by AIDS for a longer period of time or have higher levels of HIV infection in their populations, or both. Although data concerning mortality due to AIDS are scarce, AIDS is likely to be the leading cause of adult death in a number of other African cities also, and the disease may already be affecting certain standard demographic parameters (14).

REFERENCES AND NOTES

1. P. Piot *et al.*, *Science* 239, 573 (1988).
2. J. M. Mann *et al.*, *J Am. Med. Assoc.* 255, 3255 (1986).
3. K. Odehouri *et al.*, *AIDS* 3, 509 (1989).
4. K. M. De Cock *et al.*, *Lancet* ii, 408 (1989).
5. World Health Organization, *Wkly. Epidemiol. Rec.* 61, 72 (1986).
6. Serodiagnostic algorithm and criteria for test interpretation are described in K. M. De Cock *et al.*, *AIDS* 4, 443 (1990).
7. R. Widy Wirski *et al.*, *J. Am. Med. Assoc.* 260, 3286 (1988).
8. B. Barrere, Estimation de la structure per age et sexe, population de la ville d'Abidjan—Population des quartiers d'Abidjan. Rapport complementaire, March 1989. Unpublished background document available on request.
9. Centers for Disease Control. *Morb. Mortal. Wkly. Rep.* 35, 1S (1986).
10. For the United States, YPLL are calculated from deaths before a predetermined end point set at 65 years *(9)*. Since life expectancy in the Ivory Coast is between 50 and 55 years for men and women, and official retirement is at 55 years, YPLL in this study have been calculated based on an expected age of 55 years.
11. B. Barrere, Estimation de la structure per age et sexe; Population de la ville d'Abidjan—Population des quartiers d'Abidjan, December 1988. Unpublished background document available on request.
12. ————, unpublished estimations of mortality rates in Abidjan.
13. J. W. Curran *et al.*, *Science* 239, 610 (1988).
14. A. Rosenfield, *J. Am. Med. Assoc.* 262, 376 (1989).
15. Review of records in the hospitals associated with the study mortuaries showed that death rates (deaths per 1000 admissions) in medical patients increased by 54% between 1983 and 1988, with increases of 106 and 98% in men aged 20 to 29 and 30 to 39 years, respectively, and 199 and 42% in women of the same age ranges. Over the same period, official Abidjan mortality statistics showed an increase in mortality rates (deaths per 100,000 per year) of 54% in men aged 20 years and older and of 28% in women aged 30 years and older. For discussion of possible demographic consequences of AIDS in developing countries, see R. M. Anderson, R. M. May, A. R. McLean, *Nature* 332, 228 (1988).
16. We thank the Ministry of the Interior of the Ivory Coast for permission to examine vital statistics; the Ministry of Public Health and Population of the Ivory Coast; the heads of University Hospital Departments for access to records; the laboratory staff of Project RETRO-CI; the United States Embassy, Abidjan, for logistic support; staff of the Division of HIV/AIDS, Centers for Disease Control (CDC); A. Nelson, Project SIDA, Kinshasa, Zaire; R. L. Colebunders, Institute of Tropical Medicine, Antwerp, Belgium; I. Tafforeau, Free University of Brussels, Belgium; and M. Papaioanou, Division of HIV/AIDS, CDC, for discussion. See A. Nelson *et al.*, Fourth International Conference on AIDS, Stockholm, 12 to 16 June 1988 (abstract 5035).

STUDY QUESTIONS

1. Why did this research study cadavers rather than living people?
2. What does "YPLL" mean?
3. How did the researchers calculate AIDS-specific mortality rates in this study?

4. How did the researchers assess the representativeness of the deaths they studied?
5. In what age group are the highest expected percentages of AIDS-related deaths? How does this differ for men and women?
6. Why do the authors assert that their figures are probably underrepresentative of AIDS-related deaths in Abidjan and the surrounding area?

Suggested Additional Readings

R. M. Anderson, R. M. May, M. C. Boily, G. P. Garnett, and J. T. Rowley, "The Spread of HIV-1 in Africa: Sexual Contact Patterns and the Predicted Demographic Impact of AIDS." *Nature,* vol. 352 (August 15, 1991):581–588.

R. Biggar, "AIDS in Subsaharan Africa." *Cancer Detection and Prevention Supplement,* vol. 1 (1987):487–491.

F. Clavel, K. Mansinho, and S. Chamanet, "Human Immunodeficiency Virus Type 2 Infection Associated with AIDS in West Africa." *New England Journal of Medicine,* vol. 316 (1987):1180–1185.

Kevin M. De Cock and F. Brun-Vezinet, "Epidemiology of HIV-2." *AIDS,* vol. 3 (1989):S89–95.

Kevin M. De Cock, F. Brun-Vezinet and B. Brun-Vezinet, "HIV-1 and HIV-2 Infections and AIDS in West Africa." *AIDS,* vol. 5 (1991):21–28.

Douglas A. Feldman, "The Sociocultural Impact of AIDS in East and Central Africa." Richard Ulack and William F. Skinner, editors. *AIDS and the Social Sciences* (Lexington, KY: University of Kentucky Press, 1991):124–133.

N. Miller and R. C. Rockwell, editors. *AIDS in Africa: The Social and Policy Impact* (Lewiston, NY: Edwin Mellon, 1988).

"Posters from the Visual AIDS Exhibition, London Regional Art and Historical Museums." James Miller, editor. *Fluid Exchanges* (Toronto: University of Toronto Press, 1992):177–184.

T. Quinn and J. Mann, "HIV-1 Infection and AIDS in Africa." R. Kaslow and D. Francis, editors. *The Epidemiology of AIDS* (New York: Oxford University Press, 1989).

CHAPTER 8

Gender

Interpersonal Power and AIDS

• • •

The selections in Chapter 8 focus on the global implications of gendered interpersonal power relationships for the HIV/AIDS health crisis. **HIV: The Global Crisis** advances a compelling analysis of the impact of HIV/AIDS on women's lives. Across cultures, male sexual behavior—multiple partners, undisclosed bisexuality, a reluctance to wear condoms—combine with structural conditions that have feminized poverty and generally placed men in a position of dominance over women. The results are expressed in terms of greatly heightened risk for HIV/AIDS among women and children. Efforts to arrest the spread of HIV, the author suggests, will be successful only to the extent that these efforts also foster profound changes in the structural conditions of women's lives.

    Sex, Gender and Power: Young Women's Sexuality in the Shadow of AIDS examines the special difficulties young heterosexual women face in the HIV/AIDS pandemic. As the pandemic neared the end of its first decade, rates of heterosexual HIV infection seem to have remained relatively low in industrial societies. At the same time, however, in some urban areas that were earlier described as Pattern I epidemics, AIDS is now the primary cause of death among women in their childbearing years. Epidemiologists also predict that as the epidemic proceeds through its second decade, heterosexual women in their teens and twenties are likely to be profoundly affected by the HIV/AIDS epidemic. Gendered reproduction decisions about contraception, abortion, pregnancy, and childrearing complicate young women's sexual identity and sexual behavior and enhance their risk of HIV infection. Ideological forces, particularly the tendency to use romantic and sexualized relationships to define personal identity, have placed young women in a position of relative sexual powerlessness and heightened vulnerability to HIV. Both selections trace this heightened vulnerability for women during their childbearing years to women's structural and interpersonal powerlessness.

HIV: The Global Crisis

Marcia Ann Gillespie

It's been little more than a decade since we first began to hear disquieting rumors of a new, deadly communicable disease in our midst. At first erroneously and homophobicly labeled the "gay men's disease," or dismissed out of ignorance and bias as an African or Haitian scourge, it would eventually be recognized for what it always was: a deadly viral disease, primarily sexually transmitted, that could place all sexually active people at risk. Sadly, the racism, sexism, classism, and homophobia that so distort our society—overlaid with fear, mass hysteria, and denial—continue to slow our response to and understanding of this disease.

Today, with 157 countries reporting AIDS cases, the world has come to accept the terrible fact that the human immunodeficiency virus (HIV) along with the acquired immune deficiency syndrome (AIDS) that it creates is of pandemic proportions. The World Health Organization (WHO) estimated that at the end of the last decade 8 to 10 million people were HIV-infected, and most of those infections occurred in the early to mid-1980s.

Still, what far too many people fail to understand is that HIV/AIDS has become a family disease, affecting both genders, all ages, the sick and the well.

First, the numbers—as best we know them. During the first decade of the HIV/AIDS pandemic there were about 500,000 cases of AIDS in women and children, most of which went unrecognized. By early 1990, the WHO conservatively estimates that more than 3 million females, most of them women of childbearing age, were infected with HIV. Approximately 80 percent of them are in sub-Saharan Africa, where there are cities in central Africa with up to 40 percent of the 30- to 34-year-olds infected and countries with a higher incidence of infection among women ages 15 to 24 than among their male counterparts. While many in the United States may view HIV and AIDS as something that only happens to other people, no such illusion of safety exists for millions of the world's women. And because of the limited data available on women and children, the WHO cautions that its projections may fall far short of the actual scope of infection.

Even so, numbers don't begin to address the epidemic's potential impact if it goes unchecked. At best, they only begin to tell the story of the many ways women's lives will be forfeit, put at risk, and dramatically changed. Here we have a disease that is not curable and only marginally treatable, with treatments often unavailable to most of those in need. All that we do know is that by drastically reducing high-risk behaviors, its spread can be contained.

Reprinted with the permission of *Ms.* Magazine (© 1991) from *Ms.,* vol. 1, no. 4, new series (January/February 1991):17–22.

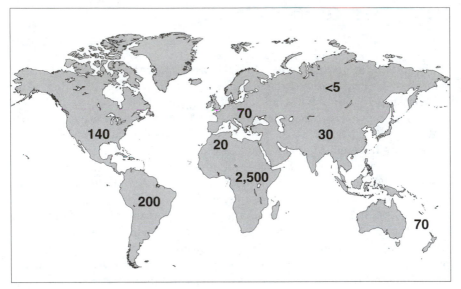

Source: J. Chin, *LANCET*, 7/20/90

HIV Infections per 100,000 Adult Women

In the best of circumstances, discussion of sexual behavior can open a Pandora's box. How we perceive ourselves as sexual beings and how we act upon the impulse—with whom, the endless variety of positions and erotic locations—has as much to do with social conditioning, mores, economics and power, belief systems, and habit as it does with biological urge. It also varies from situation to situation within a culture. Today, because of HIV, our need to understand sexual practices has never been more acute, but the very labels used in the Western world—hetero-, homo-, and bisexual—often obscure rather than illuminate. Human sexuality is far more complex and fluid than such labels would allow. But in any culture where the concept of manhood has been tied to heterosexuality, men find it difficult if not often impossible to admit to any "deviation." Therefore it should come as no surprise that current AIDS research indicates that bisexuality is far more widespread than had been previously thought. Unfortunately, those men who refuse to acknowledge their homosexual encounters, particularly those in Western countries where the incidence of infection among homosexual men is high, may place women at risk.

So much of the male behavior that puts women at risk—multiple partners, bisexuality, reluctance or refusal to wear condoms—cannot be changed by women alone. And so many of the attitudes that pervade societies about women's worth and place and men's rights make effective prevention campaigns extremely difficult to achieve. That women are often denied equal access to education, training, health care, property and legal rights, and independent incomes increases our vulnerability. Even when informed of the risk, women too rarely have the power to protect themselves. In every society, women are subservient to men. Depending on the degree of pressure on her to be submissive in sexual and social matters, a woman who tries to use information to prevent infection may become the target of mockery, rejection, stigmatization, economic reprisal, violence, and death.

In a country like Brazil, a husband can cite an offense to his honor as justification for the murder of his wife. A woman may know that her husband's behavior puts her at risk, but she also knows that her attempts to intervene could be met with charges of unfaithfulness, physical violence, and death. A recent story in the New York *Times* detailing the travails of one Ugandan woman gave poignant proof of the possible economic and social repercussions. Because she refused to have sex with her HIV-positive husband, she was treated as a pariah by his family. After his death, they stripped her of all her possessions and evicted her and her children from their home.

A layer of risk to women comes from the need to blame someone or some group that continues to haunt those caught in this epidemic. Sexually transmitted diseases (STDs) are almost universally thought of as women's diseases, a fact that increases the potential for scapegoating and violence, as does the generally misplaced focus of so much attention on "prostitutes." The term carries negative, antifemale bias and fails to recognize economic and power realities of women's lives; it is sometimes used inappropriately to describe female sexual behavior in societies where there is a very real distinction between "free" women and women working in prostitution. For example, it is not uncommon to find women living independent of men in many of the urban African settings where HIV is prevalent. These women, who are often denied job opportunities or consigned to low-paying jobs, may at times seek payment for sexual favors from their lovers to keep themselves and their children afloat. And it is customary in parts of Africa for a man to give a woman he's sexually involved with gifts of goods or money; this is no more or less a sign of prostitution than what happens when voluntary sex follows a dinner date in the U.S.A.

Almost invariably women described as prostitutes are targeted as disease carriers and blamed for the spread of HIV. Already there have been reports of groups of such women being forced out of several African cities, while in India, women working in prostitution who tested HIV positive have been thrown in jail. Although one can find prevention campaigns targeting these women in almost all countries reporting cases of AIDS, the fact remains that rarely do they have the power to insist on condom usage. The more fragile their economic situation, the less likely they are to refuse to have sex with clients who won't wear condoms. Meanwhile, only a few programs even try to provide economically viable alternatives.

Given the feminization of poverty and the limited economic options available to nations already overburdened with debt, prostitution increasingly becomes the sole means of survival for many of the world's poorest women. As a recent United Nations report concluded, "Even when prostitution seemed to have been freely chosen, it was actually the result of [economic] coercion." Such women, and the growing legions of street children who are also ensnared in the sex industry, easily fall prey to this epidemic. But it is these women and children, the weakest among us, who become targets for condemnation, not their male clients who may be the source of infection and who may spread the virus to their families and other sex partners. In addition, as one report stated: "The comparatively new phenomenon of international sex tourism, associated as it is not only with the power of men over vulnerable women, but also with the power of men from rich countries to purchase sexual activities from poor women in developing countries, adds an international dimension to the spread of HIV infection." One should not assume that the women in the developing world targeted for sex tours are the source of the infection. For example, HIV infection among women and children in prostitution in the Philippines has been traced to the U.S. military and other foreign clients.

In Bangkok, it is unofficially estimated that there are one million prostitutes, of whom some five to eight hundred thousand are women. And studies indicate that in some Thai cities, the increase in HIV among females in prostitution has been as much as 50 percent. Chantawipa Apisuk, the head of EMPOWER (Education Means Protection of Women in Recreation), is all too aware of the realities that these women face. "Of course it is better for women to become prostitutes than to live in poverty, suffer from hunger in the villages, or be raped by relatives. AIDS or no AIDS, these women have to earn a living; you cannot eat a plate of morals." She has concluded, with a certain fatalism, that "prostitution is here to stay. What we want to do is minimize the suffering."

The precarious state of women's reproductive health in so many of the world's poorer countries also increases their chance of infection. The lifetime risk of dying of causes related to pregnancy in the developing world is 200 times that for women in the industrialized nations. And in the developing world, most of the blood transfusions go to women, usually in connection with obstetric complications, and to children. But the resources and equipment needed for routine screening of blood supplies are not readily available, especially in rural areas. As a result, women can be caught in a deadly cycle. Not only is there the risk of HIV infection due to contaminated blood, but because pregnancy, studies have indicated, may act to accelerate the disease, the combination of pregnancy and HIV leads to ever higher mortality rates.

There is also strong evidence to suggest that the presence of other STDs—such as syphilis, herpes, and cancroid that often cause genital ulcers and sores—leaves one more susceptible to HIV. Not only are we seeing dramatic increases in such diseases among teenagers and young adults in the U.S., but they are widespread throughout Africa in countries with insufficient resources to treat infection. Vaginal tears, abrasions, and lesions may also increase risk; these are common among women where the lack of female lubrication during sex, or an extremely tight vaginal passage, is thought to heighten male pleasure, as well as where female circumcision is practiced.

Terrible as rape is under any circumstance, the threat of HIV makes it even more ominous. The more violent the attack, the more likely it is that a woman will suffer internal bruising, lacerations, and bleeding. Just how many women become infected this way is not known, but given how frequently rape occurs and how widespread this particular form of violence is, the risk is clear. Adolescent girls may become particular targets for rape. The low incidence of HIV among girls may encourage some men to seek them out, and it is not unheard of for young girls to be seduced or raped by men who believe that sex with a virgin cures sexually transmitted diseases.

Too often rape and war go hand in hand, and in many countries, HIV infection rates within the military are alarmingly high. According to a recent report in *AIDS and Society,* "military units in some central African states are reported to be over 50 percent seropositive." As a result, the recent invasion of the central African nation of Rwanda by a rebel force of exiled Rwandans out of Uganda carried the very real threat of HIV transmission to women, both through consensual sex and rape. Similarly, the presence of large standing armies in so much of the world where the incidence of HIV is high poses an ongoing threat. *Africa Analysis* reported last year that throughout sub-Saharan Africa, "armies are regarded as being the main disseminators of the AIDS virus"; and that up to half of Zimbabwe's 46,000-strong army is HIV positive.

Although pregnancy may hasten the progression of illness caused by HIV infection, abortion is often neither available to or chosen by women. In much of the world, a woman's identity and status are tied to her ability to bear healthy children, and, to many African and Asian people, children are considered necessary to maintain ancestral ties. A woman may well risk HIV infection by having unprotected sex in order to become pregnant. She may not learn that she is infected with the virus until pregnancy or until her child falls ill. Even if she knows she is infected, she may still attempt pregnancy in the hopes of having an uninfected baby. And wherever the Catholic church holds sway—in the Philippines, for example, or countries in the Caribbean and Central and South America—abortion is even less of an option and deep resistance to the use of contraception is prevalent.

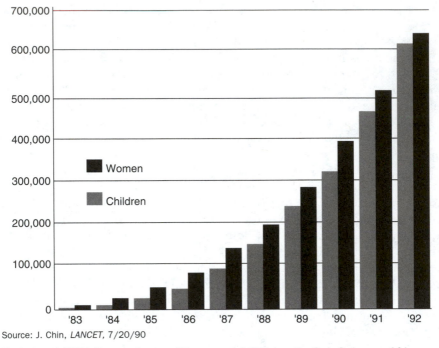

Source: J. Chin, *LANCET,* 7/20/90

Estimated AIDS Cases Among Women and Children in Sub-Saharan Africa

As of the end of the last decade it's estimated that 2.5 million African women were HIV-infected. These women gave birth to 2 million infants, of whom about 500,000 are thought to be infected. The WHO estimates that worldwide, by the end of 1992, about 4 million babies will have been born to HIV-infected women; one million of these babies are expected to be infected, and in some areas of the continent, there will be more children than women with AIDS. The majority of children born infected are not expected to survive beyond their fifth birthdays. But the early deaths of HIV-infected mothers place their children, both the well and the sick, in terribly precarious situations. In Africa, the numbers of orphans may well overwhelm the extended family that traditionally provided for them. In one section of Uganda, there are reports of some 40,000 children orphaned, many as a result of this epidemic. And throughout the developing world, nations will be hard pressed to provide facilities and care. Given that the world already allows some 100 million children and adolescents to live most of the time in its streets, it seems almost inevitable that many AIDS orphans will end up joining their ranks.

This epidemic also increases the burden on women who are the primary caretakers of children, the sick, and the dying. Although older women are less likely to become infected, it is they who often must shoulder the responsibilities of caregiving. They nurse and bury their children and kin;

they take in their orphaned grandchildren. In those parts of Africa where the epidemic has made its most serious inroads, roles have been reversed. Older women who once relied on their children now provide the support; invariably increased poverty results.

The situation for adolescent girls may become increasingly difficult. Because the incidence levels among children five to 15 are still low, older men may begin to seek ever younger wives, thus increasing the risk of infection among the young. The epidemic may also decrease a girl's chances for education due to early marriage, or, as families become increasingly impoverished by AIDS, the tendency to spend whatever school fees are available for the education of her brothers.

Increased poverty is the one inevitable outcome of this epidemic. AIDS has taken its greatest toll among people in the prime of their lives, the sole or major providers of family income. The very people forced by poverty to make extreme choices—the Caribbean farm workers who toil in the U.S., the men who migrate from all over southern Africa to work in South Africa's mines, the women in prostitution—become the first casualties. The absence of their incomes, no matter how meager, endangers whole families. The disease also takes its toll among the developing world's educated and skilled urban populations, depriving nations of valued workers and leaving large networks of families destitute. Its spread into rural areas in nations already struggling and failing to feed themselves raises the specter of increased starvation.

The levels of risk for women are clear to anyone who cares to look at these worldwide patterns. In a speech delivered in Paris in 1989, Dr. Jonathan Mann, the former director of the WHO Global Programme on AIDS, spoke pointedly: "For women, AIDS is just the tip of the iceberg—of poverty, lack of access to adequate health care, disenfranchisement, and discrimination." And yet, as a recent article in *Lancet* noted: "The social, economic, and demographic impacts on women and children have until now been largely neglected. Only recently has the growing magnitude of HIV infection in women and children been recognized outside a few geographic areas. Economic studies of the HIV infection/AIDS pandemic have paid little or no attention to the special problems of women, especially mothers and children." The rationale often given for this neglect is that during the early stages of the epidemic the majority of the cases were among men. But such neglect comes as no surprise, given that the plight of the world's women and children, the issues as they affect our lives, are too often given low priority, misaddressed, or ignored. Yet any success in arresting the spread of HIV can only come as a result of profound change in the condition of women's lives.

At some point in time, historians may look back and see this epidemic as a turning point in human history. Perhaps they will speculate about what might have happened if the numbers had been reversed, with heterosexuals in North America and Europe the ones most at risk. Despite the work of dedicated people in this and other industrialized nations, a cynicism taints public discussion and policy. From time to time the suffering of African, Asian, Caribbean, Central and South American people moves us—"We Are the World"—but too many of us have come to see death and poverty in the developing world as fated, an ugly but acceptable reality. It's a notion fueled by the unspoken assumptions of racial and cultural superiority.

While we seek vaccines—"magic bullets"—that no doubt will be tested on the very people we so distance ourselves from, we expend no concurrent effort to make today's treatments accessible to them. No public cry is raised to fund and field a massive drive to eliminate all the other curable sexually transmitted diseases that facilitate HIV infection. And even if by some stroke of luck or genius, a shot guaranteeing immunity is perfected, a cure found and made readily available to the world's people, all the underlying conditions will still remain.

HIV/AIDS has been described as a disease of development, its spread in so much of the developing world spawned by rapid urbanization and the attendant deterioration of living conditions and changes in behavior. It is in these cities that the epidemic has made its most dramatic impact. Some think that this is but the first of many such developmentally linked infectious diseases. If that's true, then unless there is a concerted effort to redress the economic imbalance between rich and poor nations, we may see untold millions of people die. And if all the factors that impoverish women, that silence and render them invisible, are not seriously addressed, the overwhelming majority of those who suffer will be brown, beige, and yellow women and children.

STUDY QUESTIONS

1. How does the author establish parallels between women in developing nations and women in industrialized nations?
2. What is the nature of the connection between the feminization of poverty and HIV transmission?
3. Why does "the precarious state of women's reproductive health" in developing nations place women at greater risk of HIV infection and AIDS than men?
4. What kinds of political conditions heighten women's vulnerability to HIV infection?
5. In what ways does HIV/AIDS expand the burden of older women in developing nations and among poor people in all places?
6. Why has HIV/AIDS been characterized as "a disease of [economic] development"?
7. In what ways does this author's analysis of prostitution differ from that advanced by Charles Hunt in his essay, "Migrant Labor and Sexually Transmitted Disease: AIDS in Africa" in Chapter 7?

Sex, Gender and Power

Young Women's Sexuality in the Shadow of AIDS

Janet Holland, Caroline Ramazanoglu,
Sue Scott, Sue Sharpe, and Rachel Thomson

AIDS, Young Women and Risk

With the exception of the labelling of prostitute women as a high risk group, there has been relatively little discussion of women in the epidemiological literature (Richardson 1990). In the US, however, women are proportionately the fastest growing group of people with AIDS; in New York City, AIDS is the primary cause of death for women between 25–29; in Africa and the Caribbean 50 per cent of people with AIDS are women, and in Western Europe 9 per cent of reported AIDS cases are women (PWA Coalition 1988). On a global scale AIDS is clearly an issue for women.

We are not suggesting that, on the basis of this evidence, heterosexual women should now be identified as yet another 'high risk group'. Understandings of risk are contested, but have been shifting from a focus on membership of specific groups to a concern with the kinds of sexual and other practices which seem to be more or less effective in spreading HIV infection (Aggleton and Homans 1988; Aggleton *et al.* 1989). Safer sexual practice appears to be one of the main ways in which this epidemic can be limited. There is already evidence that the rate of HIV infection is falling where gay men and prostitutes have become well informed about sexual risks (Carne *et al.* 1987; Fitzpatrick *et al.* 1989; Johnson and Gill 1989; English Collective of Prostitutes 1988; Panos Institute, 1988; Plant 1990). A rational choice model does not, though, seem appropriate for young women's decisions about their sexual behaviour.[1] Much of the emphasis in public health campaigns around HIV/AIDS in the UK has been placed firstly, on the acquisition of knowledge in order to dispel ignorance, and secondly on condom use as protection against infection. These are strategies which take little account of the barriers which young women face in attempting to put this knowledge into practice in their sexual encounters. While women's sexual beliefs and practices are critical factors in understanding the nature of risk, and how it is managed, we argue that the very variable ways in which young women negotiate their sexual practices can be seen as responses to contradictory social pressures.

Information on young women's conceptions of personal risk and safety in sexual activities is critical for effective health education. We argue that

This selection is based on a survey of 496 young women between the ages of sixteen and twenty-one in Manchester and London, England, and supplemented by in-depth interviews with 150 of those respondents.

Reprinted with the permission of Blackwell Publishers from *Sociology of Health and Illness*, vol. 12, no. 3 (1990):336–348. © 1990.

ways in which young women understand risk, negotiate sexual relationships and develop strategies for safer sex will play a significant part in the spread or limitation of AIDS.

Sexuality, Femininity and Power

By sexuality we mean not only sexual practices, but also what people know and believe about sex, particularly what they think is natural, proper and desirable. Sexuality also includes people's sexual identities in all their cultural and historical variety.[2] This assumes that while sexuality cannot be divorced from the body, it is also socially constructed (Turner 1984). The negotiation of desires and practices occurs in social contexts in which power is embedded. Age, class and ethnicity are examples of sites of power differences, but what is particularly significant in the negotiation of safer sex in heterosexual encounters is the power which men can exercise over women. Sex, as it is currently socially constructed in its various forms, cannot simply be understood as a pleasurable physical activity, it is redolent with symbolic meanings. These meanings are inseparable from gendered power relations and are active in shaping sexual interaction.

Identifying the relevant power relationships is no easy task since young people engaging in sexual encounters may well be unaware of what Foucault has called the 'best hidden things in the social body' (1988:118). Some of our informants are well aware, although in differing ways, of the existence of men's power over women, and of a double standard in sexual activity. But the discovery of hidden power relations is particularly difficult because, however they are experienced, they must be conceptualised in order to be recognised. Young women are encouraged to attach themselves socially to young men in order to succeed as conventionally feminine women, but they are then inhibited from seeing this desired and expected relationship as a structurally unequal one.

The control which young women can exercise over the risks or safety of their sexual practices is constrained by the confusion of their notions of sexuality with their expectations of romance, love and caring. Just as we lack a clear discourse for 'normal' heterosexual practices, so there is a lack of a clear female heterosexual identity. Sexual identity for heterosexual women is ideologically constructed in a context which defines sex in terms of men's drives and needs (Jackson 1978, Jackson 1984). Women tend to be seen, and to see themselves, as passive receptacles of men's sexual passions. Sexually active women are in constant danger of having negative identities attributed to them (Lees 1986). The positive identities available to young heterosexual women tend to be linked to their social relationships with men as girlfriends, wives, or objects of love. Our respondents tended to explain their sexual activity in other terms than those of sex or sexual pleasure.

We have used young women's own accounts of the social processes involved in their sexuality and sexual experience to conceptualise the particular processes through which the power relations embedded in sexual relations are produced and reproduced and through which they become part of individual sexual identity. We have found wide variations in knowledge and experience of sexual matters amongst the young women in our sample, but, with few exceptions, they lack a positive sense of their own sexual identity. Women who seek their own sexual pleasure with different partners were seen by some of our informants as 'slags' or as 'doing what lads do'. Others saw sex primarily as what you do to keep your boyfriend happy or, more negatively, what you do to keep him. It is difficult for young women to insist on safe sexual practices, when they do not expect to assert their own needs in sexual encounters.

The prevailing definition that heterosexual sex is penetration of the vagina by the penis, was accepted by most of the young women we interviewed. This definition in terms of men's 'natural' sex drive, and men's need for sexual fulfilment left little space for the 'normal' and successfully 'feminine' woman to assert needs and desires that might differ from those of men and which might imply an active, and therefore 'unnatural' female sexuality. Women who challenge male definitions by revealing their own needs and desires for sex have negative images as rapacious and devouring, or as sluts. 'Sex' was very generally taken to mean vaginal intercourse with male orgasm, although it was acknowledged that the term also has other meanings. Some young women were clear that vaginal intercourse was not particularly pleasurable for them but, with few exceptions, they assumed that this was what men wanted. A number said that they had never experienced orgasm through penetrative sex and that they much preferred other sexual activities. Their definition of heterosexual sex in terms of male objectives impeded their capacity for making their own desires known, or even recognizing what these might be. Most of our respondents felt unable to ask for what they wanted. Their reluctance to express their desires and needs was sometimes explained in terms of superior male knowledge about sex, or their own embarrassment.

Young women's strategies for achieving safer sex then develop in social contexts characterised by gendered power relations, sexual hierarchy and male dominance. Feminist theory from the 1960s initially asserted women's common experiences of male domination, but the current focus is on the diversity of women's experience, cut as it is by other social divisions such as race, class and sexual orientation (Ramazanoglu 1989). We would not suggest, therefore, that young women's experience of heterosexuality is a unified phenomenon, but would argue that while their experiences, and the strategies which they adopt, will vary, the discourse of 'normal' heterosexuality through which they must negotiate safer sex has many common contours.

We have also to recognise that patriarchal power is not necessarily unified, coherent and centralised. It should more properly be seen as 'dispersed constellations of unequal relationships' (Scott, J. 1986) which leaves spaces for human agency, in contrast to a conceptualisation of patriarchal power which suggests a unified subordination of women. While we argue that sexuality is a socially constructed rather than a wholly biological phenomenon, it is not our intention to imply by social construction that young women's sexuality is passive and simply moulded by patriarchal power relations. There is certainly evidence from our interviews that young women can be very active in resisting men's power, but their resistance may not necessarily be effective (see also Halson 1987). It is clear from our respondents' accounts that young women are actively engaged in constructing their femininity and sexuality, but it is also clear that the negotiation of sexual encounters is a contradictory process in which young women generally lack power.

Sex and Violence—Giving Way to Risk

We have argued elsewhere (Holland *et al* 1990c) that taking a sociological perspective on the AIDS epidemic can shift understandings of safe sex from a focus on fragmented individual responsibility for personal behaviour change, to seeing safer sex as located in the context of social relationships. One of our initial findings is of the amount of pressure from men which many women experience as part of their sexual relationships. The control which young women have over the progress and content of heterosexual relationships appears to be quite limited. Where women have adopted passive feminine sexual identities which assume male superiority, men can control sexual encounters without exerting pressure. Feminist theory, however, has used women's experiences to show the very general exercise of power, aggression and violence which structures social relationships. Male control over female sexuality is then taken to be a crucial mechanism for the reproduction of sexual hierarchy, and male violence against women an important instrument in maintaining that control (Hanmer and Maynard 1987). Both form an essential part of the construction of masculinity and masculine sexual identity. Feminist research has established the extent of male violence against women, and the power that this violence has to control women's lives (Stanko 1985; Hanmer and Saunders 1984; The London Rape Crisis Centre 1984).

Our informants indicated a wide range of pressures in operation, and reported quite frequently being coerced by men whose objective is penetrative sex. Some of these stresses were more obvious to them than others, but they range on a continuum (Kelly 1988) from mild persuasion to give way sexually or to accept unprotected intercourse, through varying degrees of force, to assault and rape. While women have some power to identify and resist these pressures, they do not necessarily want to resist, when love, romance and the fear of losing a boyfriend are critical issues. Only a handful of young women managed to develop relationships in which their needs

could be asserted and given importance, including the need to refuse intercourse at times. (As only young women were interviewed in this study, this
proportion might well increase in samples of older women). In these rare
cases, some women had been able to define safe sex as nonpenetrative and
to teach their male partners how to give pleasure as well as to experience
it. Yet they were often frustrated by their treatment by their partners and
their inabilities to put their own beliefs into practice. These young women
were characterised by the stance they had taken in relation to what they
perceived as unsatisfying sex. They had to be assertive in defining their own
desires and had to be prepared to lose their boyfriend if their definition of
a satisfactory sexual relationship was not achieved. Some of these women
had been subject to sexual pressures in previous relationships and one had
been raped in very violent circumstances.

We do not want to suggest that all male sexual partners are personally
dominant or violent. Young men, like young women, have many personal
styles of coping with the uncertainties of sexual encounters, and many
degrees of learning from experience. What we are suggesting is that we can
locate these styles in the context of an institutionalized heterosexuality
which defines male dominance as normal, defines sexual intercourse in
terms of men's satisfaction and turns sexual encounters into potential power
struggles. Even when violence is overt, it only becomes a social problem
when it is named and resisted by women. It is clear from preliminary analysis of our data that while some women can redefine their femininity so that
they are able to make choices at least with some sexual partners, most
women do not resist pressure from men most of the time, even when they
object to what is happening (Holland *et al* 1990a, 1990b).

It is clear from our informants' accounts that being able to achieve some
measure of sexual safety in a particular relationship, or at a particular stage
of a relationship, is no guarantee that the same protection can be ensured
with another partner or as the relationship develops. Safer sex is not just a
question of using protection or avoiding penetration, it is also an issue of
trusting the one you love. Sexual strategies which assume that your partner
could be a source of infection become hard to sustain in longer term relationships. At the same time, brief relationships or one night stands can
counter mistrust with passion, spontaneity and hopes of love. It is these
contradictory pressures which make it so difficult for young women to take
responsibility for sexual safety.

Contradictions in the Negotiation of Safer Sexual Encounters

Contradictions arise in sexual encounters because women are pulled in different directions by conflicting social pressures. Passion, romance, trust and
what you should be prepared to do if you really love a man are inconsistent
with mistrust of strangers, social subordination to men, fear of unprotected

sex, the use of physical force and concern for reputation. Feminine identity and expectations of sexual passivity pull against the need to be assertive in order to enjoy sex and to ensure personal safety.

The imbalance of power in sexual negotiations coupled with social pressures on young women to guard their reputations, reduces the amount of control which young women have over the practice of safer sex. This renders their decision-making about sexual safety somewhat unpredictable. If, for example, a young woman feels that she should not be engaging in sexual activity, or at least not planning it in advance because of an ideology of femininity which equates sex with romantic love and being swept off your feet, then she may well reject the arguments for carrying condoms. On the other hand, if fear of pregnancy is a prime concern, she may reject condoms in favour of the pill. For many of the young women we have spoken to the immediate risks to their reputation from being seen to be sexually active, or from becoming pregnant, were much more real than a fear of AIDS.

Public education campaigns which equate safer sex with condom use would appear to have been highly successful at the level of information, as almost all our respondents identified safer sex with using condoms. This connection, however, tells us nothing about whether the use of condoms can actually be negotiated in any given sexual encounter. Our evidence is that condom use and safer sex more generally is not a simple matter of making rational decisions based on a knowledge of the facts (see also Watney 1990). Condom use is unpredictable because of the contradictory pressures operating in sexual encounters. Women who can achieve safer sex by using condoms with one partner cannot necessarily negotiate their continued use as the relationship progresses, nor ensure that they can be used with subsequent partners.

Many young women seem to have internalised a negative view of condoms. They argue that condom use 'breaks the flow', makes you 'lose the moment', spoils the romance and turns the event into a mechanical, physical activity. These views can be understood as a product of a dominant ideology which equates sex with men's needs for penetration and ejaculation. A number of our respondents express negative feelings about condoms from what could be defined as a male perspective. Many argue that condoms are unacceptable to their current partner, or are generally rejected by men, because the male sexual drive brooks no interruption. This view embraces a mechanistic and biological understanding of sexuality but one which is equally resistant to the 'rational' decisions which are assumed by public health educators. Women's resistance to condoms can also come from young women having experienced sex as a somewhat alienating experience, as something which is done to them.

If, however, a young woman does make a decision to use condoms in order to protect herself from HIV, then she must find a way to negotiate their use with her male sexual partner or partners. Our data suggest that this is no easy matter and that there are a number of barriers to be negotiated along the road to safer sex. Many of the young women we spoke to viewed 'sex' as something which you do only if you love someone, love having taken the place of marriage as justification for sex. Indeed sex is often seen as a *means* of demonstrating that you love and trust someone. Several of them commented that they would not be sleeping with their partner if they did not trust him. The expression of this sentiment though did not indicate any common degree of trust. It was the expression of love that defined the nature of the relationship (see also Abrams *et al* 1990).

As a result of this view there is a tendency to go on the pill as a means of indicating the seriousness of a relationship. Some even say 'I went on the pill for him'. As love and trust develop, women may then be safely carried away as far as pregnancy is concerned, but still be engaging in unsafe sex in relation to STDs and HIV. There seems to be an assumption of monogamy regardless of whether this is realistic. Young women who are already on the pill sometimes conceal this from new partners in order to justify asking for condoms to be used. Condoms tend to be used in situations where partners are not to be trusted. The transition from condom use with new partners, to the pill in steady relationships is highly symbolic and can be used to signify the seriousness of a relationship (see also Elmslie 1989). It can be the passage of time which enables trust to be built up and changes the basis for negotiating condom use. There is, however, a great deal of pressure on many young women to define relationships as serious in order to justify sex, and the passage of time may be brief. Trust, therefore, while carrying symbolic meaning, may offer little protection from HIV. Our data indicate that while condoms are seen as the best protection from HIV infection, and while they may be used in the early stages of a relationship or in the context of brief encounters, the barriers to the negotiation of their long term use are significant.

Education for safer sex which assumes that women have a positive sexual identity, and that they are in control of the negotiation of sexual encounters, will pass most young women by. Public health messages need to be couched in terms of images with which women can identify, and strategies which are realistic in contradictory situations. The effectiveness of health education for women will depend on the effectiveness of education for men.

Notes

1. For the purposes of this paper we are considering only heterosexual young women and their sexual relationships with men.
2. Since sexuality is culturally and historically variable we are generalising here only about the dominant form of western sexuality. Further research is needed on variations in this form of sexuality.

REFERENCES

Abrams, D., Abraham, C., Spears, R. and Marks, D. (1990) AIDS invulnerability: relationships, sexual behaviour and attitudes among 16–19 year-olds. In Aggleton *et al.* 1990.

Aggleton, P. and Homans, H. (eds) (1988) *Social Aspects of AIDS,* London: Falmer.

Aggleton, P., Hart, G. and Davies, P. (eds) (1989) *AIDS, Social Representations, Social Practices,* London: Falmer.

Aggleton, P., Davies, P. and Hart, G. (eds) (1990) *AIDS: Individual, Cultural and Policy Dimensions,* London: Falmer.

Carne, C., Johnson, A., Pearce, F., Tedder, R., Weller, I., Loveday, C., Hawkins, A., Williams, P. and Adler A. (1987) Prevalance of antibodies to human immunodeficiency virus, gonorrhea rates and changed sexual behaviour in homosexual men in London, *Lancet* (1), 656–8.

Elmslie, K. (1989) AIDS and women. *AIDS Care.* 1, 219–22.

English Collective of Prostitutes (1988) *Prostitute Women and AIDS: Resisting the Virus of Repression* London: Kings Cross Women's Centre, PO Box 287, London, NW6 5QU.

Fitzpatrick, R., Boulton, M. and Hart, G. (1989) Gay men's sexual behaviour in response to AIDS. In Aggleton *et al.* 1989.

Foucault, M. (1988) (ed Kritzmann, L.D.) *Politics, Philosophy, Culture: Interviews and Other Writings,* 1977–1984 London: Routledge.

Halson, J. (1987) 'Going with boys': Girls 'being bad' unpublished paper.

Hanmer, J. and Maynard, M. (1987) *Women, Violence and Social Control* London: Macmillan.

Hanmer, J. and Saunders, S. (1984) *Well-Founded Fear: a Community Study of Violence to Women* London: Hutchinson.

Holland, J., Ramazanoglu, C., Scott, S., Sharpe, S. and Thomson R. (1990a) 'Don't die of ignorance', I nearly died of embarrassment: condoms in context, paper given at *The Fourth Conference on the Social Aspects of AIDS,* London, April.

Holland, J., Ramazanoglu, C. and Scott, S. (1990b) Managing risk and experiencing danger: tensions between government AIDS education policy and young women's sexuality, *Gender and Education.* 2 (2) June.

Holland, J., Ramazanoglu, C. and Scott, S. (1990c) AIDS: From panic stations to power relations, *Sociology.* 24 (3) August.

Jackson, M. (1984) Sexology and the social construction of male sexuality. In Coveney, L. *et al* (eds).

Jackson, S. (1978) *On the social construction of female sexuality* (Explorations in feminism No. 4) London: Women's Research and Resource Centre Publications.

Johnson, A. and Gill, O. (1989) Evidence for recent changes in the sexual behaviour of homosexual men, *Phil. Trans. R. Soc. Lond.* B325, 153–61.

Kelly, L. (1988) *Surviving Sexual Violence* Cambridge: Polity Press.

Lees, S. (1986) *Losing out: Sexuality and adolescent girls* London: Hutchinson.

London Rape Crisis Centre (1984) *Sexual Violence* London: The Women's Press.

Panos Institute (1988) *AIDS and the Third World* London: Panos Publications.

Plant, M. (ed.) (1990) *AIDS, Drugs and Prostitution* London: Tavistock/Routledge.

PWA Coalition (1988) An open letter to the planning committees of the third international conference on AIDS. In Crimp, D. (ed) *AIDS Cultural Analysis/ Cultural Activism,* Cambridge (Mass.): MIT Press.

Ramazanoglu, C. (1989) *Feminism and the Contradictions of Oppression* London: Routledge.

Richardson, D. (1990) AIDS education and women: sexual and reproductive issues. In Aggleton *et al.*

Scott, J. W., (1986) Gender: a useful category of historical analysis, *The American Historical Review.* 91 (5).

Stanko, E. (1985) *Intimate Intrusions: Women's Experience of Male Violence* London: RKP.

Turner, B. (1984) *The Body in Society* Oxford: Blackwell.

Watney, S. (1990) Plenary address at *The Fourth Social Aspects of AIDS Conference* Polytechnic of the South Bank, London.

STUDY QUESTIONS

1. Why do the authors distinguish between the ability to *implement* knowledge about HIV transmission and knowledge about HIV/AIDS in and of itself? In what ways is this distinction a crucial key to preventing the sexual transmission of HIV/AIDS?

2. What factors, according to the authors, limit young women's abilities to exercise control over their own (high-risk) sexual behavior?

3. How did the young women respondents in this research tend to define differently the meaning of sex for women and for men? What do those differences in definition suggest about gendered constructions of interpersonal power?

4. What strategies do men tend to use to weaken young women's control over their own sexual behavior and activities?

5. What kinds of social pressures foster an imbalance of power in sexual negotiations?

6. What strategies can HIV education/prevention programs use to equalize the balance of power between women and men in sexual negotiation?

Suggested Additional Readings

The ACT UP/New York Women and AIDS Book Group, *Women, AIDS and Activism* (Boston: South End Press, 1990).

Kate Bagley and Alida V. Merlo, "Controlling Women's Bodies." Alida V. Merlo and Joycelyn M. Pollock, editors. *Women, Law, and Social Control* (Boston: Allyn and Bacon, 1995):135–153.

Carole A. Campbell, "Women and AIDS." *Social Science and Medicine,* vol. 30 (1990):407–415.

Carole A. Campbell, "Women and AIDS: The Growing Crisis." *HIV/AIDS Prevention Newsletter* (1991).

Gena Corea, *The Invisible Epidemic: The Story of Women and AIDS* (New York: HarperCollins, 1992).

Fran Peavy, *A Shallow Pool of Time: An HIV+ Woman Grapples with the AIDS Epidemic* (Philadelphia: New Society Publishers, 1990).

Ines Rieder and Patricia Ruppelt, editors. *AIDS: The Women* (San Francisco: Cleis Press, 1988).

Andrea Rudd and Darien Taylor, editors. *Positive Women* (Toronto: Second Story Press, 1992).

Beth Schneider, "Women, Children, and AIDS: Research Suggestions." Richard Ulack and William F. Skinner, editors. (Lexington: University of Kentucky Press, 1991).

United Nations Development Programme. "Young Women: Silence, Susceptibility and the HIV Epidemic." (New York: United Nations, 1992).

CHAPTER 9

Core Groups

Commercial Sex Workers in Latin America and the United States

• • •

Core groups are social networks from which an infectious disease radiates. The pattern of an infectious disease epidemic, particularly one like HIV/AIDS that is transmitted in large part through social behaviors, is shaped by four major characteristics of the core group: (1) the geographic boundaries of the group's contact network; (2) the age range of group members; (3) sex and ethnic and racial composition of the group; and (4) of particular interest in the case of sexually transmitted diseases, the predominant sexual orientation of the group. While commercial sex workers are only one type of HIV/AIDS core transmission group (injection drug user and casual, noncommercial sexual networks also being important HIV core transmission groups), the selections in Chapter 9 focus on the social and cultural forces that shape commercial sex workers as a core group for HIV transmission in Pattern II and I/II AIDS epidemics.

For obvious reasons—particularly a high number of sexual partners and a high incidence rate of other sexually transmitted diseases—commercial sex workers tend to have relatively higher rates of HIV infection than the general population. In urban sub-Saharan Africa, for example, HIV infection rates among sex workers range from 30 to 50 percent. In Latin America, although the data are anecdotal, HIV infection rates reach 40 percent. And in Asia—available data are drawn from India and Thailand and, given the relatively recent onset of the epidemic in Southeast Asia, must be regarded as preliminary—the HIV infection rates among commercial sex workers range from 20 to 40 percent. Given these high prevalence rates, the organization of the commercial sex industry and the networks of transmission shaped through interactions between sex workers and their clients are crucial to an understanding of the HIV/AIDS global health crisis.

Inevitably, commercial sex workers expand the geographic boundaries over which HIV can travel. At the same time, the sexual exchange is transacted within and shaped by political, economic, and cultural environments. As a result, the commercial sex industry within any given sociocultural setting is varied and stratified, reflecting and paralleling already-established social and economic arrangements. The two selections in this chapter illustrate the diversity of the commercial sex industry in two Pattern I/II settings, Latin America and the urban United States. **Global Warning** describes the dynamic relationship between prostitution and the AIDS epidemic in San Pedro Sula, Honduras, a city of 600,000 in Central America, a place not so remote from the United States as it might initially appear. Here, where machismo prevails, prostitution and male bisexuality serve as major vectors for HIV transmission. Similarly, as the research summarized in **Sexual Behavior and AIDS Knowledge of Young Male Prostitutes in Manhattan** indicates, male bisexuality also plays an important role in HIV transmission in New York City.

Global Warning

Mary J. McConahay

Veronica Pineda rides cradled in her brother's arms from the taxi door to the plain yellow house—they look like an odd, living pietà crossing the hot, empty street. Inside, Dr. Carlos Lopez examines the thirty-nine-year-old woman. He thinks she may die quickly, yet part of him rejoices that these poor, scarcely educated people have found their way to his new and specialized clinic. Lopez is here, after all, to confront the wave of AIDS that is breaking over Latin America, and Veronica Pineda is his first patient.

Like much of urban Central America, San Pedro Sula, the steamy Honduran industrial hub where Pineda and Lopez live, is jumping in size—from a population of 150,000 a decade ago to 600,000 today. Tropical palms punch at the radiant white sky, and a flood of flowering bushes in bright, wild colors flows through the concrete downtown and meanders among sun-faded wood houses built when this place was best known as a crossroads between the interior and the banana republic coast. It is a languid and sensual town after dark, with residual heat and the smell of night blooms in the air. Veronica Pineda is in many ways a typical resident, and as it happens, she also fits the profile of the fastest-growing and least-noted class of people now becoming infected with the AIDS virus: monogamous heterosexual women.

Until she got sick, Veronica was an aspirant to the working middle class that fuels this city's expanding economy. She began married life as the wife of a banana farm worker, then moved up to earning $11.20 a week sewing skirt pockets in a factory that exports clothes to stores in the United States. Tall, dark eyed, with a natural grace, by early last year Veronica could no longer work. She wears cotton dresses so threadbare and ironed so shiny that they fall like old silk on her thin frame.

AIDS—sometimes called here the new disease—is so mysterious and stigmatizing that Veronica has kept its name secret from her neighbors,

Reprinted with the permission of the author from *Vogue,* vol. 182, no. 1 (January 1992):149–151, 194–195. Mary J. McConahay is Central America editor of the Pacific News Service.

other immigrants from the countryside who live in jerry-built houses spread over farmland to the east of the city. When I visit her there, she looks at rest, though the ordinary noises of a crowded neighborhood break through the thin walls of her wood-plank shack like cymbals on unaccustomed ears—arguments, infant cries, a loud, suddenly cruel educational radio jingle that announces, "AIDS equals death."

Veronica sits propped up on pillows in a spare, spotless room as if in a cocoon, surrounded by loving women. Her eighteen-year-old daughter, Janira, cooks soup on the single-ring hot plate in the shack's only other room, a tiny kitchen. Veronica's sister Marina checks in every day and helps bathe her. And her big-eyed twelve-year-old daughter, Jenny, sits for hours at the foot of her mother's bed, both of them watching a black-and-white television. It doesn't matter what is on; it is a way they have of being together now that Veronica can hardly talk. She hasn't the strength to travel the half hour to Carlos Lopez's clinic, either. "I don't feel too well," she says in keen understatement. So Lopez visits her at home—when the clinic has enough money for gas.

Veronica professes a deep religious faith that accepts misfortune as the will of God, so I am surprised when she answers without equivocation when I ask what is to blame for her fate.

"My husband," she says.

Santos Rosales, a preacher at the local Protestant evangelical church, died of AIDS in 1989 at the age of thirty-nine; he probably became infected from a brothel visit. This is no secret to the girls. "But you pardon him, don't you?" Marina asks Janira several times, until Janira nods a reluctant-looking yes.

At a time when North Americans are struggling to learn the rules of prevention and the most optimistic reports suggest that the disease is peaking among us, the epidemic is beginning to hit the southern half of our hemisphere with a vengeance. Today some two-thirds of the AIDS cases in the Americas are in the north—mostly the United States—and one-third are in the south, or Latin America. Within only ten years that proportion will be reversed, say international health officials. The surge in the south is part of the global spread of AIDS: by the year 2000, forty million men, women, and children worldwide will be infected. The number of AIDS orphans, or uninfected children whose parents have died of the disease—when I think of them I see Janira and Jenny alone in the wooden house—will exceed ten million worldwide by the end of the decade.

Our worlds north and south are increasingly enmeshed: thousands of American military and civilian-aid workers are stationed everywhere from Guatemala to Panama; business ties, immigration, and two-way tourism are surging. We cannot close our borders to the virus, and arguably, AIDS will not come under control in countries like our own until it is also vanquished in developing regions like Central America.

But there is another reason for watching the plague abroad: to learn from it. Jim McDermott, a doctor and Democratic congressman from Washington who cochairs the congressional International AIDS Task Force, believes that a second wave of HIV infection will inevitably break back upon the United States, hitting predominantly non-drug-using heterosexuals, taking advantage of "our own cultural reluctance to deal honestly with our sexual behaviors." The problems that health workers like Carlos Lopez face in Latin America confront us, too.

On the wall of Lopez's clinic in San Pedro Sula is a telling hand-lettered poster bearing the silhouette of a young man with AIDS titled "I Look like a Leopard." "I believe my life of homosexuality caused me this," the poster reads. "I wish I might have had children. I always wanted to have a family and a wife. I want to die as soon as I can."

Lopez, a family physician pulled into AIDS work in the absence of far-reaching government action, is a convert to one of Latin America's fast-growing evangelical Protestant sects, and his clinic is modestly financed this year by the missionary organization World Vision. But in the year since Veronica Pineda became his first patient, new cases at the clinic have grown from one a week to three a day, and Lopez says he has become realistic about many things, including the variety of people who contract AIDS, and yes, about homosexuality, which both the traditional majority Roman Catholics and the evangelicals consider immoral.

"We are not judges. We do not say you have AIDS because you sinned," he says. Then he looks across his desk graced with a blue New Testament and stacks of manila folders holding case reports. "This is my motto: live and let live."

Lopez looks tired this morning. At 2:00 A.M. he awoke to a call from the anguished mother of a seventeen-year-old glue-sniffing boy named Giovani, who may have contracted AIDS by prostituting himself for glue. The boy has just died, his mother said. Should they bury Giovani right away, or is a wake permissible? "Yes, have the wake, just don't prepare the body," Lopez told her.

Lopez and his colleagues at the Program for the Fight Against AIDS in Honduras miss every minute of lost sleep, since they receive only a bare-bones salary from the clinic and must make ends meet for their families by working in hospitals or with private patients. By next summer the church funding for the clinic will run out, and Lopez is racking his brain to figure out ways to raise money—something he's never had to do before.

He looks weary, too, from an increasingly complex clinic schedule. New patients are drawn by word of mouth, sent by other doctors who can't or won't take them or by sympathetic priests to whom the ill have gone for help. Often the infected men have been maintaining two households, which means Lopez must somehow contact both "wives" (most people don't have telephones) and convince each to come in for examination and education—but at different hours so they don't meet in the waiting room. (It was a lesson learned after several fights erupted.) The doctors have even started to send out word that gays are welcome to come to the clinic and learn about AIDS, and a small group has begun to meet weekly, "the infected helping us with the noninfected."

"We are not endorsing their lifestyle," Lopez says carefully, "but yes, now we are advocating for them, that they be protected. No one else is doing it. And if a life can't be, well, corrected . . ." Then he shoots me a what-the-heck grin and opens a huge drawer, as packed with condoms as a kid's sack is with candy on Halloween.

Lopez shuts the drawer when a knock sounds, and a twenty-two-year-old named Armando strides in, wearing cutoff jeans, the brave, thin mustache of an adolescent, and a bright, open look only slightly skewed since AIDS-related disease destroyed the sight in his left eye.

Armando says he became infected from a prostitute in Mexico after a frustrated attempt to cross the border into the United States to join a brother living in Los Angeles. "The *migra* [U.S. Border Patrol] caught me in a ditch with about a thousand other people." He grins ruefully. Now he is trying to figure out a way to get the drug AZT, which doctors believe might prolong his life. It looks out of the question: Armando can't work, most of his remaining eight siblings can't help, and his father, a lottery-ticket seller, makes only $120 a month. A fifteen-day supply of AZT costs $150. There is no government insurance safety net.

"It's a little sad . . . a sickness without a cure," Armando says, falling into a chair with all the familiarity of a young man in his living room. He boasts that he avoided alcohol and women but says, "I guess the women finally got me." Lopez rolls his eyes good-naturedly as the youth elaborates on his self-description, drawing the picture of an apprentice Don Juan with incredibly bad luck. It is clear they have come to like each other since the day a few months ago when Armando came into the clinic "just looking" for vitamins. If he contracted AIDS from a homosexual encounter, it isn't likely that Armando—who identifies himself as "normal," or heterosexual—would admit it. What North Americans think of as bisexuality simply isn't recognized as such here. "He who penetrates believes he is not committing a homosexual act," one doctor explained.

If Armando had had more information about AIDS, of course, he might have avoided the disease. But if AIDS education is difficult in a secular country like the United States, where most people can read, imagine the task in a country like Honduras, where illiteracy can run 90 percent in the countryside, where superstition—not faith in science—remains a determining force, and where it is difficult to overestimate the influence of religion.

Some evangelicals, for instance, consider AIDS another in a series of disasters, like war, that must be withstood by the faithful in preparation for the Second Coming, when mankind will be freed from the trials of this world. While the belief may comfort some, it can also encourage passivity in the face of the disease.

Health workers also complain that the Roman Catholic church prevents authorities from forcefully promoting condoms, which the church believes encourages promiscuity. The church's AIDS campaign—and it is a serious one, involving health and social workers in even far-flung villages, and stressing the need to treat victims with dignity—instead sees family stability and monogamy within marriage as the answer to the crisis.

What's left for the government-sponsored education campaigns are, mostly, ineffective extremes: terror tactics, such as the radio jingle played near Veronica's house equating AIDS with hopelessness, as well as a proliferation of highway billboards showing cuddly, faithful sheep ("Each sheep with its partner") and posters showing a presumably suggestive humming-bird with its beak in a golden flower proclaiming that fidelity is "the most sure and noble way to avoid contagion."

Armando died just as the insupportable heat of San Pedro Sula eased with seasonal rains. He became one of the statistics compiled across town at the government's Social Security Hospital, where Dr. Ada Rivera de Romero is keeping tabs on local growth of the disease with funding from Scandinavian Red Cross societies. Seven hundred eighty men and 416 women have died since the first death was recorded in 1985, that of a fifty-five-year-old orthodontist who traveled often to San Francisco and Los Angeles. The number of cases is doubling every year. But behind the numbers, Romero sees attitudes that long precede AIDS.

"Parents are so afraid their boys will be homosexuals they may take their sons to prostitution houses at age thirteen or fourteen," says Romero matter-of-factly. Then her voice takes on tones of wonder and frustration. "I confronted one of my own nurses who did this, bringing up the risk of AIDS she knows well, and she just shrugged. It's the same machismo that cuts through classes and entraps all of us, because women have it too, insisting so much on the virility of the man."

Promiscuous heterosexual men are the greatest source of infection, says Romero. Infected women generally practice serial monogamy. (Intravenous drug use and sex for drugs—big factors in the U.S. spread of AIDS—are negligible here.) "Another problem we identified is that the men don't want to use condoms. Many think the frequency is what counts. They say, 'We just have sex once in a while, so we don't need a condom.'"

Romero is a good example of a highly qualified, dedicated public-health worker crippled by the government's archaic organization, lack of equipment, and shortage of personnel and money. Like virtually every other health professional involved with AIDS I talked to over six months, she now must split her time to prepare for cholera, too, which is threatening the Latin American continent for the first time in a century. Sensitive to what tells a story best, Romero picks up a completed questionnaire at random from a pile, blocks out the man's name, and lets me jot quick notes, typical answers to the Red Cross survey from a laborer stricken with AIDS:

How many women can a man have before he's considered a womanizer?
  Answer: five.
Yes, I believe prostitution is necessary for the man.
No, I don't know any homosexuals.
Women become prostitutes because they've been tricked into the life or they
  like it.

In red crayon letters, scrawled across the bottom of the survey: "Died, December 13, 1990."

By June, Veronica Pineda's body can no longer withstand the onslaught of the disease. In Central America a person diagnosed with AIDS lives an average of six months; poorer general health means opportunistic diseases like tuberculosis and simple diarrhea take a quick toll. (The U.S. survival rate is moving toward nine years after HIV infection.) Because women here are in even poorer health than men, those infected by their husbands generally die first. Veronica is an exception to that rule.

"But now everything is out of control," Carlos says to me one day as we drive the narrow unpaved road to Veronica's house. "High blood pressure. Uric acid. Gout. . . ." I have seen him with several patients over the months, concerned but professionally cool, but somehow Veronica's case has gotten to him. This skinny, bedridden woman's refusal to slip away when medical sense says she should have been gone months ago is, I suspect, making him root for a miracle.

"She doesn't want to leave her girls yet," Marina tells me. Daughter Janira is warming towels with an iron, and Marina applies them to Veronica's knees. We help Veronica turn—she can't even do that by herself now. Carlos has brought along a gallon of disinfectant concentrate, blood red and creamy, and dispenses some into a bottle so they can continue to bathe a wound on Veronica's forehead, which she suffered in a fall while trying to go to the bathroom by herself. "But be careful not to touch the blood," he warns. On the TV screen, *The Golden Girls,* the women looking incredibly plump compared with the women in this room, chatter and pull faces in black and white while the laugh track punishes the air. It is all too surreal for a twelve-year-old, no matter how much she loves her mother, and little Jenny bolts out of the room toward the sunshine.

"This is what hurts me the most," whispers Veronica, and it's clear she means leaving her daughters. It is also clear there will be no miracles. Carlos excuses himself, saying he needs a break for a soda. When he returns half an hour later, it is with the forced smile and the cracked voice of a man who has been crying.

I stoop by the side of the bed to stroke Veronica's arm and also because I can't make out what she is saying from where I stand. The arm is alarming—just bone really—and she looks at me when I touch her as if to say, "You see how it is?" We are quiet for a while until she murmurs something

I can't make out. I look helplessly at Marina. "She is asking you, 'Why live if it is like this?'"

When a friend discovered I was looking at AIDS in Central America, she warned me passionately not to focus on prostitutes as carriers, "or they'll be blamed for something that isn't their fault." Blame, no. But anyone who ignores prostitution local-style in the fight to stop the disease's spread will deny a phenomenon of truly destructive—even evil—proportions.

Prostitution here reflects ideas about sex, servitude, and the role of authorities that in many ways have gone unchanged since the Spanish conquest five hundred years ago. Like the arms trade, the sex trade represents big money, it is beyond the reach of public outrage, and it has protectors in high places. Often it's most visible where soldiers hang out, on sleazy strips in provincial towns frequented by the wide-eyed conscripts of the region's bloated armies, in slicker discos and hotel lobbies where one sees some of the thousands of U.S. (and in Belize, British) military personnel based in the region. But prostitution is elsewhere, too, in market towns and migrant camps where peasants live while picking cotton or coffee, in glittering urban clubs where the young moneyed go to have fun, and in private networks that cater to businessmen.

It is ten o'clock on a weeknight, and I am sitting on a single bed in a dank room, the center of the universe for a twenty-five-year-old woman named Santos. It is the size of a walk-in closet. Above the bed is a rack of short skirts and dresses. On one wall are a picture of Santos looking very dignified, the kind of black-and-white photograph a young person might order when she wants to apply for a job and show she is serious and responsible; and another photo in color of herself and a girlfriend smiling in the open air, the scene a relic from another world. There is no picture of her ten-year-old son, also called Santos. She last saw him a year ago, before she was traded to this brothel for five hundred dollars by a woman who lured her to the city from her rural home with a vague promise of work.

The world of the white slave—a woman or a girl held unwillingly for the purposes of prostitution—is dreary. Escape is impossible. The police—in league with brothel owners—will bring her back, and she'll get another beating for her trouble. In this room are no books or magazines, no pencil or paper, no other furniture except a small table on which are arranged three oranges, some eye shadow, three bottles of shampoo, and an iron. There are nine rooms just like this one around us, inhabited by women in the same situation as Santos, who can't leave the brothel until she pays back the five hundred dollars the owner paid the woman broker. That may take a long time to earn. Santos is expected to turn in chits for twenty tricks a week, at four dollars a trick, but three dollars is deducted from each encounter for room, food, and cosmetics. Since Santos must pay the brothel owners for clothes, too, which must be new and snazzy to attract clients, the remaining dollar a trick [earns] disappears as if to a company store, and in fact she is in debt far beyond the original five hundred dollars.

"We are conquered," Santos tells me. "But it's no use crying, because that just takes away from your life." How long will she have to work here? "I'll die here," she says.

Like other prostitutes I talk to in San Pedro Sula, even those who are not part of the *trata de blancas,* or white-slave system, Santos says she knows what AIDS is, but she doesn't dwell on the consequences of contracting it. The apparent passivity—it looks to me like a survival tactic—recedes only once, when her eyes flare in anger at the brothel owner, on whose behalf she may already have become infected. "I'm afraid of it, yes. But it's like a lot of things where somebody else enjoys the fruit of the work and you pay the price."

Leaving Santos's airless stall, I pass the smelly communal toilets to reach the barroom and dance floor, where clients are arriving for the evening. The decor of the big room is a mix between the O.K. Corral and the Circus of Horrors, with wood-slat tables and low clouds of half-deflated colored balloons. It occurs to me that this is the kind of place where Veronica's husband contracted the disease that tore their family apart and left her across town immobile on the clean white bed, hostage to the dull gray eye of the television set. I listen to a couple of songs the women play on the juke-box with coins the men have given them and walk out with their titles in my head: "Your Prison" and "Love Without Words."

In a 1989 study of 338 local prostitutes, municipal social worker Ricardo Ruiz found 69 with AIDS, many of whom had five sexual encounters a day. "Multiply that," he says. (Another health official, in Tegucigalpa, the country's capital, estimated that a third of the region's prostitutes were infected by now.) Even those who solicit on the streets or work in "date houses," who are ostensibly more independent than women like Santos, are not truly free to turn down a man who won't use a condom, Ruiz says.

"I asked the women, 'Aren't you afraid of getting AIDS?' 'Yes,' they'd say, but they are just very poor. 'Look, the customer is paying me twelve dollars,' they'd say. 'I have three children. I can't say no.'"

When Ruiz's team tried closing brothels for not providing condoms, owners relocated their women to other houses. Today that AIDS program is abandoned, and Ricardo Ruiz has a new job, running the city's Department of Environmental Health and Cemeteries. But during the time I spent in San Pedro Sula, Ruiz agreed to go with me to his former working turf, to places where the sex trade flourishes and with it the risk of AIDS. These were not like the white-slave houses, where I met women like Santos, but they still had guards armed with rifles and pistols to keep away trouble.

Our trips take in rich neighborhoods and poor—the business covers the map. At one blue house distinguished only by a red porch light in a quiet residential tract, the brothel owner delivers young girls in a station wagon at the beginning of the evening, as if to a high school dance. In a rougher barrio, where vendors cook cheap food over open fires on the sidewalk, a twenty-three-year-old mother named Jackie with a peroxide wash on her pretty long hair sits on a cement block in a littered dirt yard and tells me her dreams of working as a hairdresser in Los Angeles. Inside, clients lounge on frayed flowered couches under walls draped with a huge American flag and posters of Bruce Lee. ("We like the colors," one of the children who live in the brothel tells me.) Very late that night Ruiz leads me to Cleo's Barr, near the railroad tracks that lead to the banana ports on the sea. Here the prostitutes call themselves waitresses, make twenty-five dollars a month after room rent, and like to kick off their high heels and slip into a back chamber to play with the two-month-old pale-eyed son of a thirty-one-year-old named Juana, who keeps the child covered with clean rags next to cases of empty pop bottles.

What all the women around town have in common is a frightening lack of knowledge about the plague in their midst. Carmen, who has worked at Cleo's Barr for nine years, explains the disease to me in a typical way: "If you catch it early, you take some pills and don't stay up too much at night. You need plenty of sleep with AIDS. If you do that you'll be all right."

In the early hours of one morning, Ruiz escorts me back to my hotel but looks startled to see the somber-eyed woman I have noticed for several nights apparently soliciting sex out front. "Where do you know her from, the brothels?" I ask.

"No," he says. He recognizes her from his new job, which takes him regularly to the city's cemetery. The woman, who has three small children, comes every day to visit the grave of her husband, who died about six months ago. "I guess it's her way of supporting the family," Ruiz says. I leave him gently greeting the woman, who looks embarrassed but grateful to see a friendly face under the streetlight.

> The extent of its ravages was never known, not because this was impossible to establish but because one of our most widespread virtues was a certain reticence concerning personal misfortune.
>
> —Gabriel Garcia Marquez, *Love in the Time of Cholera*

In some ways, we may never know how hard AIDS is hitting Central America. The region is just beginning to recover from two decades of political violence costing 250,000 lives; both war and AIDS strike economically active young men and women. What are the real numbers? In a regional population of some thirty million, where many people don't see doctors, deaths from AIDS can easily blend unrecognized into deaths attributed to tuberculosis, diarrhea, or "bad airs." Officially Honduras, which may have the most government support behind its health ministry's AIDS programs, counts 1,344 cases, or 50 percent of the region's total, while Nicaragua reports what health experts consider a ridiculously low 11 cases. Health workers in neighboring countries—El Salvador, Guatemala, Panama, and to a lesser extent, Costa Rica—also agree that reported figures are not yet an accurate indicator of the breadth of the crisis.

What does seem clear is that the social sins of past decades—for that is the language that might be used in these cities and mountains—have come back to haunt the moment, making prevention and treatment of "the new disease" hard. You cannot, as one Catholic activist on the National AIDS Commission tells me, effectively treat the medical problem if women have no recourse to laws that protect them and have little say in their own homes. You cannot, as one public-health doctor tells me, insist on a share of extremely limited government funds for treating AIDS patients, who will certainly die, when there are so many cases of infant malnutrition, "against which we have a chance." A local director of the La Leche League says you cannot tell women with AIDS not to breast-feed, despite the odds of infection, when they are so poor they can't afford store-bought milk or medicines and breast milk may save babies from the bigger odds of death by diarrhea.

"We have no more cases of rabies in humans, and instead of a polio epidemic every four years, we haven't had a single case in two years," Dr. Enrique Zelaya, the government's chief epidemiologist, tells me proudly in Tegucigalpa. But now Zelaya has AIDS and cholera to deal with at the same time. "Cholera and AIDS have something in common," he says. "Both *desnudan,* reveal to the naked skin, the poverty factors that hurt prevention: the lack of education, the lack of means even to keep yourself clean."

The last day I spend with Carlos Lopez is unforgettable. Inevitably, given a disease that recognizes no barriers of geography or economic class, Carlos has discovered that someone close to him—his own brother—has become infected. He confesses he hasn't told him yet, wondering which words to use and seeking "the right moment." He is no longer strictly on the outside: AIDS has hit home in a way Carlos might never have imagined when he opened this clinic over a year ago.

Carlos Lopez's reticence to inform his loved one right away is not just the full flowering of some Latin characteristic that Garcia Marquez describes —it feels universal. "But, Carlos," I ask, "isn't this denial on your part, just like some of your patients? While you hesitate, doesn't it mean someone else might get infected as a result?"

"No," he says, too defiantly, but offers nothing more.

The door isn't closed firmly to the empty waiting room, and now the wind that precedes the night storm blows it ajar.

"Well, you can rest now," I say. "Look, no patients."

He composes his drawn face and smiles, professional again.

"There will be more tomorrow," he says.

On Veronica Pineda's fortieth birthday, a Tuesday, she seems happier than she has been in weeks. Her brother has brought a half dozen church members to sing joyous hymns around her bed. She asks her daughter for help with the clapping, so Janira takes one of her mother's hands in each of her own and brings them together over and over to the rhythm of the music. Veronica mouths the words, and her eyes sing, "I praise you with prayer,/If I don't have voice I praise you with my hands."

On Thursday Janira wakes to find Veronica has died in her sleep in the bed next to hers. Little Jenny runs crying across the street for help, to find a neighbor with a motorcycle who can take her to find her uncle. They bury Veronica in a free space in an old cemetery that is hardly visited anymore, where funeral offerings gone feral form a wild, but not unattractive, backdrop to her grave.

STUDY QUESTIONS

1. What were the circumstances surrounding Veronica Pineda's infection with HIV?
2. According to McConahay, how is the distribution of AIDS cases in the Americas likely to change over the 1990s?
3. What impact is the increase of HIV/AIDS in Latin America likely to have on the distribution of HIV/AIDS in the United States?
4. What cultural factors currently limit HIV/AIDS education in Latin America?
5. How do culturally specific ideas about sexuality support and foster prostitution in Latin America?
6. How has prostitution become a major vector of HIV/AIDS transmission in Latin America?
7. How does the limited legal recourse available to Latin American women foster HIV transmission?

Sexual Behavior and AIDS Knowledge of Young Male Prostitutes in Manhattan

Richard R. Pleak and Heino F. L. Meyer-Bahlburg

Male prostitutes for men ("hustlers") are thought to constitute a large proportion of the prostituting population.* Kinsey and his colleagues estimated that male "homosexual prostitutes are, in many large cities, not far inferior in number to the females who are engaged in heterosexual prostitution" (Kinsey,

---

* The authors intend this generalization to refer to the gendered structure of prostitution in the United States.

This selection has been edited. Readers interested in the details of subject selection and statistical analysis should refer to the original article.

Reprinted with permission from *The Journal of Sex Research,* vol. 27, no. 4 (November 1990):557–587. © 1990 by The Society for Scientific Study of Sex.

Pomeroy, & Martin, 1948), although no epidemiological data exist to verify this estimate even now. Male prostitutes, who largely are engaged in sexual activities with multiple male partners, have been presumed to act as an important vector in the transmission of the ascribed etiologic agent of AIDS (acquired immune deficiency syndrome), HIV-1 (human immunodeficiency virus, type 1) (e.g., Coutinho, van Andel, & Rijsdijk, 1988; Velimirovic, 1987).

Recently, male prostitutes have been studied in greater depth, due primarily to their presumed role in the AIDS epidemic. In a model HIV antibody prevalence protocol, Elifson and colleagues (Boles, Elifson, & Sweat, 1989; Elifson, Boles, Sweat, & Darrow, 1989a; Elifson, Boles, Sweat, Darrow, Elsea, & Green, 1989b) reported on 194 male street prostitutes in Atlanta. They conducted brief interviews focusing on sexual history, drug use, social networks, and health issues. Blood samples were collected in the street areas, with at least two investigators present at all times (Mike Sweat, personal communication, 1989). Of their 194 subjects, 24.7% were found to be HIV-1 antibody positive (Elifson et al., 1989a), about the same incidence (or slightly higher) as gay men in Atlanta (Mike Sweat & Kirk Elifson, personal communication, 1989). This HIV antibody seropositivity was significantly associated with presence of hepatitis B antibodies, presence of syphilis seromarkers, practice of receptive anal intercourse, intermittent condom use, and hustling for at least 10 years, but was not associated with sexual orientation (their sample was approximately 44% heterosexual, 27% bisexual, and 29% homosexual, by self-identification). Coutinho, van Andel, and Rijsdijk (1988) did HIV antibody testing on 32 male prostitutes from brothels in Amsterdam and found 13% to be seropositive, less than the prevalence of seropositivity in homosexual men in Amsterdam (about 31%). Chiasson, Lifson, Stoneburner, Ewing, Hildebrant, and Jaffe (1988) determined HIV-1 antibody status in people attending a New York City clinic for sexually-transmitted diseases. Of 961 individuals, 32 males admitted to prostitution with men, and 17 (53%) of these were seropositive (none admitted to intravenous drug abuse). There were 52 males who admitted to prostitution with women, and 5 (10%) were seropositive (1 was also using IV drugs, and 3 had engaged in homosexual activity).

In another model protocol, Lauderback, Waldorf, Marotta, and Murphy interviewed 180 male street prostitutes and 180 call men from 1987 to 1989 in San Francisco, using a chain referral or snowball method of recruitment (Lauderback & Waldorf, 1989; David Lauderback, personal communication, 1989). These paid interviews covered life history, sexual behavior, and AIDS knowledge. The street subjects were younger (mean age 25 years) and less well educated (mean of 11 years of school) than the call men (mean age 31 years, mean of 13 years of school). Twenty-five percent of the street subjects were transvestites, transsexuals, or drag queens. Sixty percent of the subjects had been tested for HIV antibodies, with 10% of the street subjects and 23% of the call men reporting positive results. Ten percent of the subjects had symptomatic HIV infection, and 2% had AIDS. The subjects generally had high scores on their AIDS knowledge test, and 65–81% knew someone with AIDS. Approximately 50% were intravenous (IV) drug users (predominantly injecting methamphetamine), and 70% of these were sharing needles. Condoms were frequently used for anal intercourse, more so by the call men than the street subjects.

HIV antibody seropositivity studies including male prostitutes have also been recently initiated or completed in London, England (Peter Davies, personal communication:, 1989); Toulouse, France (Puel, Gayet-Mengelle, Averous, & Bazex:, 1989); Sao Paulo, Brazil (Santos-Ferreira, Mazza, Lourenco, Focaccia, & Veronesi, 1989; Ayroza, Suleiman, & Suleiman, 1989); Bangkok, Thailand (Sittitrai, Phanupahak, Satirakorn, Elweera, & Roddy, 1989); Northeast Italy (Tirelli, Vaccher, Bullian, Saracchini, Errante, Zagonel, & Serraino, 1988); and Sydney, Australia (Alan, Guinan, & McCallum, 1989).

The existing studies lead to several conclusions. The investigator must rely on convenience samples recruited from locations where prostitutes are known to work, as representative sampling cannot be done with male prostitutes due to the absence of epidemiologic data on this population. The samples which have been studied and are currently under study are heterogeneous in their composition in regard to such variables as age, ethnicity, socioeconomic status, sexual orientation, gender role (masculine, cross-dressing, transsexual), mode of operation (street work, bar solicitation, advertisements, etc.), and drug abuse. Given this variability in sample composition, it is not surprising that the existing reports on male prostitutes differ considerably in their HIV antibody seroprevalence findings. Nevertheless, the studies are in agreement that the seroprevalence among male prostitutes is much higher than in the general population and, therefore, male prostitutes have to be considered an "at risk" population.

The aim of the current study was to conduct a comprehensive behavioral investigation of young male prostitutes for men in New York using semi-structured and structured instruments to cover patterns of sexual behavior, knowledge of AIDS, current and past psychopathology, history of gender-role behavior, and factors associated with entering prostitution. The long-range goal was to provide data sufficient for designing and implementing intervention programs for male prostitutes in New York, which could be assessed for efficacy using methods employed herein for initial and follow-up interviews. The current report presents the data on sexual behavior patterns and on AIDS knowledge.

Results

Subject Characteristics

Fifty out of 58 male prostitutes (86%) who were approached for this study were interviewed, 25 from the street and 25 from bars and theaters. All 50 completed the sections on sexual behavior and AIDS knowledge. None of these subjects objected to or refused to answer any questions in these sections. Three male prostitutes declined to be interviewed, 2 because the study payment was lower than they could receive in the same amount of time by prostituting, and 1 because he thought he would not be a good candidate, since he provided only companionship and not sex for his clients.

The age range for the 50 subjects was 14–27 years, with a mean of 20.7 years. Street subjects were significantly younger (range 14–27, mean 19.3 years) than bar/theater subjects (range 17–26, mean 21.7 years). The ethnic composition for the whole sample was 42% white, 22% Hispanic, 12% mixed Native American/white or black, 10% mixed Hispanic/white, 8% black, 4% mulatto, and 2% Indian. The street subject group, compared to the bar/theater group, had less whites (28% vs. 56%), more Hispanics or mixed Hispanic/whites (52% vs. 12%), more blacks or mulattos (20% vs. 4%), and had no Native Americans (0% vs. 24%). The subjects had a mean of 12.26 ($SD \pm 2.44$) years of school. Their parents had a mean of 12.94 (±2.84) years of school, and mean Hollingshead (1975) occupational level of 4.87 (±1.91). Other demographic characteristics will be reported elsewhere.

Sexual Behavior

None of the subjects had ever been involved in sex rings or had had pimps. Six had been involved in escort service work, and 3 were actively involved in pornographic magazines and movies/videotapes which involved anal intercourse without condoms. Two subjects had cross-dressed when younger for the purpose of prostitution. Two of the street subjects were also occasionally hustling in bars or theaters, and one of the bar/theater subjects was also occasionally hustling on the streets.

The subjects had been involved in homosexual prostitution for an average of 3.0 years (range: 3 days to 14 years), having started at an average age of 17.6 years (range: 12–24 years). Almost half of the subjects had at times been paid for sex with drugs. The mean number of subjects' lifetime (male) clients was 495, median 90 (range: 1–9,980), with a mean of 835 sexual encounters, median 142.5 (range 1–14,000). Table 1 shows the number of subjects engaging in various sexual activities with men, the number of times for each activity, the mean percentage of condom use for each activity, and the mean percentage of unprotected ejaculation for each activity in the 3 months prior to being interviewed. Forty percent of subjects had not engaged in active (insertive) anal intercourse with men in these 3 months, while 67% had not engaged in passive (receptive) anal intercourse. Twenty-nine percent had not engaged in either form of anal intercourse. None of the subjects had been involved in fisting or in serious sadomasochistic or scatologic sex in these 3 months, i.e., sex intentionally involving urine, blood, piercing of body parts, or other serious bodily harm. During sex with

Table 1 • Subjects' Sexual Activities and Condom Use
in Three Months

Sexual Activity and Partner Type	Street Subjects ($N = 25$)			
	Number of Subjects	Mean Number of Times	Mean Percentage Condom Use	Mean Percentage Unprotected Ejaculation
Subject Fellated (Passive)				
Male for money	23	31.7	42.7	18.0
Male for pleasure	4	25.8	25.0	50.0
Female for pleasure	11	19.5	9.1	27.0
Female for money	1	12.0	0	0
Subject Fellates (Receptive)				
Male for money	14	42.6	59.0	2.9
Male for pleasure	3	26.3	66.7	0
Anal Intercourse, Receptive				
Male for money	3	11.0	100	0
Male for pleasure	1	3.0	100	0
Anal Intercourse, Active				
Male for money	11	13.8	89.1	9.1
Male for pleasure	2	18.0	4.2[a]	41.7
Female for pleasure	5	5.4	6.0	0
Female for money	0	—	—	—
Vaginal Intercourse				
Female for pleasure	16	25.4	37.5	26.3
Female for money	0	—	—	—
Rimming, Active				
Male for money	1	1.0	—	—
Male for pleasure	0	—	—	—
Rimming, Passive				
Male for money	9	7.2	—	—
Male for pleasure	3	8.0	—	—

Continued

men, 60% and 72% reported having been sometimes or always under the influence of alcohol or drugs, respectively.

Sixteen subjects had also been involved in heterosexual prostitution, with a mean of 3.4 lifetime (female) clients, median 2 (range: 1–10) for a mean of 18.7 sexual encounters, median 3.5 (range: 1–200). For each of these 16 subjects, their activity in homosexual prostitution exceeded that in heterosexual prostitution. One subject had begun prostituting heterosexually as a gigolo, later moving on to sex for pay with men. The others became involved in sex for pay with women later and more incidentally, such as being picked up by women while soliciting for men. All but 1 of the 50 sub-

Table 1   continued

Sexual Activity and Partner Type	Bar/Theater Subjects (N = 25)			
	Number of Subjects	Mean Number of Times	Mean Percentage Condom Use	Mean Percentage Unprotected Ejaculation
Subject Fellated (Passive)				
Male for money	23	53.8	33.7	1.8
Male for pleasure	20	16.8	18.2	3.0
Female for pleasure	7	24.0	0	5.2
Female for money	1	14.0	0	14.3
Subject Fellates (Receptive)				
Male for money	16	15.6	64.1[b]	0
Male for pleasure	19	15.5	21.2[b]	2.0
Anal Intercourse, Receptive				
Male for money	8	19.8	80.0	0
Male for pleasure	12	13.7	80.7	2.4
Anal Intercourse, Active				
Male for money	14	30.4	90.0	0.1
Male for pleasure	14	14.6	82.2[a]	11.8
Female for pleasure	2	4.9	25.0	25.0
Female for money	1	2.0	0.0	100
Vaginal Intercourse				
Female for pleasure	7	40.1	16.2	31.2
Female for money	1	14.0	0.0	71.4
Rimming, Active				
Male for money	3	10.7	—	—
Male for pleasure	8	6.9	—	—
Rimming, Passive				
Male for money	17	11.1	—	—
Male for pleasure	12	8.6	—	—

Continued

jects had had sexual encounters with women in their lifetime (for payment or pleasure), with a mean of 42.4 partners, median 10 (range: 1–1,000) for a mean of 179.9 sexual encounters, median 29 (range: 2–2,000). Ten subjects had paid female prostitutes for sex, with a mean of 2.7 prostitute partners, median 1 (range: 1–6) for a mean of 14.0 sexual encounters, median 2.5 (range: 1–100). Street subjects did not significantly differ from bar/theater subjects in these lifetime measures.

In the 3-month period prior to the interviews, only 2 subjects had engaged in heterosexual prostitution, each with 1 client for 12 and 14 sexual encounters. Twenty-four subjects had had sex for pleasure with women

Table 1   continued

	All Subjects (N = 50)			
Sexual Activity and Partner Type	Number of Subjects	Mean Number of Times	Mean Percentage Condom Use	Mean Percentage Unprotected Ejaculation
Subject Fellated (Passive)				
Male for money	46	42.8	38.2	9.9
Male for pleasure	24	18.3	19.4	10.8
Female for pleasure	18	21.2	5.6	18.5
Female for money	2	13.0	0	7.1
Subject Fellates (Receptive)				
Male for money	30	28.2	61.7[c]	1.3
Male for pleasure	22	17.0	27.4[c]	1.7
Anal Intercourse, Receptive				
Male for money	11	17.3	85.4	0
Male for pleasure	13	12.8	82.1	2.2
Anal Intercourse, Active				
Male for money	25	23.1	89.6	4.1
Male for pleasure	16	15.1	72.4	15.5
Female for pleasure	7	5.0	50.0	7.1
Female for money	1	1.0	0.0	100
Vaginal Intercourse				
Female for pleasure	23	29.9	31.0	27.8
Female for money	1	7.0	0.0	71.4
Rimming, Active				
Male for money	4	8.3	—	—
Male for pleasure	8	6.9	—	—
Rimming, Passive				
Male for money	26	9.8	—	—
Male for pleasure	15	8.5	—	—

[a]Significant difference between street and bar/theater subjects, $t = 3.4$, $p < 0.005$.
[b]Significant difference between male partners for money and pleasure, $t = 4.4$, $p < 0.0007$.
[c]Significant difference between male partners for money and pleasure, $t = 2.4$, $p < 0.03$.

in this period, with an average of 9.1 partners, median 2.5 (range: 1–100) for a mean of 36.5 sexual encounters, median 11 (range: 1–300). The number of subjects engaging in various sexual activities with women, the number of times for each activity, and the percentage of condom use for each activity over 3 months are shown in Table 1. During sex with women, 52% and 44% reported having been sometimes or always under the influence of alcohol or drugs, respectively.

HIV Status and AIDS Knowledge

Twenty-eight subjects reported having been tested for HIV antibody at least once, usually at city HIV antibody testing centers, city STD clinics, or private physician offices. Two subjects did not return to learn their results, 25 reported negative results, and 1 reported a positive result. None reported any clinical signs of HIV infection or AIDS, and none appeared overtly symptomatic. Regardless of stated test results, subjects were asked what they thought their chances were of having been infected with the virus that causes AIDS. Eight subjects (7 street and 1 bar/theater) thought their chances were zero, 17 thought their chances were from 1–10%, 8 thought 12–20%, 8 thought 25–40%, 4 thought 50%, 2 thought 60%, 1 thought 90%, and 1 (aside from the subject who tested positive) thought 100%. Overall street subjects did not significantly differ from bar/theater subjects on this measure. Thirty-two subjects reported having had at least one sexually-transmitted disease (STD) in their lifetime: 22 having had crabs (lice), 18 gonorrhea, 8 syphilis, 5 nonspecific urethritis, 2 anal warts, and 1 herpes.

Twenty-six percent of the sample knew at least one person (range: 1–30 people) personally who tested positive for HIV antibody, but who was not symptomatic. Forty-eight percent knew someone (range: 1–5 people) with what has been called ARC (AIDS-related complex, now subsumed into symptomatic HIV infection or HIV-spectrum disease) or with AIDS, including one subject who had a sibling with AIDS. Fifty-four percent knew someone (range: 1–10 people) who had died of ARC or AIDS. Altogether, 84% knew someone in one of the 3 above categories (HIV antibody positive, has ARC/AIDS, or died of it). Only 3 subjects reported having had sex with someone they knew, or later found out, to have tested positive to HIV antibodies or to have ARC or AIDS.

On the Safe Sex Awareness Scale, the subjects rated such activities as dry kissing, massaging, and mutual masturbation to be safe (means from 1.1–1.4 on a 5-point scale, where 1 = safe, 3 = possibly safe, and 5 = unsafe). Tongue kissing, unprotected (without a condom) fellating without ejaculation, and anal intercourse using a condom were rated possibly safe (means from 2.3–3.8). Swallowing semen and unprotected anal intercourse (active or receptive) were rated unsafe (means 4.2–5), with unprotected receptive anal intercourse with ejaculation rated 5 by all subjects.

The mean score on the total AIDS Knowledge questionnaire was quite high, at 85.7% correct. These scores were positively correlated with age and with education. Although bar/theater subjects appeared to score significantly better than street subjects on 4 components and the total, these differences, except for the Transmission component, became nonsignificant trends (in the same direction) when subjects were matched for age. Individual items with mean scores below 75% correct included knowing that: most people infected with HIV look healthy (52%), most people infected with HIV don't have AIDS (52%), it is easier for a man to give AIDS to a woman than vice versa (52%), lambskin condoms are less safe than latex ones (60%), needles sterilized with bleach or vodka are safer than unsterilized ones (62%), and tongue kissing has not been known to lead to AIDS (66%).

Substance Abuse and Dependence

The subjects' rates of current substance abuse or dependence diagnoses (DSM-III-R, American Psychiatric Association, 1987) were high: 18% for alcohol, 30% for marijuana, 26% for cocaine (including crack), and 8% for other drugs (stimulants, opiates, hallucinogens). Forty-four percent had at least one current substance abuse/dependence diagnosis. There were no significant differences between numbers of street vs. bar/theater subjects with these diagnoses. Only 3 subjects reported to have ever injected drugs intravenously, and all denied sharing needles.

Associations

Percentages of condom use were not significantly correlated with age, education, Kinsey score, age at starting prostitution, duration of prostitution, perceived chance of being infected with HIV, number of people known who have tested positive for HIV antibodies or who have ARC/AIDS or died of ARC/AIDS, nor history of STDs. Psychopathology was not associated with condom use, except for a trend towards lesser use in those subjects with major depression. Drug and alcohol abuse were not associated with less condom use; indeed, many subjects reported *more* condom use when using cocaine, since the cocaine made them feel more "paranoid." Ethnicity was also not associated with mean percentage of condom use, except in vaginal intercourse, where whites used condoms less than the other ethnic groups combined. Subjects' condom use for various sexual activities correlated weakly and positively with their ratings of the unsafeness of each activity, except for a strong correlation of their rating with unprotected receptive anal intercourse without ejaculation.

Greater AIDS knowledge also appeared to be associated with less ejaculation by subjects inside their male partners. Percentage of unprotected ejaculation for the subjects' being fellated by their male clients correlated significantly and negatively with several AIDS Knowledge scales. Also, a trend toward significance was found for negative correlations of AIDS knowledge with unprotected ejaculation in active anal intercourse with male clients and partners for pleasure. No such association was found for unprotected ejaculation inside female partners nor inside the subjects themselves.

Those subjects who abstained from any anal intercourse with men ($N = 14$) tended to score lower on AIDS knowledge than those who participated in anal intercourse ($N = 34$); however, these differences were not significant by t test. The abstainers also tended to be younger than the participators (mean age 19.6 years vs. 21.1 years), which again was not significant by *t* test.

Discussion

The present study confirms results from other studies showing that male prostitutes can be heterosexual, bisexual, or homosexual (see also Hoffman, 1972). However, studies done in the later 1970s and the 1980s, including the present report, have found increasing proportions of male prostitutes to be bisexual or homosexual. Based on observations from the present study that some male prostitutes deny pleasure from most of the sexual activities they engage in for pay, Kinsey ratings of prostitutes' sexual behavior should differentiate between sex for pay and sex for pleasure. Ratings for sexual behavior for pleasure can then be combined with ratings for erotic fantasy, as has been done in the present study. Many of the self-identified straight objects in this study, when interviewed in depth about their sexual responsiveness during sex for pay with men, admitted to sometimes being erotically aroused my their male clients and sometimes having homosexual fantasies during masturbation.

Condoms can provide an effective barrier against HIV (Rietmeijer, Krebs, Feorino, & Judson, 1988), they are widely promoted as a means of increasing the safety of sex, and they have been shown to be effective in reducing rates of HIV antibody seroconversion. The extensive condom use shown in this study was higher than expected by the authors, particularly for anal intercourse. This may be due to exaggeration by the subjects, perhaps to make themselves appear to be less at risk. However, few subjects reported 100% condom use, differential frequencies of condom use were found for different partners, and subjects were not reluctant to report on other risky activities. This makes it less likely that subjects grossly exaggerated condom use. The subjects, as expected, were safer with their male clients than with their male partners for pleasure. This possibly is due to the subjects' perceptions of higher risk for HIV infection/AIDS with clients than with their lovers, whom they presume to know better. It may also be due to the subjects' not wanting to be perceived as possibly unsafe by their lovers ("If I ask to use a condom, he'll think I'm unsafe or fooling around"). The subjects were least safe with their female partners, where perceived risk is low. These patterns of differential condom use (higher with clients or casual partners than with lovers, lower with female than male partners) have also been observed in San Franciscan male street prostitutes and call men by Lauderback and Waldorf (1989); male street prostitutes in Atlanta by Sweat (personal communication, 1989); young male and female prostitutes in Sydney, Australia, by Gold, Griggs, Toomey, Alan, Turbitt, Anns, and McElwee (1989); Canadian adolescents who were school dropouts and/or homeless by Radford, Warren, and King (1989); and by Rekart, Manzou, and Loftus (1989); homosexual men in

England by Boulton, Fitzpatrick, Hart, Dawson, and McClean (1989); hetero-sexual Amsterdam men with female lovers and prostitute partners by Hooykaas, Van der Pligt, Van Doornum, Van der Linden, and Coutinho (1989); and Californian college adolescents by DiClemente, Forrest, and Mickler (1989). Such differential condom use between sexual activities and types of partners shows the importance of obtaining detailed information on condom use. Studies asking simply how often a subject uses condoms are not particularly useful for planning and assessing intervention programs, and such data cannot be compared to results from other studies.

Subjects indicated that they were more likely to use condoms if their peers were using them. This peer-based identification in condom use has also been observed among male prostitutes in Toronto (Danny, Cockerline, personal communication, 1989) and in Californian adolescents (DiClemente & DuNah, 1989). The 27 subjects involved in rimming (oral-anal contact) did not use protection other than washing, except for one subject who used plastic wrap or latex for both active and passive rimming. Rimming was perceived to be a moderate-risk activity which does not yet have peer- or community-based norms for protection. Most subjects saw fisting as a high-risk activity, and all abstained from it.

It should be noted that many of the subjects' paid encounters with clients involved mutual masturbation as the only sexual activity, or did not involve sex at all. For example, the client might pay the subject to undress, to accompany him to a restaurant or show, or to go on vacation with him. Explicit data on the numbers of such nonsexual encounters were not obtained. Of all sexual encounters with customers, 86% involved masturba-tion, 71% involved fellatio (22% subject fellating client), and only 17% involved anal intercourse (4% subject receptive).

The subjects had a very good overall didactic knowledge about AIDS and HIV and appeared more knowledgeable than either youths in shelters or gay youths. (Rotheram-Borus, Bradley, Pleak, McCandless, & Martin, 1987), although this difference is probably due to the older age range in the prostituting sample. Such a high level of AIDS knowledge was also found in Lauderback and Waldorf's (1989) sample. The subjects were most defi-cient in knowledge about the latency period between infection and symp-toms, generally believing that most people infected with HIV are ill and will show signs of this illness that the subjects can recognize ("I can tell by bumps and rashes, or if he's skinny and dirty, then I won't go with him"). The subjects in the present study also tended to believe that a man was just as likely to acquire HIV from a woman as vice versa. Although this would seem to indicate equal safety in sex with men or women, the subjects per-ceived their own female partners as being safe, even though some of these female partners had multiple partners and/or were involved in prostitution themselves. This seemed to be accompanied by denial or underestimation of the subject's chances of being infected and his own ability to transmit the virus to others. None of the subjects gave any indication that he actively and overtly wished to infect others.

AIDS knowledge in this group is related to less condom use for lower risk activities such as oral sex, and more condom use for higher risk activities such as anal sex. This finding contrasts with other reports which have shown little relationship between AIDS knowledge and sexual risk behavior, e.g. in adolescents (McCandless, Rotheram-Borus, Bradley, Pleak, & Martin, 1988) or in adult gay men (Kohn, Gibson, & Bolan, 1989). Many of the more knowledgeable subjects were aware of 1988–1989 changes in guidelines for safer sex by AIDS organizations in Toronto and New York, which they felt supported their not using condoms for fellatio. Some subjects regularly read reports about AIDS in the New York *Native* or in *The New York Times* and based their willingness to have unprotected fellatio upon such reports, while practicing protected anal intercourse if any. In general, however, the subjects perceived their risk for HIV infection to be low even though they engaged in high-risk activities at times. This was especially true in the younger subjects, which may reflect the adolescent sense of invulnerability. The lack of significant associations between condom use and other variables was surprising, especially for the subjects' personal knowledge of people with HIV infection and/or AIDS. This may be due to actual lack of association, or may be due to the small sample size with lack of power to find such associations significant.

Although drug abuse/dependence was frequent, intravenous drug abuse was reported by few of the subjects. This may be due to underreporting by the subjects as a result of sample bias in excluding the frequently cross-dressing street hustlers who, from clinical observations by the first author, appear to be greater drug abusers (of heroin and other IV drugs as well as crack) than the subjects. The 3 subjects who were using IV drugs stated they did not share needles and that sterile needles were readily purchasable on the street. The subjects had high rates of substance abuse during sexual encounters, most of marijuana, cocaine, and alcohol. Although intoxication may make safer sex less easy to maintain, such an association was not found here.

The findings from this study indicate that Manhattan male prostitutes are engaging in safer sexual practices to a large degree with their customers, but there is room for further reduction in risk, especially in sex for pleasure. It is impossible to know how much these prostitutes' sexual behavior has changed because of the AIDS pandemic, since no detailed sexual behavior data are available for comparison. Deficits on some of the AIDS Knowledge questionnaire items and informal conversations with subjects lead the authors to believe that AIDS education in this group should be focused upon the risks of transmission by and to the male prostitute even in early, asymptomatic stages of HIV infection. Intervention programs appear more likely to succeed if selected male prostitutes (or former ones) are trained to educate their peer prostitutes about HIV/AIDS and safer sex practices and to distribute condoms. These peer counselors may provide role models and greater acceptance for safer sex among male prostitutes, as has occurred in Toronto (Cockerline, 1989, and personal communication 1989) and in Sydney (Gold et al., 1989). Additionally, informing street prostitutes about their right to health services and providing them with health referral information has been effective in Rio de Janeiro (Wiik, Filguerias, Castro, 1989). These intervention methods may be more cost-effective than attempting large-scale purely educational programs in this oftimes transient and mobile population.

References

Alan, D. L., Guinan, J. J., & McCallum, L. (1989). HIV seroprevalence and its implications for a transsexual population. V International Conference on AIDS, Montreal, Quebec, June 4–9, Abstract #W.D.P.34.

American Psychiatric Association. (1987). *Diagnostic and statistical manual for mental disorders, third edition—revised.* Washington, DC: American Psychiatric Association.

Ayroza, G., Suleiman, J., & Suleiman, G. (1989). HIV seroprevalence in transvestites in the city of Sao Paulo. V International Conference on Aids, Montreal, Quebec, June 4–9, Abstract #T.A.P.17.

Boles, J., Elifson, K., & Sweat, M. (1989). Male prostitutes and their customers and lovers. 142nd meeting of the American Psychiatric Association, San Francisco, May 6–11, Abstract #92D.

Boulton, M., Fitzpatrick, R., Hart, G., Dawson, J., & McClean, J. (1989). High risk sexual behavior and condom use in a sample of homosexual men in England. V International Conference on AIDS, Montreal, Quebec, June 4–9, Abstract #M.D.P.15.

Chiasson, M. A., Lifson, A. R., Stoneburner, R. L., Ewing, W., Hildebrandt, D., & Jaffe, H. W. (1988). HIV-1 seroprevalence in male and female prostitutes in New York City. IV International Conference on AIDS, Stockholm, Sweden, June, Abstract #4116.

Cockerline, D. (1989). Whorephobia. *Advocate,* 535, 4–6.

Coutinho, R. A., van Andel, R. L. M., & Rijsdijk, T. J.. (1988). Role of male prostitutes in spread of sexually transmitted diseases and human immunodeficiency virus. *Genitourinary Medicine, 64*(3), 207–208.

DiClemente, R. J., & DuNah, R. (1989). Influence of perceived referent-group normative behavior on adolescents' use of condoms. V International Conference on AIDS, Montreal, Quebec, June 4–9, Abstract #T.D.P.91.

DiClemente, R. J., Forrest, K., & Mickler, S. (1989). Differential effects of AIDS knowledge and perceived susceptibility on the reduction of high-risk sexual behaviors among college adolescents. V International Conference on AIDS. Montreal, Quebec, June 4–9, Abstract #T.D.P.92.

Elifson, K., Boles, J., Sweat, M., & Darrow, W. (1989a). Risk factors for HIV infection among male prostitutes in Atlanta. V International Conference on AIDS, Montreal, Quebec, June 4–9, Abstract #W.A.P.38.

Elifson, K. W., Boles, J., Sweat, M., Darrow, W. W., Elsea, W., & Green, R. M. (1989b). Seroprevalence of human immunodeficiency virus among male prostitutes. *New England Journal of Medicine, 321*(12), 832–833.

Gold, J., Griggs, L., Toomey, M., Alan, D. L., Turbitt, P., Anns, M., & McElwee, P. R. (1989). The development of a street based outreach programme to reach young male, female and transsexual, street based prostitutes in Sydney,

Australia. V International Conference on AIDS, Montreal, Quebec, June 4–9, Abstract #M.D.O.12.

Hoffman, M. (1972). The male prostitute. *Sexual Behavior, 2,* 16–21.

Hollingshead, A. B. (1975). Four factor index of social status. New Haven, CT: Privately printed.

Hooykaas, C., Van Der Pligt, J., Van Doornum, G. J. J., Van Der Linden, M. D., & Coutinho, R. A. (1989). High risk heterosexuals: Differences between private and commercial partners in sexual behavior and condom use. V International Conference on AIDS, Montreal, Quebec, June 4–9, Abstract #T.A.P.14.

Kinsey, A. C., Pomeroy, W. B., & Martin, C. E. (1948). *Sexual behavior in the human male.* Philadelphia: W. B. Saunders.

Kohn, R., Gibson, P. M., & Bolan, G. (1989). AIDS knowledge and unsafe sexual practices at an STD clinic. V International Conferences on AIDS, Montreal, Quebec, June 4–9, Abstract #M.D.P.30.

Lauderback, D., & Waldorf, D. (1989). Male prostitution and AIDS: Preliminary findings. *Focus: A Guide to AIDS Research,* Jan., 3–4.

McCandless, W. H., Rotheram-Borus, M. J., Bradley, J., Pleak, R. R., & Martin, J. A. (1988). AIDS education: Assessing the relationship between increased knowledge and behavioral change among runaway and gay youth. Eastern Psychological Association annual meeting, Buffalo, New York.

Puel, J. M. L., Gayet-Mengelle, C., Averous, S., & Bazex, J. (1989). La diffusion du VIH-1 dans la population du prostituees de Toulouse (France). V International Conference on AIDS, Montreal, Quebec, June 4–9, Abstract #M.A.P.46.

Radford, J. L., Warren, W. K., & King, A. J. C. (1989). Adolescents at risk of HIV infection. V International Conference on AIDS, Montreal, Quebec, June 4–9, Abstract #M.D.O.8.

Reitmeijer, C. A. M., Krebs, J. W., Feorino, P. M., & Judson, F. N. (1988). Condoms as physical and chemical barriers against human immunodeficiency virus. *Journal of the American Medical Association, 259*(12), 1851–1853.

Rekart, M. L., Manzou, L., & Loftus, P. (1989). Knowledge, attitudes and behavior of street-involved people in Vancouver. V International Conference on AIDS, Montreal, Quebec, June 4–9, Abstract #T.D.P.8.

Rotheram-Borus, M. J., Bradley, J. S., Pleak, R. R., McCandless, W. H., & Martin, J. A. (1987). General and personalized knowledge of AIDS among runaway, high school, and gay youth. 34th meeting of the American Academy of Child and Adolescent Psychiatry, Washington, DC, October.

Santos-Ferreira, M. O., Mazza, C., Lourenco, M. H., Focaccia, R., Veronesi, R. (1989). HIV-2 infection in female and male Brazilian prostitute groups. V International Conference on AIDS, Montreal, Quebec, June 4–9, Abstract #M.A.P.84.

Sittitrai, W., Phanupahak, P., Satirakorn, N., Ekweera, E. W., & Roddy, R. E. (1989). Demographics and sexual practices of male bar workers in Bangkok. V International Conference on AIDS, Montreal, Quebec, June 4–9, Abstract #M.D.P.19.

Tirelli, U., Vaccher, E., Bullian, P., Saracchini, S., Errante, D., Zagonel, V., & Serraino, D. (1988). HIV-1 seroprevalence in male prostitutes in Northeast Italy. *Journal of Acquired Immune Deficiency Syndromes, 1,* 414–417.

Velimirovic, B. (1987). AIDS as a social phenomenon. *Social Science and Medicine, 25*(6), 541–552.

Wiik, F. B., Filguerias, A., & Castro, M. L. (1989). Street teenagers and an AIDS prevention program in Brazil. V International Conference on AIDS, Montreal, Quebec, June 4–9, Abstract #M.E.O.9.

STUDY QUESTIONS

1. What percentage of the male prostitutes in this study had sex with both men and women? What are the implications of these findings for the Pattern I/II epidemic in the United States?
2. What might be the reasons that these male sex workers tend more often to use condoms with clients than with lovers?
3. How did knowledge about HIV/AIDS change their sexual behavior?
4. How do the authors explain the unusually high levels of condom use reported by these male sex workers?
5. Why do the authors recommend peer counselors to promote safer sexual practices among commercial sex workers?

Suggested Additional Readings

David J. Bellis, "Fear of AIDS and Risk Reduction Among Heroin-Addicted Female Street Prostitutes: Personal Interviews with 72 Southern California Subjects." *Journal of Alcohol and Drug Education,* vol. 35 (1990):26–37.

Thomas Calhoun and Brian Pickerill, "Young Male Prostitutes: Their Knowledge of Selected Sexually Transmitted Diseases." *Psychology: A Journal of Human Behavior,* vol. 25 (1988):1–8.

Carole A. Campbell, "Prostitution, AIDS, and Preventive Health Behavior." *Social Science and Medicine,* vol. 32 (1991):1367–1378.

Jim A. Cates and Jeffrey Markley, "Demographic, Clinical, and Personality Variables Associated with Male Prostitution by Choice." *Adolescence,* vol. 27 (1992):695–706.

W. W. Darrow, "Assessing Targeted AIDS Prevention in Male and Female Prostitutes and Their Clients." F. Paccaud, J. P. Vader, and F. Gutzwiller, editors. *Assessing AIDS Prevention* (Basel, Switzerland: Birkhauser Verlag, 1992):215–231.

Edward S. Herold and Carla van Kerkwijk, "AIDS and Sex Tourism." *AIDS and Society,* vol. 4, no. 1 (1992):1, 8.

A. S. Klovdahl, "Social Networks and the Spread of Infectious Disease: The AIDS Example." *Social Science and Medicine,* vol. 21 (1985):1203–1216.

Richard G. Parker, *Bodies, Pleasures and Passions: Sexual Culture in Contemporary Brazil* (Boston: Beacon, 1991).

John L. Peterson, Thomas J. Coates, Joseph A. Catania, Lee Middleton, Bobby Hilliard, and Norman Hearst, "High Risk Sexual Behavior and Condom Use Among Gay and Bisexual Men." *American Journal of Public Health,* vol. 82 (1992):1490–1494.

Photo Essay

The Politics of AIDS

Kennebunkport, Maine, September 1991. Approximately 1,500 people join an ACT UP demonstration to demand more action from then-President George Bush to end the AIDS crisis. (©1991 Marilyn Humphries/Impact Visuals)

Atlanta, Georgia, December 1990. Women living with AIDS march around the Centers for Disease Control in another ACT UP demonstration, demanding a redefinition of CDC guidelines for an AIDS diagnosis. (© 1990 Allan Clear/Impact Visuals)

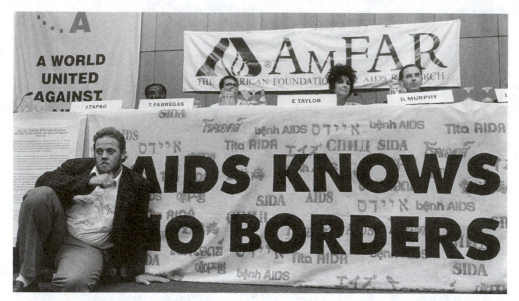

The Eighth International AIDS Conference, Amsterdam, the Netherlands, July 1992. Actress Elizabeth Taylor joins an American Foundation for AIDS Research (AmFAR) press conference concerning immigration restrictions imposed on people infected with the HIV virus and living with AIDS. (© 1992 Allan Clear/Impact Visuals)

The Eighth International AIDS Conference, Amsterdam, July 1992. French citizen Fernand Beauval displays his passport to journalists. In violation of the 1988 WHO mandate that urged member nations not to discriminate people with HIV/AIDS, Beauval's passport had been stamped by the American consulate in Paris with a code indicating that he had AIDS. (© 1992 Allan Clear/Impact Visuals)

Department of Health, New York City, January 1991. ACT UP members deliver used dirty needles, collected during the group's needle exchange program, to the City Department of Health. (© 1991 Allan Clear/Impact Visuals)

Washington, D.C., October 1992. At an ACT UP political funeral march from the Capitol to the White House, a man holds the ashes of his lover, who died from AIDS. (© 1992 Vincent Cianni/Impact Visuals)

Global Concerns

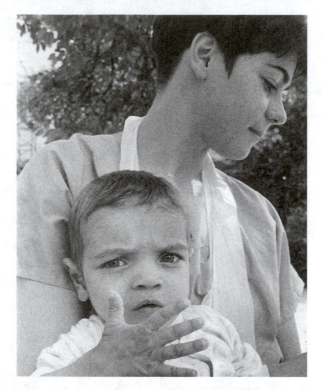

Colentina Hospital, Bucharest, Romania, August 1990. A health care worker holds an HIV-positive orphaned child. International publicity surrounding the conditions of HIV-infected children—many of whom were infected by contaminated blood and dirty syringes—pressured the Romanian government into permitting foreign health care workers into the country. (©1990 Andrew Lichtenstein/Impact Visuals)

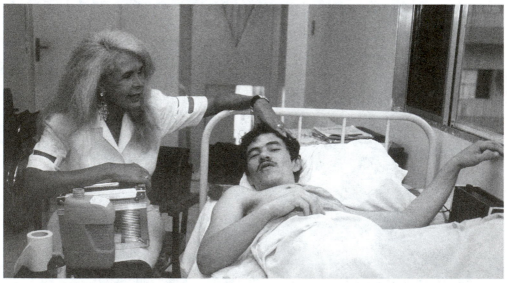

Brenda Lee House, Sao Paulo, Brazil, October 1990. Brenda Lee cares for one of her patients. HIV prevalence rates in Sao Paulo are among the highest in South America—as high as 75 percent among injection drug users. (© Armando Waak/Pan American Health Organization)

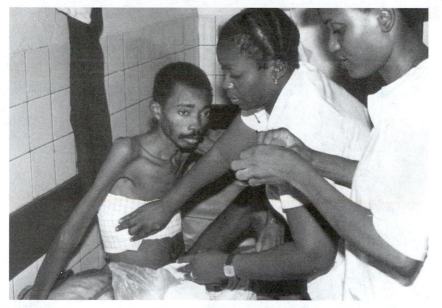

Zaire, 1993. A man with AIDS receives medical care for an AIDS-related opportunistic infection. In the African AIDS belt, the disease is called "Slim" because of the extreme wasting that is associated with it. Sub-Saharan Africa accounts for two-thirds of the global HIV/AIDS case load. (H. Anenden/World Health Organization)

The Eighth International AIDS Conference, Amsterdam, July 1992. Protesters publicize governmental persecution of commercial sex workers in Southeast Asia. Thailand had deported Burmese sex workers, and the Burmese government administered cyanide to HIV-infected sex workers. (© 1992 Allan Clear/Impact Visuals)

Education

San Francisco, May 1992. A man adorns himself with packets of condoms during the Cinco de Mayo parade as part of the Latino outreach project of the San Francisco AIDS Foundation. Encouraging condom use has been a major component of safer-sex education. (© 1994 Rick Gerharter/Impact Visuals)

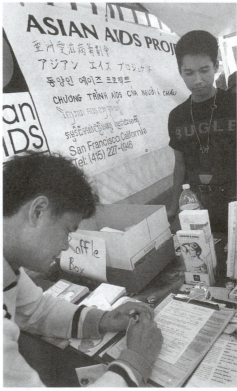

San Francisco, September 1993. A safer-sex outreach worker surveys a visitor at the Asian AIDS Project booth at the Folsom Street Fair. In San Francisco and other urban areas, reaching out to people of diverse ethnic and cultural backgrounds is a top priority in AIDS education. (© 1993 Rick Gerharter/Impact Visuals)

Seward Park High School, New York City, December 1991. High school students learn about AIDS, the immune system, and alternative ways to combatting disease. (© 1991 Allan Clear/Impact Visuals)

Living with AIDS

New York City. Ira Rosenbaum, living with AIDS, takes part in an aquarobics class at Manhattan Plaza. (© Allan Clear/Impact Visuals)

Housing Works, New York City, December 1993. Gladys Algarin, a recovering drug addict who is HIV positive, participates in an art project at Housing Works, a community-based organization that provides housing and supportive services to homeless families and individuals living with HIV and AIDS. (© Carolina Kroon/Impact Visuals)

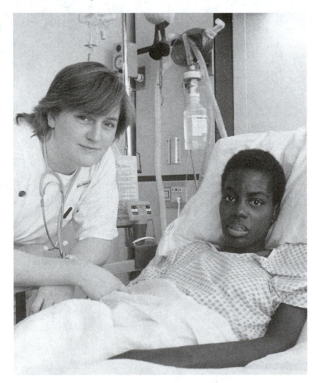

St. Vincent's Hospital, New York City, 1991. Marilyn Spruill is being cared for by her nurse. See Chapter 12 for readings on how HIV/AIDS has affected the relationship between patients and health care workers. (© 1991 Ansell Horn/Impact Visuals)

Remembrance

Trafalgar Square, London. At an AIDS vigil, those who have been felled by the epidemic are remembered. According to the World Health Organization estimates, more than 14 million adults worldwide had been infected by HIV by late 1993. As the global health crisis enters its second decade, there have been more than 3 million cumulative AIDS cases in adults and children throughout the world. (© Allan Clear/Impact Visuals)

PART

IV

Pattern III Epidemics and AIDS in the 1990s

Asia and Global Concerns

• • •

As recently as 1987, reported AIDS cases in Eastern Europe, the Middle East, North Africa, Asia, and the nations in the Pacific Basin (other than Australia and New Zealand) accounted for slightly less then 1 percent of the total HIV/AIDS cases monitored by the World Health Organization. Yet in Asia and the nations of the Pacific Basin, and particularly in India, Thailand, and Myanmar (formerly Burma), the speed at which the epidemics have progressed anticipates a massive health crisis scenario in the region. By 1993, that figure had increased to between 1.5 and 2 millions, and the World Health Organization estimates project that by the year 2000, 90 percent of the world's HIV-positive people will be from Asian nations.[1] While the earliest reported AIDS cases in these regions could be traced to sexual contacts in Pattern I and Pattern II areas, indigenous transmission tended to occur within core groups—primarily commercial sex workers and injection drug users. The evidence of a new cluster of AIDS epidemics, described as Pattern III epidemics, was unmistakable.

In part, Pattern III epidemics are marked by a relatively late onset, but in other respects—particularly the configuration of transmission vectors—the epidemiological profiles of Pattern III epidemics vary widely. In Eastern Europe, for example, the ratio of male-to-female HIV/AIDS infection in 1992 was 10:1. However, in Northeast Asia the male-to-female ratio was 5:1, and in Southeast Asia the ratio was 2:1. This is one indicator of greater variation in transmission

---

[1]"Recent HIV Seroprevalence Levels by Country: June 1993." Health Studies Branch, Center for International Research, U.S. Bureau of the Census (Research Note No. 9, June 1993). Tony Kahane, "Noise About AIDS." *Bangkok Post,* June 17, 1993:36.

vectors among Pattern III epidemics.[2] Pattern I and II epidemics have been generally defined in terms of the dominant mode of sexual transmission—heterosexual versus homosexual—and the ratio of male-to-female prevalence rates has traced multiple, and only gradually converging, sexual HIV transmission vectors. In contrast, the ratio of male-to-female prevalence rates in Pattern III epidemics is shaped in a more complex fashion by a shifting equation of intersections among injection drug user networks, the commercial sex industry, male homosexuality/bisexuality, and noncommercial heterosexual transmission vectors. Likewise, the percentages of all reported HIV/AIDS cases among children are varied in Pattern III regions. In Eastern Europe, where HIV/AIDS mirrors the United States epidemic of the early and mid-1980s, pediatric cases accounted for less than 1 percent of the total reported HIV/AIDS cases in 1992. In Southeast Asia, however, which in some respects resembles the Pattern II sub-Saharan African epidemic, pediatric cases accounted for slightly more than 3 percent of the total cases. The pediatric cases in Southeast Asia are but one early warning of a rapidly escalating HIV prevalence rate in Pattern III epidemics, where sexually constructed transmission vectors have intersected very early in the course of local epidemics with vectors formed by networks of injection drug users. As a result, preliminary projections of the HIV/AIDS epidemic in Asian regions anticipate a potentially devastating health crisis that will be measured not only by death rates but also by economic and social costs to families, communities, and nations ill-prepared to bear them.

The global HIV/AIDS health crisis of the 1990s, in many respects a "second wave" of HIV/AIDS epidemics, is likely to be characterized by an increasing incidence of the disease among groups and populations who in the mid-1980s were regarded as at relatively low risk. Yet this "second wave" of epidemics is not clearly separated from the first wave. At the beginning of the eleventh year of the global HIV/AIDS health crisis, no community or nation that had previously reported the presence of HIV/AIDS was able to claim a reduction in either incidence or prevalence rates. To the contrary, all the evidence suggests that at the global level and at the level of the many smaller epidemics, HIV/AIDS will continue to spread.

At the beginning of the 1990s, 71 percent of all adult HIV transmissions had occurred through heterosexual intercourse, 15 percent had been transmitted homosexually, 7 percent through injection drug use, and 5 percent through blood transfusions or other medical procedures. Within this broad skeletal framework local and regional HIV/AIDS surveillance reports actually reflect

[2]Jonathan Mann, Daniel J. M. Tarantola, and Thomas W. Netter, editors. *AIDS in the World* (Cambridge, MA: Harvard University Press, 1992):20–21. In comparison, in North America, where male homosexuality still accounts for the numerical majority of the reported HIV/AIDS cases, the male-to-female ratio is 8:1, while in sub-Saharan Africa, where HIV/AIDS is a heterosexually transmitted disease, the ratio is 1:1. In Latin America and the Caribbean, areas that began as Pattern I epidemics but shifted during the 1980s to Pattern I/II, the male-to-female HIV/AIDS ratios are 4:1 and 1.5:1, respectively.

many small epidemics. In Norway and the former Yugoslavia, for example, the core transmission groups are networks of injection drug users, whereas in Czechoslovakia and Paraguay they are gay men. In India and Thailand, commercial sex workers are the most heavily infected, and in San Francisco there are marked ethnic variations in infection rates among gay men. The selections in Part IV explore the frightening potential of HIV/AIDS to disrupt the fabric of communities and nations and suggest the challenges that the HIV/AIDS health crisis will continue to present to public health policy and health care delivery systems throughout the world.

CHAPTER 10

Asia

• • •

Typical of the Pattern III epidemics, AIDS began to appear in Southeast Asian nations during the latter years of the 1980s, and the conditions that have forged transmission vectors in this region foreshadowed an explosion of HIV/AIDS epidemics in the coming decade. While networks of injection drug users account for a substantial portion of the HIV/AIDS cases in Southeast Asia, the commercial sex industry, particularly in Thailand and India, has also served as a major HIV springboard, and an epidemic within Asian gay communities seems inevitable.

A Plague Awaits describes the international appeal of Bangkok brothels at the beginning of the HIV/AIDS epidemic in Thailand. A combination of intense poverty, which informed family decisions to "sell" their children to commercial sex traders, and official denial of the impending epidemic fueled the spread of the disease during the late 1980s. In Bangkok, connections between the commercial sex and drug industries and the enormous profits of the commercial sex industry fostered political corruption and compromised the legal system. As a result, HIV transmission vectors radiated out from a complex and highly stratified commercial sex worker core group.

Despite government-based "anti-AIDS" programs, HIV transmission continues, and reported HIV/AIDS cases multiply in both Thailand and India. **AIDS in Asia, the Africa Syndrome** describes the combination of factors that thwart the Indian government's AIDS education and prevention efforts: the cultural acceptance of commercial sex, the dense and feminized poverty that also characterizes sub-Saharan Africa, and high illiteracy rates, particularly in villages and among poor people, which limit access to HIV/AIDS prevention information.

Readings from _WorldAIDS_ revisits familiar environments of HIV transmission: commercial sex, injection drug use, and gay male subcultures, offering a closer view of the interaction between transmission vectors and the cultural contours of three Asian nations. "Fighting Against Fate" describes the equation of powerlessness and social stigma that simultaneously overwhelms young Nepali women who have been drawn into the region's commercial sex industry and compromises government programs designed to combat HIV transmission. As is the case in Europe and the United States, throughout Asia HIV infection rates are very high among injection drug user networks. "Turning the Tide" describes Vietnam's injection drug user subculture and illustrates how organized HIV/AIDS education programs can capitalize on the social organization of injection drug user communities to introduce and implement hygienic measures that slow HIV transmission. "No Safer Sex for Pakistan's Gays" describes the climate of underground sex and homophobia that will continue to fuel HIV transmission among gay communities in Karachi and elsewhere in Asia as surely as it has among gay communities in Western nations. Clearly, HIV transmission vectors are built on a foundation of culturally specific beliefs, attitudes, and values combined with local and national political and economic exigencies. Yet, as **Socioeconomic Implications of AIDS in Developing Nations** argues, the long-term consequences of all HIV/AIDS epidemics will entail devastating public costs and private tragedy.

A Plague Awaits

Steven Erlanger

If you don't see the coffin, you shed no tears.

—Thai proverb

Four Thai men, cigarettes in hand, sit on a rough bamboo bench, staring across a packed dirt floor.

Five young women in casual clothes sit opposite them on similar benches, but behind a display window of cheap glass. They chat among themselves, brushing each other's hair or playing with the brothel dog.

In the unshaded light of a pink fluorescent tube, their makeup looks coarse, their lipstick purple. One young woman wears a "Snoopy and his friends" T-shirt dress. Over her breast is a blue, heart-shaped pin with a number. Some women wear yellow pins. These are price tags.

In this establishment, with its chatty mamasan, shrine to the Buddha and small table of snacks for indecisive clients, a half-hour of sex with a woman with a blue pin costs 65 baht, or $2.60; with a yellow pin, $2.

These young women live at the brothel, a shabby building of bamboo and thatch, roofed with tin, in the Thai city of Chiang Mai. They are always on call, and each has between 10 and 20 customers a day. In this area, in this kind of brothel, four of five women carry the AIDS virus.

Thailand is in the grip of a hidden AIDS epidemic. On average, in testing done in December for the Government's semiannual survey of AIDS, 17.3 percent of brothel prostitutes nationwide carried the virus, an increase of 26 percent over June. Some 4.2 percent of "indirect prostitutes," those who solicit in massage parlors, go-go bars and the like, are infected nationwide, while in Bangkok, 7.9 percent are. In June 1989, 3 percent of Bangkok's brothel prostitutes were infected; by last December, 18 months later, the figure was 20.6 percent.

But the disease, spread by the brothels, is by no means confined to them. At least 14 percent of the young men here in northwest Thailand, ages 20 to 24—like the ones in this brothel—carry the virus, too. Within six years, the World Health Organization estimates, half of those infected will be dead. In time, since AIDS is always fatal, the others will die as well. So the sexual and commercial transactions in this brothel, common throughout Thai society at every level, are a form of indirect murder or suicide.

The eerie quality of the raging AIDS epidemic in Thailand is its invisibility. Doctors and scientists estimate that at least 300,000 Thais are infected with AIDS, and thousands more are being infected every month. By 1997, according by W.H.O., between 125,000 and 150,000 Thais will have died from AIDS. This is a conservative estimate. The Population and Community Development Association of Thailand estimates that AIDS could infect as many as 5.3 million by the year 2000, with more than a million dead by then.

But the disease is still so new here that very few Thais have died or even fallen sick, and only a tiny number of those infected know that this modern plague is already killing them. So sexual behavior has hardly begun to change.

Dr. Surasing Visrutaratna, the assistant chief medical officer of Chiang Mai Province, points proudly to a sign on the brothel window: "We welcome only guests using condoms." Showing rare initiative in centralized, hierarchical Thailand, he has made his singular, urgent effort to diminish the tidal wave of death that Thai doctors know is coming, but that many politicians and bureaucrats don't seem to want to see.

There is another sign in Thai: No foreigners allowed. Surasing laughs a little. "They still think foreigners bring AIDS," he says. "But it is already here."

It is also out of control.

Prostitution is illegal in Thailand, but it is practiced everywhere. Thousands of brothels, massage parlors, bathhouses, bars, clubs, teahouses, coffee shops and even barbershops serve as fronts for the selling of sex. Some of these establishments are for tourists, especially in parts of Bangkok, Pattaya and the southern city of Hat Yai, near Malaysia. And some foreigners still arrive on packaged sex tours, especially from Germany and Japan.

But Thailand's AIDS epidemic is now a Thai–Thai affair, and it is raging in cheap brothels like this one and in thousands more like it in the countryside, where 80 percent of Thailand's 56 million people live. According to reliable surveys of sexual behavior, every day at least 450,000 Thai men visit prostitutes. More than 75 percent of Thai males have been to prostitutes, and 75 percent of them go to the cheapest brothels, where the AIDS infection is most prevalent. Then they spread it to their lovers, wives, and unborn children.

Yet the Government is only slowly waking up to the severity of the epidemic. Indeed, many in the bureaucracy still want to minimize the problem for fear of hurting Thailand's expanding tourist industry, already the country's largest source of foreign exchange.

The dimensions of the Thai AIDS epidemic approach those of the more publicized disaster in Uganda, where the Ministry of Health estimates that about 1.2 million Ugandans out of a population of 17 million are infected and more than 80 percent of prostitutes carry the disease.

In the United States, a country with more than four times the population of Thailand and where AIDS has been a decadelong experience, the Public Health Service estimates that AIDS infects about a million Americans, with deaths put at about 100,000.

But the AIDS epidemic in America is not a heterosexual one on the African model, and it has already prompted significant behavioral change on the part of high-risk groups like homosexuals and intravenous drug users. More important, America does not share the Thai appetite for commercial sex.

"It will be horrible, utterly horrible," says Dr. Vicharn Vithayasai, director of immunology at Chiang Mai University's Faculty of Medicine. "But I'm afraid that for behavior to change, we need many more Thais to die."

The epidemic is most advanced in the provinces of northwest Thailand, which are said to have the country's most beautiful women and to which Thai tourists go for sex. According to a survey by Vicharn in late 1989, 72 percent of the prostitutes in Chiang Mai's cheapest brothels carry the AIDS virus. At the cheapest brothels, he said, "they're surely all HIV positive now."

According to the Royal Thai Army, which is now testing 20,000 young male recruits a year, 14 percent of the young men from Chiang Mai Province, aged 20 to 24, are HIV positive. Moreover, 3 to 4.5 percent of pregnant women tested randomly at prenatal clinics in Chiang Mai Province are also HIV positive, an extraordinary finding. Pregnant women are significant because, of all the groups in the Government's survey of AIDS, they are regarded as the most representative of the general population.

"This is a problem of Thailand," says Vicharn. "It's the fault of our Thai behavior, and our behavior will destroy Thailand. Thai men go to prostitutes at every level of society. Half of boys by 14 have been to a prostitute. And if the prostitutes are so infected, everyone's at risk."

Aren't these brothels a form of indirect murder? Vicharn lifts his eyes to the ceiling. "Of course," he says. "But we think for now we should keep these women in the brothels, where we can check them and teach them to use condoms. Otherwise, they will go underground and spread over the country, infecting many more."

Chiang Mai, a city of only 250,000 people, has nearly 3,000 prostitutes in two brothel districts. In the older one, Kampaeng Din, near the commercial district, is the Angel Cafe. There is a bar, tables with chairs, roses on the tables. About 25 young women sit on stepped benches with a backdrop of horses running through a field. They watch television while the patrons, all university students, watch them through the glass.

There are four price tags here: yellow, $4; blue, $8; red, $12; clear, $20. At such prices, these prostitutes have far fewer partners than the women in the cheap brothels. Still, according to Vicharn, nearly one in five is HIV positive.

Some of the students are drunk, laughing among themselves, but most seem quiet, intent on the women, their drinks or their cigarettes. From time to time, someone will saunter over to talk to the manager. A few minutes later, behind the glass, a young woman will shrug and stand, gathering up a little purse, and exit through a small door in the back. Often, the women will turn back to catch a last glimpse of the show on TV.

In Thai universities, there is a traditional initiation called *ruen pee, ruen nung,* or upperclassmen, lowerclassmen, in which older male students take younger ones to a brothel and buy them prostitutes.

In one indication of changing attitudes, students at Khon Kean University, in northeastern Thailand, abandoned the practice last year, citing AIDS. But the tradition continues at other universities, including those in Chiang Mai. "If you refuse to go along," one young man says, "they call you gay or reject you."

A young Thai woman, 24 years old, speaks unusually frankly about her sexual life. While a university student, she had a boyfriend, she says, and slept with him, taking birth control pills. Did he ever go to the brothel? She pulls her hair in front of her face and runs her fingers through the ends. "Yes," she says, "once a month, with his friends." Did she ask him to use a condom with her? "No," she says. "I couldn't. Then I couldn't even say the word."

Prime Minister Anand Panyarachun, the head of an interim Government installed after a military coup, is trying to explain Thai behavior. While Thai men will wear condoms for family planning, he says, they object to them with girlfriends and prostitutes. Of the 450,000 Thai men who go to prostitutes every day, he says, only half wear condoms.

Condom use is increasing, but most doctors believe Anand's percentage is too high. A 1990 survey by a Thai market research company, Deemar, found that 59 percent of Thai men say they never use a condom, 26 percent had multiple sex partners in the last six months and 86 percent think there is very little chance of getting AIDS.

"This is a very permissive culture, where *sanuk,* or fun, is a prime virtue," says Werasit Sittitrai, director of the Institute of Population Studies at Chulalongkorn University. Thai men think it is their right to have cheap sex, he says, and there are enough poor Thai women to make it possible.

This has been true for many years, even going back to the time of Kings Rama III and IV in the 19th century. The Thai tradition of "minor," or secondary, wives is also longstanding. The Vietnam War and the popularity of Thailand as a rest and recreation center for American soldiers made the sex industry both more important and more obvious. The Americans also introduced coyer fronts for sex, like go-go bars, clubs, and massage parlors.

Nowadays, Thai businessmen and officials do a lot of entertaining in massage parlors and private clubs. When their superiors visit from Bangkok, etiquette still dictates the offer of an attractive prostitute or a visit to a sex establishment. Senior officials are often presented their pick of provincial beauty contestants. When Thai men travel, many do not feel they have visited a province unless they have slept with a local girl.

"When they come to Chiang Mai," says Surasing, "first they go to the temples. Then they taste the food, and then they taste the girls."

How does a young Thai woman, normally very shy, dance naked in front of strangers or sleep with them? "You make yourself very empty," says Noi, a former prostitute who now sells cosmetics. Tonight she is visiting old friends at the bar where she used to work.

Would she ever go back to the bar, where she could make about four times what she makes now? "No," she says, but then points to one of her friends, sitting on a customer's lap. "They say, 'Why work in a factory for 2,000 or 3,000 baht a month [$80 to $120], when one man for one night is maybe 1,000 baht?'"

Maybe it means dying, too "Yes," she says, "maybe."

The Thai epidemic has had three main phases. The HIV virus arrived here comparatively late, brought by Thai homosexuals returning home from the West, sometimes to die, and by foreign tourists and drug users who came to northern Thailand for sex and cheap heroin. The first Thai to die from AIDS, in 1984, was a homosexual who had lived for some years in the United States.

This first phase, before 1987, was largely among homosexuals and intravenous drug users. From 1987 to 1989, the epidemic exploded among drug users in Bangkok, who commonly shared needles. Many of these drug users also had sex with low-cost brothel or sidewalk prostitutes, who had many other partners. Since most Thai male prostitutes are bisexual or heterosexual, and also use drugs, the disease began to spread heterosexually. Now, in the third phase, heterosexual transmission is the main mode, and the virus is spreading rapidly and dramatically through prostitutes to the general population.

There are no reliable figures for male prostitutes or for homosexuals, but doctors say condom use among them is now common. The national rate of infection among intravenous drug users, too, seems to have stabilized at about 35 percent, with education at drug clinics and free bleach to clean needles.

But not enough is being done to educate female sex workers and the general population, where the epidemic has quickly spread. "The main problem is that every time we think we've reached the bottom," says a W.H.O. official, "we find there's another bottom."

The Ministry of Public Health says there are 86,000 sex workers, known politely in Thai as those "who sell their gender." After a two-year study, Werasit, of the Institute of Population Studies at Chulalongkorn University, thinks that figure is ridiculously low. While some put the total at 500,000, Werasit believes the number is about 210,000, which includes about 10,000 male and child prostitutes. Fewer than 20 percent work in Bangkok.

Women become prostitutes for a few main reasons: subsistence; a financial emergency at home; as a way to return to their village farther up the social ladder, with a house and the chance to marry a decent husband; to help their older parents, or to finance the education of a sibling. Some, of course, simply freelance, working weekends in a massage parlor to afford a more comfortable or stylish life.

Poverty is an accelerator of prostitution, not its primary cause, says Suvit Yodmani, a minister in the Prime Minister's office and a former Government spokesman. "The main causes are demand and the value system of the people. Some parents don't mind, and kids are brought up to feel they should pay somehow for being born. Then there is the attraction of the big city. People aren't starving in the villages, but they're bored."

Modernization and sophisticated advertisements have also brought new desires for consumer goods to villagers and a shift toward a cash economy. Dr. Debhanom Muangman, dean of the School of Public Health at Mahidol University, has asked mothers why they sell their daughters. "They say they're poor, and I say, 'You own land, a house, you have enough to eat,' but they say, 'I want money.'"

Chantawipa Apisuk runs Empower, an organization that works with prostitutes. Typically, she says, well-dressed agents working for brothels visit villagers, offering between $160 and $800, depending on the beauty of their daughters, as an "advance" on salary. Sometimes agents will convince monks, in return for contributions to the temple, to hold beauty contests on temple grounds.

In areas of the north known for beautiful women—Chiang Mai, Chiang Rai, Lampang and Phayao, provinces that also have the highest rates of HIV infection in Thailand—the agents may also offer refrigerators, television sets and jewelry. With AIDS, Chantawipa says, there is a premium on pretty virgins from remote areas, "who are becoming as rare and valuable as white elephants," the symbol of Thailand.

These young women are bonded to brothels like indentured servants and must earn back their debt. Like migrant farm laborers in America, they must buy from the company store at inflated prices, while money is deducted from their earnings for days lost to illness or menstruation, or for sloppiness or laziness or any of many other sins.

Most prostitutes are not allowed by brothel owners to refuse a customer who won't wear a condom. Many women, fearing loss of income, don't insist. "If the man seems clean and healthy, I say, 'O.K.,'" says Daeng, a Bangkok bar girl. "If the man comes to me often and is nice to me, I say, 'O.K.' If he offers me more money, I say, 'O.K.' A man asked me if I feared AIDS and I said, 'I'm poor.'"

To make money more quickly, Werasit says, many women work through their menstrual period, when they more easily get and give the disease, by inserting a small tampon. If a customer notices blood, the woman will say, "Oh, you're so big and macho, I couldn't stop myself."

Some of these brothels are nationwide businesses, and young women are shipped around the country so customers don't get bored. If they become infected, they may be sent home with nothing. Sometimes they continue working in a rural brothel.

"People just want to talk about prostitutes and penalize them," says Chantawipa. "They don't want to talk about the profiteers." It's not the poor who need to be controlled, she says, but the rich, not the women, but the men. "Changing women isn't difficult; they're ready to change. Why not open factories instead of brothels and bars?"

Part of the answer is that many politicians, officials and policemen invest in the sex trade or benefit from it. In the northern province of Phrae, a senior Thai official says, policemen own some of the brothels. Thai newspapers sometimes suggest that certain politicians own chains of brothels.

Thais, who are deferential to authority figures, become nervous when faced with questions of corruption, especially when they involve the powerful military. Thais protect and supplicate their superiors, and for reasons of face avoid public discussion of unpleasant matters.

So while a fatal epidemic rages among Thais, especially in the countryside, officials tend to blame foreigners. "The Government promotes tourism and the sex industry, but they shut their eyes to what is happening," Chantawipa says. "There's a big fear of losing face. They're not so much trying to solve the problem as to clean their image." But many Thai doctors hope that the new Government, though interim, will do better at actually doing something.

Still, W.H.O. officials say, Thailand has done more than any other country in Southeast Asia to combat AIDS. The Thais began working seriously with W.H.O. in 1988, and in April 1989 began the region's first W.H.O.-approved plan against AIDS.

Among the positive results, W.H.O. officials say, is that the blood supply is now considered safe, at least in the provincial capitals, and anti-AIDS ads have begun running on television and radio. In America, the first national

TV ad did not run until 1987. Authorities have also tried to insure that condoms of reasonable quality are more widely available, and the involvement of private agencies like Empower is welcome.

In addition, the military was persuaded to get serious about AIDS, testing and teaching draftees and putting the first anti-AIDS ads on military-run radio and TV stations. Princess Chulabhorn, the youngest daughter of Thailand's revered King, has spoken out about the disease and its victims.

But an internal review by the Ministry of Public Health points up serious shortcomings in its AIDS program. In the report, obtained by The Times, the ministry says much data is inadequate; condom supplies are insufficient and of indifferent quality; little is being done in the provinces; educational efforts are insufficient, and "direct political commitment from the highest national authority" is still lacking.

W.H.O. officials agree. "Nothing's really moving," one W.H.O. official says. "They're not acting with any real urgency." The biggest problem for prevention is in the rural areas, where the sex industry continues to grow. But in Thailand, everything stops at provincial capitals, whether the effort is blood screening or the prevention of tuberculosis.

"The challenge we really face," the W.H.O. official says, "is to reach the kids, 11 to 14 years old, and the housewives and the pregnant women, and to help produce policies for the time when thousands of people are going to the hospitals with full-fledged AIDS."

As it stands now, thousands will die before behavior alters, he says. "But we're at least a couple years away from that, and for now the epidemic goes on and it worsens. Every month we wait, thousands more are infected."

Bamras Naradura Hospital, near the Bangkok airport, contains Thailand's showcase AIDS ward and training center for doctors and nurses, set up in 1987. There are 18 patients. Some are homosexual or bisexual and were infected abroad; some are intravenous drug users; a few are women; two are babies.

A young man, 36, was told this morning that he had full-blown AIDS. His parents are dead. "If they knew. . . ," he says, and starts to cry. Does he think about dying? "No! I don't want to die. I just picked the black pot."

Another young man, bisexual, seems more reconciled. "I'm just as afraid of dying as you are," he says. "But in Buddhism we call this karma, so never mind. I feel like it's a debt to pay. To pay is to die. I accept it."

Downstairs, in the women's ward, watching her baby struggling to breathe, is a victim of the next generation. Prapai Pokamor is 19; her baby son, Maladung, is 8 months old, the skin of his arms and thighs wrinkled and loose. At 15, Prapai was working in a Bangkok restaurant when she met a regular customer nicknamed Gob, or Toad. He chatted her up and eventually invited her home. In fact, she says, he took her to Nakhon Pathom Province, west of Bangkok, and sold her to a brothel for $200.

There were 110 girls there, she says, aged from 15 to 17. How many men did she sleep with? She shrugs, "I don't know," she says quietly, "maybe seven or eight a day, and at night, too."

Men paid 60 baht for her, or $2.40. Half was supposed to be credited against her debt, but she never saw any money. She was moved to different brothels until she became too pregnant to work. Then she was given $4 in bus fare and returned to Bangkok.

Her family took her to a hospital. A month before Maladung was born, she was found to be HIV positive, as is her dying son.

"I didn't do anything wrong," she says, playing with Maladung's wrinkled arms. "If I had not gone with Gob, it wouldn't have been like this."

Whom does she blame? "A few men are good," she says, bending down to listen to her baby struggling to breathe. "But it's hard to find a good man, very hard. Men are not honest with women."

STUDY QUESTIONS

1. What cultural factors in Thailand foster a permissive attitude toward prostitution?
2. What strategies do sex traders use to recruit young women into the Thai sex industry? What personal and family motives buttress these strategies?
3. How and why do local politicians and law enforcement agencies support the Thai sex industry?
4. How does the Thai government explain the failure of the official HIV/AIDS education and prevention program?
5. What are the similarities between the commercial sex industry in Thailand, sub-Saharan Africa, and Latin America? What are the differences?

AIDS in Asia, the Africa Syndrome

India Confronts the Spectre of a Massive Epidemic

Hamish McDonald

Sitting at her desk in the microbiology department of Madras Medical College, Suniti Solomon says the coming of AIDS to India has transformed her sense of Indian identity. "I now know that we are not what we think we are." For a long time, she and many other prominent Indians believed that India's deep-seated family traditions, social conservatism and spirituality would protect it from the ravages of the global AIDS epidemic, unlike the more "promiscuous" cultures to the west and east. Solomon, for one, sees things differently now.

Reprinted with permission from *Far Eastern Economic Review* (February 20, 1992):28–29. © 1992 by *Far Eastern Economic Review*.

In the five years since HIV was first found among prostitutes in Madras, the dimensions of the AIDS plague have multiplied alarmingly, particularly the way the epidemic is spreading virulently in Maharashtra (the state surrounding Bombay) and Tamil Nadu (around Madras). These two states with a combined population of 135 million, notes New Delhi's Directorate-General of Health Services in its latest AIDS Update, "resemble the pattern of Sub-Saharan Africa where the principal mode of transmission is through heterosexual contact."

So far only 103 AIDS cases have been reported in India, and 6,400 cases of HIV infection, a minuscule number in a population of 844 million. Yet no health workers believe that more than a fraction of the total picture has been drawn in. "It can only be a guestimate," said S. P. Tripathy, director-general of the Indian Council of Medical Research (ICMR). "You take the number of prostitutes, multiply by the average number of clients, and the efficiency of infection—some say one in 100 encounters, some say one in 1,000. The answer may be somewhere between 100,000 and 1 million. But it's anybody's guess."

The spectre of massive depopulation of sexually active age groups in Africa has caused the Indian Government to speed up drastically its current Rs 200 million (US$7.75 million) anti-AIDS programme. It is designed to block paths of infection like contaminated blood supplies, and attack heterosexual transmission through education and promotion of condom use. Another target is an AIDS epidemic in the Northeastern states along the Burmese border, spread by widespread intravenous (IV) heroin use. The tendency to blame it all on outsiders—Tripathy's predecessor suggested banning sex between Indians and foreigners—has gone.

Last year, India became the second country after Zaire to accept foreign loans for its AIDS programme. It will get US$85 million from the World Bank over five years, in addition to special funding from the World Health Organisation and the US Government.

Like many other professionals grappling with this new enemy, Solomon has become familiar with many subcultures of India previously kept out of sight or ignored: "Before we started working on AIDS we didn't know so many things: that there were so many prostitutes, IV drug users or homosexuals. Now I know not only that, but where to find them."

On a night-time tour of Madras, S. Sundararaman, a young psychiatrist who heads the city's privately funded AIDS Research Foundation of India, points out the coded commerce of sex in a port metropolis that officially has no red light district or homosexual precinct. "I grew up in this area, but I went around like a blind man," he said.

Apart from the activities of a small cosmopolitan elite, extra-marital sex in India tends to be what most AIDS workers call, in a cautious neutral way, commercial. Women engage in it for survival. Or they submit to sexual demands to obtain work.

In some cities commercial sex is highly visible and organised: Bombay has an estimated 100,000 women in organised prostitution serving a large population of unattached men; Madras has about 50,000 women in the trade at any one time, moving to and from the hinterland. Women in squatter settlements sell sex for as little as Rs 5 on the Madras beach, along canal banks, in vacant lots or city parks. "Prostitution is illegal here, but anyone can find a woman," said Sundararaman. "It takes only 10 to 15 minutes of effort."

Their clients come from all social backgrounds. Labourers and dockworkers use the cheapest open-air prostitutes. Even the brahmins have their own channels: in certain Hindu temples the elderly women who mingle with worshippers will arrange a rendezvous with part-time prostitutes. Male prostitution is largely unorganised. Teenagers and young boys who sell peanuts on the beach during the day sell their bodies at night when large crowds move around the seashore.

The possibility of women or boys forcing clients to use condoms is very low. They know the client can simply move on to the next person. Brothel owners are uncooperative, said Sundararaman. "Unlike in other countries they do not feel the women are an investment," he said. "They are moved on every 45 days. They are expendable, because there is an endless supply. This creates a degree of powerlessness among the women."

But many prostitutes have only a vague idea of health measures. Lalitha, a 20-year-old from Madurai, has been selling sex for five years to one or two men a day. She uses no contraception and has had two abortions since the birth of her child at 15. She has not heard of AIDS. "I deal only with better people and I trust they do not have any problems so there's no need for condoms," she said. "We have an intuition who could have a disease so we don't go with these clients."

In a Madras park frequented by homosexuals after dark, Anthony and six friends sat smoking a marijuana joint. All are rent-boys, who work the trains for male clients. "We have been doing it for 8 years and we don't have AIDS," Anthony said, "Homosexuals don't get AIDS."

When prostitutes do take precautions against sexually transmitted diseases (STDs), they are often half-measures. Scattershot prescription of penicillin by bucket-shop doctors has produced resistant strains of diseases. Few women inspect themselves or worry about genital sores until they grow painful enough to prevent them from working. As a result, the risk of heterosexual transmission of HIV is greatly increased. Already, ICMR head Tripathy estimates that 30% of Bombay and Madras prostitutes are infected.

Ignorance also abounds among the clients, and infections are taken back to wives in the villages. India is currently supplied with about 1 billion condoms a year, a small number considering its population. As well as the stationary workforce who might use a prostitute on pay-day, there is a large contingent of itinerant workers: seasonal plantation labourers, peddlers, transport workers, construction labourers.

As in Africa, Indian truck drivers are emerging as a key vector of HIV infection, with sampling in Tamil Nadu showing an incidence of about 3%

positive. Women from impoverished villages stand by bridges or culverts and flag down trucks, or hang around the *dhabas* (tea shops). "If a truck parks nearby other trucks will stop and form a queue," said Sundararaman.

In southern India, folklore about health depending on a balance of heat and cold makes sex essential. "Driving long distances definitely transfers heat from the engine into the body," said Farhad Basha, 28. "Sex is the only way to get it out." Basha always takes a condom on trips—to patch up leaks in his air-brake hose. "You rarely use it for sex, unless you definitely know someone is unhygienic," he said. "How can four inches of rubber help in reducing the risk of AIDS, when there is so much body contact and the disease travels by air, from the breath?"

Surjeet Singh, 33, a Sikh trucker who plies the route between Delhi and Bombay, said the heat theory was prevalent among southerners, but 85% of his colleagues had sex along the way "just for the pleasure" and rarely used condoms. "Once you are past Jaipur, there are whole villages devoted to prostitution," Singh said. Singh and two colleagues had not heard of AIDS. "We know of some sexual diseases, but not this one," he said.

The drug-abuse path of AIDS infection is turning into a heterosexual one as it spreads from addicts to their sexual partners. The northeastern state of Manipur is estimated to have about 30,000 addicts among its 1.8 million people, according to narcotics-control agencies. The number is thought to be doubling each year, and among 3,000 recently tested for HIV 54% showed signs of the virus.

The network of defences provided by the government's AIDS programme is scant. Efforts are being made to ensure safe blood supplies in the four big metropolitan health services by testing all units of blood. However, clerical errors have led to infection in one case, and it will be a month or two before laboratories have testing kits that can detect antibodies for the HIV-2 virus, which is also believed to have reached India. In Tamil Nadu, only about 25% of the total blood supply in all hospitals and clinics is being tested.

When blood tests indicate HIV contamination, the blood is simply destroyed and no attempt is made to inform or maintain contact with the donor. "If we contact the person, tomorrow no one will come forward to donate blood," said Solomon. "They will say the government will send someone to your house and everyone will know about it. It will damage the voluntary system. We tell the donors that if you want to know about your test, come forward and we'll tell you."

In one celebrated case, a group of 834 Tamil prostitutes "rescued" from Bombay and sent back to Madras in May 1990 were given the preliminary HIV test, showing a 65% positive result. Most of the young women subsequently disappeared from the authorities' view. Two are known to have developed AIDS, and at least one committed suicide.

Ignorance and panic has led to the imprisonment of people infected with HIV without any legal basis. Several hundred drug-users with HIV are locked up in the Imphal Central Jail in Manipur. Even in hospitals, people with HIV tend to be shunned. A major task for the Health Ministry has been to dispel myths among doctors and nurses about the way HIV is spread.

As yet, an obvious gap separates the health educators and the people they need to reach. Mass-media education is becoming more explicit, but is still constrained in explaining the use of condoms. It fails to reach the truck drivers, most of whom have never met a health education worker or seen any government advertisement relating to STDs.

The urgency is penetrating top levels of officialdom. Tamil Nadu's health minister participated in World AIDS Day in December 1991 for the first time. The dean of a women's college bought T-shirts advising condom use and distributed them to all her students. The real impact of the epidemic will come as the suspected vast number of HIV-positive cases start developing into AIDS. "People have not yet seen AIDS patients," said Solomon. "They have not seen anyone they know dying of it."

STUDY QUESTIONS

1. Why does Suniti Solomon admit that "the coming of AIDS to India has transformed her sense of Indian identity"?
2. With only 103 reported cases of AIDS in a population that exceeded 844 million in 1992, why are Indian public health officials concerned about an epidemic of HIV/AIDS?
3. What is unusual about the Indian government's HIV/AIDS education and prevention program?
4. What popular misconceptions about HIV transmission fuel the spread of the virus in India?

Readings from *WorldAIDS*

Jan Sharma; Tony Kahane; Mohammed Hanif*

Fighting Against Fate

When life became difficult in her native village of Melamchi in the Nepali hills, Geeta moved to Kathmandu where she worked as a housemaid. When her cousin promised her a better job in a carpet factory in India, she jumped at the opportunity.

---

*"Fighting Against Fate" (March 1994:11) was written by Jan Sharma, "Turning the Tide" (July 1993:2) was written by Tony Kahane, and "No Safer Sex for Pakistan's Gays" (January 1993:11) was written by Mohammed Hanif.

Reprinted with permission from *WorldAIDS*, a bimonthly magazine about AIDS and development published by the Panos Institute in London.

"I didn't realise that I was sold to a Nepali brothel keeper in India until the lady told me to engage in business," she said. "I wept and wept. I was shocked to be sold by my own relative. I went mad. They admitted me into a mental hospital. After a year, I was ultimately forced into prostitution. I never liked it—that was not what I had wanted. But you can't fight against luck and fate."

Thousands of girls from Nepal meet Geeta's fate every year. They are promised an attractive salary and a film heroine's lifestyle by the pimps and 'dream merchants' who travel through Nepal's villages.

In India, where Nepali girls are considered sexually attractive and are in high demand, they are sold to brothel keepers. Many resist but are beaten and repeatedly raped until they submit. The girls are then held in the brothel until they can pay back the owner the amount spent for them. In Bombay brothels alone, there are at least 20,000 Nepali girls, and more than 200,000 in the country as a whole.

But now the Indian health authorities are testing prostitutes for HIV, an increasing number of them—like Geeta—are sent back to Nepal when they test HIV positive.

Up to 25% of prostitutes are HIV positive in some Indian cities—and the rate is even higher for Nepali prostitutes, reaching 35% in places, according to the Kathmandu-based Women's Rehabilitation Centre, who provide support for some returning girls.

But the facilities for those women are few and far between. Eighteen-year-old Laxmi, who was diagnosed with HIV after escaping from a Bombay brothel, found that her parents refused to take her back when she came home to Nepal. After a brief spell in hospital, she was discharged and disappeared in Kathmandu. "We discharged her because we could do so little for her," explained Dr. Gopal Gajurel. "Another reason was that local youths made a beeline to her cabin in the evenings and nights."

Prostitution is illegal in Nepal, but many returning prostitutes are "doing brisk business back home", say senior police officials. An estimated 25,000 girls, many of them infected with HIV, are engaged in prostitution in Kathmandu. Rejected by their families, unskilled and stigmatised, most of them have no other option to survive.

AIDS is already a political issue in the Himalayan kingdom, where at least 5,000 people are estimated infected with HIV. According to Dr Bal Gopal Baidya, of the National Planning Commission, many factors facilitate the spread of HIV in Nepal. These include large-scale migration across the 2,000-mile open border with India, widespread sexually-transmitted diseases and drug use, inadequate health care and a low level of condom use—even by South Asian standards.

Opposition MP Asta Laxmi Shakya has already raised the issue of AIDS and women in parliament: "There is an urgent need to provide proper treatment to the AIDS-infected women returning from India in order to check the spread of the disease," she said. She alleged that women who tested HIV positive were being discriminated against by medical staff in hospitals.

AIDS carries a heavy stigma in Nepal. When Maya, another returning prostitute, died of AIDS in a Kathmandu hospital, her body was removed and buried with the help of bamboo sticks—no-one dared even touch her body for fear of infection.

Geeta was sent home with 200 Indian Rs (US$6.50) for her transport after she tested HIV positive. Back in Melamchi, she found her mother had died and her father refused to take her back. Determined to begin a new life, she rented a liquor shop with her savings. The shop was successful until her HIV status became known in the village—then business collapsed and she was forced to close down.

Geeta is now sheltered at a home for HIV-infected girls run by the Women's Rehabilitation Centre in Kathmandu, learning to knit sweaters to earn a living. But homes are not the answer.

"It's financially and practically impossible to open hostels for all these girls because of their sheer numbers," says Dr Aruna Upreti, who works with the Centre. "To make the girls' rehabilitation sustainable, efforts have to be made in the family, in the society and the native villages of the girls themselves."

Turning the Tide

American Jon Stuen-Parker, a former drug addict who studied public health at Yale University, has been at the forefront of a clean needle campaign in Vietnam. He is founder of the Boston-based National AIDS Brigade which has 200 workers throughout the United States providing AIDS information and running needle exchange schemes. Some are war veterans, most are former drug users, and many are HIV positive.

This year, the AIDS Brigade agreed to work in Vietnam. At a veterans' AIDS drop-in centre in Boston, a group of Vietnam war veterans raised money for Stuen-Parker's trip. "These men want to give something back to the country they helped to devastate," says Stuen-Parker. "They want to help prevent the spread of AIDS through ignorance. Doing this makes their difficult lives seem worthwhile."

According to the Vietnamese government there are some 120,000 injecting drug users in Vietnam. Other estimates go as high as 800,000 in a population of 67 million. Of the 332 cases of HIV infection officially notified by May this year, over 90% are drug-related. There has been a rapid spread of HIV infection through the sharing of dirty needles and equipment.

For the most part, HIV is concentrated in Vietnam's southern provinces, although seven cases have been reported recently in central Vietnam, all involving drug users.

On his visit in March, Stuen-Parker made contact both with officials in Hanoi and Ho Chi Minh City, formerly Saigon. Assisted by a Vietnamese outreach worker, he set up a programme of needle exchange in the main areas of Ho Chi Minh City frequented by drug users.

Stuen-Parker was surprised by the positive reception they received in Vietnam. "The idea of needle exchange is no great legal problem in Vietnam, unlike the United States," he says. "People are pragmatic, and there is no controversy around the idea."

The most common injected drug is liquid opium, almost certainly produced locally in Vietnam. The opium is partly refined, but not enough to be white, like heroin. It remains a muddy sort of colour, and is made into a powder, and then liquefied.

To get any effect from liquid opium, a large quantity has to be injected, and because of this large syringes must be used. This makes it very difficult for people to inject themselves—a large vein has to be located, and the injection needs accuracy and skill. This is the job of the 'community injector'. Each group of about 20 addicts will tend to have its own injector.

The injectors are not trained, but they work with a steady hand. Addicts queue for their turn. The injector, using the same needle for everyone, injects a solution of liquid opium into the large vein in the leg or thigh. There is no sterilisation of equipment. The addict then pays and leaves.

There is, paradoxically, an advantage to this system, as regards HIV prevention. As Stuen-Parker says, "outreach work is very much easier because of the existence of a group of injectors. Since most people don't inject themselves, but go to a small number of professional injectors, it is necessary only to teach the injectors about sterile needles and clean paraphernalia—and of course make sure they practise what they are taught."

Liquid opium is cheap and easily available, often from mobile vendors who operate in that way to evade arrest. According to Stuen-Parker, "the problem here is that needles are more expensive than the drugs."

An alternative approach to needle/syringe exchange is being adopted by Care International. They are proposing a scheme to clean needles using bleach—both for medical use and for injecting drug users. Barbara Franklin, AIDS consultant for the agency, says that the method is simple: syringes are filled twice with water which is then spurted out, twice with bleach, and twice again with water.

Dr Do Hong Ngoc, the liberal-minded director of the Health Information and Education Centre in Ho Chi Minh City, has produced pamphlets promoting the bleach strategy. The literature is awaiting approval from higher up before being released. "Bleach and condoms are the backbone of HIV prevention," Barbara Franklin says.

Jon Stuen-Parker, however, cautions about too carefree an adoption of bleach. "Some new findings in the US have shown that just swishing around with bleach can be ineffective for HIV. The needles and syringes must soak for at least 30 seconds to become sterilised. And it must be 100% bleach, not a 10% solution. Otherwise it may not be any good."

Jon Stuen-Parker and a colleague, Roy Nickerson Jr—a retired fireman and founder of the Vietnam Veterans with AIDS Committee—are planning a second trip in July.

"Our aim on our next visit," says Stuen-Parker, "is to train Vietnamese workers in needle exchange so they can continue the programme, and to convince the authorities the strategy is the right one. It's still possible for Vietnam to avoid the AIDS epidemic which is already devastating so much of South and Southeast Asia."

No Safer Sex for Pakistan's Gays

KARACHI: As night descends over the smog-ridden skyline of Karachi, Ali dons his bright yellow shirt and hits the road. For those who are not familiar with him, he is just another lad standing on a busy street waiting for a lift back home. But those who know him, know that Ali is a male prostitute who never says "no", does not bargain very hard and is available in one of Karachi's city centre parks anytime. He is one of the thousands of invisible male prostitutes on the prowl in packed buses and dark corners of public parks. Ali knows the ins and outs of Karachi's gay scene; his clients cut across age and class barriers. From feudal politicians to labourers on holiday from the gulf states, he seems to have slept with them all. Ask him about condoms and he laughs. "These things are for those who want to avoid pregnancies," he says. He doesn't have any such problems, thank you very much.

Ali as well as his numerous friends and clients who stalk the streets of Karachi probably have not read some of the statistics recently released by the National AIDS Control Programme: during the last 10 months alone, the officially recognised number of HIV cases has doubled from 67 to 120. And although the AIDS programme jealously guards the identities and histories of these cases, the sources claim that more than 20% of these cases are avowedly homosexual. But there is no way of knowing how many of these are really bisexual. Those who have been identified seldom admit to having had sex with men.

Male homosexuality is far more common in Pakistan than many care to acknowledge even though it has been recognised throughout the ages as part of subcontinental culture. Classical Urdu poets have rhapsodised about it and Sufi poets have made explicit references to male lovers in their poetry. But, given the country's puritanical ethos, it is rarely talked about and virtually never acknowledged in polite society. In fact, any discussion of sexuality per se, much less homosexuality, is absolutely out of the question in Pakistan's mainstream discourse and media.

So although homosexuality is rampant, a gay community in the Western sense of the word does not exist—except for a few odd groups of educated youths in Karachi who get together once in a while to party. "It's all strictly sexual," says JT, one of the very few gays in Pakistan who does not try to maintain a straight facade. "Very few are ready to own up to it as their identity and certainly nobody is ready to acknowledge that every time you drop off your pants in front of a stranger you are exposing yourself to AIDS."

Experts insist that a majority of men who have sex with men are not gay at all: "It has got more to do with our social conditions than anything else," says a doctor. "In a segregated society it's not a matter of one's sexual preference, it is more a matter of availability." And in a country where police can regularly stop any heterosexual couple at night and ask for marriage papers, homosexual prostitutes openly ply their wares on the streets. People are regularly arrested and punished, at times even flogged, for committing adultery, yet rarely has anyone been arrested for having sex with another male even though it is also punishable by law.

"It is a lot safer," says a 26-year old government servant who has been Ali's steady client for more than two years. "If I got myself a woman there would be lots of problems. She would be expensive, and it would be difficult to take her anywhere with me."

No-one in Pakistan disputes the fact that a very large number, a majority in fact, of males have some sort of homosexual experience in their lifetime. As far as the threat of AIDS is concerned, the statistics may not seem as frightening as figures available in other Asian countries, but health workers believe that officially acknowledged AIDS cases are only a fraction of the actual figure. "It's just the tip of the iceberg," says Hilda Saeed, the editor of *National Health,* a leading health magazine. About 24 government-run AIDS laboratories have screened only about 250,000 people out of a population that is well over 100 million now.

The first four HIV positive cases detected in Pakistan included one gay male, one bisexual male and his wife and child. Most of these figures appeared in the English language press. At the same time the state-run radio and television, which reaches all corners of the country, has made no attempt to educate the public about AIDS.

Although medical experts say that the data is too scant to form an opinion, 55 out of the 130 HIV cases have been detected in Northwest Frontier Province of Pakistan (NWFP) which has only one-sixth of Pakistan's total population. There are various factors which might explain the high number of cases in this province. Segregation of the sexes is most stringent in the province and Pukhtoon society is known for its openness towards homosexual practices. It is in fact the only part of Pakistan where it is socially acceptable for a man to have a young male lover. Even so the existence or even prevalence of homosexual practices in Pukhtoon society is ambiguous. For though active homosexuality is not seen as perverse or blameworthy, passive homosexuality may compromise the honour and claim to virility of a man in what is an uncompromisingly patriarchal society. As one Pathan watchman puts it, " a (passive) homosexual is not a man. He is a coward." So while the active partner stands to gain honour in the exercise of his virility, the passive partner earns shame and ridicule.

Perhaps another reason for the seemingly higher proportion of AIDS in NWFP is that many foreigners—including journalists, aid workers, gun runners and spies—have been concentrated in the province for the last 10 years in connection with the Afghan war.

In any event, the cause of safe sex in Pakistan seems to be a lost one. The few educated gays who have tried to preach the virtues of safe sex in their circles are frustrated by the response they get. "I tried distributing condoms to some of my friends who I knew were prostituting on the side," says JT, "and they just laughed at me." Another gay doctor who has been trying to encourage his friends to use condoms has given up now: "All of them tell you the same joke about eating candy with the wrapper on." "It is quite futile actually," says a gay doctor, "you cannot teach safe sex in a society which refuses to acknowledge its own sexuality. The only safe sex you can have here is just sitting at home and masturbating."

STUDY QUESTIONS

1. How has the Indian government's deportation policy fueled the regional HIV/AIDS epidemic? What resources—family, community, governmental—are available to HIV-infected women in Nepal?
2. What factors have fostered a positive reception to the needle exchange program in Vietnam? What lessons about effective HIV/AIDS education might be learned from this program?
3. How have public and private perceptions of homosexuality in Pakistan fueled the HIV/AIDS epidemic there? Why do these perceptions act as inhibitors for effective HIV/AIDS education and the introduction of safer sex behaviors?

Socioeconomic Implications of AIDS in Developing Countries

Jill Armstrong

In the mid-1970s, the scientific community first became aware of an illness that was striking predominantly adults in various parts of the world. Those affected by the disease would gradually waste away and not respond well if treated for common illnesses. But it was not until the early 1980s that this syndrome was identified as the Acquired Immune Deficiency Syndrome (AIDS), the final and fatal stage of infection with the human immunodeficiency virus

Reprinted with permission from *Finance and Development,* vol. 28 (December 1991): 14–17. © 1991 by International Monetary Fund.

(HIV). Now, barely a decade later, the AIDS epidemic has reached global proportions. The World Health Organization (WHO) estimates that in 1991, there were nine million adults and almost one million children worldwide infected with the virus, with over 80 percent of those in developing countries. As the numbers of those infected continues to increase—with the developing world accounting for a growing share—finding a cure, or vaccine, looms as one of the greatest challenges to modern science.

To date, most of the discussion surrounding the AIDS epidemic has focused on the devastating human toll and the serious strains that no doubt will be placed on national health care systems. But as many developing countries—particularly the poorer economies of Sub-Saharan Africa—are already discovering, the epidemic is not solely a health issue and cannot be dealt with as such (see box). Rather, it threatens to alter dramatically the economic and social fabric of many societies, raising serious questions about the development process itself. Although not the biggest killer—far more people in the developing world succumb to childhood diseases, such as respiratory ailments, diarrhea, and measles—AIDS strikes young and economically productive adults. Moreover, given the large numbers of individuals infected with the HIV virus, AIDS may well turn out to be an even more serious problem in the years to come. This article takes a look at the potential social and economic consequences of AIDS for developing countries, drawing on initial World Bank work in this area.

Status of Epidemic

For policymakers in countries that have been hit hard by AIDS, the need to design effective policies to prevent the further spread of the disease and to mitigate the negative consequences of the epidemic takes on increasing urgency with each passing day. But epidemiologists and statisticians are finding AIDS to be one of the most difficult diseases that they have ever tried to model. Unlike previous epidemics—such as the Black Plague, which ravaged Europe in the Middle Ages—AIDS has a long gestation period and can be transmitted sexually. As a result, researchers must try to predict human (i.e., mostly sexual) behavior—a formidable task.

Although AIDS is still a relatively new phenomenon—in effect, a breakdown of the body's immune system, which leaves it vulnerable to "opportunistic" infections that would normally be treatable—scientists already know a great deal about its epidemiology or transmission. To begin with, AIDS can be transmitted in three ways: through sexual intercourse, which globally accounts for approximately 80 percent of all HIV infections (of these, only 10 percent are estimated to have been due to homosexual exposure); through infected blood or blood products (this includes not only blood transfusion, but contact with HIV-contaminated drug-injecting equipment and the well-publicized, albeit rare, needle-prick exposure of health personnel); and from a mother to her fetus or infant, also known as peri-natal transmission, which accounts for another 10 percent.

Researchers also know that progression from the time of infection with the virus to the onset of full-blown AIDS is not immediate. In fact, there is a long incubation period—about ten years—during which individuals are already infectious but may show no signs initially of being ill. For children, however, the time from infection to developing AIDS is much shorter, usu-ally less than five years. Average survival after the onset of AIDS for both adults and children in developing countries is less than one year.

What researchers do not know enough about is sexual behavior in given populations and the potential changes that current prevention campaigns might bring. Questions also surround the efficiency of transmission (notably, the probability that a mother will pass AIDS on to her fetus or infant; estimates range from 30–50 percent), as well as the exact number of those infected but not yet ill (data are particularly poor in developing coun-tries). As a result, it is extremely difficult to forecast with any certainty at what point the epidemic will peak and stabilize in various regions, let alone in individual countries. Even so, conservative WHO estimates predict that nine million adults will develop AIDS during the 1990s, on top of one mil-lion AIDS cases in the 1980s. By the turn of the century, as many as 30 mil-lion adults and 10 million children will have been infected with HIV, gen-erating one million annual AIDS cases—over 90 percent of which will occur in Africa.

Certainly the epidemic has spread the most quickly in Sub-Saharan Africa, which WHO now estimates accounts for roughly two thirds of the HIV infections worldwide. But unlike in developed countries, in Africa, AIDS has struck men and women in an almost even ratio, and this means—especially when fertility rates are high—that many infants are also at risk. The industrialized countries come next, at 17 percent, with most cases still involving homosexual men. Increasingly, however, there has been a rise in heterosexual transmission, probably through infected drug users to their partners in the United States, as well as in Latin America and the Caribbean. So far, South and Southeast Asia have escaped the high tolls seen in other regions, although there are indications that the epidemic is beginning to take hold in highly populated India and Thailand.

By the turn of the century, however, some dramatic changes are antici-pated. Although the rate of increase of new cases is expected to slow in industrialized countries, in large part because of behavior change among high-risk groups, the numbers will continue to climb sharply throughout the developing world. By the year 2000, over 90 percent of those infected with HIV will be in developing countries, with half in Sub-Saharan Africa and a quarter in South and Southeast Asia. The current trend among high-risk groups in Thailand and India is particularly disturbing. What started in Thailand as a problem among intravenous drug users now has spread to the

Uganda: A New Approach to Combating AIDS

AIDS began to spread in eastern Africa along the shores of Lake Victoria in the mid-1970s. Today, of just under 17 million Ugandans, 1.3 million carry the HIV virus, most in their prime productive and most sexually active years. If the epidemic continues unabated, more than a million Ugandans—including nearly 400,000 children—will have died from AIDS by the turn of the century. Already, indicators of child survival and life expectancy are well below what they would have been without AIDS (see charts in box), and these estimates are conservative, given the number of uninfected children that will be losing primary caretakers—their mothers.

Faced with this crisis, Uganda has been one of the most forthright governments in Africa in admitting the seriousness of the problem. Indeed, it was the first, with help from WHO, to develop and adopt a Medium Term Plan to control AIDS, implemented by a special unit in the Ministry of Health that was established in 1986. These early efforts concentrated on developing and disseminating health education messages, screening blood supplies, and establishing a surveillance system to track the disease's spread. But in April 1990, the Government of Uganda turned to the World Bank for additional help, although traditionally the Bank has not been involved with the control of epidemics.

The Bank responded to the Government's appeal by forming a multidonor mission in September 1990, consisting of senior representatives from WHO, the United Nations Development Programme (UNDP), the United Nations Children's Fund, the United Nations Population Fund, Britain, Denmark, Norway, Sweden, and the United States. The objective was to pinpoint Uganda's emerging and unmet needs in the area of AIDS prevention and control. Questions raised by concerned Ugandans included: (1) how to provide cost-effective patient care for the tens of thousands developing symptoms of full-blown AIDS, including highly contagious tuberculosis; (2) how to provide basic needs, including school fees, for anywhere from 500,000 to 1 million orphans; (3) how to develop and spread health messages through more channels than only the Ministry of Health; and (4) how to assess the long-term economic ramifications, particularly in terms of per capita income and productivity.

continued

heterosexual community. In June 1989, about 3 percent of Bangkok's estimated 100,000 prostitutes were HIV positive; 18 months later, the figure was up to 20 percent, and the disease is likely to spread quickly from infected clients to their spouses.

Socioeconomic Impact

What costs can countries expect to bear as a result of the AIDS epidemic, especially in the developing world, where many are already struggling with

continued

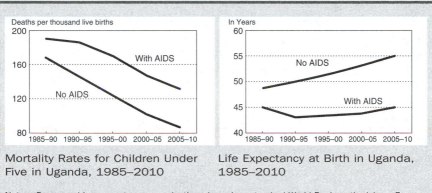

Mortality Rates for Children Under Five in Uganda, 1985–2010

Life Expectancy at Birth in Uganda, 1985–2010

Note: Demographic parameters are projections based on standard World Bank methodology. For Uganda, the World Bank average decline in mortality of causes other than AIDS was assumed, while fertility decline was assumed to follow a slow decline pattern. The "With AIDS" scenario is based on a World Bank simulation model.

Source: World Bank staff estimates, 1991.

As the mission participants worked closely with government officials and local NGO representatives, they quickly discovered that the impact of AIDS extended far beyond the health sector. Moreover, since Uganda was one of the first countries affected by the AIDS epidemic, early indications of some longer-term economic consequences were already becoming evident. The answer was to develop a multisectoral approach, with discussions centering on how to devise both a strategy and an appropriate institutional structure to ensure that the problem was effectively tackled. This theme was pursued by a follow-up Bank mission, jointly supported by WHO and UNDP.

The structure that emerged in early 1991 was a National AIDS Commission, chaired by the President of Uganda and comprising key ministers from a wide range of sectors. Its chief function is to set broad policy and provide high-level political support for the multisectoral AIDS activities. The Commission is supported by a full-time Secretariat, which is now working with relevant ministries and NGOs to develop a national AIDS strategy. Once this is done, the Secretariat will be instrumental in mobilizing—but not necessarily directly channeling—resources, as well as coordinating interventions, to stem further infections and mitigate the devastating consequences of AIDS.

high debt loads, fragile economies, famine, scarce human capital, and, in some cases, civil wars? Increasingly, the evidence shows that the ramifications will cut across all sectors, implying that many countries may need to look at the implications for development itself.

Demographic Effects

First and foremost, AIDS is a human tragedy, as captured by the changes in social indicators increasingly used as a proxy to monitor the development process. In Africa, where HIV prevalence rates have reached 10 percent and greater, deaths due to AIDS among children are already negating gains made by child survival programs in reducing mortality. Anticipated declines in adult mortality rates, too, are beginning to show signs of reversal. WHO has estimated that over 1985–90, AIDS added 10 percent on average to annual death rates for adults aged 15–49. In five years, these rates will increase by an additional 40 percent, and for some age groups, mortality rates could double or even triple. Gains in life expectancy, too, will be eroded as AIDS strikes adults in their prime productive years. The impact of AIDS on population growth rates will be noticeable—most models estimate that population growth rates in severely affected countries will be reduced by one half to one percentage point annually in the next two decades. But predictions of negative growth and shrinking populations are very unlikely, particularly where underlying growth rates remain high, such as in Sub-Saharan Africa. And, in spite of the AIDS epidemic, the promotion of family planning services should remain on the priority agenda.

Economic Impact

Assessing the magnitude of the economic impact hinges, of course, on the difficult task of determining the course of the epidemic itself. Based on anecdotal evidence at the household and firm level, however, a reasonable hypothesis is that the impact on the productive sectors will be channeled through changes in the size and quality of the labor force. Given the scale of the epidemic in some hard-hit countries, it is conceivable that long-run growth in per capita output will be constrained.

AIDS predominantly affects adults in their prime sexual and most productive ages, and unlike many other diseases afflicting adults in developing countries, it is fatal. Furthermore, this disease does not spare the occupational or urban elite, who are arguably among the more productive members of the economy. It is thought that the virus first spread among higher socioeconomic classes in African capitals. Indeed, infection rates in African urban centers are often double those in rural areas (AIDS is already the leading cause of adult death in Abidjan, and about 20 percent of adults in Kampala are infected).

Formal Sector

The spread of AIDS in cities in the developing world has implications for the development of the service and industrial sectors, the expansion of the private sector, as well as capacity-building efforts in countries where human capital is scarce. At the firm level, morbidity reduces productivity and boosts firms' medical expenses; eventual mortality also means increased outlays for death benefits. Replacement and retraining costs in hard-hit industries are already beginning to escalate.

Agriculture

The rural sector will not escape the touch of the epidemic, either. Although infection rates are lower in rural areas, throughout much of the developing world, most people still live there, making the absolute numbers of infected persons much higher. For countries where the bulk of agricultural production is very labor intensive and grown on smallholder plots, shortages of able-bodied adults may lower overall agricultural output. In addition, in the early phases of HIV-related illnesses, individual productivity will be reduced, other household members will need to devote time to caring for the patient, and household resources—otherwise used to purchase agricultural inputs—may be diverted for medical treatment.

Coping mechanisms involving labor allocation decisions are not well understood. The contribution of children's labor may be increased as families struggle to maintain current cropping patterns, and nonessential activities, such as weeding and pruning, may be curtailed. The key constraint will surface during periods of peak labor demand. If a household becomes unable to either supply labor internally or hire temporary workers, the composition of crops may be altered, and established patterns of many smallholders indicate that subsistence needs are usually met first, with marketable crops grown thereafter. It is conceivable that farmers will incrementally reduce labor-intensive or cash crops, but the extent to which this occurs will depend on these types of coping mechanisms, as well as underlying factors, such as population density, soil fertility, and rural infrastructure.

Overall, as was the case with many plagues and epidemics in the past, the short-term socioeconomic consequences could be severe, but there will no doubt be adjustments in the long term. Families, communities, and nations will adapt in an effort to cope with the increased mortality. If labor becomes a truly binding constraint, technological changes to save labor will emerge. If AIDS becomes severe, relative prices will adjust over time, and as wages get bid up, migration could play an equilibrating role. What is clear, however, is that more information is needed not only about the path of the epidemic but also about how the disease will alter development prospects in individual countries with different resource endowments.

Human Capital

One of the most troubling aspects is the possible implications for human capital formation—a key ingredient for successful development, as underscored in the World Bank's *World Development Report 1991*. Investing in people through improved health, education, and nutrition—particularly women, who constitute half of the developing world's population—holds the key to higher productivity and output in the long run, as well as being a desirable end in itself. But the AIDS epidemic poses a serious threat to the further development of human capital, potentially reversing the gains already made.

Education

Families with an AIDS illness or death will be less able to afford school fees, in part because of other expenditures on medical care, and children may be required to spend more time at home performing chores normally carried out by adults. In addition, university students, entering sexually active ages, are at increasing risk of contracting HIV, and their loss has a compound effect—not only have many years of education been foregone, but often limited university positions have been denied to others, as well.

Health

Even before AIDS, many developing countries were straining to improve the general health status of their populations. Now they must also cope with growing demands for hospital beds, health personnel, and drugs—in some parts of Africa, over half the occupants in many hospital wards are HIV-positive. The opportunity costs of temporarily treating illnesses of terminal AIDS patients could be enormous, as patients with curable ailments are crowded out. Expensive drugs available to those suffering with AIDS in industrialized countries are well beyond the reach of both public sector health care budgets and most individuals. Expenditures for health care are unlikely to expand at the same rate as new AIDS cases, despite the desperate need for them to do so to reach even basic primary health goals. Costly drugs are not recommended in WHO treatment guidelines for AIDS. One exception is to fully treat tuberculosis—a communicable disease now known to increase with AIDS—to prevent secondary infections.

Food Security and Nutrition

The links between AIDS, nutrition, and food security are complex. Extreme weight loss is one of the key symptoms of AIDS, caused by difficulties in food intake because of HIV-related illnesses. But distinguishing between AIDS and acute malnutrition is very difficult without testing for HIV. This is especially true for children, as chronic malnutrition (i.e., stunted growth) will only show up in children over time, and pediatric AIDS cases are unlikely to live long enough to show signs of stunting.

Even more disturbing are the indirect effects of AIDS within households on the food security and the nutritional status of surviving family members. Because AIDS is spread heterosexually, it is not uncommon for more than one adult per family to carry the virus. Household productive capacity, purchasing power, and per capita food availability are all likely to be reduced in the event of an adult's death from AIDS. Disruption—and even dissolution—of family structures because of AIDS is likely to increase food insecurity and malnutrition. Extended families that take in orphans could find food resources spread more thinly.

Women and Children

As heterosexual exposure takes over as the main mode of transmission worldwide, women and children will become more and more vulnerable, both as potential AIDS casualties and as survivors. The implications are quite serious, given that in many developing countries—particularly in Africa—women are not only the main providers of care but also the ones largely responsible for food production, agricultural labor, and the raising of children. The evidence from Africa increasingly shows that women are more likely to be infected than men and at an earlier age. This happens, in part, because women tend to have little control over the sexual behavior of their husbands, either in terms of their own relationships or those outside the union. Moreover, as mentioned earlier, women infected during peak child-bearing years also expose unborn children to the virus.

Another cause of deep concern is that by the year 2000, there may be an estimated five to ten million orphans in Africa alone—a region that has never had to deal with an orphan problem, thanks to extended families—on top of the ten million children that are projected to be infected. Orphanages hold little hope as a solution because of the sheer numbers involved, and extended families in parts of Africa are already beginning to feel the strains; often, the responsibility to feed, clothe, shelter, and educate the children falls on elderly grandparents, with little means of financial or physical support. Of growing concern is the ability of widows and orphans to acquire property rights (i.e., land) after the death of a male head of household. Without access to means of production, widows and children may be forced into petty theft or prostitution to support themselves.

What Can Be Done?

The AIDS epidemic poses an unprecedented challenge to policymakers—a challenge that must be met on two fronts. First, in keeping with the strategy long urged by WHO, the emphasis should be on prevention, especially in areas where the epidemic is in its earliest stages (as in Asia). Short of a vaccine, an unlikely development before the year 2000, this means changing sexual behavior. But as many prevention campaigns have demonstrated, improved knowledge does not necessarily lead to reformed behavior. The use of condoms and the treatment of other sexually transmitted diseases can also help—Thailand, for example, has a well-established and highly visible program to deliver contraceptives, especially condoms, which could be tailored quickly to promote safe sex. Blood screening, use of protective medical garments (gloves), and clean syringes add to the effort.

But even if all new transmissions were stopped tomorrow, there would still be a staggering number of AIDS cases, especially in Africa, with potentially profound implications for human resource development and economic growth. Thus, policymakers must also concentrate on designing measures to mitigate the consequences of the epidemic, which will involve taking stock of the potential magnitude of the epidemic as it affects various economic sectors. Since AIDS is no longer solely a health issue, ministries across the board should be involved in both planning interventions to mitigate the consequences (e.g., school fees for orphans and labor-saving technologies) and disseminating prevention messages (e.g., through teachers, agricultural extension agents, political organizations, social groups, and religious bodies). Local communities and nongovernmental organizations (NGOs) must also be enlisted—indeed, in many instances, they have already been instrumental in responding to the needs of patient care and providing for orphans.

What started out as a disease of concern to national health ministries and international health organizations has now become a problem with many dimensions. It is imperative in countries where the epidemic has already made inroads, that governments openly acknowledge the seriousness of the problem and take urgent action to stem the further spread of the virus. Even where the incidence of HIV infection is low—but where there are factors known to facilitate its transmission—early prevention measures, such as information campaigns, should also be promoted. The challenge for the donor community is to identify areas of comparative expertise and move forward quickly in a coordinated approach. Failure to do so will only exacerbate what is emerging as a major challenge to economic and social progress in developing countries and, above all, a human tragedy of massive proportions.

STUDY QUESTIONS

1. Why does Armstrong argue that HIV/AIDS poses severe threats to the economic fabric of developing nations?
2. In what ways do the Patterns II and III epidemics in developing nations create a larger health crisis than the Pattern I epidemics in industrialized nations?
3. How is the HIV/AIDS health crisis likely to affect population growth in developing nations over the next decade?
4. In what ways will developing nations experience the economic impact of HIV/AIDS during the next decade?
5. Why will HIV/AIDS have long-term consequences for agricultural production in developing nations?
6. How will HIV/AIDS affect family life and childhood in developing nations during the next decade?
7. Why does Armstrong believe that AIDS is *more* than a health crisis in developing nations? What strategies does she propose for managing HIV/AIDS in these nations?

Suggested Additional Readings

G. G. Bhava et al., "HIV Serosurveillance in Promiscuous Females of Bombay, India." Presented at the Sixth International Conference on AIDS, San Francisco (June 1990).

David E. Bloom and Joyce V. Lyons, editors. *Economic Implications of AIDS in Asia* (New Delhi: United Nations Development Program, Regional Office for Asia and the Pacific, 1993).

A. Cabello et al., "The Risk of Sexually Acquired HIV Infection in Paraguay." Presented at the Seventh International AIDS Conference, Florence, Italy (July 1991).

Dale D. Chitwood, "Annotation: HIV Risk and Injection Drug Users—Evidence for Behavioral Change." *American Journal of Public Health,* vol. 84 (March 1994):350.

Don C. Des Jarlais and Kachit Choopana, "AIDS Risk Reduction and Reduced HIV Seroconversion Among Injection Drug Users in Bangkok." *American Journal of Public Health,* vol. 84 (March 1994):452–455.

Paul Handley, "Catch It If Catch Can: Thailand Moves to Stanch the Virus." *Far Eastern Economic Review,* vol. 155 (February 1992):29–30.

Paul Handley, "Pumping Up Condoms: Family Planning Minister Turns His Talents to AIDS." *Far Eastern Economic Review,* vol. 155 (February 1992):31.

The Hidden Cost of AIDS: The Challenge of HIV to Development (London: The Panos Institute, 1992).

"Termites in the Basement: (AIDS Spreads in Thailand, India and the Philippines)." *The Economist,* vol. 328 (September 1993):42.

G. A. Williams with D. Bjerregaard, editors. *Community Responses to HIV/AIDS: Experiences from India and Thailand* (New Delhi: United Nations Development Program, Regional Office for Asia and the Pacific, 1993).

Thailand Ministry of Public Health. National Sentinel Seroprevalence Survey (August 1991).

World Health Organization Global Programme on AIDS. "HIV/AIDS in Countries of Central and Eastern Europe: Epidemiology, Prevention and Control." Report of the Global Programme on AIDS/EURO (Copenhagen, July 24, 1991).

Dialogues

Politics and Public Health Policy

• • •

"AIDS has refashioned America," Steven Findlay observed in the *U.S. News and World Report* as the nation and the world entered the second decade of a largely unsuccessful battle against the HIV virus.[1] While in part that refashioning remains problematic, there can be no question that the public face of AIDS has changed in the United States, and with that different public face there have been other changes as well. In 1991 more than 1.5 million Americans were infected with the HIV virus. Compared to one decade earlier, proportionately fewer of them were gay men, and more of them were young heterosexual women and men, infants, and children. New infections were occurring at the rate of forty to sixty thousand each year—about 150 new cases diagnosed every day, on the average. The national HIV/AIDS medical bill was soaring toward $8 billion. At the beginning of the second decade of the HIV/AIDS health crisis in the United States, AIDS was no longer the remote disease or the Pattern I epidemic that it had been during the early 1980s. **Needed (for Women and Children):** reflects some of the ways in which the changed public face of the HIV/AIDS health crisis has initiated restructured thinking about public health programs and policy.

With no effective medical therapies and a continuing increase in reported HIV infections and AIDS cases, previously tried (and rarely successful) public health measures—mandatory testing, mandatory name reporting, contact tracing, and quarantine—still surface for discussion. However, the discourse surrounding those debates is transformed. People like Sandor Katz—who have consistently opposed mandatory HIV testing, mandatory name reporting of HIV-seropositive people, quarantine, and similar control measures during the early years of the decade—no longer fashion their opposition in the vocabulary of civil rights and individual liberties. Faced with a continuing health crisis of ever-increasing proportions, the concerns have become pragmatic: Is it likely that this will work? **HIV Testing—A Phony Cure** takes such a measured and practical stance opposing mandatory testing.

During the 1980s, community-based, grass-roots organizations—the Gay Men's Health Crisis in New York, the San Francisco AIDS Foundation, and then ACT UP/ACT NOW, along with many smaller groups throughout the nation—

---

[1]Steven Findlay, "AIDS, the Second Decade." *U.S. News and World Report* (June 17, 1991):20.

266

countered government inertia in AIDS-related public health programs. The daily struggle against AIDS that was and is carried on within those organizations has required an enormous expenditure of focused human energy. **Battle Fatigue** describes the physical and emotional exhaustion of the people who have led that daily struggle and the structural rearrangement of HIV/AIDS activists. Many have fashioned working partnerships with the public health community, and others, like Bob Hattoy, have claimed a visible space in the national political arena. Tracing the politics of neglect that punctuated the 1980s, Hattoy called for a suspension of the moral judgments that had been attached to HIV and for a national health care policy that would protect HIV-seropositive people from the economic exploitation of the drug industry and insurance companies. In his five-minute endorsement speech of Bill Clinton's candidacy for U.S. presidency, Hattoy also signaled the transformation of public perceptions about HIV/AIDS, that "refashioning of America" to which Steven Findlay referred.

Needed (for Women and Children):

Suki Ports

AIDS is the major killer of women between the ages of twenty-five and thirty-four in New York City. In December of 1985, there were 487 women and 103 babies with AIDS. The majority were black, Hispanic, Asian, Native American, and "unknown other." Exactly two years later, in December 1987, the numbers in New York had risen to 1,364 women with AIDS and 231 pediatric cases—with the majority again being disproportionately from minority communities. AIDS occurs mainly among the poor, whose opportunities for obtaining comprehensive services during pregnancy or illness, at death, and for survivor children are slight. Appropriate housing, family case management, child care, and mental health support systems are even more limited, and AIDS has only exacerbated this situation.

Women are normally the care givers for the ill, so when they themselves become ill, who will care for them? There is no inclusive coordinated care system in place for them. We must not continue the patchwork, band-aid approach to AIDS care for women. Comprehensive extended support systems must be developed for families—whether traditional nuclear families, extended families, single sex couples and lovers with children, or the growing numbers of single parent families.

Reprinted with the permission of MIT Press from Douglas Crimp, editor, *AIDS: Cultural Analysis, Cultural Activism* (Cambridge, MA: MIT Press, 1991):169–176. © 1991 by Massachusetts Institute of Technology and October Magazine, Ltd.

The fastest growing numbers of AIDS cases are among women, and, again, this means primarily minority women (eighty-four percent in New York City). While black and Hispanic women are disproportionately and increasingly affected by AIDS, the media insensitively and incorrectly tells us that the heterosexual spread of AIDS is not really a threat. How does a black or Hispanic woman feel when she hears this? Prostitutes, of course, continue to receive headlines, but only to be scapegoated as "vectors" of the disease, even though female-to-male transmission is considerably less common (or documented) than male-to-female transmission. Women have not achieved full equality in the job market, let alone in bed, and yet condom ads continue to place the necessity of protected sex on women.

While women have displayed incredible stamina, courage, and resourcefulness, AIDS has played a cruel trick upon their coping skills. Their strength is sapped caring for children, preparing meals, cleaning, shopping, and doing laundry—leaving little energy for personal care or the mother's additional duties of relating to schools, taking her children to the park or on special outings. Exhaustion is compounded by a sense of isolation. Among the factors that contribute to this additional impact of AIDS upon women are fear of eviction if neighbors find out that they or their children have AIDS, loss of support if the extended family finds out, loss of a lover or husband, "coping" if drugs are in any way involved, dismissal of their children from school if other parents or school board members find out. The low-income mother faced—alone—with these seemingly never-ending problems does not have recourse to, say, insurance-paid psychiatric counseling—a need that is of primary importance for anyone faced with HIV infection, both at the time of diagnosis and during the extended process of explaining such information to children, family, or friends.

Counseling, as an aid to coping and healing for those affected by AIDS, is generally frustrated by the limited availability of personnel who can relate to specific ethnic, racial, class, or language needs. The counselor must be able to deal effectively and with compassion with a broad range of psychosocial concerns, often including confronting a drug problem in whatever way it might be manifested. For adults, there is the need to face death and to make practical as well as emotional decisions about children. For children in a family affected by AIDS there are equally powerful and emotionally complex issues. One young nine-year-old recently stated, "When Mommy dies, it will be my fault." No counselor of the same ethnic background was immediately willing to visit the home of this young boy. AIDS often means that young people must come to an understanding of the illness and/or death of the person closest to them. It also means that they must comprehend why certain other parents might forbid their children to play with them, or why even a family member might shun them. And it means they have to face the fears they have now and, more frighteningly, an ultimate grief upon the death of a loved one, which they might have to bear alone or with little immediate or sustained empathy.

NEEDED: An appropriate means of dealing with death in a family, tailored to the needs of individual children of different ages. If we do not train people now, we will face—unprepared—thousands of children left behind by the deaths of their mothers, fathers, or both. This loss, this legacy of children left behind and unable to cope with their grief, will precipitate a crisis that we have yet to tackle in any nationwide or community-specific manner. We have an entire generation of physically well (or possibly potentially ill) children to plan for and protect.

—Originally diagnosed and hospitalized with tuberculosis, Jane, the grandmother of a three-year-old boy, was soon diagnosed with AIDS. Because there was no nursing home willing to care for her, she lived the next seven—and final—months of her life in a major urban hospital. Already over-burdened with an average daily caseload of forty-five people with AIDS or other HIV-related illnesses, the hospital's infectious disease, psychiatric, and social support personnel interpreted Jane's early signs of AIDS-related dementia as nothing other than a grandmother's senility or lack of cooperativeness. Generally on alternate-level (as opposed to acute) care, Jane was resented by a staff forced to attend to her when they knew that what she really needed was a nursing care facility. Jane, in turn, resented their lack of attention. At some point during her hospitalization, her lower plate was lost, and its replacement was not a high priority on anyone's list but Jane's. Her once dry sense of humor and winsome smile contrasted sharply with the erratic and uncooperative behavior of this often cranky and complaining woman, whose facial appearance had now changed as much as her temperament. On one of my visits to another patient in her room I discovered that Jane and I were "twins"—sharing the same birth date and year. We compared stories of our "grands," and she always spoke of her sadness at missing out on seeing her grandson grow up. The little boy finally did see his grandmother . . . he was all dressed up in a gray suit and matching tie, shiny black shoes, and a look of puzzlement as he was walked past her open coffin.

NEEDED: A change in funding streams, which will provide, from the federal to the city level, housing for indigent seniors, including and especially those with AIDS. A little far-sightedness will ultimately result in fiscal soundness. The needs of senior citizens are the same as those of PWAs—ramps, handrails, elevators, doors with wheelchair and/or stretcher access, and spaces for group social activities including meals, family meetings, outpatient medical care, and private counseling. The housing required by both groups could be built into any rehabilitation of abandoned structures. Per diem costs would be far less than the toll now paid in actual dollars and in the demoralization of personnel, to say nothing of that of clients.

NEEDED: The funding necessary to enable care givers to get special training that would not only provide them with the most accurate and updated AIDS information to help them respond to PWAs' myriad questions, but take into account the extraordinary stress and strain of such a health care service by building in adequate internal support and respite systems for all workers. AIDS care must not be static, lacking in compassion, or inadequate because of ignorance or overwork.

NEEDED: The ability to provide other than acute medical care for low-income PWAs, i.e., dental care, mental health counseling, and planning for legal and other business needs for both PWAs and their families.

NEEDED: Additional auxiliary personnel who have the time to consider and plan for the fulfillment of human needs. Jane, whose long life ended separated from family, and with the added indignity of not being able to eat well due to the lack of lower teeth, is but one painful example of an overburdened system's turning its back on the needs of individuals. Low-income communities cannot produce the same numbers of volunteers ("candy stripers") as the more affluent communities, which have both public and private hospitals within their boundaries.

—Mary was a tall, statuesque, thiry-one-year-old woman who became weak and thin almost before your eyes. Oral thrush made it difficult for her to talk and, consequently, difficult for her boyfriend to communicate with her. He eventually became discouraged by this, as well as by Mary's countless trips to the hospital's inpatient and outpatient clinics, and so he left her—which, needless to say, sent Mary into a deep depression. Only the stern intervention of a very caring infectious disease physician made the boyfriend see the vital role he played in both her physical and emotional health.

NEEDED: Time and funds for additional trained staff to participate in the education of family members—including lovers—and neighbors of PWAs. Where appropriate, family reconciliation needs to be nurtured.

—Betty, who had a teenage daughter, acted like a spoiled, manipulative adolescent herself. She frequently suffered from boredom, which caused her moods to swing dramatically from those of a crying, wily childlike person, who begged for cigarettes and specific candy or food, to a completely uncooperative patient whose abusive behavior was directed primarily at the overburdened nursing staff.

NEEDED: The availability of a TV in a social setting. This space might also serve as a place where some vocational or other training classes (i.e., writing skills or crafts) might be taught. Such an allotted space within an institution would allow patients who are sometimes in the hospital for long periods of time the opportunity to occupy themselves, while also providing them with valuable information that we mistakenly assume they get by osmosis. It could be the location for the dissemination of reading materials and information about AIDS, ranging from general home precautionary guidelines to practical nutrition recommendations. Nutrition information cannot be taken for granted within poor communities. AIDS care is completely out of step with the needs of people who must make their purchases on food stamps or whose ethnically oriented local grocery stores limit the availability of certain foods.

—Rosa, with five children from ages two to twenty, struggled with her religious upbringing and country of origin's traditions and finally decided it would be most responsible if she aborted her sixth child and had her tubes tied. She did not count on the fact that this very difficult personal decision would be met by a three-week delay due to fear and unwillingness to deal with an HIV-infected woman on the part of a surgeon, a lab technician, and a nurse. After going through the humiliation of rejection by one medical staff person after another, she finally was scheduled for an overnight stay. We asked the appropriate city agency that child care be provided by a caretaker who was familiar to the children and who was willing to spend the night, although existing norms place children in temporary foster care. During the surgical procedure Rosa's uterus was perforated, thus requiring that a total hysterectomy be performed. She remained in pain many hours after returning to her room because no one had written orders for medication for this procedure. Given the lack of attention to Rosa's immediate health needs, it should come as no surprise that no one authorized the extension of the child care for the entire week now required for her hospitalization.

NEEDED: Coordination and sharing of information and training of all hospital personnel, particularly those who might come into contact with AIDS-related problems, and not only those in infectious disease units. Social services must be sufficiently organized and coordinated with medical personnel so that, for example, the infectious disease staff can alert general surgery (or others) when a particular patient might be hospitalized for a reason other than AIDS.

NEEDED: Child and family care based upon a Family Case Management system responsive to the needs of any member of a family in which there is a person with AIDS or HIV infection. This seemingly simple and common-sense need is not met because of existing rules for reimbursement, job definition, union work regulations, and scope of training. A major overhaul of child care and home care is long overdue, but AIDS-related needs have created a new crisis, and the gaps are glaring, as are the ramifications for affected families. In many cases the lowest-paid women are asked to provide the most support for difficult situations—without provisions for their own health, vacation, and other benefits.

—A mother with an income in the low twenty-thousand-dollar range has to quit work to take care of her child, who is HIV positive, because her income is too high to be eligible for free child care and too low to pay the going rates for private care. She cannot put her daughter in day care, as the child must be taken to a clinic weekly for medication and checkups. The mother's welfare payments do not cover her rent increase, the extra carfares needed to go to and from the hospital, extra pampers and special foods required by the child so as to avoid effects of diarrhea. As if it were not enough that this woman, who has never been on welfare, must face the emotional stress of a change in financial status and the painful realities of a child sick with a life-threatening disease (which might engender feelings of guilt and inadequacy on her part), she must also deal with the possibility of losing her home.

—Another mother is single and weak with AIDS. She qualifies for home care, but her children, who are healthy, might be sent to foster care because the adult-care worker is reporting that the mother neglects her children. Existing regulations do not require or even permit the home attendant assigned to an adult to feed the children the same food prepared for the mother. A duplication of workers is provided only after further reports of "neglect." This loving mother, who wishes to keep her family intact as long as possible, is faced with the "choice" of sending them to foster care or having neglect charges filed against her. The final result was that her children were placed in the home of strangers.

NEEDED: The development of a new definition of AIDS family care givers, with special training in AIDS care for any and all members of a "family." Perhaps the Peace Corps could serve as a model for a program that would draw people from a variety of backgrounds, including mothers whose children have grown up and left the nest, recent graduates with related academic interests who are undecided in career choice; these people might also include women who had been incarcerated and had received a special training certificate while institutionalized, or women on welfare who would be allowed to augment payments or who could get off welfare entirely, having been trained with skills for a new family health care career.

The foregoing examples of women who have experienced a multitude of problems with the onset of AIDS or HIV infection—either their own or that of a member of their family—represent but a glimpse of the multi-dimensional effects of AIDS upon women. But of what women are we speaking? For the most part, women who have lived difficult lives already: women who are (or were) drug users or who have been sexually involved with a drug user. They are also women who generally have low incomes, who have had little opportunity for higher education, and who have limited job opportunities. In the United States they are, for the most part, black and

Hispanic. As a group of women at the Third International Conference on AIDS in June of 1987 stated, "AIDS offers a paradigm for all of the critical issues which impact upon women."[1]

—A young black mother recently stated, with tears in her eyes, gripping the hand of her husband, "If it was not for Robert's support and being there, I would have committed suicide. When my baby was born she was beautiful. Now my baby is dying of AIDS."

—Lisette, when well enough to be ambulatory, helps older patients eat, combs their hair, acts as a nurse's aide and personal care giver, and is generally an outgoing spirit-picker-upper. But she has recently been depressed. She worries about her baby (age three) who is now seropositive, and her only healthy child (an adolescent), who just had an abortion. Lisette lost her husband, middle child, and a stepsister to AIDS. She has tried to commit suicide. Abused as a young girl, Lisette escaped from the world of school into a world of sex and drugs and became pregnant at sixteen. She cautions young women, "Learn more about life and yourself before trying to raise a family."

But we must ask: What are responsible adults doing to ensure that adolescents are getting specific AIDS prevention information? What is the prevailing knowledge among teenagers? What precautions are they taking?

In the December 1987 issue of *New Youth Connections, NYC,* the results of a survey from the previous month were printed in an article entitled "Thinking About AIDS." It is a sobering look at what teens believe in the city with the highest case incidence of AIDS in the world:

—Thirty-three percent think that you can only get AIDS by having sexual relations with a gay man.

—Sixty-eight percent of the sexually active readers who responded either never or only sometimes use a condom.

—Forty-two percent know people who shoot drugs.

While young people continue to shoot drugs, have unprotected sex, and get pregnant at the same alarming rates as before the advent of the AIDS epidemic, adults on school boards and boards of education are embroiled in emotional, diversionary controversies about sex education—how explicit to be about sex and drugs; whether methods of birth control, which are the only available artificial methods of preventing AIDS, should be discussed, displayed, or distributed.

If we are to ensure the well-being of our children, we must aggressively pursue the education, follow-up education, and, even more importantly, the follow-up counseling of adolescents, who are at the stage in life during which they are least receptive to adult intervention—when they are confronted with adulthood themselves, an adulthood that includes the challenge and excitement of sex and drugs.

If we are to ensure and encourage stable environments and compassionate care for PWAs, we must educate family members and communities to respond to those in need of care. Family case management is critical, but existing informal networks must also be encouraged. Only such steps will help kill the climate of fear about AIDS.

If we are to ensure that those already infected receive the best care, regardless of insurance coverage or class status, we must provide ongoing education to current care givers, create new sources of care givers, and provide respite and support for those providing care.

Because AIDS has disproportionately affected black and Hispanic women and children, future planning must involve the input of black and Hispanic women at the highest levels. We must base care and planning upon the most accurate knowledge and the most creative and promising guesses we can make, while also providing the compassion and coordination of services so lacking now. We must anticipate; we cannot luxuriate in testing the limits of women's endurance. Prevention, yes, and foresight based upon what is happening now. New policy issues will be arising in proportion to new situations, such as the lack of housing for adolescents with AIDS or HIV positivity. In New York City we must develop policy recommendations based upon large minority caseloads in a city torn apart by racism. While we may have the ability, the question is whether we have the will, the will to act immediately—to provide care and services for those already affected/infected and to inform and protect others from contracting this devastating disease.

NOTES

1.   See The International Working Group on Women and AIDS, "An Open Letter to the Planning Committee of the Third International Conference on AIDS." Douglas Crimp, editor. *AIDS: Cultural Analysis, Cultural Activism* (Cambridge, MA: MIT Press, 1991):166–168.

STUDY QUESTIONS

1. How do the special needs of women and children with HIV/AIDS differ from the needs of men?
2. How will "a change in funding streams" meet the unique needs of women who are living with HIV/AIDS?
3. What kinds of nonmedical support services does Ports advocate to meet the needs of women who are living with HIV/AIDS?
4. What is a "Family Case Management"system, and how would it better serve the needs of women and children who are living with HIV/AIDS?
5. What is an "AIDS family care giver," and how would that care giver function in the Family Case Management system that Ports advocates?
6. What impact does the intersection of HIV/AIDS and racism in urban America have on HIV/AIDS prevention and education programs?

HIV Testing—A Phony Cure

Sandor Katz

As the AIDS crisis in the United States accelerates into its tenth year, panicked health authorities are adopting counterproductive and coercive policies instead of confronting the difficult realities of treating people with AIDS and halting the spread of HIV, the virus believed to cause AIDS. Policy-makers in search of a magic bullet have focused on testing people for the presence of HIV antibodies, reporting to health authorities the names of people who test positive and finding and notifying their sexual and needle-sharing partners. Despite evidence that these measures discourage those at greatest risk of getting AIDS from seeking information and care, almost half the nation's states now report, in most or all cases, names of people who are HIV positive. This past December the American Medical Association officially endorsed mandatory name reporting and called for aggressive contact tracing as well (contact tracing is when authorities notify sexual or needle-sharing partners of the HIV infected that they are at risk). But aside from advocating widespread HIV testing, "most of the nation's physicians are still failing to take part in the fight to treat and control the deadly disease," according to a recent investigation by Bruce Lambert of *The New York Times*. The medical establishment's response to AIDS mirrors that of the federal government and many states and localities, where the focus of AIDS policy is identification of the infected rather than care and prevention.

Social control in the name of public health has a long and illustrious history in this country. The legacy of wholesale quarantines of immigrants and prostitutes gives other disenfranchised groups good reason to fear name reporting of people who are HIV positive. Given the stigma of AIDS and the vulnerability of the groups hardest hit by it so far—gay men, drug addicts and their partners and children—there is an ever-present danger that public health officials will trample on civil liberties in their zeal to do something (or at least to appear to be doing something) to fight AIDS. New York's recently departed Health Commissioner, Stephen Joseph, was condemned by virtually every AIDS service–providing agency in the city for his proposal to compile lists of the names of people testing HIV positive. In a *New York Times* Op-Ed piece in February, Joseph wrote, "Concern for the individual liberties of those currently infected must take second place to the protection of the uninfected and the larger community."

But do the civil liberties of the HIV infected really conflict with the protection of the uninfected? Dr. Mervyn Silverman, president of the American

Foundation for AIDS Research and the former San Francisco Health Commissioner who made the controversial decision to close the gay bath-houses in that city in 1984, thinks not. "Whenever there is a conflict between public health and civil liberties, public health always wins," he says. But in the case of AIDS, he continues, "they are consonant. If I can make it safe for you to come in [for testing and health care], you'll do it. If you think you'll lose your civil liberties, you won't come in." Ronald Johnson, executive director of New York's Minority Task Force on AIDS, concurs in saying that any public health policy that arouses fears of repression "would be counterproductive to public health goals because it would drive people away" from testing and care.

HIV testing has raised the specter of discrimination in employment, housing, health insurance and other areas. When the HIV test was still in development in 1984, for instance, Florida health authorities received a request from a school district to use the test to screen out gay teachers, which they properly denied. A recent national survey conducted by the Robert Wood Johnson Foundation and the University of California at Los Angeles found that, despite promises of confidentiality, two-thirds of the nation's hospitals indicate HIV status openly on patients' medical charts, and many hospitals routinely test patients without their knowledge or consent. Stories abound of test results leaking out, and insurance companies routinely test applicants and share the names of HIV-infected individuals. Due to the lack of effective legal protection from discrimination on the basis of HIV status, most AIDS activists have opposed anything but anonymous and voluntary testing. Blood samples tested anonymously are identified by a number to insure that the name of the tested individual is never known.

The appeal of name reporting for health authorities is that it gives them greater control over any follow-up procedures. But there is convincing evidence that such policies backfire. A now-classic University of South Carolina study, presented at the Fourth International Conference on AIDS in Stockholm in 1988, charted changes in HIV testing patterns after South Carolina repealed anonymous testing in 1986 and established mandatory name reporting. The number of gay men tested dropped by 51 percent. While the total number of people tested increased slightly, the overall rate of seropositivity among those being tested decreased by 43 percent. The study demonstrates that ending anonymous testing and requiring the reporting of names serve to scare away from diagnostic information and health care those people at greatest risk. Despite the evidence that mandatory reporting is a counterproductive health policy, it is winning widespread support. With the passage of a New Jersey law earlier this year, twenty-five states now require name reporting in most cases; nine of those states do not allow anonymous testing at all.

Mandatory name reporting is usually accompanied by contact tracing. It is desirable for people to inform past and present partners who may be at risk and not know it. Discussion of notification procedures is an important component of the post-test counseling process, and every state has voluntary partner notification programs in which people can ask counselors to notify partners for them. But contact tracing raises frightening civil liberties questions when it moves beyond the purely voluntary. Patients can feel coerced into revealing the names of partners, fearing that services will be withheld if they don't, and doctors and health authorities frequently breach confidentiality to inform partners without the patient's consent. Because of the stigma attached to AIDS and the sexual and drug-using behaviors with which it is generally associated, people often are afraid to inform partners. Many doctors and public health authorities feel that, justified though the fear of telling partners may be, it is unconscionable not to tell them, and that it is their medical duty to inform the partners if the HIV-infected patient refuses to do so. The gay community has taken a firm position opposing such breaches of confidentiality, arguing that, as with name reporting, the threat of such action is *precisely* what will keep people away from testing and health care. "If your primary goal is to notify unsuspecting partners," says Nan Hunter, director of the A.C.L.U.'s AIDS and Civil Liberties Project, "you can be damn sure you'll never get to them if their partners don't come in in the first place."

There is no unanimity among AIDS activists on contact tracing; class, race, gender and sexual orientation all come into play. "I think the gay community has valid and serious concerns about contact tracing," says Debra Fraser-Howze, executive director of New York's Black Leadership Commission on AIDS. But Fraser-Howze believes that for women the issues are different: "We are beginning to ask, Why are we not letting these women know they are at risk?" For Marie St. Cyr, executive director of New York's Women and AIDS Resource Network (WARN), the question of breaching confidentiality is more complex. "Contact tracing tends to be coercive and punitive toward women," she says, noting that partner notification for HIV-positive women often results in physical violence against them from the men informed.

Opponents of contact tracing also note that it can drain resources from treatment and education programs. Multiple contacts, and lack of information about how to reach them, create vast logistical challenges. "A lot of people can be going on a lot of wild-goose chases," cautions St. Cyr. A study of the contact-tracing provisions of Representative William Dannemeyer's Proposition 102, defeated by California voters in 1988, estimated initial costs of $765 million and ongoing costs of $25 million a year for a state in which total AIDS spending in the 1988–89 fiscal year was below $75 million. This study's authors, University of California, Berkeley, economists Robert Anderson and John Quigley, concluded that "adoption of Proposition 102 would have required a massive diversion of funds from other programs, including, in all likelihood, proven programs for prevention of HIV transmission."

The spread of AIDS can be halted only by appealing to the rationality of human beings bent on personal survival. If human behavior can be changed—and the experience of the gay male community in the first decade of the epidemic suggests that it can—it will take aggressive education efforts. This entails explicit risk-reduction information from an early age, targeted education efforts, mass-media reinforcement and support from existing institutions, from health and social service agencies to churches and schools. "If we are looking seriously at prevention, it needs to be a global approach," St. Cyr says, in support of the idea that locating and testing identified contacts solves nothing when everyone is potentially at risk. Mervyn Silverman concurs: "Our goal is to get the emphasis and mind-set on educating everybody."

The alternative places the full burden of responsibility on the HIV-infected individual. This is the view that supports breaches of confidentiality and the logic of incarcerating people who have sex without announcing they are HIV positive. Indiana's health department, under Dr. Woodrow Myers, put two HIV-infected people in "isolation" and issued pre-quarantine warnings to ten others, threatening that "engaging in an intimate sexual act *even with the use of barrier technique* (condoms or rubbers), without informing your partner that you carry HIV," could lead to detention. [Emphasis added.] Myers has since been named New York City Health Commissioner by Mayor David Dinkins, over the vocal objections of the AIDS Coalition to Unleash Power (ACT UP) and many AIDS service providers and gay groups.

Many public health advocates and civil libertarians interviewed in the course of researching this article believe there are behaviors that expose others to HIV risk and should be subject to state control, such as quarantine. They recount worst-case scenarios which vary in detail but generically consist of a vindictive "AIDS monster" deliberately infecting scores of innocents, à la Gaetan Dugas as he was sensationalized as "Patient Zero" in Randy Shilts's book *And the Band Played On*. But even in the worst-case scenarios, punishing such individuals as a matter of public policy would do little to protect anyone from AIDS, for it does nothing to alter anyone else's risky behavior.

The HIV virus is not easily transmitted. It can be forced on a well-informed person only through rape or physical assault. Aside from those exceptions, people can protect themselves from it. But they can protect themselves only by behaving as if every sexual partner is HIV infected. Screening partners is ineffective. The facts of HIV are that it takes from several months to several years after transmission of the virus to develop antibodies, and people can live with HIV for many years without symptoms. If people know what sexual acts are unsafe and how they can be made safer with condoms and dental dams (for cunnilingus), then it doesn't matter what a partner's status is, whether the partner knows his or her status or whether the partner chooses to share that information. A urine test to detect HIV antibodies has been developed by New York University researcher Alvin Friedman-Kien, who envisions its use as a home test to "check out your lover" before having sex. Such screening promotes a false sense of security, due to the lag between the time of HIV infection and the appearance of antibodies. People who engage in unsafe behavior do so at their own risk. Until there is a cure, we are all living with AIDS.

Regarding the possibility of quarantine, the A.C.L.U.'s Nan Hunter says that "it's certainly conceivable that it could be justified," so long as the state "first exhausts every possible less restrictive alternative, proves that there is an imminent risk to others and affords full due process." But these lines are already being crossed. In Indiana an HIV-infected person (and the state knows who that is, thanks to name reporting) is considered an imminent risk to others if he or she does not announce his or her HIV status to sexual partners, even if they are practicing safer sex. Some states' HIV laws refer not only to people infected with HIV but those "suspected" of it. "Remember, there is an attitude that the people involved in this [AIDS] are disgusting scumbags to begin with," notes Rodger Pettyjohn, a nurse formerly at New York's Community Health Project who has AIDS himself. The prospect of quarantine laws being abused is a chilling one. What could be more appealing to opportunistic politicians functioning in a climate of panic?

No less horrific a figure than Adolf Hitler devoted his attention to the control of syphilis. In "the medical struggle against the plague," the Führer wrote in *Mein Kampf,* "there must be no half-measures; the gravest and most ruthless decisions will have to be made. It is a half-measure to let incurably sick people steadily contaminate the remaining healthy ones." Hitler's ideological descendants recognize AIDS as a potent issue to mobilize fear. North Carolina Senator Jesse Helms advocates universal testing and says, "I think somewhere along the line we are going to have to quarantine, if we are really going to contain this disease." Lyndon LaRouche's unsuccessful 1986 ballot proposition calling for the quarantine of all HIV-positive individuals was supported by 2 million California voters. In this atmosphere, would you want the government to know you were HIV infected?

It is against this backdrop that the overall role of HIV testing in the fight against AIDS must be understood. One important political appeal of testing is that it is cheap and easy. Public health officials generally view testing as part of prevention. But where is the rest of the strategy? Providing drug treatment to intravenous drug users is difficult and expensive, and provision of explicit safer-sex education and clean needles is controversial and therefore easier not to do. The isolationist approach to AIDS prevention, which costs relatively little compared with universal education and gives the appearance of action, is HIV testing, contact tracing and the threat of quarantine.

Increasingly, the HIV test is being viewed as a diagnostic tool for purposes of treatment. Aerosolized pentamidine can prevent pneumocystis carinii pneumonia, the single biggest killer of people with AIDS, and low doses of AZT, or azidothymidine, may slow the virus's effects. With the advent of such early intervention treatments for asymptomatic HIV-infected people, many AIDS activists have begun to warm to testing, although generally with the caveat that the decision of whether to get tested is complex and must remain up to the individual.

For most AIDS activists, the primary consideration in thinking about testing is access to quality health care (as well as supportive social services), without which it is not possible to take advantage of early intervention therapies. And, as Stephen Beck, former executive director of the National Association of People with AIDS, points out, "That's not a reality for most people." In New York, waits of several days in hospital emergency rooms are common, while waiting lists for primary health care clinics are measured in weeks and months. St. Cyr of WARN laments, "Without the support network, I really have to think, What is it that I am offering someone [by getting them tested]? What is the level of psychological punishment that I am asking people to take?" Rodger Pettyjohn asks, "Since the needs of people already diagnosed aren't being met, how are we supposed to believe that the government will do anything more for more people?" The expected passage of $600 million in emergency federal AIDS assistance will be an important step in the right direction, but providing adequate health care will require a far greater commitment of spending.

Federal AIDS research has so far yielded little, being driven more by scientific egos and the pursuit of pharmaceutical profits than by health needs. While the National Institutes of Health reorganizes its data, new drug trials are being held up. (ACT UP plans to storm the N.I.H. on May 21 [1990].) Progress has instead come out of places like New York's Community Research Initiative, where the tests for aerosolized pentamidine were conducted, and which the feds have refused to fund. In case after case, the Food and Drug Administration has failed to release promising drugs until AIDS activists forced them to.

The government is not mobilizing to help people with AIDS survive or to stop the spread of HIV. "All across the country there is a cry for leadership from the Federal Government," stated the National Commission on AIDS in its April report to President Bush, who has refused to address the Sixth International Conference on AIDS being held in San Francisco next month. This dismal record leaves AIDS activists suspicious of the focus on testing and frightened of what the future appears to hold.

STUDY QUESTIONS

1. What are the specific public health control measures to which Katz objects?
2. Who is Stephen Joseph, and what did he advocate for New York City?
3. How does Dr. Mervyn Silverman's statement weigh the balance between public health needs and civil liberties?
4. What are the potential negative outcomes of HIV testing, according to Katz?
5. What happened in South Carolina when the state repealed anonymous HIV testing in 1986?
6. What is contact tracing? Why does Katz argue that it is ineffective in controlling HIV transmission?
7. How did Indiana introduce the possibility of quarantining people with HIV/AIDS?
8. What are the medical advantages to HIV testing? Why does Katz say the HIV screening "promotes a false sense of security"?
9. What alternatives to social control would foster what Katz believes to be the only effective measure of control over HIV transmission?

Battle Fatigue

Five years ago, Peter Staley abandoned his job as a Wall Street bond trader to become a hotshot fund-raiser for the AIDS activist group ACT UP, and he also emerged as one of the leaders of its Treatment and Data Committee, which became instrumental in reforming the policies of the Food and Drug Administration and the National Institutes of Health. Staley, a wealthy white businessman, was an unusual recruit to grass-roots politics. He persuaded ACT UP to mass-market T-shirts bearing its slogan, "Silence = Death," and solicited donations by direct mail—tactics that were initially greeted as politically incorrect but helped accelerate the startling momentum of ACT UP.

The original New York chapter, founded in 1987, spawned sister organizations in other cities, some of them overseas, and the group brought the issue of AIDS to center stage by mounting smart, brash protests. Staley got himself and four other ACT UP members onto the floor of the Stock Exchange, for example, and they handcuffed themselves to a balcony railing, blew foghorns, and unfurled a large banner urging traders to sell Burroughs Wellcome stock, because the company was charging astronomical amounts for the drug AZT. Later, three members of ACT UP sneaked onto the set of "The CBS Evening News" and disrupted the broadcast, while over at PBS additional members were attempting unsuccessfully to chain themselves to Robert MacNeil, of

"The MacNeil/Lehrer Newshour." At other protests, seas of people turned up wearing googly-eyed Cardinal O'Connor masks or spacey George Bush faces. By creating vivid controversies, ACT UP has inspired speedier trials of new drugs, and, most recently, it played a part in forcing the government to acknowledge tens of thousands of cases of AIDS among women and intra-venous-drug users whose illnesses hadn't been included in the official defin-ition of the disease. "Perhaps because of the need, the tragedy, without know-ing it we were making history," says the playwright Larry Kramer, who found-ed the original group. "We were able to work together in harmony in a way that members of the gay and lesbian community had never seen before. The love and respect of each for each was so heavy it was tangible."

But the world of political organizing is a volatile one. Rancorous factional disputes in the last two years helped bring about the departure of Staley and other prominent activists last winter and left ACT UP's New York chapter a small-er, poorer, and less effective organization. In a recent series about its troubles, *QW,* a gay-oriented magazine, cited membership and fund-raising figures that tell the story eloquently: the number of people who attend the group's week-ly meeting—formerly the place to be on Monday nights if you were gay and lived in New York—dropped from seven hundred at its peak, two years ago, to a hundred and fifty earlier this year; the amount of money raised decreased from a million dollars two years ago to a fourth of that amount this year; and the number of demonstrations staged by the group has slipped. Kramer, who is among the disenchanted, says of the current meetings, "It's like going to Miami and seeing all the old folks on the beach—you recognize the faces, but that's about it. All the energy is gone." Some members consider this an over-statement and claim to see signs of a revival, but even they recognize that there has been a decline. In the face of the Bush Administration's unreceptive atti-tude, and of the seemingly insurmountable medical challenges posed by AIDS, some members just lost hope. Others, including some of the group's key fig-ures, died of the disease. Membership also dwindled because some members went to work on AIDS-related causes full time.

And, inevitably, there was infighting, as complicated issues were hashed out in large groups. In particular, there was a history of tension between ACT UP's Treatment and Data Committee and the New York chapter as a whole. Treatment activists on the committee, like Mark Harrington and Jim Eigo, are so well educated on the subject of AIDS that they are considered honorary scientists. Kramer, a treatment activist himself, recalls a meeting between members of the committee and executives of the pharmaceutical company Bristol-Myers: "Mark would go in, and Jim, too—they never took baths, and they smoked incessantly, and they looked like terrorists, but they opened their mouths and you couldn't believe the quality of the knowledge that came out." In a way, that very expertise created friction. Government offi-cials tended to accord credibility only to activists well versed in the medical issues, most of whom happened to be gay white men, and those activists were subsequently criticized for failing to speak for other people with AIDS, who lacked the time and resources to study the disease themselves. Most treatment activists will tell you that they tried to do so, and they say that it was hard, after working around the clock, to come to the weekly meetings and be greeted like the enemy. There was jealousy, too—some members resented the attention accorded the prominent treatment activists—and no formal mechanism had ever been created by which to settle the disputes.

Last January, Staley led a dozen prominent members to break with ACT UP's New York chapter and form an autonomous organization called the Treatment Action Group, or TAG. It wasn't an easy decision. "I think that forming TAG was not a happy experience for any TAG members," he says. "All of us were freaked out by it. ACT UP was my family. It was also my life support. It was my social life. It was everything to me. I left Wall Street for ACT UP. I really felt that the organization was keeping me alive. Feeling that that family had turned against me, and that there were enemies in the family, was devastating." In an effort to avoid infighting, TAG admits members only by invitation—a policy that is anathema to many in ACT UP. But among the accomplishments of TAG has been an extensive report on the N.I.H.'s AIDS budget, outlining inefficiencies and redundancies in government spending. The group is also preparing a report on the gaps in the understanding of AIDS and is identifying scientists who are willing to do the necessary research.

TAG is not the first independent organization to evolve from ACT UP—early initiatives on housing and on needle exchange also grew into full-fledged autonomous entities—but the members of TAG were among the group's stars, and their decision to work independently has raised questions about the future of ACT UP as a whole. Kramer says, "We conquered the world, but we failed utterly, and I don't know how else to say it." But Ann Northrup, a longtime member who remains involved, says, "I don't think TAG's splitting off destroyed ACT UP at all. Any movement like this has to have constant turnover of personnel. No one person is indispensable."

Study Questions

1. Who is Peter Staley?
2. What does "ACT UP" mean? How does the name of the organization reflect the group's political philosophy?
3. Why does ACT UP use the slogan, "Silence = Death"?
4. What are some of the explanations for the high burnout rate of ACT UP members?
5. What is TAG, and why did Peter Staley initiate its organization?
6. How does TAG avoid the internal political turmoil that has plagued ACT UP? Why did some members of ACT UP find this policy "anathema"?
7. What leads Ann Northrop to conclude that "any movement like this [ACT UP] has to have constant turnover of personnel"?

Address to the Democratic National Convention, New York City, June 1992

Bob Hattoy

Thank you, Gay and Lesbian Community. Thank you, Congresswoman Pat Schroder. Thank you, Aretha Franklin.

I am here tonight because of one man's courage and conviction, one man's dedication and daring and —yes—one man's true kindness. He's my boss, Bill Clinton. (cheering) You see, I have AIDS. I could be an African American woman, a Latino man, a ten-year-old boy or girl. AIDS has many faces, and AIDS knows no class or gender, race or religion, or sexual orientation. AIDS does not discriminate, but George Bush's White House does. (cheering) AIDS is a disease of the Reagan–Bush years. The first case was detected in 1981, but it took forty thousand deaths and seven years for Ronald Reagan to say the word "AIDS." It's five years later. Seventy thousand more are dead, and George Bush doesn't talk about AIDS, much less do anything about it. Eight years from now there will be two million cases in America. If George Bush wins we're all at risk in America. It's that simple. It's that serious. It's that terrible. (cheering—no second term)

I am a gay man with AIDS, and if there's any honor in having this disease, it's because it's an honor being part of the gay and lesbian community in America. (cheering) We have watched our friends and lovers die, but we have not given up hope. Gay men and lesbians created community health clinics, provided educational materials, opened food kitchens, and held the hands of the dying in hospices. The gay and lesbian community is an American family in the best sense of the word. (cheering) President Bush, we are a million points of light. You are just too morally blind to see us. Mr. President, you don't see AIDS for what it is. It's a crisis in public health that demands medical experts, not moral judges. And it's time to move beyond your politics of denial, division and death. It's time to move George Bush out of the White House. (cheering)

We need a President who will take action, a President strong enough to take on the insurance companies that drop people with the HIV virus, a President courageous enough to take on the drug companies who drive AIDS patients into poverty and deny them life-saving medicine; and we need a President who isn't terrified of the word "condom." (cheering)

Every single person with AIDS is someone worthy of caring for. After all, we are your sons and daughters, fathers and mothers. We are doctors and lawyers, folks in the military, ministers and priests and rabbis. We are Democrats and, yes, Mr. President, Republicans. We are part of the American Family, and, Mr. President, your family has AIDS. We're dying, and you're doing nothing about it.

Listen! I don't want to die, but I don't want to live in an America where the President sees me as the enemy. I can face dying because of a disease, but not because of politics. So I stand here tonight in support of Bill Clinton, a man who sees the value in each and every member of the American Family. And although I am a person with AIDS, I am a person with hope, because I know how different my life and all our lives could be if I could call my boss "Mr. President."

Martin Luther King once said that our lives begin to end the day we become silent about things that matter. 50,000 people took to the streets in New York today because they will no longer be silent about AIDS. Their action gives me hope. All of you came here tonight. Millions more are watching on [American television]. Obviously, we have hope, and hope gives me the chance of life. I think it's really important to understand that this year more than any other year we must vote as though our life depends on it. Mine does. Yours could. And we all have so much to live for. (cheering)

Act Up! Fight Back! Fight AIDS!

STUDY QUESTIONS

1. What does Hattoy's open admission from the podium of the Democratic National Convention that he is a gay man with AIDS suggest about the shifting American attitudes toward homosexuality and toward AIDS?
2. How do Hattoy's public presence and the linguistic texture of his remarks signal a strategic change in the politics of HIV/AIDS activists?
3. What rhetorical and psychosocial strategies does Hattoy employ to connect the struggle of people with HIV/AIDS to other civil rights movements?
4. In what ways has the Clinton administration delivered and made good on Hattoy's hopeful expectations?

Suggested Additional Readings

Elliot D. Cohen and Michael Davis, editors, *AIDS: Crisis in Professional Ethics* (Philadelphia: Temple University Press, 1994).

Michael Cunningham, "If You're Queer and You're Not Angry in 1992, You're Not Paying Attention." *Mother Jones* (May/June 1992):60–68.

Ann M. Hardy et al., "The Economic Impact of the First 10,000 Cases of Acquired Immunodeficiency Syndrome in the United States." *Journal of the American Medical Association* (1986):209–211.

Imani Harrington, "American Quarantine: Isolation, Alienation, Deprivation." Andrea Rudd and Darien Taylor, editors. *Positive Women* (Toronto: Second Story Press, 1992):179–180.

David Leavitt, "The Way I Live Now." *New York Times Magazine* (July 9, 1989):29ff.

"On the AIDS Barricades." *The Economist* (June 30, 1990):79–81.

Jeffrey Schmalz, "Whatever Happened to AIDS?" *New York Times Magazine* (November 28, 1993):56–60, 81ff.

CHAPTER 12

Dialogues

Politics and Health Care Delivery

• • •

Problems of health care delivery have long been a part of the HIV/AIDS health crisis. The slow and circuitous responses by politicians, public health officials, and professional medical organizations to these problems began with the ponderous 1984 deliberations concerning the screening of HIV-seropositive blood from blood bank donations. Competing interpretations of the individuals' right to privacy punctuated those debates, but the issues were never entirely resolved. The Kimberly Bergalis case several years later served as a lightning rod for a fierce debate about the extent to which the principle of informed consent overrides health care workers' right to privacy. Bergalis may have been infected with the HIV virus by her dentist, Dr. David Acer, and her death in 1991 at the age of twenty-three marked the end of a highly publicized private tragedy.[1] The circumstances surrounding her infection, as well as the infection of several other patients of Acer's, have never been fully clarified; yet, by the sheer force of her public presence, Bergalis forced the medical and political communities in the United States to grapple with the apparently conflicting civil rights of medical patients (their right to be informed of *all* risks, including the risk of HIV transmission from the attendant medical worker during a particular medical procedure) and the civil rights of health care providers (their right to privacy regarding their HIV status). The debate that Bergalis initiated has been controversial and often acrimonious, and the conflicted legacy of that ongoing debate is outlined in Chapter 12.

The selections in this chapter examine three aspects of the continuing American search to locate the balance between the individual right to privacy and the urgent health care issues that are embedded in effective delivery of HIV/AIDS-related health care: (1) the legal and ethical responsibility of physicians to disclose the risk of HIV transmission to their patients—an application of the informed consent principle; (2) the legal and ethical responsibility of health care systems to provide medical care to HIV-infected people; and (3) the special health care needs of HIV-seropositive women.

There have been no easy answers to the questions the Kimberly Bergalis case raised: Do patients have a right to know their physicians' HIV status? Conversely, do physicians have a right to know their patients' HIV status? Should

---

[1]See especially "Private Grief." *National Review*, vol. 23 (July 29, 1991):14–16.

health care workers be required by law to be tested for HIV? Should they be required to disclose the results of those tests? Should HIV-seropositive health care providers be limited in the kinds of medical procedures they can deliver? **A Surgeon with Acquired Immunodeficiency Syndrome** traces the process by which these concerns have been addressed. The American Medical Association issued a policy statement that requires physicians' disclosure of their seropositive status for medical procedures that carry an *identifiable* risk of HIV transmission to patients and for procedures that require a patient's informed consent. Almost simultaneously, the Centers for Disease Control recommended that patients be notified of their physician's seropositive status before allowing invasive medical, surgical, or dental procedures, but remanded responsibility for defining *exposure-prone* procedures to local professional organizations and medical institutions. In October 1991, the U.S. Congress enacted legislation that required all states to either adopt CDC guidelines regarding disclosure of physicians' seropositive status or to draft similar guidelines by October 1992. Failure to comply will result in a loss of federal funds for public health programs.[2]

Yet, Bergalis's legacy can be measured only in part by the federally mandated legislation that aims to protect the public from HIV-seropositive health care workers. Her compelling campaign may have obscured the equally crucial matter of how health care workers, confronting the infectious and deadly nature of HIV, can both effectively and safely continue to practice their healing art and craft. Many argue that the rights of patients must be balanced against the rights of health care workers, that there is a statistically greater probability that health care workers will be infected by HIV-seropositive patients than will patients by seropositive health care workers. **A Drop of Blood** examines the fears and concerns of a physician who, although still willing to treat HIV-positive patients, has come to question his unconditional commitment to treat his patients despite the risk of contracting the virus from them. **The Long Goodby** focuses on the dynamic and complex relationship between physicians who choose to provide ongoing health care and the HIV-seropositive people who depend on those physicians for hope and guidance through the course of their disease.

Physicians and their HIV-seropositive patients do not always agree on what constitutes "appropriate" health care or medical treatment. **How It Was and How It Will Be** traces one case of such disagreement, the question of whether or not an HIV-seropositive woman should continue a pregnancy—or become pregnant—after learning her HIV status. "Mrs. R" made a difficult decision: to proceed with her pregnancy "against medical advice." As she learned, this decision initiated a chain of disapproving responses—from the health care delivery system and from the community—that implicitly challenged the right of people who are HIV seropositive to determine their own destiny.

---

[2]For an assessment of the potential administrative challenges posed to health care facilities by this legislative mandate, see Kevin Lumsdon, "HIV-Positive Health Care Workers Pose Legal, Safety Challenges for Hospitals." *Hospitals* (September 20, 1992):24–32.

A Surgeon with Acquired Immunodeficiency Syndrome

A Threat to Patient Safety?
The Case of William H. Behringer

Evelyne Shuster

A year ago, the New Jersey case of William H. Behringer, the surgeon with acquired immunodeficiency syndrome (AIDS), caused health experts to focus on health care workers infected with human immunodeficiency virus (HIV) and to call for new policies and guidelines to protect patients against infection. After a year of acrimonious debate over the proper approach to the issues discussed in Behringer, no consensus has emerged. The Centers for Disease Control has quietly abandoned its plan to ease its July 1991 guidelines that call for infected professionals to cease performing invasive procedures or disclose their conditions to their patients. It has now decided to let each state set its own rules and regulations in compliance with its guidelines, or risk financial penalties.

The issues discussed in Behringer *have remained controversial. This case provides an opportunity to identify reasonable actions that may ensure patient safety without inciting public fears, unduly restricting individual freedom, or violating human rights.*

Has the time come to reverse our decade-old policy on acquired immunodeficiency syndrome (AIDS) and begin to routinely screen physicians and their patients? Recent surveys [1] indicate that more than 60% of physicians believe that they should be able to order AIDS tests for patients without their consent, and more than half hold that they, themselves, should be subject to mandatory testing for human immunodeficiency virus (HIV). Almost 90% of people have said they want to know their physician's HIV status [1]. With physicians and patients claiming a "right to know," routine or mandatory HIV screening, once widely condemned, has become more appealing to both sides.

On the other hand, the Centers for Disease Control (CDC), which thus far has effectively set AIDS policy for U.S. health care institutions, has consistently advised against HIV screening and recommended universal barrier precautions as the best means of preventing HIV transmission [2]. It has been thought that mandatory or routine screening would not reduce the risks of infection but could further exacerbate an AIDS-related "underclass" in terms of stigmatization, discrimination, and human rights' violations [3].

Reprinted with permission from *The American Journal of Medicine*, vol. 94 (January 1993):93–98. © 1993 by Cahners Publishing Company.

Do we need new laws and regulations to control the AIDS epidemic, and if so, what should they be? Among hundreds of thousands of infected people, only five have been identified as presumably having contracted the disease from a health care practitioner, a dentist, Dr. David Acer [4].

Yet, on January 17, 1991, the day before the CDC published a description of the Acer case, the American Medical Association (AMA) issued a statement saying:

> Physicians who are HIV positive have an ethical obligation not to engage in any professional activity which has an *identifiable risk* of transmission of the infection to the patient. Physicians must abstain from performing invasive procedures which pose an "identifiable risk of transmission," or "disclose their seropositive status prior to performing a procedure and *proceed only if there is informed consent*" [5]. (Emphasis added.)

By the end of 1991, when Kimberly Bergalis, the first patient of Dr. Acer to be diagnosed with AIDS, died at the age of 23, the CDC had already published new guidelines recommending that HIV-infected physicians "should not perform exposure-prone procedures unless they have sought counsel from an expert review panel and been advised under what circumstances, if any, they may continue to perform these procedures" [6]. The CDC further recommended that exposure-prone procedures should be identified by medical/surgical/dental organizations and institutions at which the procedures are performed and that prospective patients should be notified of the health care worker's seropositivity before undergoing these procedures [6]. By October 1991, Congress had passed legislation requiring each state to adopt the guidelines of the CDC or similar guidelines by the following year, or risk losing federal funding for public health programs. Because professional organizations refused to provide lists of exposure-prone procedures, in November 1991, the CDC issued draft revisions of its July 1991 guidelines, now recommending that local committees review HIV transmission from health care workers to patients on a case-by-case basis [7].

Courts have also begun to take a position. In April 1991, a New Jersey superior court judge rendered an influential opinion on the case of William H. Behringer, a surgeon with AIDS [8]. This was the first superior court to rule on these issues.

After more than a year of controversy over the proper approach to the issues discussed in *Behringer* [8], no consensus has emerged. Regulating the practice of HIV-infected health care workers remains among the most contentious medical and public health policy decisions. The New Jersey case illustrates the enormous difficulties of both hospitals and courts in addressing the problems of HIV-infected physicians and those with AIDS.

The Surgeon With AIDS: The Case of William H. Behringer [8]

At age 40, William H. Behringer, an otolaryngologist and plastic surgeon, was diagnosed with AIDS at Princeton Medical Center where he was on staff. Concerned that this information could have a devastating effect on his practice, Dr. Behringer sought a transfer to another facility. After attempts at securing treatment elsewhere failed, Dr. Behringer decided that he would be treated at home. Within hours of his discharge, colleagues, friends, and patients knew of his condition. The president of the medical center, Dennis Doody, unilaterally ordered the suspension of his surgical privileges and required mandatory disclosure under the informed consent doctrine. Ultimately, based in part on the AMA's "identifiable-risk" position, the hospital's trustees adopted a policy that stated:

> A physician or health care provider with known HIV seropositivity may continue to treat patients at the Medical Center at Princeton but *shall not* perform procedures that pose *any risk of HIV transmission* to the patient [8]. (Emphasis added.)

Dr. Behringer never performed surgery after his AIDS diagnosis. His office practice, where he remained until his death in July 1989, rapidly declined, resulting in emotional suffering and financial loss. The Behringer estate sued the medical center for breach of confidentiality and for violation of the New Jersey Law Against Discrimination (LAD). After a bench trial, Superior Court Judge Philip S. Carchman ruled in favor of Dr. Behringer on the charge of negligence in maintaining confidentiality. However, the judge upheld the hospital's decision to suspend the surgeon's clinical privileges and affirmed a patient's right to know under the doctrine of informed consent. In essence, the court ruled that Dr. Behringer, as a patient, but not as a physician, was entitled to privacy, for once the information about his HIV status was disclosed, there could be no obligation for maintaining confidentiality.

Obviously, patient safety must be a paramount concern to hospitals and physicians. Hospitals and health care providers must take appropriate measures to reduce risks of infection in the workplace. But are exclusion policies and mandatory disclosure appropriate to this goal?

The Court's Opinion

Dr. Behringer consented to be tested for HIV on the condition that the test results remain confidential. The surgeon claimed that, instead, "the results were available for placement on the chart without restriction, and no special measures were implemented to ensure confidentiality" [8]. In his words:

> Nothing is clinically gained by charting the test results without restriction. The knowledge of a patient's HIV status should not reduce the need for

[universal barrier] precautions that must be taken at all times, and for all patients. When a patient is a practicing physician, special measures need to be implemented to ensure confidentiality. Access to the chart should be limited to persons within the clinical realm having a "need to know", i.e., those persons who demonstrate to designated record-keeper a *bona fide* need to know. [The] breach of confidentiality was less the charting of the test results *per se* than its easy access [8].

Undoubtedly, an essential aspect of the physician–patient relationship is the opportunity for the physician and patient to speak freely and openly with each other [9]. Historically, the law has protected physician–patient communication, understanding that confidentiality is necessary to promote effective therapy. Recently, the disclosure of an individual's HIV-related status has been subject to stringent regulation with few exceptions [10]. Statutes have been promulgated to ensure that information gained as a result of HIV testing remains confidential. The legislature has recognized a person's right to privacy and justified disclosure of information only when there is a "compelling need" to know, i.e., when health care workers are directly involved in the patient's care [10].

On the other hand, Dr. Behringer knew or should have known that, in modern hospitals, almost everyone has access to a patient's medical record [11]. Even if access on the "need to know basis" is strictly regulated, so many people fit into this category that it is unrealistic to believe that strict confidentiality can be ensured. One may question Dr. Behringer's judgment to be tested for HIV at the very medical center where he was also a practicing surgeon. But poor judgment does not relieve the medical center from its obligation to prevent an outright violation of privacy.

Judge Carchman ruled that the patient's trust was violated, his care undermined, and thus, the medical center was guilty of negligence.

Dr. Behringer further contended that mandatory disclosure and the suspension of his medical privileges violated the New Jersey LAD [12]. The LAD (like the federal Americans With Disabilities Act of 1990 [13]) has established a comprehensive prohibition on discrimination against persons with disabilities and holds that AIDS is a handicap within the meaning of laws prohibiting handicap discrimination. Antidiscrimination laws specifically prohibit employers from discriminating against handicapped persons on account of their handicap, unless the handicap "reasonably precludes the performance of the particular employment" [13]. Dr. Behringer noted that there is no scientific or medical evidence that demonstrates significant risks of professional-to-patient HIV transmission. Had it not been for the exaggerated fear, or prejudices associated with AIDS, he would not have been excluded from practicing. His exclusion was therefore discriminatory, absent a demonstration of a "significant risk" or a "direct threat" to others.

Referring to the hepatitis B virus (HBV) model, Dr. Behringer pointed out that, HBV, which is transmitted like HIV, is common among health care workers. Infected HBV patients incur substantial risks of morbidity and mortality. However, there have been "no restrictions placed on HBV-infected physicians" [8]. Thus, an exclusionary policy that applies only to HIV infection is unjustified, prejudicial, and discriminatory. Finally, he argued that the risks of professional-to-patient HIV transmission are not so significant as to create an affirmative duty to warn patients about such risks. Nor are they significant enough to warrant a patient's "need to know." In Dr. Behringer's words:

> While a patient *might "want" to know* the health status of the physician, the risk *is not* so "significant" that a patient *would "need" to* know the information because this is not a risk within a reasonable medical opinion [9]. (Emphasis added.)

The court readily recognized that the New Jersey LAD [12] requires an employer to demonstrate a "reasonable probability of substantial harm to others," and "a materially enhanced risk of serious injury" to warrant exclusion. However, having stated these legal requirements, the court practically ignored them, saying "the risk of transmission is not the sole risk involved." Patients can be exposed to the surgeon's infected blood (e.g., surgical accidents), and the mere possibility of exposure is sufficient to make it a significant risk whether or not HIV transmission actually occurred. Thus,

> Not only does the *actual risk* of HIV transmission *need to be considered* but also the *effects of HIV exposure on a patient.* The impact of [such exposure] is enormous and could be avoided if patients were informed of the surgeon's condition before the procedure occurs, and obviously, before a surgical accident. Notwithstanding what a physician *knows or should know* about a patient's informational need, he or she *must make a reasonable disclosure* of the information and *those risks* which a reasonably prudent patient would consider material or significant to the decision about a course of treatment [8]. (Emphasis added.)

The judge concluded that if any risk of HIV transmission exists, patients, not physicians, should be the "ultimate arbiters." In the judge's words:

> The way to control *"any risk"* is to reduce it to *"no risk at all"* and to include in the decision making process the most critical participant, the patient. . . *If there is to be an ultimate arbiter of whether the patient is to be treated invasively by an AIDS positive surgeon, the arbiter will be the fully informed patient. The ultimate risk is so absolute,* so devastating that *it is untenable to argue against informed consent combined with a restriction on procedures which present "any risk" to the patient* [8]. (Emphasis added.)

In the opinion of the judge, the medical center met the burden of demonstrating that Dr. Behringer did present a risk to patients, and thus, exclusionary policy and mandatory disclosure applied.

Comments

The decision in *Behringer* manifests a trend that has developed in American society [14]. Within a week of the ruling, the New Jersey Medical Society called for HIV testing of all hospitalized patients and health providers and asked the state legislature to make mandatory screening a matter of law [15]. A bill was passed in the United States Senate calling "for prison terms for physicians who know they are HIV positive, but do not notify their patients" [16] (the bill was ultimately rejected by a House–Senate committee). States have considered—or passed—laws requiring physicians to disclose their HIV infection or barring them from "doing any medical work" [17]. A Pennsylvania state superior court has relied extensively on *Behringer* [8] and ruled that the "disclosure of information regarding the condition of a physician with AIDS is necessary to prevent the spread of AIDS" [18]. A federal court has upheld the firing of a licensed practical nurse because he refused to disclose his HIV test results [19]. Recently, the executive editor of the *New England Journal of Medicine* defended "a patient's right to know" and called for screening of pregnant women, hospitalized patients, and health care professionals [20].

This trend raises several questions: Is all of this necessary? Why would we now want to deviate from an AIDS policy that has been thus far reasonably effective? Are exclusionary policies necessary to enhance patient safety and public health? Is informed consent relevant to this debate? What could possibly justify each state having its own set of rules and regulations? Over a decade of widespread HIV infection across the United States, the one identified and reported case of professional-to-patient HIV transmission has been a "mystery, which may never be solved" [21]. Two physicians calculated that "the risk of getting AIDS from a physician whose HIV state is unknown is 1 in 21 million per hour of surgery, and 1 in 83,000, if the surgeon is known to be HIV positive" [22]. They concluded that the "risks are clearly low and might have about the same magnitude as fatal injury to the patient en route to the hospital" [22].

Cases such as *Behringer* [8] and *Acer–Bergalis* [4] have prompted the CDC to conduct major studies of patients known to have been treated by HIV-infected health care workers [23]. Of 15,795 patients in 32 practices, the CDC has found only 84 patients to be HIV positive, and not one single confirmed case of HIV transmission from a health care worker to patients [23]. As ironic as it might seem, the CDC has provided some reassurance about the risks of physician-to-patient HIV transmission. Despite this reassurance, the CDC has not rescinded its July 1, 1991, guidelines (even though opposition to the guidelines has left them in abeyance) and is now calling for each state and local health department to decide what kind of care HIV-infected health workers can provide. However, should exclusionary policy be adopted?

Exclusionary Policy

Clearly, the court in *Behringer* has been unable (or unwilling?) to distinguish between the *risk of harm* and *harm* itself, when harm is death caused by AIDS. Studies to date have not implicated HIV-infected surgeons in the transmission of disease to their patients [24]. The CDC, itself, estimates the average risk of sporadic HIV transmission from an HIV-infected surgeon to a patient during an invasive procedure to be 2.4 to 24 per million procedures [25]. Federal and state laws against discrimination support policies of exclusion only when significant risks to others exist [26]. These laws do not consider as significant the possibility of risks of HIV transmission, recognizing that "social perceptions, attitudes, and prejudices are inextricably interwoven with the disease itself" [26]. By emphasizing the "significant risk standard," the framers of the laws intend to protect physicians and patients from inchoate public perception and suspicions. The *Behringer* court, however, took the position that, in the case of AIDS, only a "no risk at all" standard is acceptable. When the slightest possibility of risk, even fear, of being infected exists, the risk must not be taken. Not only is this "zero tolerance" approach toward HIV infection unique in medicine, since it has never been applied to any other clinical context, it is also unrealistic, prejudicial, misleading, and unfair. It is unrealistic because risks are intrinsic to living, and individuals routinely accept much greater risks in life. It is prejudicial because patients may subjectively perceive as objectively material and significant the risks of HIV transmission, regardless of probability. Health care workers perceived at a greater risk for HIV infection because of their risk-group status could be singled out for HIV testing, while others, not so perceived, could continue their practices. It is misleading because policies of exclusion will not substantially increase patient safety, since they only apply to those health care workers whose HIV seropositivity is known to the medical facility. Health care workers whose behaviors put them at significant risk for HIV infection may not want to be tested or learn about the best infection control practices because of fear of being the object of discrimination and losing their jobs. Those who are already infected may not be encouraged to seek treatment, could find ways of protecting their careers, and quietly change the way they do their jobs [26]. It is unfair because health care workers are at significantly greater risks of contracting HIV from patients than patients are of contracting infection from them [25]. Those who are not infected may refuse to treat HIV-infected patients and risk their livelihoods. Those who are infected may be willing to treat infected patients, and thus, would bear all the burden of care. The cost of these policies could ultimately be enormous to society in terms of expenditures, loss of professional resources, social services, delays or outright refusals to treat HIV-infected patients, and unjust treatment.

The AMA's "Identifiable Risk" Position [5]

The AMA's position on "identifiable risk" creates different problems when it states that physicians must abstain from performing procedures that pose an "identifiable risk" to patients [5]. This position seems to treat all risks the same regardless of probability. A 1 in a billion risk of becoming infected with HIV during a procedure, a 1 in 100,000 risk, or a 1 in 2 risk are all identifiable risks. For instance, the risk of being infected by a surgeon known to be HIV positive and the risk of death from anesthesia during surgery (which is comparatively 10 times greater) are identifiable risks, and thus, they should be considered the same [27]. For good reasons, the AMA has never claimed that anesthesia should not be administered. Not only does the AMA position foster a false and misleading view that "identifiable risks" can always be eliminated, it also means, taken literally, the end of medicine. No surgeon would ever operate, no physician would ever diagnose, treat, or prescribe medications, because these activities all involve identifiable risks. Glantz and colleagues [27] pointed out that the AMA may have applied that "identifiable risk" standard to HIV because the organization believes that AIDS should be treated differently from any other type of risk. As an example, 20 patients per day die in New York state as a result of negligence [28]. These deaths are identifiable risks. However, "there has been no response from the AMA calling for measures to reduce the risks, urging physicians to avoid sending their patients to New York hospitals or requiring physicians who have been guilty of negligence to so notify their patients" [27].

Informed Consent

The patient's "right to know" requirement is equally misguided. Historically, informed consent has been developed to assist patients in making decisions about the benefits and risks of medical treatment, because of the inherent uncertainties of therapy [29]. Patients have a right to know what is materially relevant to a proposed therapy. The informed consent requirement has never been a screening process. Its purpose is not to identify HIV-infected or otherwise unqualified, impaired, handicapped, or dangerous physicians. These problems should be remedied by professional standards and licensing requirements. Surgeons are either qualified or not qualified to operate on patients. If they are unqualified, the patient's consent does not make them qualified. If they are qualified, giving patients a "de facto" authority to disqualify them under mandatory disclosure only promotes unjustified stigmatization and discrimination. If the hospital where a surgeon practices knows the physician is unqualified, it has the obligation, and indeed, the responsibility, to prohibit that physician's practicing, and licensing boards should suspend or revoke the license of unqualified physicians. Whether or not patients consent to be treated by an unqualified or dangerous physician does not change the moral and legal responsibility of hospitals to prevent that physician from practicing. For instance, in criminal law, consent has never been recognized as a defense to such crimes as voluntarily and knowingly transmitting HIV to a consenting adult [30]. Thus, by upholding a patient's right to know, the *Behringer* court misapplied the informed consent doctrine or ignored what the doctrine represents. Had it seriously wanted to protect patients, the court would have focused on infection control strategy, rather than on the infection status of the surgeon.

The risks patients incur in the ordinary course of receiving care far exceed any risks an HIV-infected physician presents [31]. Yet, patients are not routinely informed about all that could adversely affect therapeutic outcomes. The "right to know" requirement that singles out HIV infection while overlooking or choosing to ignore other such significant risks as HBV transmission, a surgeon's wound infection rates, history of substance abuse, financial or family problems, and fatigue or mental stress is discriminatory and prejudicial. For instance, to this date, the medical profession stands accused and condemned, and properly so, of never having responsibly dealt with HBV-infected surgeons, even now that a vaccine is available (Shrager MW, oral communication). Barnes *et al* [32] observed that the CDC has thus far allowed HBV-infected health care workers to continue full practice, including highly invasive procedures. The risk of HIV transmission should not be trivialized, but it should be addressed in the context of the true issue of patient safety. The "right to know" approach toward HIV infection is a "clear illustration of the double standards at work in HIV-related injuries, a phenomenon that should be tolerated neither by law nor by public health" [32].

A More Reasonable Approach

Modern medical facilities remain hostile to both patients and physicians despite the high standards set for performance, the use of equipment, infection control, and health hazards. To be sure, the risk of HIV transmission in the workplace is real. However, unusual circumstances should not dictate broad policy questions because these circumstances instinctively prompt emotional and phobic reactions that fail to address the central question: how can we best protect patients (and physicians) from HIV infection? The transmission of HIV from health care workers to patients is likely to increase during procedures in which the operative field cannot be fully visualized [6]. Factors like the duration of an operation and/or the frequent use of sharp instruments in body cavities also increase the risks of HIV infection [6]. Therefore, policymakers should turn their attention to those particular practices and procedures that facilitate HIV transmission and to the need for proper disinfection of instruments that otherwise could result in cross contamination from patient to patient. The use of universal barrier precautions, to date, has resulted in a reduction of the frequency of some type of blood exposure [24]. To further reduce this risk, the development of new technologies and techniques should be encouraged. Scrupulously enforced infection control practices of all surgeons, not just those who are HIV infected, could be a far better and more effective means of reducing exposure to blood-borne pathogens than attempts at removing infected health care workers from the workplace. Obviously, the use of precautions will not reduce the frequency of surgical accidents (e.g., needle-sticks or other sharp injuries) [24]. Thus, there should also be mandatory ongoing education and training of all health care professionals in both hospitals and private practices in the use of instruments and techniques. For example, the New York State Department of Health has called for mandatory infection control training for purposes of licensing of *all* health care workers, recognizing that "HIV infection alone is not sufficient justification to limit the professional duties of health care professionals unless specific factors compromise a worker's ability to meet infection-control standards or to provide quality patient care" [33]. This is, I believe, one step in the right direction.

Medical centers and service chiefs should: (1) discuss and monitor a physician's competence to perform medical and surgical procedures that lead to HIV transmission; (2) institute good infection control policies and practices; (3) scrupulously examine all surgeons' and physicians' techniques and procedures; and (4) reinforce compliance with the policy of universal barrier precautions and infection control practices. Noncompliance could be deterred by the threat of professional (or legal) sanctions, or other relevant disciplinatory actions. All parties need to be educated about the *actual* risk or *absence* of risk of HIV transmission and *to explicitly agree* on the private and confidential nature of these discussions.

There may come a time when it is determined that a significant risk of transmission does exist, despite appropriate precautions and training. For instance, studies of HBV outbreaks have identified certain procedures such as vaginal hysterotomy as inherently more likely to lead to infection in patients. When this determination is established for HIV through prospective studies like those conducted by Tokars *et al* [34], it would be appropriate to limit the practice of health care professionals to procedures that do not present such risks. But restriction must be addressed within the context of "true" patient safety.

Conclusion

More than a year after the *Behringer* decision, experts continue to discuss the proper approach to the issues of policy restrictions and patients' right to know, and there have been almost no changes in laws or policies. This is because society is looking for someone to blame, and discrimination and punitive reactions against patients with AIDS have sadly remained prominent almost everywhere. A (mis)perception exists that HIV-infected individuals ought to be punished for their "unacceptable," "dangerous," or "immoral" behaviors. Ultimately, as it is always the case in the time of an epidemic, perceptions are more important to public policy making than is reality, and public health officials must address these perceptions accordingly. If these perceptions cannot be persuasively dispelled through explicit and culturally appropriate education, i.e., behavioral changes towards patients with AIDS, then sound scientific, epidemiologic, and medical evidence may have only a modest influence on national health policy. Failure to dispel such perceptions could result in more panic and fear among patients and no improvement in the safety of health care for either patients or physicians.

References

1. Survey finds doctors and nurses favor getting AIDS tests. New York Times, June 15, 1991: A-11; Many doctors infected with AIDS don't follow new US guidelines. New York Times, August 18, 1991: A-20.
2. Centers for Disease Control. Recommendations for preventing transmission of infection with human T-lymphotropic virus type III/lymphadenopathy associated virus in the workplace. MMWR Morb Mortal Wkly Rep 1985; 34: 681–95.
3. Gostin LO. The AIDS litigation project. A national review of court and human rights commission decisions. Part 1: the social impact of AIDS; Part 2: discrimination. JAMA 1990; 263: 1961–70, 2086–92.
4. Centers for Disease Control. Update: transmission of HIV infection during an invasive dental procedure—Florida. MMWR Morb Mortal Wkly Rep 1991; 40: 21–7, 33.
5. American Medical Association. Statement on HIV-infected physicians. January 17, 1991.
6. Centers for Disease Control. Recommendations for preventing transmission of human immunodeficiency virus and hepatitis B virus to patients during exposure-prone invasive procedures. MMWR Morb Mortal Wkly Rep 1991; 40: 1–9. No. RR-8.
7. Centers for Disease Control. Revised recommendations for preventing transmission of human immunodeficiency virus and hepatitis B virus to patients during invasive procedures. Draft. November 27, 1991.
8. *William Behringer v. The Medical Center at Princeton.* N.J. Superior Court Law Division, Mercer County. Docket No L 88-2550. Decided: April 25, 1991.
9. Annas GJ, Glantz LH, Mariner WK. The right of privacy protects the doctor–patient relationship. JAMA 1990; 263: 858–61.
10. The Confidentiality of HIV-Related Information Act, 35 P.S.; 7601–12 (Purdon Supp. 1991)
11. Siegler M. Confidentiality in medicine—a decrepit concept. N Engl J Med 1982; 307: 1519–21; Annas GJ. The rights of patients. Totowa, NJ: Humana Press, 1992: 160–74.
12. *New Jersey Stat.* Ann:10:5–4.
13. The Americans With Disability Act of 1990. H. Rept. 101-558. Washington DC, Government Printing Office, 1990.
14. Hopkins to alert patients of doctor who died of AIDS. The Sun (Baltimore), December 2, 1990: A-1; 5,000 told their doctor had AIDS. Philadelphia Inquirer, June 2, 1991: A-14; Doctor infected with AIDS virus urges his patients to get tested. New York Times, June 17, 1991: A-13; Doctor has AIDS virus, 442 are informed. New York Times, June 20, 1991: A-15.

15. Test all hospital patients for AIDS, New Jersey doctors urge. New York Times, May 1, 1991: B-1.
16. Medical groups balk at rules for AIDS risk. New York Times, August 30, 1991: A-1, 19.
17. Many states tackling issue of AIDS-infected health care workers. Boston Globe, May 27, 1991: 29.
18. Application of Milton S. Hershey Medical Center of Pennsylvania State University and Harrisburg Hospital; Appeal of: John Doe, M.D. Pennsylvania, Superior Court, 1991, Lexis 2178.
19. *Leckelt v. Board of Commissioners of Hospital District 1*. 909 F 2d 820. 5th cir. 1990.
20. Angell M. A dual approach to the AIDS epidemic. N Engl J Med 1991; 324: 1498–500. See also: Bayer R. Public health policy and the AIDS epidemic. N Engl J Med 1991; 324: 1500–4, and Brennan TA. Transmission of the human immunodeficiency virus in the health care setting, time for action. N Engl J Med 1991; 324: 1504–9.
21. Palca J. CDC closes the cases of the Florida dentist. Science 1992; 256: 1130–1. See also: Smith TF, Warweman MS. The continuing case of the Florida dentist. Science 1992; 256: 1155–6; and Ou CY, Ciesielski CA, Myers G. *et al.* Molecular epidemiology of HIV transmission in a dental practice. Science 1992; 256: 1165–71.
22. Lowenfelds AB, Wormser G. Letter. N Engl J Med 1991; 326: 12.
23. Centers for Disease Control. Update: investigations of patients who have been treated by HIV-infected health care workers. MMWR Morb Mortal Wkly Rep 1992; 42: 344–6. See also: Mishu B, Schaffner W, Horan JM, *et al.* A surgeon with AIDS. Lack of evidence of transmission to patients. JAMA 1990; 264: 467–70.
24. Nichols RL. Percutaneous injuries during operation: who is at risk for what? JAMA 1992; 267: 2938–9.
25. Bell DM. Human immunodeficiency virus transmission in health care settings: risk, and risk reduction. Am J Med 1991; 91 (Suppl 3B): 294S–300S.
26. Rogers DE, Osborn JE. Another approach to the AIDS epidemic. N Engl J Med 1991; 325: 11: 806–8.
27. Glantz LH, Mariner WK, Annas GJ. Risky business: setting public health policy for HIV-infected health care professionals. Milbank Q 1992; 70: 1: 43–78.
28. Breenan TA, Leape LL, Laird NM, *et al.* Incidence of adverse events and negligence in hospitalized patients: results of the Harvard Medical Practice Study I. N Engl J Med 1991; 324: 370–6
29. President's Commission for the Study of Ethical Problems in Medicine and Biomedical and Behavioral Research. Making health care decisions. Washington, DC, Government Printing Office, 1982.
30. When doctor has AIDS. The National Law Journal, September 9, 1991.
31. Daniels N. HIV-infected professionals, patient rights, and the 'switching dilemma.' JAMA 1992; 267: 1368–71.
32. Barnes M, Rango NA, Burke GR, *et al.* The HIV-infected health care professional: employment policies and public health. Law, Medicine, and Health Care 1990; 18: 311–30.
33. U.S. drops its plans to ease rules on doctors with AIDS. Washington Post, June 15, 1992: A-9; Altman LK. U.S. to let states set rules on AIDS related health care workers. New York Times, June 16, 1992: C-7.
34. Tokars JL, Bell DM, Culver DH, *et al.* Percutaneous injuries during surgical procedures. JAMA 1992; 267: 2899–904. See also: Mandelbrot DA, Smythe RW, Norman SA, *et al.* A survey of exposures, practices and recommendations of surgeons in the care of patients with human immunodeficiency virus. Surg Gynecol Obstet 1990; 171: 99–106.

STUDY QUESTIONS

1. Who was William H. Behringer?
2. What are the Centers for Disease Control recommendations regarding invasive medical procedures performed by an HIV-seropositive physician?
3. Why did Behringer agree to be tested for HIV? Why does the author say it may have been a "poor judgment"?
4. What argument did Behringer employ when he opposed the suspension of his medical privileges?
5. How did the judge in this case reconcile Behringer's right to privacy regarding his HIV status with his patients' right to know about the risk of HIV transmission from their physician?
6. Why is it important to distinguish between the *risk of harm* and *harm* in cases such as Behringer's?
7. What does the American Medical Association mean by *identifiable risk*? How does the author refute the AMA position on identifiable risk?
8. How does the author counter the patient's "right to know" requirement?

A Drop of Blood

J. S. David

More than two months ago, I stuck myself with an H.I.V.-tainted scalpel.

I didn't wake up that morning expecting it to happen, of course. I'm always careful: double gloves, a mask and visor. But that day, it didn't seem to matter.

I recall opening one scalpel blade, but another was on the tray. I had already cleared up the other stuff—the giant needle used in the actual liver biopsy, the needles for the local anesthetic, the scalpel blade used for the incision.

But it was that second blade. I had used it to cut up the core of tissue. It was hidden in some paper wrappings, which I grabbed to throw away. A drop of blood welled in my palm. Half a second later, I was forcing blood out of the puncture. A nurse was frantically pouring disinfectant on my hand. Even the patient seemed worried—"I sorry," she said in broken English.

The sad thing is, my record was pretty good: I figure I've had about 8,000 potential exposures to H.I.V.-positive blood in my medical career. This was chance number 8,001. I'm no longer batting 1.000, but .999 would probably get me in the Hall of Fame. In baseball, that is, not here.

Reprinted with permission from *New York Times* (January 19, 1993):A19. © 1993 The New York Times Company.

Still, the numbers are pretty good, friends said. And they are: one in 250 people exposed to H.I.V. will get it. The 249 who do not test positive will be fine. The one who does contract the virus will eventually get AIDS and die.

People suffering from AIDS and its horrible diseases should not be denied surgery and other invasive procedures that put medical workers at risk. Most procedures done on patients with AIDS (and other serious infectious diseases, like tuberculosis and hepatitis) are appropriate. And I do not agree with those who refuse to treat people who are H.I.V.-positive.

But just as financial concerns about health care are now taken into account, so too must we think more about the safety of health workers. We can't be afraid to ask uncomfortable questions like: Is a procedure that may add a few weeks to the life of a patient dying of AIDS worth the risk it poses to a healthy doctor or nurse or technician?

I got the results of my H.I.V. test: I'm negative. Still, if I had a gun with 250 chambers and one bullet, and spun the barrel and pointed it at your head, wouldn't you be just a bit anxious if I pulled the trigger?

STUDY QUESTIONS

1. How was the author exposed to HIV?
2. What are the odds that a person will contract HIV from one exposure to the virus?
3. What strategies might you devise, if you were in Dr. David's situation, for coping with the mental stress and physical danger associated with caring for an HIV-seropositive person?
4. The author asks, "Is a procedure that may add a few weeks to the life of a patient dying of AIDS worth the risk it poses to a healthy doctor or nurse or technician?" On what basis must moral choices such as this be made? Can, or should, the decision be legislated?

The Long Goodby

Abigail Zuger

She is sitting in the clinic waiting room, bent over a magazine, half an hour early for her appointment and looking fine. Year after year now, as the others sitting out there slowly fade into shadows, she alone has remained solid, substantial, voluptuous, the only image left on the screen.

She first came to our clinic four years ago for an H.I.V. test. It was her fifth. The other tests had all been positive, but refusing to believe the unbe-

Reprinted with permission from *New York Times* (July 25, 1993):Section 6:16. © 1993 The New York Times Company.

lievable, she still felt there was the possibility of a mistake and had no patience for anyone who suggested otherwise.

"I don't trust any doctor but Dr. B.," she announced, standing in the middle of my examining room and looking belligerent. She was referring to the doctor in our group who had cared for her second husband, her passport to infection, during his final days.

The temptation in these situations is always to usher the disappointed party directly into the office of the beloved, but Dr. B.'s clinic attendance was irregular and that busy afternoon his cubicle was dark. She glowered at this news, shrugged, cracked her gum and sat. We had clearly made each other's day.

She was all show. Despite the lush classical profile inherited directly from a Roman coin, despite the grating voice, the brassy hair, the stretch-denim jeans and punishing heels, despite her early departure from all forms of organized education, she proved to have the charm and savvy of an orphaned pup. By her second visit (the test was positive), she was giving me details of her love life. When Dr. B. reappeared a month later, she was unmoved. She belonged to me.

At the beginning, I didn't suspect what I was getting into. Technically speaking, in the spectrum of the H.I.V.-infected, she was, and still is, "asymptomatic." The virus, latent in her body, is causing no medical problems at all. Her immune system is still working. Technically speaking, all she would be needing from me in the clinic was a wave and a wink from time to time.

In fact, over the years I saw her at the clinic she was almost a full-time job. She had aches and twinges, numbness and tingling, rashes and wheezes, terrible breathlessness and a continual rippling of her sight. Her symptoms always came on at night, in the dark. I could never find anything wrong.

Finally I caught on. Her husband had died blind, numb and screaming, and she knew all too well what to expect for herself. "Just tell me how long," she would plead. "Just say, 'More than five years' or 'Less than five years.' Just tell me when."

It took a long time to convince her that if I could have told her I would have. Instead of a prognosis, she had to settle for statistics, and at this point the statistics are not very helpful in predicting futures like hers. The great majority of people in her situation have gone on to develop AIDS after a grace period that ranges from a few years to more than a dozen. A small, baffling minority have remained absolutely well, living with the virus with no apparent ill effects. AZT given at the right time seems to prolong the grace period for some people, but not for all. The chances are that other prophylactic regimens more successful than AZT will be developed in the near future. No one can predict quite when.

Meanwhile, they all ask us the same questions; we tell them all the same things: "Probably, but not definitely." "Nobody can predict exactly when."

They nod, shrug, smile, go home to husbands and wives, to friends, to children, to empty rooms. How do they live? That answer is never in our clinic rooms, never in our charts.

It's not in her medical record either, which, despite the false alarms, the frantic phone calls, the emergency visits, is as bland as they come. Nothing we can measure has happened to her. Her vision is fine. No blotches or bumps have ever been located by me. Her blood tests are normal. Her cholesterol's a little high. Nobody, looking into that chart, would have a clue to the H.I.V.-infected person unfolding in my clinic room over the last three years.

When we first met, she had a life composed mostly of souvenirs. Her first husband had died years earlier, leaving her with a young son. From her second husband she got her infection and the vivid nightmare of his passing. The third man in her life, and possibly worst bargain of them all, drank, used drugs and slugged her periodically as a record of his possession.

At some point after that fifth (and last) H.I.V. test, she managed to reset the balance of power. None of us can imagine how or why she found the strength to do it—and none of us ever worked up the nerve to ask her. My own theory is that she simply had to demonstrate what an outrageous error in bookkeeping somebody had made, sending her a comeuppance clearly intended for someone else.

It was quite a show. Month after month, she came into the clinic with new reports.

She got her high-school equivalency diploma. ("Do you think I could become a nurse?")

She got the guy who slugged her out of her house and life. ("I miss him but it's like, when he says he's going to be different, I don't believe him.")

She got her 12-year-old son through elementary school on the honor roll. ("Do you think I should tell him why we come to this clinic all the time?")

Slowly, she got rid of her symptoms. ("I knew you would say it was nothing, so when I looked again it wasn't there.")

And now she's gotten herself out of the South Bronx. ("I'm so scared I can't sleep.")

She borrowed money to buy a plot of land and a mobile home in North Carolina, in the community where her son's grandparents live. She's packed up her apartment and reserved a 20-foot truck. They're leaving an hour after the boy graduates from sixth grade.

Tomorrow, the clinic psychiatrist, the Legal Aid lawyer who drafted her will and I are taking her out for a goodbye lunch. This is something we don't ordinarily do. Our goodbyes are usually said at the bedside, rarely scheduled in advance over tuna. I suppose it should be a cheerful occasion—after all, how many graduations from our clinic, or from life with a slugger, or from the South Bronx, do we get to celebrate?

But what I realize now, as she looks up from her magazine in the waiting room and grins at me, is that all I want is for her to stay with us ("How long, Dr. Zuger? Just tell me how long. Can't you just say, 'Probably never'? Can't you say it just for me?") until I can tell her everything she wants to hear.

STUDY QUESTIONS

1. What was the basis for the bond between Abigail Zuger and the HIV-seropositive woman about whom she is writing?
2. How did this woman cope with her HIV-seropositive status? How did Dr. Zuger help?
3. In what ways was this "goodby" different from the usual "goodbys" between a physician and an HIV-seropositive patient?
4. How might Zuger respond, based on her experiences recounted here, to the assertion that HIV/AIDS has both challenged and compromised a physician's healing mandate?

How It Was and How It Will Be

Roseanne

It was a Tuesday morning I believe, in mid-February of 1987, when the call came. Ten days before this, I had found out that we were going to have our first child. We were both so happy at that time, so completely happy.

Then the nightmare began. "This is Dr. Smith's office calling," the voice on the other side said. "I have been asked to book you an appointment for this afternoon, Mrs. R. Could you please come in to the office about, let's say, 4:00 PM?

I had no idea at that time how drastically that call would change my husband's and my lives. The happiness we had come to know just a short time ago was about to be shattered into a thousand little pieces.

I arrived promptly at 4:00 PM. In about twenty minutes, I was called into Dr. Smith's office.

"Hello, Mrs. R," he said. "How are you today?" After some preliminaries, he got right down to the reason I was called. "I heard from your family physician that you have just been handed a positive pregnancy test result," he said.

Reprinted with the permission of Second Story Press from Andrea Rudd and Darien Taylor, editors, *Positive Women* (Toronto: Second Story Press, 1992):133–139. © 1992 by Andrea Rudd and Darien Taylor.

"Yes," I replied.

"I wish the news I have could be good news, but unfortunately it isn't."

"What is it?" I asked. "Is it the baby?"

"No," he said, "but I have some test results here that I should tell you about."

"But I haven't had any tests done in about ten months aside from my pregnancy test." I said.

"Not so. According to this, you have tested positive for the HIV antibody."

"What is that?" I asked.

"Have you ever heard of AIDS, Mrs. R? Have you ever heard of Rock Hudson?"

Then it was suddenly clear to me what this man was telling me. It was as if a sharp knife sliced through me right to the very core of my being. My life was being shattered in front of my eyes. I couldn't speak. The fear overwhelmed me. For me, for my unborn child, for my husband, for us. I wished he would just shut up. I wanted to scream but no sound came.

"I suggest that you contact your physician and discuss the details of an abortion. You will in all probability pass the infection on to your child and the baby will die."

How dare he suggest that I was going to kill my baby before it had a chance to live! How dare he tell me I was going to die! I was only twenty years old and someone had just handed me a death sentence.

I don't know how I made it home. I know I sat there and cried until there were no tears left, until I felt emotionally drained. And then my husband came home. How do you tell the man you love that someone has just sentenced you to death, and how do you explain that his unborn child may be born with AIDS? How do you explain that he himself could already be infected? There is no easy way.

But I did, and somehow I survived. The next three days passed in a haze of shock. I slept alone. He hardly slept at all. Locked away from each other, we both tried to contemplate what was happening to us. When we finally faced each other, we wouldn't touch. We just sat there and talked. We talked for about six hours and slowly through the anger and shock we decided,

> *For better and for worse*
> *In sickness and in health*
> *Till death do us part*

We had so much believed in those words, so young yet so confident that nothing bad would ever touch us.

But that was then, and it all seems so long ago. My husband went for a test and it came back negative. Through the discrimination and fear and people urging us to abort our baby, we stuck together. But "for better or for worse" became mainly "for worse." But when the labour and delivery room was ready two months ahead of time because I was a "special precautions" case, we managed to love each other.

Then one beautiful Friday morning at 8:45 AM our baby came into this world, screaming her will to live for all to hear. How proud we were and how scared for this little child, so tiny, so defenseless. We were so scared to love her, for we feared that if she should die, we would perish along with her. But she made us love her, more than life itself, for she was the continuance of life personified. She was life longing for itself and a new hope for us.

I was discharged two days later because the hospital was afraid the news of an HIV positive mom might spread around. I wasn't allowed to use the same bathroom as the other women and even had to use a completely different shower. My baby girl was with me all the time, as she was not allowed into the nursery and was an "infectious disease case" with "special precautions" labels all over. We loved her dearly and yet everytime she would get a childhood disease or infection, we would fear that this might be the last time we would hold her.

In the beginning, she tested HIV positive, but we were told that those were just the maternal antibodies passed on to the child from the mother. And with each subsequent test they went down. When our little girl was barely two months old, I decided to defy the doctors and death and I became pregnant again. Call it risky, stupid, even downright dumb, I wanted another child. It was an act of defiance. It went against everything we were told. But we had faith.

This time the pregnancy was hard. I had a baby to care for and another on the way. I had numerous colds, pelvic infections. I bled early in my pregnancy and I was worn out to the point of total exhaustion more than once. Then we got the news of work in northern Ontario and decided to go where our prospects were good. Or so we thought. What a mistake!

In the beginning things were hard but beautiful. We lived in a small town. Clean air and lots of sun was always available. Everything was expensive and we didn't make much money, but we were happy.

At least until I became sick and my doctor ordered me hospitalized in the small town hospital. Then the parade of red stickers began again. One day I learned that while I was in hospital nobody would babysit for my husband or help him with our daughter. As a result he had to skip work, and since there were lots of contractors in the town, he lost the job. How I blamed myself those days and how I hated myself for putting him through this hell!

One day we took our little girl to the only doughnut shop in town and met up with a surprise. When we entered, the place fell silent and only whispers could be heard from behind our backs. Someone spit on the floor in front of us. At this point I was nearly in tears. They knew! There must have been a confidentiality leak at the hospital. We bought our daughter her doughnut and left. Thank God she was only nine months old.

The next day we found out more devastating news. I wasn't going to be able to have my baby naturally, or in town. I was to be scheduled to be induced at a hospital in the city five hours away. I was told when to go to the city and to report to Dr. X to be induced.

The next day, while my husband waited, the doctor broke the amniotic sac of water. We spent the rest of the day wandering through the hospital. I had to carry my little girl on my hip, leaning on the wall to breathe through the contractions.

When the pain of my labour got so strong that I could hardly stand, we were faced with the problem of what to do with our little girl. It looked as if my husband and I were going to have to be apart while I had my baby. But then a small miracle happened. A woman approached my husband and told him that she had an HIV positive friend and that she was this person's nurse. She offered to babysit for us right there in the hospital. We were absolutely ecstatic. We wanted to be together when our child came into the world.

The delivery came two hours later and as our younger daughter entered this world we cried tears of joy. We were now complete. The four of us would face whatever life would bring and nothing would stop us. In the short moments after our child's birth, we decided that we were going to leave this city, the town we lived in, and take our family back home.

Our joy was premature though. The doctors miscalculated the dates and our daughter was born too early. She was a big girl at seven pounds, nine-and-a-half ounces, but there were other problems. Her bottom eyelids were turned inwards, eyes not quite ready for the outside world.

Ten days after her birth, she came down with a respiratory infection. She had to be hospitalized in the town hospital and there she suffered inhumane treatment. During the five days she was there, she was in a large metal crib, separate from the other babies. She was left to cry and at feeding time her bottle would be propped up on a blanket. How cruel to deny a ten-day-old baby human touch. The nurses only changed her when it was completely necessary. And then, they wore rubber gloves, masks, and gowns with hats. They tried to tell me that this was for my baby's protection. But if that was so, why was she plagued by a bleeding diaper rash from not being changed often enough? And why was her voice hoarse from crying? Her diaper rash cleared up when she got home, but her lungs and chest have always been sensitive and remain that way. She remained a shy and insecure child until the age of one, and to this day is afraid of strangers.

After we arranged an early release, we thought we could finally leave town. But life had other plans for us. I was so physically and emotionally exhausted by all the events and with caring for an eleven-month-old and a newborn, I came close to a nervous breakdown. I came down with severe migraines and was told that I couldn't be treated in the town hospital. I was sedated with Demerol, against my wishes, and flown to the city. There they performed a CAT scan to make sure that it was a migraine. Afterwards, still heavily sedated with Demerol, I was approached by another doctor. I remember talking with him about permanent sterilization and I know that in my state I wasn't hard to convince. The surgery was done the following day. It made me feel awful and I wondered how come they didn't want me to have babies so much. They caught me off guard and weak. I was plagued by a pelvic infection and severe bleeding after the surgery. I was also told to leave my room ten hours early and spent my time waiting for my husband in the hospital sitting room, while the staff scrubbed the room I had been in twice over, from top to bottom including the ceiling.

When the time came to leave northern Ontario, we had to sell just about everything we owned and worked so hard for. Everything went at a charity price. The town people didn't hide that they were happy to see us go. My microwave that my husband had bought me to make it easier to heat two babies' bottles had cost him 475 dollars of his hard earned money. It was still wrapped and 18 days old. They offered us a hundred dollars, and we had no choice but to accept. How much hurt I felt at this insensitive cruelty! My babies were the only bright things in our lives. We were literally run out of town. When we left, the only possessions we had were our vehicle, two baby cribs, some clothes and our dishes. We had our pillows, blankets and 980 dollars to our name to show for our move.

We have since closed a door on that chapter in our lives. Our love for each other is stronger than the hate we face. My husband remains HIV negative and our two beautiful daughters, aged two and three, are also negative. We just recently got the test results on our two-year-old with a big congratulations from our doctor. Our faith has paid off and our lives will continue in our children. We will teach them to love as we love and to respect life as we do. So maybe one day they will be able to say they were proud to be my children. I gave them life and in turn they brought hope into mine.

Back then, we lived in fear. Now we live with hope for a brighter tomorrow and we will never be sorry that we didn't listen to the doctors. For it was not their right to take a life that I had given. And I will never be sorry that I chose to do so.

STUDY QUESTIONS

1. When and how did Mrs. R learn of her HIV-seropositive status?
2. Why did her physician recommend an abortion to Mrs. R?
3. How did the community respond to Mrs. R's second pregnancy?
4. What kind of special treatment did Mrs. R receive from the hospital during her labor, delivery, and postpartum experience when she gave birth to her second child?
5. How did hospital personnel accommodate Mrs. R's sick newborn?

6. What were the circumstances surrounding Mrs. R's sterilization?
7. What are the moral debates that can be raised by Mrs. R's decision to become pregnant after she learned she was HIV seropositive, given the possibility that she might pass the virus to a baby?

Suggested Additional Readings

The Americans with Disability Act of 1990. House Report 101-558 (Washington, D.C.: Government Printing Office, 1990).

Mark Barnes, Nicholas A. Rango, Gary R. Burke, and Linda Chiarello, "The HIV-Infected Health Care Professional: Employment Policies and Public Health." *Law, Medicine and Health Care,* vol. 18 (1990):311–350.

Ronald Bayer, "AIDS and Reproductive Freedom." Dorothy Nelkin, David P. Willis, and Scott V. Parris, editors. *A Disease of Society: Cultural and Institutional Responses to AIDS* (New York: Cambridge University Press, 1991).

Centers for Disease Control, "Update: Transmission of HIV Infection During an Invasive Dental Procedure—Florida." *Morbidity and Mortality Weekly Report,* vol. 40 (1991):21–27, 33.

Joan Dworkin, Gary Albrecht, and Judith Cooksey, "Concern About AIDS Among Hospital Physicians, Nurses and Social Workers." *Social Science and Medicine,* vol. 33 (1991):239–248.

J. A. Fleishman, V. Mor, and J. Piette, "AIDS Case Management: The Client's Perspective." *Health Sciences Research,* vol. 26 (1991):447–470.

V. Mor, J. Piette, and J. Fleishman, "Case Management for Persons with AIDS." *Health Affairs,* vol. 38 (1989):139–140.

Margaret A. Sommerville, "AIDS, Law, and the Need for 'Special Law.'" James Miller, editor. *Fluid Exchanges* (Toronto: University of Toronto Press, 1992):289–302.

Designing Programs for Behavioral Change

. . .

For more than a decade the HIV/AIDS health crisis has sparked heated debates on the problem of change. Change in private sexual behavior. Change in the role public health officials can and should play in promoting that behavioral change. Change in biomedical research agendas. Change in government bureaucracies, health care priorities, funding, and health care delivery strategies. At the same time, the debates and the public discourse about these changes have masked multiple subtexts. Opposition to closing gay bathhouses and sex clubs masked the welding of sex and politics. Equivocation on the part of public health and elected officials masked a deeply embedded homophobia juxtaposed against a need to maintain publicly harmonious relationships with gay constituencies. Resistance to blood screening—from officials within the blood industry and from groups like the National Gay and Lesbian Task Force, and hemophiliacs—masked political, reputational, and even commercial interests and investments. Resistance to sex education programs has been informed by religious and moral rather than public health concerns, and resistance to education and prevention programs for injection drug users has been grounded in the notion that prevailing drug laws must take precedence over public health measures for those people who are using illegal drugs. Part V examines the ways in which those debates and subtexts have been confronted, challenged, and in some cases surmounted.

The issue of sexual behavior has proved difficult to address from the outset of the health crisis. Still, HIV/AIDS has instigated changes in the American sexual landscape. As early as 1983, even as gay men and public health officials wrestled with the problematic issue of the bathhouses and sex clubs, even before the Pasteur Institute and the National Institutes of Health had isolated the human immunodeficiency virus, before "hard" scientific evidence had documented sexual transmission, gay men in New York and San Francisco began to make changes in their sexual life-style. By 1985 gay men were voluntarily reducing their number of sexual partners, using condoms when engaging in anal intercourse and oral-genital contact, and turning in greater numbers to monogamous relationships.[1]

By 1983, physicians and epidemiologists knew that unprotected anal intercourse was not the only transmission vector for the HIV virus. Within the medical community, evidence of vaginal and perinatal transmission and transmission through blood transfusions mounted.[2] Nevertheless, sexual transmission still accounted for the majority of AIDS cases. Noting in 1985 that 70 percent of all AIDS cases were transmitted sexually, physician George H. Lundberg observed in the *Journal of the American Medical Association* that "until a technological method of prevention and treatment can be developed, it will be necessary to contain this virus by changing the life-style of many people—by no means all of them homosexual men." Prevention, Lundberg noted, "is fairly simple." In a statement that seems now apocalyptic, he advocated basic lifestyle revisions, such as not sharing injection needles or having sex with an infected person.[3] The translation of Lundberg's recommendations for defensive living in the "Age of AIDS" into effective prevention programs, however, has been one of the most difficult challenges of the HIV/AIDS health crisis. Despite the relative simplicity of the behavioral changes that Lundberg advocated, which are necessary to reduce the risk of HIV transmission, the barriers to communicating and implementing those changes have proved enormous.

David L. Cohen, assistant director of the Denver Disease Control Service, initially recommended that physicians should take the lead in fostering HIV/AIDS awareness and encouraging appropriate behavioral change among their patients. "You can't stick your head in the sand," Cohen told medical colleagues in a 1985 conference. Physicians must become willing to confront the disease themselves before they could effectively guide their patients to the understanding that "'you really need to make some changes in order to prevent infecting somebody else if you are infected, or to avoid becoming infected if you aren't.'

---

[1]For reports of local studies, see especially *The American Journal of Public Health*, vol. 75 (1985):493–496; *Journal of the American Medical Association*, vol. 254(1985): 2537–2538.

[2]The accumulating medical evidence during 1982–1985 is reflected in a substantial bibliography. For examples, see A. Rubenstein et al., "Acquired Immunodeficiency with Reversed T_1/T_2 Ratios in Infants Born to Promiscuous and Drug-Addicted Mothers." *Journal of the American Medical Association*, vol. 249 (1983):2350–2356; James Curran et al., "Acquired Immunodeficiency Syndrome (AIDS) Associated with Transfusions." *New England Journal of Medicine*, vol. 310 (1984):69–75; A. Ammann et al., "Acquired Immunodeficiency in an Infant: Possible Transmission by Means of Blood Product Administration." *Lancet*, vol. 1 (1983):965–968; Robert Redfiend et al., "Frequent Transmission of HTLV-III Among Spouses of Patients with AIDS-Related Couples and AIDS." *Journal of the American Medical Association*, vol. 254 (1985):1571–1573.

[3]George H. Lundberg, "The Age of AIDS: A Great Time for Defensive Living." *Journal of the American Medical Association*, vol. 254 (1985):3440–3441.

Now is the time," Cohen told the conferees.[4] In an ideal world, 1985 would be well past the time when effective information and education programs had altered the frightening increase in HIV/AIDS prevalence and incidence rates. In the United States, the national bill for the epidemic—a combination of direct medical costs and indirect losses in income and productivity—approached $5 billion. Education remains the key to prevention, and successful HIV prevention programs must exploit multiple information channels and multiple sources. They must address both attitudes about HIV and risky behavior. In order to transcend the barriers of misperception, bias, stigma, and overpowering psychosocial human needs, prevention messages must be culturally sensitive in design and culturally appropriate in delivery.

[4]As quoted by Donald E. Reisenberg, "AIDS-Prompted Behavior Changes Reported." *Journal of the American Medical Association,* vol. 255 (1986):171, 176.

CHAPTER 13

Global Concerns

• • •

The HIV/AIDS education and prevention efforts of the 1980s have made clear that information, even highly credible and well-planned information, will not necessarily induce the kinds of behavioral changes that are needed to disrupt transmission of the HIV virus. The selections in Chapter 14 suggest strategies for strengthening HIV/AIDS education and prevention programs. **Information and Education** summarizes both the flaws in message content and the channels that have limited the effectiveness of HIV/AIDS prevention programs: the relatively greater power of explicit messages about HIV/AIDS transmission and prevention over ambiguous ones; the impact of moral censorship on prevention and education programs; the relative advantages of electronic, print, and interpersonal communication channels in the delivery of HIV/AIDS prevention and education information. **Understanding the AIDS Pandemic** suggests that strategies to cope with the HIV/AIDS health crisis must be crafted within the demographic realities of particular epidemics. At early stages of an HIV/AIDS epidemic, when the prevalence of HIV infection is relatively low, education and condom distribution within targeted high-risk core groups will be more effective than at later stages, when such efforts must be directed toward a wider population. Together these two selections suggest strategies for redesigning HIV/AIDS prevention programs.

Information and Education

Jonathan Mann, Daniel J. M. Tarantola,
and Thomas W. Netter

For many, information was thought to be the key to behavior change.[1] Therefore, prevention programs usually focused on increasing awareness about modes of HIV transmission and information on how to avoid becoming infected. Examples abound of increased awareness following information campaigns.

Reprinted with the permission of the publishers from Jonathan Mann, Daniel J. M. Tarantola, and Thomas W. Netter, editors, *AIDS in the World* (Cambridge, MA: Harvard University Press, 1992):330–337. © 1992 by the President and Fellows of Harvard College.

Even so, experience over the past decade has shown that by itself information is insufficient to change behavior. For example, at one time it was commonly believed that the possibility of dying of AIDS would prompt individuals to change their behavior. Widely disseminated information about the risk of AIDS, however, has failed to achieve such a result. This failure of information to lead reliably, regularly, or predictably to behavior change has been documented repeatedly in varying cultures and contexts and underscores the need for a comprehensive approach to prevention, combining the three elements essential to its success.

Relying solely on information also has risks. Misperceptions and misunderstandings have been common in AIDS information programs and serve as barriers to adopting preventive behavior. Correcting such misperceptions has been a theme of HIV prevention programs in many settings (see box 13.1). Unfortunately, even with complete and accurate information, adoption of prevention behavior is far from assured.

When a person sees AIDS as inevitable, there is little motivation to change behavior; people must have hope that preventive behavior will reduce their chances of infection. Prevention programs which provoke anxiety have been associated with adopting preventive behaviors, but extreme anxiety can lead to denial, avoidance or a sense of fatalism.[2]

The search for love and intimacy may also create an obstacle to adoption of safer sex practices. The belief that steady partners are "safer" than occasional partners is widespread and persistent.[3] Therefore, beyond information, the interaction between partners is an important factor in deciding to practice and maintain safer sexual behaviors.

Messages

Messages are more effective when they can be directed toward a specific target population. The language and the approach must be shaped to reflect specific needs and solutions that are appropriate for different communities.

An analysis of the information/education programs of 38 national AIDS programs revealed that in over 90 percent of both industrialized and developing countries, the main messages were caution about lifestyle and correcting misperceptions. About 80 percent of the countries surveyed have provided information about how to assess personal risk. Far fewer countries included messages countering discrimination, partner negotiation, and testing; partner negotiation and testing messages were more commonly reported from industrialized countries.

Most countries surveyed reported that their main prevention themes aimed at reducing sexual transmission of HIV, include using condoms, reducing the number of partners, and preventing and treating sexually transmitted diseases (STDs). Each of these approaches was cited slightly more

Early Perceptions and Misperceptions About AIDS in Tanzania

Justin Nguma
Muhimbili College of Health Sciences, Dar es Salaam, Tanzania

In many countries around the world, the onset of the AIDS pandemic was met with varied perceptions both at the community and government levels. For example, in the late 1980s most Americans perceived AIDS to be a disease of homosexual men, injection drug users, and people of Haitian origin because they were the ones most affected by it. Thus, individuals who did not identify with these groups falsely believed that they were safe from AIDS. In Tanzania, AIDS took its first toll in the Kagera region on young men and women involved in illegal trade across the border with Zaire, Rwanda, and Burundi. The trade flourished on illegal buying and selling of currency, minerals, alcohol, and basic commodities that were in short supply in Tanzania, especially after the border war with Uganda in the late 1970s.

One commodity that made history in this trade was colorful shirts, some of which had an eagle emblem on the back or the inscription "Juliana." The shirts became very popular among the youth and spread like fire around the country. As the death toll continued to rise among these traders, the Kagera communities started to perceive the disease as having something to do with the nature of the trade. In particular, they believed that witchcraft was the main cause of these deaths and that the dying were bewitched by their colleagues (as a result of cheating in their business deals) or by their competitors. The communities named the disease Juliana, symbolizing a disease resulting from the trade on Juliana shirts. A majority of Tanzanians, therefore, perceived AIDS as a disease of illegal traders and smugglers. As in the case of homosexuals and injection drug users in the United States, those who did not identify themselves with this trade falsely believed that they were not susceptible to HIV infection. Because the majority of AIDS patients, particularly those suffering from diarrhea and fever, were noticed to lose a lot of weight, the communities later renamed the disease "Slim."

The new name, "Slim," came to serve as a community's visual criterion for determining who could be carrying the AIDS virus. Just as homosexuals, Haitians, and injection drug users were being discriminated against in the United States as possible carriers of the AIDS virus, slim people, especially when they happened to be strangers, were often discriminated against in casual sex situations based on this perception. People were more likely to have casual sex with strangers who were plump and overweight than with those who appeared extraordinarily slim. This misconception became the major target of the early IEC [Information, Education, and Communication] messages. It was critical to dispel this myth and alert the public that anyone could be carrying the AIDS virus irrespective of his or her physical appearance.

frequently in industrialized than developing countries, with the exception of prevention and treatment of STDs, which received more emphasis in developing countries. Fewer countries selected abstinence as a major theme; industrialized countries were about twice as likely to promote abstinence as developing countries.

Message *content* is more effective when it is clear and unambiguous. Yet the past decade has revealed how cautious many HIV prevention messages have been when talking about sex, condoms, and drug injection. Prevention messages have been full of inferences to sexual practices which were as likely to confuse as to inform. For example, the warning against exchanging "bodily fluids" may have avoided offense, but it was interpreted incorrectly as including sweat, saliva, and tears, for which there is no evidence suggesting a possible role in HIV transmission.[4]

Ambiguous messages can result from lack of cultural sensitivity, self-censorship, and imposed censorship. Among adolescents and young adults who say they have adopted monogamy, further probing may reveal a pattern of serial monogamous relationships lasting from only a few weeks to several years.[5] In another instance, a campaign was conducted in the Netherlands to counter common misunderstandings about HIV. The format was purposefully ironic, and their research found that as much as 25 percent of the population failed to understand the irony.[6] As an example of censorship, the first brochures in England about safer sex were confiscated as obscene.[7] Indeed, nongovernmental organizations often produce more provocative messages and images than governments—sometimes in opposition to government policy and other times with its consent.[8,9] (See the *AIDS in the World* survey of nongovernmental organizations, Chapter 17, "AIDS Service Organizations in Transition.")

A further barrier to HIV prevention through information is the gap between the literacy level of the audience and the level at which a brochure or pamphlet has been written. A study in the United States reviewed 137 HIV-related brochures and found that between 2 and 16 percent of the target audience were at a reading level below that of the material. Two studies evaluated the readability of inserts in condom packages and concluded that all texts required a reading level above the education level of many people at risk for HIV.[10]

Material can be pretested with the intended audience for comprehension and impact. The audience can then provide feedback to the producers of the material, and necessary changes can be made to improve design. This type of research contributed greatly to the success of interventions such as the social marketing campaigns of condoms in Zaire,[11] the "Hot Rubber" campaign in Switzerland,[12] and in-school prevention material in the Congo.[13] Pretesting also has the advantage of obtaining the cooperation of key members of the target populations.

In the future, more emphasis needs to be given to messages emphasizing partner negotiation, as partner interaction is one of the most powerful influences on adoption of safer sexual behavior. In addition, an immense gap remains between the receipt of a message and subsequent behavior.

Channels

Developing clear and appropriate messages is an essential part of the information/education component of the HIV prevention process. Making sure they are heard is another. Few programs start with a formal analysis of their communications environment, and many fail to consider the best combination of channels for reaching a particular target audience: radio, newspapers or television; brochures or posters; counseling, theater or outreach and self-help groups. Instead, most programs start with a channel in mind because it is the predesignated choice or simply the channel already available to the program.

Reach and frequency must be considered when selecting and evaluating the effectiveness of a communications channel. Reach refers to the number of people who can potentially be exposed to the message. Frequency refers to the number of times the message is repeated. HIV prevention messages in the mass media are often published or broadcast as public service announcements, often at the discretion of television or newspaper managers. Little information has been collected on the frequency with which they are shown; thus, one of the key variables for mass communication is often uncontrolled.

Data on the number of brochures printed are often used by programs as an indicator of activity. Less frequently, are there records of the quantities delivered to various distribution points. Stockpiles of brochures are sometimes found in warehouses and storerooms without any systematic plan for distribution. Most programs are constrained by the small number of counselors, teachers, and outreach workers that can be hired. Consequently, there is rarely an attempt to calculate the overall reach of the program.

There is consensus that mass media channels create awareness and set the agenda, while interpersonal channels are more likely to influence behavior.[14-16] In developing a media plan, the per contact cost and the overall budget for the program are key variables. Per contact, mass media costs significantly less than counseling or other types of personal contact, and when trying to reach the general population, the reach of the message may be greater than for other channels. Still, the absolute cost of producing the message and arranging or purchasing media time may be quite high.

Lower cost channels and specialized media may be more efficient, however, when programs target specific populations such as sex workers or gay men. Gay newspapers have clearly been effective in reaching gay men.[17-20] Newsletters have been created to reach commercial sex worker groups, and workbooks have been created to reach students. In addition, the use of popular culture is particularly effective in increasing awareness; some of the

more innovative channels used to reach populations have been performances and music.

The *Aids in the World* survey indicated that in industrialized countries,
print media are used most frequently, followed by targeted media, electronic media, and school courses. Training of trainers is used most frequently by developing countries, followed by targeted media, printed
media, and electronic media. School courses are used more frequently by
industrialized countries, while performances are used more frequently by
developing countries.

NOTES

1. For further discussion of the uses of information, see P. Brown, "AIDS and the
   Media," and P. Piotrow, "AIDS and Mass Persuasion," in Chapter 16 [of *AIDS
   in the World*, from which this reading is taken].
2. L. A. Kurdek and G. Siesky, "The nature and correlates of psychological ad-
   justment in gay men with AIDS-related conditions," *Journal of Applied Social
   Psychology* 20(1990):846–60.
3. A. Prieur, "The dangers of love," in *Changing Sexual Behaviors in the Shadow
   of AIDS*, ed. M. Cohen (New York: Plenum, forthcoming).
4. K. Siegel, P. Grodsky, and A. Herman, "AIDS risk-reduction guideline: A
   review and analysis," *Journal of Community Health* 2(1986):233–43.
5. E. de Vroome, M. E. Paalman, T. G. Sandfort, et al., "AIDS in the Netherlands:
   The effects of several years of campaigning," *International Journal of STDs
   and AIDS* 1(1990):268–75.
6. K. de Vries, E. de Vroome, T. G. Sandfort, et al., The effectiveness of the 1989
   multi-media safe sex campaign in the Netherlands, presented at the I European Conference on Effective Health Education, Rotterdam, Netherlands,
   December 1989.
7. P. Weatherburn, P. Davies, and A. Hunt, "The response to AIDS in the London gay community," in Cohen, *Changing Sexual Behaviors*.
8. B. Robert and S. Rosser, "Evaluation of the efficacy of AIDS education interventions for homosexually active men," *Health Education Research* 5(1990):
   299–308.
9. M. Cohen and T. Sandfort, Theory: A practical guide to synchronizing HIV
   prevention with stage of the HIV epidemic, presented at the V Conference on
   the Social Aspects of AIDS, London, U.K., March 1991.
10. R. Mullins, "Reading ability and the use of condoms," *Medical Journal of
    Australia* 151(1989):358–59.
11. J. Drosin, J. Price, J. Spilsbury, and W. Martin, Condom sales and protection
    through non-traditional outlets: An evaluation of the Zaire social marketing
    program, presented at the 1991 AIDS Prevention Conference, USAID, Rosslyn,
    Virginia, November 1991.
12. F. Wasserfallen and R. Staub, "The gay community response to AIDS in
    Switzerland," in Cohen, *Changing Sexual Behaviors*.
13. P. M'Pelé, personal communication, Congo, 1992.
14. R. C. Hornik, "Channel effectiveness in development communication pro-
    grams" (Philadelphia: Annenberg School of Communications, 1991).
15. T. Edgar, S. Hammond, F. Lee, and S. Vicki, "The role of the mass media and
    interpersonal communication in promoting AIDS-related behavioral change,"
    AIDS Public Policy Journal 4(1990):3–9.

16. E. Stoller and G. Rutherford, "Evaluation of AIDS prevention and control programs," *Current Science Ltd.* 3(1989):S289–96.
17. J. Martin, L. Dean, M. Barcia, and W. N. Hall, "The impact of AIDS on a gay community: Changes in sexual behavior, substance abuse, and mental health," *American Journal of Community Psychology* 17(1987):269–293.
18. R. Stall and J. Paul, "Changes in sexual risk for infection with the HIV virus among gay and bisexual men in San Francisco," in Cohen, *Changing Sexual Behaviors.*
19. G. Dowsett, S. Kippax, R. W. Connell, and J. Crawford, "The contribution of the gay community to sexual behavior change among homosexually active men in Australia," in Cohen, *Changing Sexual Behaviors.*
20. T. Myers, D. McLeod, and L. Calzavara, "Responses of gay and bisexual men to HIV/AIDS in Toronto, Canada: Community-based initiatives, AIDS education, and sexual behavior," in Cohen, *Changing Sexual Behaviors.*

STUDY QUESTIONS

1. Why do information-based AIDS education programs often fail to induce changes in sexual behavior?
2. What are the crucial elements of message content for AIDS prevention programs?
3. What psychosocial factors are likely to act as barriers to AIDS prevention messages?
4. How does the impact of information delivered via mass media channels differ from the impact of information delivered via interpersonal channels?
5. What circumstances led to an initial association between AIDS and illegal trading/smuggling in Tanzania?
6. How did AIDS come to be named "Slim" in Tanzania?
7. How did Tanzanian AIDS prevention programs address the misperceptions about HIV transmission?

Understanding the AIDS Pandemic

Roy M. Anderson and Robert M. May

To assess the demographic impact of AIDS in the worst-afflicted regions of the world, we must develop models that combine descriptions of HIV spread and of population growth. The first analyses in 1988 suggested that AIDS is capable of turning positive growth rates into negative rates over time scales of a few to many decades. Even the annual growth rates of 3 percent or more in sub-Saharan Africa could be converted to negative rates. Much controversy surrounded these early predictions, mainly because of the uncertainties in assigning parameters and the failure to account adequately for differences in sexual activity between and within communities.

More recently researchers have accumulated data to help in estimating the most important epidemiological parameters, but considerable uncertainty still surrounds many of these efforts. Studies in developed countries appear to show that the average incubation period of AIDS in cases transmitted from infected mother to unborn infant is one to two years. Roughly 13 to 30 percent of infants born to infected mothers in developed countries appear to acquire the infection; the number is closer to 40 percent in Africa.

The greatest uncertainty in assessing the rate of transmission centers on the prevailing patterns of sexual behavior within and between communities. The World Health Organization has initiated wide-scale surveys on sexual behavior in Africa, and data are beginning to accumulate. At present, our meager understanding of the processes that dictate sexual behavior in different societies is for the most part anecdotal in character.

Under these circumstances, mathematical models can once again offer guidance, this time in identifying the linkages between sexual activity and the observed pattern of HIV spread. In the past few years, models have been developed that address various aspects of these issues, although it must be emphasized that theoretical developments have greatly outstripped the available data. The major role of such models is to provide qualitative guidelines concerning the interpretation of observed patterns. The model should also provide a framework within which to assess the potential impact of different interventions. Understanding is best developed by the gradual inclusion of complexity, in a manner akin to that adopted by the experimental scientist, who changes one factor at a time, while holding the other factors constant.

As an illustration of what these models can show us, we consider two examples of the effect of variability in sexual contact on the potential effect of AIDS in Africa. Our first example deals with the influence of contact patterns between different age classes of the two sexes. In particular, we focus on the tendency of African men to form sexual partnerships with women who are five to 10 years younger than themselves. Other factors being equal, models that take into account the observed age bias suggest a significantly enhanced demographic impact as compared with predictions based on restricted contact within the same age class. The increased impact is a consequence of the concentration of infection in young women who are just entering childbearing age. The models also suggest that the ratio of HIV infection in men and women will change over the course of the epidemic. This shifting ratio may help explain why widely different figures have been reported in Africa, ranging from a male to female ratio of close to 1:1 to 1:2.

Our second example concerns the patterns of mixing between men and women with high and low rates of sexual-partner change. The simplest of models—based on the stratification of the population by sex and classes of sexual activity—illustrates well the significance of sexual-contact networks.

When high-activity men (such as migrant male laborers in urban centers) have greatest contact with high-activity women (such as female prostitutes) but also have some contact with low-activity women (wives or girlfriends), a multiple epidemic may occur. First comes a rapidly developing epidemic in the small proportion of high-activity men and women. A more slowly developing, but much larger, epidemic follows the initial outbreak. The second epidemic involves the low-activity men and women who constitute the majority of the population. The epidemic in the high-activity classes serves to seed the slower-growing epidemic, and the peaks in the two classes may be separated by a decade or more.

The scenario predicted by this simple model may reflect what is actually occurring in cities such as Nairobi. There, levels of infection are high in female prostitutes (60 to 80 percent), moderate to high in their male clients (20 to 40 percent) and low in pregnant women in the general population (5 to 6 percent). The model suggests that the low levels in the general population will rise over the coming decade. This increase will herald a second and much larger epidemic, similar to what has already happened in the cities of Malawi, Tanzania and Uganda.

Available facts indicate that in the absence of major changes in behavior or the development of better drugs, AIDS is likely to cause serious demographic changes in some African countries over the coming decades. It also appears increasingly likely that the pattern will be repeated in parts of India and Southeast Asia.

What can be done to reduce the spread of infection? Models that assess the influence of behavioral changes on the rate of advance show the importance of the timing of these changes. The effects of timing are not necessarily intuitively obvious, given the nonlinear character of the epidemic. Changes introduced early in the course of the epidemic have a disproportionately greater effect than similar changes introduced later. As a consequence, significant resources should be directed toward inducing behavioral changes to try to prevent a widely disseminated lethal epidemic some 10 to 20 years from now.

Targeting education and condom distribution at high-risk groups will always be beneficial in the early stages of the epidemic, when infection in the general population is limited. Such a policy would clearly be beneficial in countries, such as Nigeria, where the levels of HIV infection in high-risk groups such as female prostitutes and their male clients are low to moderate and the levels are very low in pregnant women. If mixing patterns are highly assortative, an approach aimed at high-risk groups is particularly worthwhile. It may even turn out that the rates of sexual-partner change in the general heterosexual population are insufficient to maintain the transmission of HIV. If infection has taken hold to a significant degree within lower-risk groups, however, as is the case in Malawi, Tanzania and Uganda, education and condom distribution must be aimed more widely. Indeed, in these circumstances models suggest that much is to be gained by focusing efforts on young teenagers before they become sexually active.

The subtle interplay among rates of sexual-partner change, patterns of mixing between sexual-activity classes and the need to balance supply with demand for sexual partners can trigger perverse outcomes. Reducing rates of sexual-partner change in the general population offers an interesting example. Suppose a community has liberal attitudes regarding the formation of sexual liaisons. Most men and women will have a number of different sexual partners every year, with the result that the men have limited contact with female prostitutes. If education reduces partner-change rates among women, which concomitantly means that men have more frequent contact with prostitutes, the result may be an acceleration in the rate of spread of the virus in the general population in the short term. In the long term, however, the overall size of the epidemic would be reduced. The example illustrates the need to assess the influence of education not only on rates of sexual-partner change but also on the pattern of sexual mixing within a given community.

More generally, a growing body of evidence points to the importance of other sexually transmitted diseases (STDs). These diseases seem to enhance the likelihood of HIV transmission, presumably through the genital lesions that STDs can cause. This evidence shows the need to control the spread of STDs in developing countries, particularly in Africa. Simple models of concomitant STD and HIV transmission lend support to such an effort. Another advantage of improving control of STDs is that the programs facilitate counseling and condom distribution to a high-risk segment of the population.

Developed countries have another option for minimizing the effects of AIDS: the use of zidovudine [AZT] and other drugs that appear to slow the progression of the disease. A randomized trial in the U.S. tested two dosage levels of zidovudine (500 or 1,500 milligrams a day) and a placebo on asymptomatic patients. The trial was halted prematurely because patients being given zidovudine showed a considerable reduction in rates of progression of AIDS and advanced AIDS-related complex (ARC).

Zidovudine treatment may, under certain circumstances, have a negative side. Although the treatment is life-prolonging and therefore good for the individual, there are situations where it can be detrimental for the community. Depending on the extent to which the treatment reduces infectiousness, which is currently uncertain, it could be that lengthening the incubation or symptomatic periods in treated individuals can increase the incidence of HIV within the community. In extreme circumstances, the outcome could be an increase in the AIDS-related death rate in the community. Given that AIDS is a lethal disease and that zidovudine appears to slow its progression, it would certainly be unethical to refuse treatment to individuals. Nevertheless, mathematical models confirm the possibility that what is beneficial for the individual is not necessarily so for the community.

Clearly, there is a need for virological research of a quantitative nature to measure the impact of drug treatment on infectiousness and for reduced infectiousness to be part of the protocol of drug development. Moreover, these considerations highlight the desirability of linking treatment with counseling to promote safe sex practices among treated individuals.

In the absence of effective drugs and vaccines, changes in sexual behavior provide the only weapon against AIDS. Mathematical models, with their sometimes surprisingly counterintuitive revelations, can channel those changes into the most advantageous paths.

STUDY QUESTIONS

1. What elements must mathematical models of HIV/AIDS epidemics incorporate in order to be useful to AIDS prevention programs?
2. What predictions about the future of an epidemic can be made from the observed high rates of HIV infection among commercial sex workers?
3. When is the most appropriate point in an HIV epidemic to target core groups for AIDS prevention information and programs?
4. When is the most appropriate point in an HIV epidemic to target low-risk groups?
5. Why do the authors say the mathematical models may yield "counterintuitive revelations," and how may these results pose ethical questions in containing the epidemic?

Suggested Additional Readings

Marshall H. Becker and Jill G. Joseph, "AIDS and Behavioral Change: A Review." *American Journal of Public Health,* vol. 78 (April 1988):394–410.

Jeffrey A. Kelly et al., "HIV Risk Behavior Reduction Following Intervention with Key Opinion Leaders of Population: An Experimental Analysis." *American Journal of Public Health,* vol. 81, no. 2 (February 1991):168–171.

Gerardo Marin and Barbara VanOss Marin, "Perceived Credibility of Channels and Sources of AIDS Information Among Hispanics." *AIDS Education and Prevention,* vol. 2, no. 2 (1990):154–161.

Thomas R. Prohaska, Gary Albrecht, Judith A. Levy, Noreen Sugrue, and Joung-Hwa Kim, "Determinants of Self-Perceived Risk." *Journal of Health and Social Behavior,* vol. 31 (December 1990):384–394.

CHAPTER 14

Educating Within Communities

• • •

By the mid-1980s HIV/AIDS education and prevention programs in the United States, as elsewhere around the globe, had met with complex and thickly textured psychosocial obstacles. Physicians as a group had not met David Cohen's challenge to educate themselves and their patients, and broader prevention efforts had mired in morality debates and politics. **Education to Change Risky Behavior** reviews the performance of public health and elected government officials during the early 1980s and suggests how these two groups of potential leaders might have responded differently to the HIV/AIDS health crisis had the "at risk" population been heterosexual rather than gay.

The early mismanagement of HIV prevention programs contains powerful lessons for the future. In the absence of a vaccine and effective medical therapies to combat the HIV virus, education remains the key to prevention and the Gordian knot of the HIV/AIDS health crisis. **Voices** describes an HIV/AIDS education and prevention program that employs trained peer educators and that has demonstrated success in changing attitudes as well as behaviors. The ACE design suggests an effective educational strategy that can reach populations at particularly high risk for HIV infection.

Knowledge About HIV and Behavioral Risks of Foreign-Born Boston Public School Students and **HIV Infection and Homeless Adolescents** direct attention to factors that are shaping the "second wave" HIV/AIDS epidemics of the 1990s and that must be considered as HIV/AIDS education and prevention programs are designed. The lessons of the 1980s—that knowledge alone will not support behavior change, that HIV will not quickly dissipate within particular core transmission groups, that the HIV/AIDS health crisis has wide-reaching and devastating potential—provide clear guidance for organized, focused, and effective prevention programs in the 1990s.

Education to Change Risky Behavior

Charles Perrow and Mauro F. Guillen

We believe that a vigorous education campaign in the first year of the epidemic could have saved several thousand lives. Changing gay men's sexual behavior was a priority for some medical people from the start, but individual and organizational resistance was strong among gays. Despite early evidence that the disease was being spread by a few highly active homosexual men, largely through gay clubs and the bathhouses of San Francisco and New York, the gay community (and the owners of the profitable bathhouses) resisted any restraints on its behavior. In his detailed account of the bathhouse polemic, Ronald Bayer, a professor at Columbia University's School of Public Health, documents the inaction of the gay press and such influential groups as the Gay Men's Health Crisis (GMHC), which bluntly refused even to talk about regulating or conducting education campaigns at the bathhouses.[1] There were, however, many gay physicians and groups, like the National Gay Task Force, pressing for some sort of regulation.[2] Public health officials were also cautious to an extreme, perhaps because of gay political pressure or the controversial nature of the establishments and of such drastic action. In any case, the bathhouses remained open during the first three years of the epidemic.

Closing the houses was not discussed seriously until May 1982, eleven months into the crisis. As late as May 1983, when the country had 1,450 reported cases, 45 percent of them in New York City, an official of that city rejected suggestions for education, saying that gay men were providing it themselves, and turned aside concerns about the bathhouses with the libertarian argument that the "city should not tell people how to have sex." By February 1985 the city's AIDS cases surpassed 3,000, yet the New York City Health Commissioner, Dr. David Sencer, maintained that education was adequate and dismissed the idea that there was a crisis in New York City. Governor Mario Cuomo of New York, a liberal Democrat, assured gay leaders that the bathhouses would not be closed and, for the second year in a row, opposed allocating any funds to fight AIDS.[3] Owners resisted any suggestion that bathhouses should be the location for education regarding AIDS and had to be ordered to put up warning posters. (The resistance to posters was based not only on a commercial argument but also on a civil liberties argument; a similar resistance by the National Organization of Women to posters in bars warning women about the effects of alcohol on the fetus was based on the right to privacy.) San Francisco bathhouses were ordered to

Reprinted with permission from Charles Perrow and Mauro F. Guillen, *The AIDS Disaster* (New Haven, CT: Yale University Press, 1990):28–38. © 1990 by Yale University Press.

put up warning posters in June 1983, but a survey in March 1984 indicated only feeble compliance. Closings started in September 1984 (T-39) in San Francisco, and bathhouses were closed in many cities in the rest of the nation by mid-1985, though they remained open in Los Angeles, at least.

Closing the houses was clearly not easy. The Director of Public Health in San Francisco during this period was Dr. Mervyn Silverman, who later was co-founder of the American Foundation for AIDS Research (AmFAR). Initially he was against closings but favored regulation.[4] He later changed his mind and in October 1984 ordered the closings of the gay bathhouses and clubs, but the civil liberties issues were serious. A few weeks after the closings a superior court ordered that they be reopened on the ground that public health and civil liberties concerns should be balanced,[5] although one gay physician, Marcus Conant, testified that some gay men infected at bathhouses would return to them and "not feel guilty about giving it back."[6] But Silverman, a vigorous advocate for more education and more care, offered a striking observation a year later in an interview with Sandra Panem. Silverman said that Dianne Feinstein, then mayor of San Francisco and very supportive of the gay population, had remarked, " 'If this had been a heterosexual disease, I would have closed the bathhouses immediately.' And she's right, because it wouldn't have been a bathhouse; it would have been a whorehouse," and that would be easier to close. Presumably Silverman meant that straight "johns" were not as well organized as gay men.[7]

One argument against closing bathhouses was that frequent anonymous anal sex would "go underground." As Shilts notes with bitter irony, however, sodomy in public parks and neighborhood bushes by "unrestrained sex fiends," predicted even by New York State Commissioner of Health David Axelrod, who initially opposed the closings, did not occur.[8] The opportunity to use the houses as places to inform highly active homosexual men of the risk—something most bathhouse owners strongly resisted because it would undoubtedly diminish the attraction of the institutions and reduce their profits—not only was never realized, but was probably unlikely from the start. At least one bathhouse in New York City handed out condoms and displayed posters, according to a GMHC official, but there is no evidence that a serious effort was made. It was not until October 1985 that Axelrod and Cuomo, side by side, announced the closing of the bathhouses. In New York City, Mayor Koch and Commissioner Sencer decided to postpone implementation of the new state directive and were moved to act only under direct pressure from Albany.[9]

The problem of highly efficient transmission of the virus through central locations such as bathhouses persists and probably always will. A survey in 1986 of 807 men leaving seven bathhouses in Los Angeles found that while all but 2 percent reported familiarity with the AIDS information that was distributed in the bathhouses, 10 percent continued to practice anal intercourse without a condom. These were likely to be the poorer, younger, less-educated members of the sample (though the patrons as a whole were prosperous), and they were more likely to have had five or more partners in the previous month.[10] From 2,000 to 4,000 males visited bathhouses in the Los Angeles area each week. Bathhouses remained closed, technically, in New York City, but some gay cinemas and clubs apparently provided opportunities for risky sex at the close of the 1980s (and may still). One gay cinema, recently closed after repeated warnings, had, among other things, provisions for the "glory holes" that were featured in the San Francisco Castro district in the 1970s.[11] These are plywood partitions with holes cut into them, to permit thoroughly anonymous anal sex on a production-line basis. It is hard to conceive of a more efficient transmission device; it is even harder to see how it could operate in 1988, given all the publicity about AIDS. Obviously more than education is required to convince *everyone* to give up risky behavior. But an epidemic cannot be sustained if there are only a *few* sources of transmission.

The dynamics of epidemics are somewhat counterintuitive. High success rates with prevention efforts are not necessary to stop the epidemic, though they are needed to eliminate the risk for specific individuals. For an epidemic to be sustained it is necessary that every infected person has to infect, on average, one other. Because there is a good chance that a fair proportion of the sexual contacts will occur between already infected individuals, however, an infected person contacting a variety of people in a well-defined social group will not be sustaining the epidemic if all are infected. To sustain the epidemic, therefore, those outside the group have to infect more than one person, enough to make up for those who are either not infecting anyone or contacting only those already infected. No one gets well, of course; the disease still spreads; but if it does not spread in epidemic terms it will eventually die out as the number of carriers declines.[12]

In addition to closing down transmission sites, an education campaign directed to the private physicians who serve the gay male population and to the sexually transmitted disease (STD) clinics could have prevented thousands of subsequent infections. Mass media education campaigns, while necessary, are the least effective; the most needed campaigns are those that target the most concentrated sources of infection. The presumably small proportion of the gay male population that engages in very frequent casual sex is also the population with the highest rate of sexually transmitted diseases, such as hepatitis B, syphilis, gonorrhea, and genital warts. There are successful treatments for these diseases, so these individuals visit their doctors fairly regularly. A concerted, well-funded campaign to persuade the doctors to convince their patients that they were in danger of contracting a debilitating and presumably fatal disease, and of spreading it to their partners, could have made a large difference. Even if only one-third of the highly active population took precautions or limited their participation in risky forms of sexual behavior, the spread would have been greatly reduced.

But no significant effort was made to launch an educational campaign that would reach doctors who treat gay men. Nor was any substantial effort made to flood the STD clinics with counselors or at least literature on the new risk. In those early days—say, from 1982 to 1984, when the epidemic first became apparent—most of the at-risk population was visible, accessible, and geographically concentrated in small sections of New York City and San Francisco. As AIDS spread at a slower rate into the gay population that engaged in progressively less frequent and casual sex, the difficulties of effective education increased. It was simply not inevitable that about half of all gay men in San Francisco and New York City would become HIV-positive, as estimates still suggest. Reaching the other major group, the IVDUs [intravenous drug users], would have been much more difficult, but even here it was not inevitable that from 60 to 90 percent of New York City's IVDUs would be infected (estimates vary widely). The rate in cities that are not on the East Coast is believed to be only about 5 percent.[13]

The education failure rests upon the gay community, the medical community, and above all upon public officials. The gay community was initially reluctant to recognize the problems with disseminating sources and risky behavior, but within a couple of years it was conducting educational efforts, and for several years these efforts were the only meaningful ones. The doctors in San Francisco and New York City who included gay men among their patients, and especially those that specialized in sexually transmitted diseases in males, appear to have made no organized effort to educate even their clients, let alone the population from which their clients were drawn. But the most serious failure is that of public health officials and public officials in general. For a top health official in New York City to declare proudly that he was not about to tell gay men how to have sex, when this was exactly what was needed, was to commit thousands to death. Nor can these criticisms be dismissed as hindsight. As Shilts's history of the early days repeatedly demonstrates, responsible people, including public officials, spoke out for the need for aggressive education. Nor would an education campaign have to have been 90 percent or even 50 percent effective to make a decisive difference.

Doctors' offices should have been flooded with literature about the risk. A special team should have been formed in at least the two major cities to contact these doctors, and informational packets should have been provided for them to send privately to their patients. The STD clinics should have had the same sort of literature and increases in staff as well. Special counselors should have been hired to alert gay men and spouses and lovers of IVDUs (among whom hepatitis B is widespread). The organized gay community, instead of being ignored as they clamored for help, should have been enlisted to arrange special parties, meetings, and mailings. There was great controversy over the degree of danger, the amount of denial, and the behavioral sources of risk, but government tried to avoid taking a stand. AIDS came at a time when state and municipal budgets were beginning to expand again;[14] pleading poverty, as Governor Cuomo did, for example, was mere expediency.

The education of gay men was bound to be difficult, and it is far from accomplished. There are areas of New York City today where men cruise in cars to pick up young men who sell themselves, and presumably condoms are not used. The success of the educational efforts even from a presumably trusted source, the gay community itself, is difficult to judge. Though the examples are not strictly comparable, the judgment should be in terms of efforts to persuade teenagers to use condoms (dismal success) and the campaigns against smoking, excessive drinking, excessive eating, gambling, and drug abuse—in short, to change lifestyles and sources of instant gratification. Behavioral changes in these areas, even under the threat of death in a few years, will not come easily. Education must be massive and explicit.

The record for changing drug-taking or sexual behavior for IVDUs, gay or heterosexual, appears to be dismal. Compounding this difficulty is the fact that the disease is transmitted more efficiently through needle sharing than through sexual activity.[15] An even more serious problem was the refusal of New York City's health officials even to try. A 1985 mayoral report from Health Commissioner Sencer said that drug users are "unlikely to change their risk behavior" and that "prevention of transmission in this population is unlikely." This was the same year in which Deputy Mayor Victor Botnick was quoted as saying "New York City has no epidemic, no AIDS crisis," and Patricia Maher, a member of the city's AIDS staff, quit in protest over the refusal to put warnings in subways. She was told that anybody who needs to know about AIDS already knows about it.[16]

The record for gay men is mixed, but on balance, the majority (but perhaps only a modest majority) appear to have changed their sexual behavior. For example, the rate of rectal gonorrhea fell quickly as gay men began using condoms—on the other hand, condom sales increased only 94 percent in four years and now has leveled off. Since condoms should be used by both gay men and heterosexuals, we might have wished for much more growth.[17] A survey of five hundred gay men in October 1984, forty months into the epidemic and before the bathhouses were closed, found that two-thirds had changed their sexual habits enough to remove any risk of contracting the infection.[18] In San Francisco, the proportion of gay men practicing insertive anal intercourse decreased from 40 percent in 1985 to 14 percent in 1987, and the average number of sexual partners per year had declined by 20 percent in one sample survey. A 1986 study among gay men in New York City found that the average number of sexual partners per year decreased from thirty-six prior to the onset of the epidemic to eight when it became clear that multiple partners increased the chances of infection.[19] Fifty-nine percent of IVDUs interviewed in a New York methadone clinic as early as 1984 reported some sort of behavior change to avoid infection, and a survey in 1985 found identical results.[20] The figures are only suggestive and probably exaggerate the amount of change. For one thing, the samples of gay men and IVDUs are from those most accessible to education and to change, either because they are in or seeking treatment or because they are willing to be interviewed in fairly public settings, such as outside bathhouses. We have no data on young men just beginning to engage in gay sex, on practicing homosexuals in general, or on bisexuals who are married or still "in the closet" in areas outside the major cities such as San Francisco, New York, Miami, and Los Angeles. The belief that sexual freedom is essential to a gay life-style has been found to be related to higher numbers of sexual partners and hence to increased risk of infection.[21]

Mathilde Krim, co-founder of the American Foundation for AIDS Research, told the following story to Maggie Mahar:

> Where homosexuality is less accepted than it is in New York or San Francisco, the disease could spread more insidiously: A community inclined to deny homosexuality is also denying the danger of AIDS. Recently, I gave a talk at the University of Utah and I noticed no official representatives of the local gay community in the audience. Usually, they are there when I talk. But in the back of the audience, I did notice three young men sitting together in a group, and I went up to them and asked who they were. They replied, "We're the gay community." "Just three of you?" I asked. "The rest are married," they said. That morning the Salt Lake City newspaper reported the case of a young mother diagnosed with AIDS. The article said she had no idea how she could have contracted the disease.[22]

As long as homosexual orientation is penalized, some young homosexual men are likely to be isolated from knowledge of STDs, including AIDS; and since monogamous homosexual relations are not exempt from social stigma, more easily concealed promiscuous relations in effect are encouraged. It is clear that the education of young homosexual men, especially those who were still children in the 1980s, when AIDS had such dramatic impact on the gay community, will not be easy.[23] The Institute for the Protection of Lesbian and Gay Youth in New York City recently found that attendance at its weekly discussion group dropped from fifty to two when it was announced that the subject would be AIDS. The topics generally involved "relationships," sexuality, dating, and even drugs. AIDS could be dealt with only if it was integrated into these "more comfortable" topics, we were told, which is what the institute then did.

We are only beginning to get information about the new wave of crack addiction, which presents a most formidable problem of educating female addicts who exchange sex for drugs. A recent study showed that 35 to 40 percent of those entering crack houses had previous experience with intravenous drug use. Crack houses foster marathon binges of cocaine use and a variety of sexual activities, sometimes with dozens of partners for two days or more. There is also an alarming rise in syphilis in the populations most vulnerable to crack addiction: in New York City, while it has dropped among white males in the past five years, it has increased by 150 percent among blacks, 73 percent among Hispanics, and more than doubled among women.[24] The combination of crack binges, prolonged bouts of sex,

HIV-positive IVDUs, and syphilis, it is feared, will lead to the spread of AIDS in a heterosexual population that is all but invulnerable to even the most forceful education programs (though no study has yet documented that syphilis sores are effective transmission routes). But a concerted effort starting in 1981 or 1982 to bring more IVDUs into methadone treatment centers and educate them about the transmission of AIDS through shared needles and unprotected sex would have reduced the size of the present crisis and the number of its carriers. What might appear to be a virtually hopeless education task now, with the spread of AIDS into the minority community through complex interactions (infected IVDUs, crack houses, syphilis, homelessness), was certainly more tractable in the early years.

AIDS is the only epidemic for which the means of prevention are available in the local supermarket, are cheap, and are easy to use. The resistance to using condoms and bleach or alcohol is, in one sense, extraordinary. Forgoing sex or breaking a drug habit (or forgoing the occasional injection) is admittedly harder, but neither is even necessary to avoid AIDS. An education campaign that said your life could depend upon using a condom when practicing anal sex, and flushing your syringe out with bleach or alcohol and rinsing with water before shooting up, would have been very cheap and very successful in saving lives. But such campaigns were not tried in the United States. The risk of encouraging nonmarital sex or IVDU by publicizing supermarket remedies was seen by powerful groups as worse than the risk of an epidemic of deaths.

Responsible people called for massive education; it could have had a substantial effect; it is still needed. European countries, though experiencing the epidemic later and so far in much smaller numbers, did a far better job. It is a job for organizations. They failed in a massive way, and later we shall discuss why.

NOTES

1. Ronald Bayer, *Private Acts, Social Consequences: AIDS and the Politics of Public Health* (New York: Free Press, 1989):30 and 54.
2. Bayer, pp. 54–55.
3. Randy M. Shilts, *And the Band Played On* (New York: St. Martin's Press, 1987):310, 455, 533; Bayer, pp. 32, 38, 59–61.
4. Bayer, pp. 50–53.
5. Bayer, pp. 50–53. A detailed account of the constitutional aspects of AIDS may be found in Judith A. Rabin, "The AIDS Epidemic and Gay Bathhouses: A Constitutional Analysis." *Journal of Health Politics, Policy and Law*, vol. 10 (Winter, 1986):729–747.
6. Bayer, pp. 47–48.
7. Sandra Panem, *The AIDS Bureaucracy* (Cambridge, MA: Harvard University Press, 1988):19–20.
8. Shilts, pp. 453–454.
9. Bayer, pp. 62–64.
10. Gary A. Richwald, Donal E. Morisky, Garland R. Kyle, Alan R. Kristal, Michele M. Gerber, and Joan Friedland, "Sexual Activities in Bathhouses in

Los Angeles County: Implications for AIDS Prevention Education." *Journal of Sex Research*, vol. 25 (1988):169–180.

11. Robert McFadden, "Health Department Closes Down Gay Cinema." *New York Times*, October 1, 1988. The owners of the establishment acknowledged to city officials that they were aware of the risky sexual practices and would assign personnel to "discourage sexual activity among the patrons." But they left in place, and in use, seven cubicles and partitions with small holes to accommodate anonymous contacts. Thomas B. Stoddard, executive director of Lambda Legal Defense and Education Fund, objected to the closing of the cinema: "We generally oppose all acts of this kind by the government. Consensual sexual activities by adults out of public view should always be beyond the eye and the arm of the government." Two other gay cinemas were closed a few months later. The action was opposed by gay rights advocates and the New York Civil Liberties Union. See Thomas Waite, "New York Shuts 2 Gay Theatres as AIDS Threats." *New York Times*, February 12, 1989.

    On the Castro scene, see Frances Fitzgerald, *Cities on a Hill: A Journey Through Contemporary American Cultures* (New York: Simon & Schuster, 1986).

12. The dynamics of the AIDS epidemic was first explored in Robert M. May and R. M. Anderson, "Transmission Dynamics of HIV Infection." *Nature*, vol. 326 (March 12, 1987):137–142. Edward Kaplan and his co-authors have explored the policy implications of intervention strategies with reference to the important but neglected matter of sexual mixing and the high utility of even quite imperfect education programs. See Edward H. Kaplan, "Can Bad Models Suggest Good Policies? Sexual Mixing and the AIDS Epidemic," *Journal of Sex Research*, vol. 26 (1989):301–314, and Edward H. Kaplan and Paul R. Abramson, "So What If the Program Ain't Perfect? A Mathematical Model of AIDS Education," *Evaluation Review*, vol. 13 (1989):107–122. The classic (and fascinating) historical discussion of epidemics is William H. McNeill, *Plagues and Peoples* (Garden City, NY: Doubleday, Anchor Press, 1976).

13. Maggie Mahar, "Pitiless Scourge; Separating Out the Hype from Hope on AIDS." *Barron's* (March 13, 1989):16.

14. Between 1982 and 1986 state and city government budgets grew at approximately the same rate as the Gross National Product, both in the nation as a whole and in New York. Vernon Renshaw, Edward A. Trott, Jr., and Howard L. Friedenberg, "Gross State Product by Industry, 1963–1986." *Survey of Current Business*, vol. 68 (1988):30–46.

15. Edward H. Kaplan, "Needles That Kill: Modeling Human Immunodeficiency Virus Transmission via Shared Drug Injection Equipment in Shooting Galleries." *Review of Infectious Diseases*, vol. 11 (1989):289–298.

16. Bruce Lambert, "Koch's Record on AIDS: Fighting a Battle Without a Precedent." *New York Times*, August 27, 1989.

17. Mahar, p. 16.

18. Shilts, p. 492.

19. Marshall H. Becker and Jill G. Joseph have summarized recent research findings concerning behavioral adaptions for coping with the risks of getting AIDS in "AIDS and Behavioral Change to Reduce Risk: A Review." *American Journal of Public Health*, vol. 78 (1988):394–410.

20. Becker and Joseph, p. 403.

21. Becker and Joseph, p. 395.

22. Mahar, p. 16.

23. Scientists are divided as to whether sexual orientation is genetic or acquired, but homosexuality is no longer associated with "mental illness" or "moral failure."

See Barbara Risman and Pepper Schwartz, "Sociological Research on Male and Female Homosexuality." *Annual Review of Sociology,* vol. 14 (1988):125–147.

24. Peter Kerr, "Syphilis Surge and Crack Use Raising Fears on Spread of AIDS." *New York Times,* August 20, 1988.

STUDY QUESTIONS

1. How did heterosexual mortality shape public health officials' responses to the gay bathhouses?
2. Why did San Francisco mayor Dianne Feinstein admit that "If this had been a heterosexual disease, I would have closed the bathhouses immediately"?
3. By what logic were the public health concerns about HIV transmission in gay bathhouses transformed into a civil liberties issue?
4. Why do Perrow and Guillen argue that "high success rates with prevention efforts are not necessary to stop the epidemic"?
5. According to Perrow and Guillen, what kinds of AIDS prevention campaigns were most needed during 1982 and 1983?
6. Where do Perrow and Guillen lay the blame for the failure to initiate effective AIDS education during the early years of the epidemic in the United States?
7. How do the authors propose to initiate AIDS education programs targeted at injection drug users and their sex partners?
8. How might you explain the reluctance of gay and lesbian youth to talk about HIV transmission and AIDS unless health concerns were cast into a "more comfortable" range of topics?

Voices

Women of ACE*

Introduction

We are writing about ACE because we feel that it has made a tremendous difference in this prison and could make a difference in other prisons. ACE stands for AIDS Counseling and Education. It is a collective effort by women in Bedford Hills Correctional Facility. This article will reflect that collectivity by being a patchwork quilt of many women's voices.

ACE was started by inmates in 1988 because of the crisis that AIDS was creating in our community. According to a blind study done in the Fall–Winter

*The authors of this essay are Kathy Boudin, Judy Clark, "D," Katrina Haslip, Maria D. L. Hernandez, Suzanne Kessler, Sonia Perez, Deborah Plunkett, Aida Rivera, Doris Romeo, Carmen Royster, Cathy Salce, Renee Scott, Jenny Serrano, and Pearl Ward.

Reprinted with the permission of South End Press from *Women, AIDS & Activism* (Boston: South End Press, 1990):143–155. © by the ACT UP/New York Women and AIDS Book Group.

of 1987–88, almost 20 percent of the women entering the New York state prison system were HIV infected.[1] It is likely to be higher today. In addition, women here have family members who are sick and friends who are dying. People have intense fears of transmission through casual contact because we live so closely together. Women are worried about their children and about having safe sex. All this need and energy led to the creation of ACE.

Before ACE

Prior to the formation of ACE, Bedford was an environment of fear, stigma, lack of information, and evasion. AIDS was a word that was whispered. People had no forum in which to talk about their fears. The doctors and nurses showed their biases. They preferred to just give advice, and many wouldn't touch people because of their own fears. There were several deaths. This inflamed people's fear more. People didn't want to look at their own vulnerability—their IV drug use and unsafe sex.

> I felt very negative about people who I knew were sick. To save face, I spoke to them from afar. I felt that they all should be put into a building by themselves because I heard that people who were healthy could make them sick and so they should get specific care. I figured that I have more time (on my sentence); why should I be isolated? They should be. I felt very negative and it came a lot from fear.[2]

Women at Bedford who are sick are housed in a hospital unit called In Patient Care (IPC). ACE members remember what IPC was like before ACE:

> The IPC area—the infirmary—was horrible before, a place where nobody wanted to be. It was a place to go to die. Before ACE people started going there, it looked like a dungeon. It was unsanitary. Just the look of it made people feel like they were going to die. That was the end.

There was no support system for women who wanted to take the HIV-antibody test:

> I had a friend who tested positive. The doctor told her, you are HIV positive, but that doesn't mean you have AIDS. You shouldn't have sex, or have a baby, and you should avoid stress. Period. No information was given to her. No counseling and support. She freaked out.

The Beginning of ACE: Breaking the Silence

Some of us sensed that people needed to talk, but no one would break the silence. Finally, five women got together and made a proposal to the superintendent:

We said that we ourselves had to help ourselves. We believed that as peers we would be the most effective in education, counseling, and building a community of support. We stated four main goals: to save lives through preventing the spread of HIV; to create more humane conditions for those who are HIV positive; to give support and education to women with fears, questions, and needs related to AIDS; to act as a bridge to community groups to help women as they reenter the community.

The superintendent accepted the proposal. Each of the five women sought out other women in the population who they believed were sensitive and would be interested in breaking the silence. When they reached 35, they stopped and a meeting was called.

Breaking the Silence Changed Us: We Began to Build a Community

At that first meeting a sigh of relief was felt and it rippled out. There was a need from so many directions. People went around the table and said why they were there. About the fourth or fifth woman said, "I'm here because I have AIDS." There was an intense silence. It was the first time anyone had said that aloud in a group. By the end of the meeting, several more women had said that they were HIV positive. Breaking the silence, the faith that it took, and the trust it built was really how ACE started.

Breaking the Silence Meant Something Special to PWAs

I often ask myself how it is that I came to be open about my status. For me, AIDS had been one of my best kept secrets. It took me approximately 15 months to discuss this issue openly. As if not saying it aloud would make it go away. I watched other people with AIDS (PWAs), who were much more open than I was at the time, reveal to audiences their status/their vulnerability, while sharing from a distance, from silence, every word that was being uttered by them. I wanted to be a part of what they were building, what they were doing, their statement, "I am a PWA," because I was. It was a relief when I said it. I could stop going on with the lie. I could be me. People were supportive and they didn't shun me. And now I can go anywhere and be myself.

Breaking the Silence Allowed People to Change Each Other

I was one of those people who once I knew someone had AIDS, I didn't want them around me. That was until Carmen got sick. She was my friend. When I found out she was sick I felt hurt because she didn't have the confidence to tell me. She knew my attitude and didn't want me to turn my back on her. That's when I started researching how you can and can't get the virus and my fear left. ACE also helped me with things I didn't know. Even though Carmen had AIDS and I didn't, I felt that I was living with AIDS through her. I told her that I loved her whether she had AIDS or not.

Breaking the Silence Meant Challenging Stigma

I think there has been a tremendous change in the institution. Before, if people knew about someone, it wasn't to help them, it was only to hurt them. Now people are protective about the people they used to talk about. You will still have people who will use this information as their power, like saying, "You AIDS-ridden this," but you have more people now who will protect those individuals. This is the first time that people in here had something they were doing for other people that they weren't getting something from, some payoff.

Since that beginning two years ago, ACE has gone on to develop a program of work through which we try to reach out to meet the needs of our community.

Supporting PWAs

PWAs and HIV-positive women are at the heart of our work. ACE believes that everyone facing HIV-related illness is confronting issues of life and death and struggling to survive and thrive.

We had to have some place for PWAs to share their experiences with each other. There have been numerous support groups which allowed us to express things that hadn't been verbalized but that had been on our minds. It was interesting to see that we had similar issues: how to tell significant others, our own vulnerability about being open, living with AIDS. My first group was a mixture of people. Some were recently diagnosed and others had been diagnosed for two years. It was informative and it was emotional. Sometimes we would just come to a meeting and cry. Or we might come there and not even talk about the issue of AIDS and just have a humor session because we are just tired of AIDS.

One of the first things that ACE ever did was to work in IPC.

ACE started going to IPC. We painted, cleaned up, made it look so good that now the women want to stay there. We take care of the girls who are sick, making them feel comfortable and alive. Now, women there know they have a friend. They feel free, they talk, and look forward to visits. They know they're not there to die; not like before.

Being a Buddy

I have been involved in ACE for about three years. About a year ago I started visiting the women in IPC. I was really afraid at first. Not afraid of getting sick, but of becoming emotionally involved and then have the women die. At first, I tried to keep my feelings and friendship at a minimum. The more I went, the more I lost this fear. There is one woman I have gotten closer to than the rest. She has been in IPC since I first started going there. We are buddies. For me to be her buddy means unconditionally loving her and accepting her decisions. I go almost every night to IPC. Some nights we just sit there and say nothing. But there is comfort in my presence. She had a stroke before I met her. So there is a lot she cannot do for herself. There are times when I bathe and dress her. Iron her clothes. I do not think of any of these things as chores. Soon she will be going home. I am overjoyed, but I'm also saddened knowing that I will not see her again. I will miss her hugs, her complaining, and her love. But I would do it all over again and I probably will with someone else.

Medical Advocacy

It is obviously a matter of life or death for anyone who is HIV infected to get good medical care and have a good relationship with her health providers. Medical facilities in prisons start out understaffed and ill equipped, and the AIDS crisis escalated these problems enormously. In the 1970s women prisoners here instituted a class action suit, *Todaro v. Ward*, to demand better medical care. Because of that case, the medical facilities and care at Bedford are monitored for the court by an outside expert. That expert issued a report criticizing all aspects of the medical department for being inadequately prepared to meed women's AIDS-related medical needs, and the prison faced a court hearing and possible contempt charges. Under that pressure the state agreed to numerous changes that brought new medical staff and resources, including a full-time medical director, a part-time infectious disease specialist, and more nurses. ACE was able to institute a medical advocacy plan that allowed ACE members to accompany women to their doctor's consultation visit to insure that nothing was missed. Afterward, there can be a private discussion between the patient and the advocate to clarify matters for the woman, to explore possibilities of treatment, or just to allow the person to express whatever emotions she experienced when she received the news from the doctor.

Peer Education

Our approach is *peer* education, which we believe is best suited for the task of enabling a community to mobilize itself to deal with AIDS. The people doing the training clearly have a personal stake in the community. The education is for all, in the interests of all. This is communicated from the beginning by the women doing the teaching.

Our peer education takes a problem-posing approach. We present issues as problems facing all of us, problems to be examined by drawing on the knowledge and experience of the women being trained. What are the issues between a man and a woman, for example, that make it hard for a woman to demand that her man use a condom? Will distributing free needles or advocating bleach kits stop the spread of AIDS among IV drug users?

Our educational work is holistic. Education is not solely a presentation of facts, although that is an important part of the trainers' responsibilities. But what impact do feelings and attitudes have on how people deal with facts? Why would a person who knows that you cannot get AIDS by eating from a PWA's plate still act occasionally as if you could? Why would a person who knows that sex without a condom could be inviting death, not use a condom? For education to be a deep process, it involves understanding the whole person; for education to take root within a community, it means thinking about things on a community, social level.

> Coming to prison, living under these conditions, was scary, and AIDS made it even scarier. I was part of a society that made judgments and had preconceived ideas about the women in prison.

Educating Ourselves

Workshops

To become members of ACE, women must be educated through a series of eight workshops. We look at how stigma and blame have been associated with diseases throughout history, and how the sexism of this society impacts on women in the AIDS epidemic. We teach about the nature of the virus, strategies for treatment, and holistic approaches. After the eight weeks, we ask who would like to become involved, and then there is a screening process. The superintendent has final approval. The workshops are followed by more intensive training of women who become members.

Orientation

When women enter the New York state prison system, they must come first to Bedford Hills, where they either stay or move on after several weeks to one of several other women's prisons. ACE members talk with the women when they first arrive.

> We do orientations of 10 to 35 women. We explain to them how you can and cannot get AIDS, about testing and about ACE. Sometimes the crowd is very boisterous and rude. I say "AIDS" and they don't want to hear about it. But those are the ones I try to reach. After orientation is over, the main ones that didn't want to hear about AIDS are the ones who want to talk more and I feel good about that. A lot of times, their loudness is a defense because they are afraid of their own vulnerability. They know that they are at risk for HIV infection because of previous behaviors. After I finish doing orientation, I have a sense of warmth, because I know I made a difference in some of their lives.

Seminars

One of the main ways we interact with our sisters is through seminars. We talk about AIDS issues with groups of women on living units, in classrooms, and in some of the other prison programs such as family violence, drug treatment, and Children's Center.

> The four back buildings are dormitories, each holding 100 women with double bunked beds. We from ACE gather right after count, with our easel and newsprint and magic markers and our three-by-five cards with the information on whatever presentation we're making. We move in twos and threes through the connecting tunnels to the building. When we arrive some of the women are sitting in the rec room, but many others are in their cubicles/cells. They ask why we're here. We look like a traveling troupe— and we've felt like it, not knowing what to expect. Some women are excited that we're going to talk about AIDS. Others say, "forget it," or "fuck you, I've heard enough about it, it's depressing."

But we begin, and people slowly gather.

> We ask the women to help us role-play a situation such as a woman going home from prison, trying to convince her man, who has been taking care of her while she's inside, to use a condom. Then the role-play is analyzed. What problems are encountered and how do we deal with those problems? We try to come up with suggestions that we can see ourselves using in that situation. We talk about the risk of violence.

One of the most immediate problems people have is whether or not to take the HIV-antibody test. We do not push testing. We explain what the test is and have a group discussion of things the women need to consider. A woman may be inclined to get tested, but she needs to know that she is likely to be transferred upstate before the results come back from the lab. The choice is up to her. Toward the end of the seminar, PWAs talk about their experiences living with AIDS.

> When they speak, they bring together everything that we have said. Not only that, but they let people know that living with AIDS is not instant death. It makes people realize why the struggles, working together, and being as one are so important. When I hear the women who are PWAs speak, it makes me realize that I could have been in their shoes, or I could still be, if they hadn't been willing to talk about their risk behaviors and what has happened to them. It gives me the courage to realize that it's not all about me. It's actually about us.

We end each seminar with all the women standing with our arms around each other or holding hands—without any fear of casual contact—singing our theme song, "Sister."[3] We sing, having come to a new place where we are for each other, unified. We all feel some sense of relief and some sense of hope. Talking about AIDS openly has changed how we live. We leave the seminar with the knowledge that we can talk about AIDS and that we're going to be okay.

Prerelease

This is a program for people within 90 days of going home. They confront the issues of living with AIDS within their prospective communities.

> The women are leaving to go to communities where they are frightened because they don't know if they will find any openness or dialogue. They don't know if they can take the behavior changes they have learned about in here and implement them out there.

The prerelease program also meets the specific needs of PWAs who are leaving the facility. We call this bridging—helping them to connect with follow-up care, assistance, housing. The Bedford community is much more supportive than what most people face when they go outside. During the period before a person is released, she experiences a high level of stress which we have to address on many levels: putting services in place, meeting emotional needs and anxieties, working through issues related to families. We also have to let go, because we become very bonded with each other. There is a weaning process on both ends, and we have to work on preparing both ends of the relationship for this transition.

Although the transition for PWAs may be difficult because of the community of support that ACE has created, it is also true that ACE members come out of Bedford committed and prepared to try to build the same kind of supportive community outside. ACE has created a training ground for women to become community workers in the AIDS crisis.

> . . . on the outside I live AIDS through personal experience by having AIDS, and I work at it on a 9 to 5 basis doing case work at Brooklyn AIDS Task Force; come 5 or 6 P.M., that day at the office is over and I am once again all alone. Even though I am involved in other personal AIDS projects, they all lack the closeness that Bedford and ACE provided.

Counseling

When we conduct the seminars and orientation sessions, women come up to us afterward with personal questions and problems. It could be they are HIV positive, or they are thinking of taking the test, or they have a family member who is sick, or they are thinking about getting involved with someone in a relationship. Sometimes they raise one issue, but underlying it are a lot of other issues they're not ready to talk about. Because women know we're in ACE, we're approached in our housing units, at school, on the job, in the mess hall, as we walk from one place to another. Women stop us, needing to talk. We're a haven for women because they know ACE has a principle of confidentiality. Women can trust us not to abuse the information they are sharing with us.

> Peer counseling. I'm just impressed that we can do it. I didn't know what kind of potential we'd have as peers. We talk the language that each of us understands. Even if it's silent, even if it's with our eyes, it's something that each of us seems to understand. I know I wouldn't want someone from the Department of Health who hasn't even taken a Valium to try to educate me about IV drug use. How could they give me helpful hints? I would feel that they are so out of tune with reality that I wouldn't be able to hear them.

AIDS: A Particular Problem for Women

When we begin our workshop on women and AIDS, we ask, "Why are we making a workshop just on how AIDS affects women?" The women come up with a list that answers this question:

- It's a man's world, so AIDS stigmatizes women, such as prostitutes.
- Our dependency on men makes us more vulnerable.
- We have to deal with male cheating and double standards.
- Women are caregivers: responsible for education and health of ourselves, our children, our spouses, and the people we work for.
- Women are isolated and have to deal with all this individually and alone. We need to see it as a social problem so we can act together.
- It's one more strike against Black and Latin women, already suffering from discrimination and racism.

You can't separate AIDS from all of the problems that women face—housing, economics, kids—and the women here, being the most marginalized, face the most problems. ACE tries to draw on women's life experiences to reflect on the problems that we share as women. We believe that by looking at our lives we can get individual strength and also build a social consciousness.

> I was conscious of women before I came in here, but not on that level. ACE has made it deeper. ACE made me realize that AIDS is bigger than each individual woman, that it's going to take all of us coming together. I never knew so many things affected just women. I had looked at issues as a Black woman—religious issues, being a single parent or not—but I had never reflected on being a woman in society.

A Crisis and Opportunity for Our Community

We are a small community and we are so isolated you can feel it—the suffering, the losses, the fears, the anxiety. Out in the street you don't have a community of women affected and living together facing a problem in this same way. We can draw on the particular strengths that women bring: nurturance, caring, and personal openness. So many women prisoners have worked in nursing and old age homes. Yet when they did, they were never given respect. Here these same activities are valued, and the women are told "thank you," and that creates initiative and feelings of self-worth. And ACE helps us to be more self-conscious about a culture of caring that as women we tend to create in our daily lives.

> For the first time in prison I was part of a group that cared about other prisoners in prison. What did that feel like? It felt like I wasn't alone in caring about people, because in this type of setting I was beginning to wonder about people caring.

Our Impact on Women

We know that we have played a role in communicating information about what is safe and what is not safe in sexual behavior—both between a man and woman and between two women—and we have certainly been able to create open and relaxed discussions about all this. But we know that actually changing behaviors is another leap ahead of us. We are learning that it's not a one-shot deal, that information doesn't equal behavior change, and it's not just an individual thing. Social norms have to change, and this takes time. And when you talk about women having to initiate change you're up against the fact that women don't have that kind of empowerment in this society. Women who have been influenced by ACE have experienced a change in attitude, but it is unclear whether this will translate into behavior change once they leave the prison.

> When I first started taking the workshops I was 100 percent against using condoms. And yet I like anal sex. But now my views are different. We're the bosses of our own bodies. You know, a lot of people say it's a man's world. Well, I can't completely agree.

Our Diversity Is a Strength

We are a diverse community of women: Black, Latin, and white, and also from countries throughout the world. In ACE there was at first a tendency to deny the differences, maybe out of fear of disunity. Now there is a more explicit consciousness growing that we can affirm our diversity and our commonality because both are important. In the last workshop on women, we broke for a while into three groups—Black, Latin, and white women—to explore the ways AIDS impacted on our particular culture and communities. We are doing more of those kinds of discussions and developing materials that address concerns of specific communities. The Hispanic

Sector of ACE is particularly active, conducting seminars in Spanish and holding open meetings for the population to foster Hispanic awareness of AIDS issues.

> The workshops didn't deal enough with different ethnic areas, and being Puerto Rican and half-Indian, some things seemed ridiculous in terms of the Hispanic family. Some of the ways people were talking about sex wouldn't work in a traditional Hispanic family. For example, you can't just tell your husband that he has to wear a condom. Or say to him, "You have to take responsibility." These approaches could lead to marital rape or abuse. The empowerment of Hispanic women means making sure that their children are brought up.

Working in a Prison

We have a unique situation at Bedford Hills. We have a prison administration that is supportive of inmates developing a peer-based program to deal with AIDS. However, because we are in a prison there are a lot of constraints and frustrations. Before we had staff persons to supervise us, we could not work out of an office space. That meant that we couldn't see women who wanted to talk on an individual level unless we ran into them in the yard or rec room.

You could be helping someone in IPC take her daily shower; it's taking longer than usual because she is in a lot of pain or she needs to talk, but that's not taken into consideration when the officer tells you that you have to leave immediately because it's "count-time." You could be in the rec room, a large room with a bunch of card tables, loud music, and an officer overseeing groups of women sitting on broken-down chairs. You're talking to a woman in crisis who needs comforting. You reach out to give her a hug and the C.O. may come over to admonish you, "No physical contact, ladies." Or maybe a woman has just tested positive. She's taken her first tentative steps to reach out by talking to someone from ACE and joining a support group. Days after her first meeting, she is transferred to another prison.

It's been difficult to be able to call ourselves counselors and have our work formally acknowledged by the administration. Counseling is usually done by professionals in here because it carries such liability and responsibility. We're struggling for the legitimacy of peer counseling. The reality is that we've been doing it in our daily lives here through informal dialogue. We now have civilian staff to supervise us, and Columbia University will be conducting a certification training program to justify the title "peer counselor."

After working over two years on our own, we are now being funded by a grant from the New York State AIDS Institute, coordinated by Columbia University School of Public Health and by Women and AIDS Resource Network

(WARN). The money has allowed hiring staff to work with ACE. ACE began as a totally volunteer inmate organization with no office or materials, operating on a shoestring and scrambling for every meeting. Now we have an office in a prime location of the prison, computers, and a civilian staff responsible for making certain that there is something to show for their salaries. Inmates who used to work whenever they could find the time are now paid 73 cents a day as staff officially assigned to the ACE Center. The crises are no longer centered around the problems of being inside a prison, but more on how to sustain momentum and a real grassroots initiative in the context of a prison. This is a problem faced by many other community organizations when they move past the initial momentum and become more established institutions.

Building a Culture of Survival

When, in the spring of 1987, we said, "Let's make quilt squares for our sisters who have died," there were more than 15 names. Over the next year we made more and more quilt squares. The deaths took a toll not just on those who knew the women but on all of us. Too many women were dying among us. And, for those who were HIV positive or worried that they might be, each death heightened their own vulnerabilities and fears. We have had to develop ways to let people who are sick know that if they die, their lives will be remembered, they will be honored and celebrated, and they will stay in our hearts.

> I remember our first memorial. Several hundred women contributed money—25 cents, 50 cents, a dollar—for flowers. Both Spanish and Black women sang and in the beginning everyone held hands and sang "That's What Friends Are For," and in the end we sang "Sister." People spoke about what Ro meant to them. Ro had died and we couldn't change that. But we didn't just feel terrible. We felt love and caring and that together we could survive the sadness and loss.
>
> In the streets, funerals were so plastic, but here, people knew that it could be them. It's not just to pay respect. When we sang "Sister," there was a charge between us. Our hands were extended to each other. There was a need for ACE and we could feel it in the air.

It was out of that same need that ACE was formed. It will be out of that same need that ACE will continue to strive to build community and an environment of trust and support. We are all we have—ourselves. If we do not latch on to this hope that has strengthened us and this drive that has broken our silence, we too will suffer and we will remain stigmatized and isolated. Feel our drive in our determination to make changes, and think "community," and make a difference.

NOTES

1. Perry F. Smith et al., *Infection Among Women Entering the New York State Correctional System* (1990), unpublished manuscript.
2. All quotations are from the authors' conversations with prisoners at Bedford Hills.
3. By Cris Williamson, from the album *The Changer and the Changed*, Olivia Records, 1975.

STUDY QUESTIONS

1. What is ACE? Who organized the program, and why?
2. Who belongs to ACE? How do they join the organization?
3. What are the components of the ACE program? What are the goals?
4. What are the strengths of the ACE program? What are the weaknesses?
5. How might the all-woman, all-prisoner environment of the Bedford Hills Correctional Facility help or hamper peer education and support?
6. How, according to the authors, has ACE helped PWAs prepare for life outside the prison? What particular problems might life on the outside pose for PWAs?

Knowledge About HIV and Behavioral Risks of Foreign-Born Boston Public School Students

Ralph W. Hingson et al.[*]

Introduction

Sixteen million mainland US residents age 18 and older were born elsewhere.[1] Many are Blacks or Hispanics who moved to urban areas where the incidence of AIDS has been particularly high, e.g., New York City, Miami, and Los Angeles. Little is known about their knowledge of human immunodeficiency virus-1 (HIV-1), drug use, and sexual behaviors.

Studies of adolescents particularly are needed. One fifth of the 186 895 AIDS cases nationally as of September 1991 have been in the 16 to 29-year-old age group.[2] Given the long incubation period of HIV-1, many persons in this age group probably became infected as teenagers.

[*]The other authors of this article are Lee Strunin, Beth Berlin, Donald E. Craven, Michael Grady, Nancy Strunk, and Robert Carr.

Reprinted with permission from *American Journal of Public Health*, vol. 81, no. 12 (December 1991):1638–1641. © 1991 by American Journal of Public Health. Reprinted by permission.

This study compares middle and high school students in the Boston public schools who were born outside the US mainland with students born in the US concerning knowledge about HIV-1 transmission; beliefs about the number of adolescents who engage in risky sexual practices and drug use; and intravenous (IV) drug use, sexual intercourse, and condom use.

Methods

In May 1990, 3049 students from a random sample of Boston public schools (13/19 middle schools and 9/15 high schools) completed a self-administered questionnaire about these topics in English (n = 2704), Spanish (n = 158), Chinese (n = 45), Vietnamese (n = 50), or French or Haitian Creole (n = 92). Translation and independent back translation ensured accuracy of questionnaire wording.

We attempted to survey all 8th and 10th grade students in selected schools. In response to an informational letter about the survey sent to parents of eligible students, 75 parents (1.5%) requested that their children not participate. On the day of the survey 11% of middle school students and 23% of high school students were absent. Among students in attendance, 81% (n = 1382) in middle schools and 73% (n = 1667) in high schools completed the questionnaires (overall response rate = 77%). Most nonresponse resulted from teachers not scheduling time to administer the survey. The gender, racial, and ethnic distributions of surveyed students closely matched those enrolled in the 8th and 10th grades in the targeted schools and in the Boston school system (Table 1). The questionnaires were anonymous and

Table 1 • Racial and Ethnic Background of 8th- and 10th-Grade Students, Boston Public Schools in 1990 AIDS Survey, Surveyed Schools and System-wide

Background	Students Surveyed (n = 3049)	8th and 10th Graders in Survey Schools (n = 4842)	8th and 10th Graders in Boston Public Schools (n = 8182)
White	20	19	22
Black	44	49	49
Hispanic	20	22	19
Asian	10	9	10
Other (unspecific)	6	<1	<1

Numbers are percentages of total.

were placed by students in blank manila envelopes. The response category, "prefer not to answer," was available for sexual and drug questions so students could not interpret the behaviors of fellow students by watching whether students answered each question. Teachers clarified student questions about the survey. Students were provided with an AIDS hotline number and instruction about AIDS was subsequently offered to all students.

Results

Students were asked to specify where they were born and how long they had lived in the United States. Thirty-five percent (n = 1057) of the students surveyed were born outside the US mainland. Half had lived in the United States less than 5 years and 21% for 1 year or less; 330 (11%) were Blacks, 309 (10%) were Hispanics, 252 (9%) were born in Asian countries, 34 (1%) were White, and the balance did not specify either their nationality or race. Twenty-one percent were born in the Caribbean or Cape Verde, 5% in Central or South America, and 8% in Asia.

The immigrant students were older (P < .0001): 13% compared to 5% of those born in the United States were 18 years or older. Neither the proportions in middle school or high school nor the gender distribution differed appreciably between those born in the US mainland and elsewhere.

Table 2 • Differences in Responses to Selected Survey Questions Among Students Born in US Mainland and Immigrant Students in Boston Public Schools

Question	US-Born (n = 1963)	Immigrant (n = 1057)	Odds Ratio (95% CI)
Worry a great deal about			
Getting AIDS	31	41	1.35 (1.11–1.65)
Discussed AIDS with parents	60	51	0.69 (0.59–0.80)
Where to get AIDS information	72	50	0.40 (0.34–0.46)
Ways to avoid getting AIDS	92	71	0.21 (0.17–0.26)
Where to get tested for HIV-1	56	38	0.50 (0.42–0.58)
Erroneous Beliefs			
A person would have to be			
sick to infect others	25	33	1.47 (1.24–1.73)
There is a cure for AIDS	2	7	3.25 (2.23–4.75)
Only gay men get AIDS	3	8	2.42 (1.72–3.41)

Numbers are percentages of total answering "yes"; place of birth unspecified, n = 29; CI = confidence interval. [Editor's note: In general, odds ratios and confidence intervals that are close to 0 indicate little or no difference between US-born and immigrant youth; and the greater the odds ratio/confidence interval, the greater the real difference between the two groups.]

Table 3 • Knowledge About HIV Transmission Among Students Born In US Mainland and Immigrant Students in the Boston Public Schools

Question	US-Born (n = 1963)[a]	Immigrant (n = 1057)[a]	Odds Ratio (95% CI)
Can get AIDS from			
Insect bites	17	24	1.55 (1.28–1.87)
Shaking hands	1	6	4.42 (2.79–7.01)
Being in the same room with a person with AIDS	1	10	8.47 (5.38–13.33)
Sex between a man and a woman	94	85	0.32 (0.25–0.42)
Sex between two men	84	76	0.59 (0.49–0.71)
Sex with someone who looks healthy	59	43	0.53 (0.45–0.62)
Sharing needles when injecting drugs	97	87	0.22 (0.17–0.31)
Can avoid AIDS by			
Sexual abstinence	78	56	0.37 (0.32–0.44)
Using condoms	87	70	0.35 (0.29–0.43)
Having sex with 1 person who is not infected	70	63	0.73 (0.62–0.85)
Not having sex with an IV drug user	73	64	0.66 (0.56–0.78)

Place of birth unspecified, n = 29; CI = confidence interval.
[a]Percent of subsample responding "yes."

Immigrant students were more likely to worry about getting AIDS, but less likely than US-born students to have talked to parents about AIDS and to know ways to avoid getting AIDS, where to obtain information, or where they could be tested for HIV-1 (Table 2).

Immigrant students were more likely to hold a variety of misconceptions about HIV-1 transmission. They were less likely to know that it can be transmitted by sharing needles, heterosexual intercourse, sex between two men, and sex with someone who looks healthy. They were also less likely to know ways to avoid HIV-1 transmission (Table 3). Further, they were more likely to believe that no one their age who has sexual intercourse uses condoms and that most or all people their age are injecting drugs (Table 4).

Immigrant students were less likely to report ever having had sexual intercourse. However, among those immigrants who were sexually active, a higher percentage reported having had sex with an IV drug user. Regardless of whether they were born in the United States or not, 62% of sexually active adolescents did not consistently use condoms and 2% injected illegal drugs (Table 4).

Table 4 • Perceptions of Peer Behavior and Personal Sexual and Drug-Use Practices of Students Born in US Mainland and Immigrant Students in the Boston Public Schools

Question	US-Born (n = 1963)[a]	Immigrant (n = 1057)[a]	Odds Ratio (95% CI)
Perceptions of peer behavior			
How many people your age are having sex?	64[b]	52[b]	0.61 (0.52–0.71)
How many people your age are using condoms?	6[c]	14[c]	2.29 (1.64–3.19)
How many people your age are injecting drugs?	12[b]	28[b]	2.76 (2.21–3.45)
Personal risk behaviors			
Ever had sex	53	31	0.36 (0.30–0.43)
Had sex in the past month with an IV drug user	1	4	2.86 (1.29–6.34)
Use condom because of AIDS risk	66	69	0.86 (0.65–1.14)
Use condoms past month	38[d]	38[d]	0.62 (0.45–0.86)
Use IV drugs past month	2	2	0.96 (0.54–1.71)
Ever shared needles	1	1	0.85 (0.36–2.01)

Place of birth unspecified, n = 29; CI = confidence interval.
[a] Percentage of subsample responding "yes," except as noted.
[b] Percent responding "almost all or most."
[c] Percent responding "none."
[d] Percent responding "all the time."

Hispanics, Blacks, Asians, and Whites born outside the United States were less knowledgeable about HIV transmission than students in these groups born in the United States (Table 5). Students who had immigrated to the US mainland in the previous year were less knowledgeable about AIDS and more likely to believe that their peers inject drugs and do not use condoms than those who had lived here 5 or more years. These newer immigrants were also more likely to have had sex with an IV drug user and to engage in sexual intercourse without using condoms (Table 6).

Conclusion

While most adolescents nationally[3] and in Massachusetts[4,5] know the principal modes of HIV transmission, those in racial and ethnic minorities are less knowledgeable,[6–9] particularly students from other countries and Puerto Rico now residing in the United States. It should be noted that our study reflects

Table 5 • Knowledge About HIV-1 Transmission Among Boston Public School Students According to Race and Nation of Birth

Question	Black		Hispanic		Asian		White		Other	
	US (n = 974)	I (n = 330)	US (n = 272)	I (n - 309)	US (n = 52)	I (n = 252)	US (n = 568)	I (n = 34)	US (n = 67)	I (n = 113)
Know ways to prevent getting AIDS	92	78	89	84	92	49	94	77	96	66
Where to get information about AIDS	76	57	68	61	67	30	65	44	80	47
Can get AIDS from										
Sex between men and women	93	87	95	85	96	79	96	84	97	90
Sex between two men	82	82	79	80	82	69	90	88	88	65
Sex with someone who appears healthy	54	46	48	44	73	39	71	50	73	39
Sharing needles	96	85	97	91	100	83	98	85	97	87
Toilet seats	5	11	7	14	6	13	6	15	2	18
Being in the same room with a person who has AIDS	1	8	2	6	0	15	1	6	0	14

US = survey students born in the mainland United States; I = immigrant students; numbers are percentages of totals answering "yes."

Table 6 • Selected Beliefs About AIDS and Sexual and Drug Use Practices of Students Who Lived in the US Mainland ≤1 Year Compared to Students Who Have Lived in the United States >5 Years

Question	Lived in US ≤1 year (n = 195)[a]	Lived in US >5 years (n = 369)[a]	Odds Ratio (95% CI)
Worry a great deal about getting AIDS	45	35	1.54 (1.08–2.19)
Can get AIDS from being in the same room with an infected person	20	4	6.69 (3.45–12.94)
Abstaining from sex can reduce chances of getting AIDS	56	68	0.59 (0.41–0.86)
Using condoms can reduce chances of getting AIDS	60	83	0.31 (0.21–0.46)
What proportion of people your age use condoms[b]	19	9	2.41 (1.40–4.14)
Almost all/most people your age inject drugs	32	21	1.71 (1.13–2.58)
Use condoms because of AIDS risk	50	72	0.39 (0.19–0.82)
Always use condoms past year	32	49	0.49 (0.23–1.05)
Had sex with an IV drug user in the last year	13	1	10.30 (1.91–55.47)

CI = confidence interval.
[a]Percentage of subsample responding "yes," except as noted.
[b]Percentage responding "none."

the perceptions and practices of immigrant students in the Boston public schools. Knowledge and behaviors may differ in other cities. The use of self-administered surveys often yields lower response rates and more missing data than in-person interviews. Also, absent students may have been less knowledgeable and more likely to engage in risky behaviors.

Despite these limitations, our findings underscore the importance of offering AIDS education in multiple languages in school systems that serve large immigrant populations. Students born outside the United States may bring varying notions about disease causation, prevention, and treatment, and educators should explore those beliefs in a nonthreatening fashion.[10]

Immigrant students may walk a tightrope between acculturation pressures to assume behaviors they perceive as commonplace among peers born in the United States and parental pressure to retain their cultural values and traditions. Students who immigrated to the United States in the previous year were more likely than those living here longer to believe their peers engage in unprotected sex and use IV drugs. Recent immigrants who want to "fit in" with perceived US social norms may be particularly vulnerable to pressure from other teens or adults to engage in unprotected sex or to use illicit drugs.

These students should be helped to understand that unprotected sex and illicit drug use are not as common as they may suspect. Peer-led instruction from students from their own countries who have lived in the United States for several years might be especially helpful, as would training in skills to resist peer pressure. The need for such education is magnified by findings that, like US-born students, most sexually active immigrant students do not use condoms and, although this sexually active group is small in absolute numbers, a higher proportion reported having had sex with an IV drug user compared with US-born students.

REFERENCES

1. Hendershot G. Health of the foreign born population, United States 1985–1986. *Advance Data* no. 157. National Center for Health Statistics; 1988.
2. *AIDS Newsletter Monthly*, Publication of the Massachusetts Dept. of Public Health 7;3, September 1991;7:3.
3. Hardy A. AIDS knowledge and attitudes for April–June 1989. *Advance Data* no. 179. National Center for Health Statistics; 1989.
4. Hingson R, Strunin L, Berlin B. AIDS transmission: changes in knowledge and behaviors among adolescents: Massachusetts statewide surveys 1986–1988. *Pediatrics*. 1990;85:24–29.
5. Hingson R, Strunin L, Berlin B, Heeren T. Beliefs about AIDS, use of alcohol and drugs, and unprotected sex among Massachusetts adolescents. *Am J Public Health*. 1990;80:295–300.
6. Dawson D, Hardy A. AIDS knowledge and attitudes of Hispanic Americans. *Advance Data* no. 166. National Center for Health Statistics; 1989.
7. Dawson D, Hardy A. AIDS knowledge and attitudes of Black Americans. *Advance Data* no. 165. National Center for Health Statistics; 1989.
8. DiClemente RJ, Boyer L, Morales E. Minority and AIDS: knowledge, attitudes, and misconceptions among Black and Latino adolescents. *Am J Public Health*. 1988;78:55–57.
9. Goodman E, Cobrall A. Acquired immunodeficiency syndrome and adolescents: knowledge, attitudes, beliefs, and behaviors in a New York City adolescent minority population. *Pediatrics*. 1989;84:36–42.
10. Strunin L. Adolescents' perceptions of risk for HIV infection: implications for future research. *Soc Sci Med*. 1991;2:221–228.

STUDY QUESTIONS

1. When and where was this survey conducted?
2. What differences are there in knowledge about HIV transmission between U.S.-born and immigrant teenagers?
3. What differences are there in the sexual behavior and drug use between U.S.-born and immigrant teenagers?

4. What cultural factors, according to the authors, may have contributed to the immigrant students' misconceptions about HIV transmission and about the sexual behaviors of their U.S.-born peers?
5. What kinds of educational strategies do the authors recommend for foreign-born middle and high school students?

HIV Infection
and Homeless Adolescents

Jean L. Athey

Adolescents are one group that is typically overlooked in discussions either of homelessness or HIV infection, and yet thousands of adolescents are homeless in this country and many of them are HIV infected. This article examines the risks for homeless adolescents of acquiring HIV infection and the service initiatives for meeting the challenges these adolescents present.

Considerable overlap exists in the literature with respect to "runaway" vs. "homeless" youths. Generally speaking, a "runaway" is a young person who has a safe and viable home and could return to it; "homeless" suggests that no such home exists. The safety and viability of the homes of many runaways, however, are often difficult to determine. Clear definition is complicated by the housing of some long-term homeless youths—those who find shelter and so are not technically homeless, but whose shelter is destructive to them, as, for example, that supplied by a pimp. Nearly four-fifths of all adolescent prostitutes have been estimated to be runaways [Manov and Lowther 1983]. Other shelters, such as crash pads, may not be much better. This article focuses on homeless adolescents living on the streets or in nonviable shelters.

The extent of adolescent homelessness is difficult to establish [GAO 1989]. Various community surveys and youth shelter data suggest that somewhere between one and 1.3 million adolescents are in emergency shelters or on the streets in any given year, a large proportion of whom are runaways [Robertson 1989], although a recent study suggests that the number may be closer to one-half million [Finkelhor et al. 1990]. It is also estimated that there are 900,000 adolescent prostitutes in the United States [Deisher et al. 1982]. The National Coalition for the Homeless found that unaccompanied minors accounted for over 25% of the homeless population in five major cities [National Coalition for the Homeless 1989]. Whatever the exact number, the problem of adolescent homelessness is clearly severe.

Reasons for Homelessness

Adolescents may become homeless for a variety of reasons.

"System Kids"

These are young people who have been shuffled back and forth among foster homes, psychiatric hospitals, emergency shelters, residential schools, and juvenile justice facilities. They have had little, if any, stability in their lives and have often been harmed rather than helped by child-serving systems. Studies of runaway and homeless youths consistently find large proportions with histories of multiple placements. In a study of shelter-using youths in New York City, half had previously lived in a setting provided by the child welfare system [Shaffer and Caton 1984]. Adolescents with a history of multiple placements often leave unsatisfactory settings when they finally conclude that the streets meet their needs better than the service system.

Throwaways

Some adolescents are evicted by their families, often following extensive conflict with parents, conflict that may have been exacerbated by parental alcohol or drug abuse or by mental illness on the part of a parent or the youth [Gullotta 1978]. Other youths are not welcome in their homes because of their homosexual orientation; one study in Seattle found that some 40% of the homeless youths in that city were gay [Seattle Department of Human Resources 1988].

Physical and Sexual Abuse

Many young people leave home to escape intolerable abuse from parents or guardians. Life on the streets is dangerous, but for many adolescents, the streets are safer than home. Even though young people are often reluctant to acknowledge a history of abuse, especially sexual abuse, studies of runaway and homeless youths have found the incidence of admitted sexual abuse to range between 21% and 60% [Yates et al. 1988; Rotheram-Borus and Bradley 1987; Rotheram-Borus et al. 1989], and that of physical abuse between 16% and 40% [Yates et al. 1988; Shaffer and Caton 1984; Chelimsky 1982].

Parental Homelessness

No data are available on the extent to which adolescents are homeless due to parental homelessness. Many shelters, however, will not take intact families. The 1987 report of the U.S. Conference of Mayors estimates that two-thirds of all homeless families have to be broken up if anyone in the family is to receive shelter. Those that take mothers and children will often not accept adolescents, especially adolescent boys. In short, adolescents who are part of a family that becomes homeless must typically fend for themselves; it is likely that most end up on the streets.

Thus, homeless adolescents have dealt with abuse, instability, rejection, poverty, and many other problems. It is not surprising that studies have found rates of clinical depression ranging from 29% to 83.6% [Shaffer and Caton 1984; Yates et al. 1988]. A relatively consistent finding is the high proportion of homeless/runaway girls who have previously attempted suicide—about one-third [Shaffer and Caton 1984; Rotheram-Borus and Bradley 1987]. A study of youths using New York City shelters found that the sample had a psychiatric profile largely indistinguishable from adolescents attending an outpatient clinic; 89% of the youths were either depressed, antisocial, or both [Shaffer and Caton 1984]. In short, for the most part these are highly troubled young people, many with tragic histories. The precarious living situation in which they find themselves combines with their emotional and economic problems to increase their vulnerability to HIV infection through high-risk sexual and drug use behavior.

Sexual Activity of Homeless Adolescents

Outreach workers who work closely with homeless youths report high levels of sexual activity among them, some of it voluntary and some not. The sexual activity of these young people may be categorized in three ways—rape, survival sex, or a love relationship—the classification reflecting the degree of personal control.

Rape

Girls who live on the streets are very vulnerable to rape. While no data exist on the frequency of rape among homeless girls, the rate of sexual assault on homeless women is reported to be approximately 20 times the rate among women in general [Kelly 1985]. Nationally, 50% of all rape victims are less than 18 years old [Neinstein and Stewart 1984]. Since homeless girls have the double risk factors of youth and homelessness, it can be assumed that rape is a common experience for them. In a New York City youth shelter study, 25% of the girls said that they had been raped at some time in their lives [Shaffer and Caton 1984]. Less information is available on rape of young boys, but street workers report it as not infrequent [Able-Peterson 1989]. Rapists are considered to be high-risk carriers for HIV owing to the large number of persons with whom they have sexual contact [Burgess and Hartman 1989].

The high incidence of sexual abuse reported by runaway and homeless girls prior to leaving home points to another potential route of viral transmission. Youth service workers have reported instances of runaway girls who became HIV infected as a result of earlier sexual assault by a guardian [West 1989]. The incidence of HIV infection spread this way is unknown, but it may be a significant route of infection among runaway and homeless girls. Ongoing abuse by a seropositive individual would provide multiple opportunities for infection.

Sexual abuse at home is related to HIV infection for runaway and homeless adolescents in an indirect way as well as a direct way: the abuse has been shown to lead to sexual acting out and increased promiscuity [Browne and Finkelhor 1986]. In one study, runaway and homeless girls who had been sexually abused engaged in more sexual activity than girls who had not been sexually abused; this activity was primarily unprotected [Rotheram-Borus et al. 1989]. It is not surprising then that another study found that runaway girls who had been sexually abused were more likely to have been pregnant than those who had not been abused [Shaffer and Caton 1984]. Thus, rape, including sexual abuse, may transmit the AIDS virus, and it may also lead to increased and unprotected sexual activity as a dysfunctional response to an earlier assault, increasing the risk of HIV infection.

Survival Sex

Both boys and girls on the streets frequently engage in survival sex, which may include occasionally turning a trick to get enough money for a meal, or being temporarily taken in by an older male who provides shelter and food in exchange for sexual favors. In a Los Angeles study, 26.4% of the homeless and runaway youths in the sample said that they engaged in survival sex [Yates et al. 1988]. Sometimes survival sex turns into more systematic prostitution. A study of adolescent prostitutes in Seattle by Deisher et al. [1989] describes a group of girls with long histories of abuse and unstable living arrangements, periodically moving from street to pimp/boyfriend's house and back to the streets. Most of these girls did not use condoms, or used them only sporadically. Clearly, to the extent that survival sex involves multiple partners and is unprotected, HIV risk is increased.

Sex in a Relationship

As it is for other adolescents or for adults, sexual activity in a heterosexual or homosexual relationship is common among homeless adolescents. These youths often have boyfriends and girlfriends, even if they are also engaged in survival sex, and their relationships change frequently [Athey 1990].

It appears that most of the sexual activity of homeless adolescents is unsafe sex, without the use of condoms. Although research on their use of contraceptives is limited, there is no reason to assume that homeless adolescents use contraceptives more often than do adolescents living at home, two-thirds of whom do not routinely use contraceptives [Trussell 1988]. Rotheram-Borus et al. [1989] found in a sample of runaways in New York City that only 40% of those youths who were sexually active had ever used a condom, and none had always used one during sexual intercourse. One indication of the lack of use of contraceptives, including condoms, by homeless girls, is their high pregnancy rates. A study of health care services to the homeless in 19 cities found that the 16- to 19-year-old age group had the highest pregnancy rate of any age group in the study: of all 16- to 19-year-old homeless girls seen by the health care projects, 31% were pregnant, a rate described by the researchers as "astonishing." This compares to 9% of 16- to 19-year-old girls in the control sample, derived from case records of ambulatory care physicians [Wright 1989]. Another indication of the lack of barrier contraception is the sexually transmitted disease (STD) rate. The health care for the homeless projects found that 10.8% of the homeless girls age 13 to 19 had an STD compared to 3.3% of a control sample.

In short, homeless adolescents typically have multiple voluntary and involuntary sexual experiences, most of which are unsafe and put them at risk of HIV infection.

Drug Use Among Homeless Adolescents

The rate of intravenous (IV) drug use among all adolescents its believed to be not extremely high. A 1988 random survey found that 1.1% of high school seniors reported having ever used heroin [National Institute on Drug Abuse 1989]. Although this suggests that IV drug use is a relatively low-incidence activity among adolescents, the problem is larger than these data indicate for certain subpopulations. For example, as many as 15% of the adolescent males from some inner cities have used heroin [Brunswick and Messeri 1986]. Out-of-school youths, including homeless adolescents, generally have higher drug abuse rates than those in school [Rahdert 1988]; the Los Angeles study of runaways found that 34.5% had used IV drugs [Yates et al. 1988]. Available data on IV drug use generally do not include the recent phenomenon of IV use of cocaine, but a recent study of adolescent IV drug users in Houston, most of whom were "street kids," did find that cocaine injection or cocaine in combination with another drug accounted for 82% of the 137 adolescent IV drug users in the sample [Williams 1989]. Thus, with higher rates of cocaine use, IV drug use may be increasing among certain subpopulations.

Homeless adolescents who do not inject drugs intravenously may put themselves at risk for HIV infection by engaging in sex with persons who do. Adolescent girls appear to be at particular risk for sex with an IV drug-using partner because males have higher rates of drug use than females [Mott and Haurin 1988], and because adolescent girls generally have sexual partners slightly older than themselves [Zelnik and Kanter 1980], an age group with the highest rate of illicit IV drug use [National Institute on Drug Abuse 1989]. One study [Nicholas et al. 1987] found that teenagers who reported IV drug use were also more likely to report large numbers of sexual partners.

Non-IV drug use is also implicated in the spread of HIV infection because some drugs, particularly crack cocaine, appear to enhance the probability of sex with multiple partners, as for example in crack dens.

Addicts may also increase their number of sexual partners and thus increase their risk of infection by bartering sex for drugs [Scribner et al. 1989]. Since the substance abuse rate of homeless youths is estimated to range from 70% to 85% [Shaffer and Caton 1984; Yates et al. 1988; Rotheram-Borus et al. 1989], it is clear that both IV and non-IV drug use is a major risk factor for HIV infection for these adolescents.

Extent of HIV Infection Among Homeless Youths

Although relatively few adolescents have been reported at this writing to the Centers for Disease Control (CDC) as having AIDS, they are not free of the virus. Since the latency period of the virus is now estimated to average about eight years [Liu et al. 1988], infection of most adolescents will not result in illness or be reflected in CDC statistics until the adolescent is a young adult. It is generally believed that a high proportion of persons who become symptomatic with AIDS in their twenties actually were infected in their teen years. Through January 1990 the CDC reported that 6,233 cases of AIDS had occurred among persons age 20 to 24, and 19,568 among persons age 25 to 29 [CDC 1990]. Seroprevalence data on both military recruits [Burke et al. 1987] and on Job Corps recruits [CDC 1987] reveal that the virus has moved heavily into the adolescent population. Although the extent to which homeless adolescents nationally have already become infected with HIV is unknown, some local figures are very disturbing. Covenant House in New York City tested 2,667 specimens of blood from youths using its services over the two-year period October 1987 to December 1989 [Stricof et al. 1991]. Over 5% were found to be seropositive. Infection correlated with time on the streets: the longer a young person had been homeless, the more likely he or she was to be infected. Since the older adolescents had typically been on the streets longer, they were more likely to be seropositive than younger adolescents. Of 20-year-olds tested, 8.6% were seropositive.

It is clear from this study and from the risk behaviors of homeless adolescents that at least several hundred homeless youths are already HIV positive. Many of them are just discovering their HIV status. According to reports from service providers, young people increasingly request a test. Others are having their infants tested [Athey 1990]. Besides the seropositive but nonsymptomatic youths, a small number of homeless adolescents are becoming ill with AIDS while still in their teens. In 1989, Covenant House admitted 35 youths to their residential symptomatic AIDS facility [Kennedy 1989], and Bridge Over Troubled Waters in Boston was working with about 25 youths with AIDS [Scanlon 1989]. As the epidemic progresses, it is safe to predict that more will become ill. Homeless youths need a range of supportive services even without being HIV infected, but being seropositive, symptomatic or not, creates additional needs.

A Service Strategy

Adolescents who are without a home and have no resources or adult protectors, who have been abused and are emotionally disturbed, and who
may use drugs and alcohol, are clearly in need of help. But these young
people rarely fit the requirements imposed by traditional service programs,
and consequently many programs reject them, considering them to be either
a poor risk or to carry problems too complex to handle [Athey 1990]. For
example, teen parenting programs often provide good services to some
girls, but these programs are unavailable to homeless girls [Athey 1990].
When these youths become HIV positive or sick with AIDS, the access to
services is even more difficult. A pregnant, homeless girl who is also HIV
positive, for example, faces extraordinary barriers to service.

Given the categorical nature of most health and social services plus the
variety and severity of problems of HIV-positive homeless youths, a new
model of care will need to be developed for these youths if they are to be
truly helped. It is fairly easy to identify the needs of HIV-positive homeless
adolescents: housing, medical care, mental health services, drug abuse treatment, education and jobs training, and legal access. It is also fairly obvious
that these services need to be delivered holistically and comprehensively. If
a critical service need, such as housing, is not met, other services will be
largely ineffective. Without housing, for example, health care routines cannot be easily maintained, there is no place to store medicine, and exposure
to additional environmental pathogens is likely. In short, a categorical
approach is unlikely to work well. Two models of service delivery that
appear to be quite promising for these youths and that avoid ineffective
compartmentalization are multiagency, coordinated care, with a case manager, and "wraparound" services.

Coordinated care has recently been established in a few states for emotionally disturbed children and adolescents whose needs cut across public
child-serving agencies. Like homeless adolescents, these children have generally not been well served in the past. A considerable body of research
documents the problems inherent in the fragmented system of care for
them [Stroul and Friedman 1986]; a system characterized as often inappropriate, incomplete, and not infrequently ineffective. To remedy these problems, some state mental health departments have strengthened coordination
at both the state and local levels through interagency committees, multidis-
ciplinary teams, and "blended funding," accompanied by case management
[Update 1986]. This integration of services appears to have brought about
greatly improved care for the youths served through these systems [Essex
and Jordan 1989]. Local systems of care for homeless adolescents have also
been developed in a few places [Pires and Silber 1991]. A multiagency commitment to encompass the full range of service needs of HIV-positive
homeless adolescents offers a viable model of care for these youths if necessary service modifications are made, as follows: address the dual diag-

noses of emotional disturbance and substance abuse; counseling that reflects special developmental issues (e.g., sexual identity and dealing with a foreshortened life span); treatment for the effects of past sexual abuse; and counseling on reducing suicide risk and AIDS risk for themselves and others [Garrison 1989].

A wraparound model of care is another particularly promising strategy for serving this population. The concept is simple to understand, but typically less simple to implement in bureaucratic agencies. It means that when the available services are inadequate or inappropriate for a particular child or adolescent, a commitment is made to develop and fund whatever is needed to help the child [Burchard and Clarke 1990]. In states where this is being tried experimentally—for example, with severely emotionally disturbed youths—a treatment team is formed and a creative approach to best serving that child is sought, with frequent use of nontraditional means. Thus, instead of fitting a child to a predetermined and preexisting set of programs, the child's particular needs and strengths determine what is developed. If no off-the-shelf program is available that is suitable for the child, something new is designed. Wraparound programs, such as the Alaska Youth Initiative, appear to be successful as well as cost-effective in more effectively meeting the needs of troubled youths [VanDenBerg and Minton 1987].

In short, the combination of serious and complicated problems these adolescents bring requires the services of a broad array of agencies, and services have to be modified, expanded, or developed brand-new for them. Effective service delivery models do exist; it is the will to implement them that has to be strengthened.

Conclusion

Homeless adolescents are a difficult population to serve: most have managed to survive by learning to distrust adults, but at a severe emotional and physical cost. Homeless adolescents who, in addition to their other problems, have a contagious, fatal disease reveal most acutely the gaps and deficiencies in the system of children's services. The growing population of homeless HIV-infected youths challenges these systems in a fundamental way, and if the systems are essentially unresponsive, it is not just these particular youths who will suffer more than they otherwise would and who will likely die without dignity—the others they infect and the babies they will have will also suffer and die. It is hard to imagine a more compelling case for developing a coordinated system of appropriate social, health, and mental health services.

REFERENCES

Able-Peterson, T. "The Most Forgotten Adolescents." Presentation at conference on Treatment of Adolescents with Alcohol, Drug Abuse, and Mental Health Problems, Alexandria, VA, October 1989.

Athey, J. G. Pregnancy and Childbearing Among Homeless Adolescents, A Report of a Workshop. Pittsburgh, PA: University of Pittsburgh, 1990.

Browne, A., and Finkelhor, D. "Initial and Longterm Effects: A Review of the Research." In Sourcebook on Child Sexual Abuse, edited by D. Finkelhor. Beverly Hills, CA: Sage, 1986.

Brunswick, A. F., and Messeri, P. "Drugs, Lifestyle and Health: A Longitudinal Study of Urban Black Youth." American Journal of Public Health 76, 1 (January 1986): 52–57.

Burchard, J. T., and Clark, R. T. "The Role of Individualized Care in a Service Delivery System for Children and Adolescents with Severely Maladjusted Behavior." Journal of Mental Health Administration 17, 1 (Spring 1990): 48–60.

Burgess, A. W., and Hartman, C. R. "AIDS and the Sexually Abused Adolescent." In Troubled Adolescents and HIV Infection, edited by J. O. Woodruff, D. Doherty, and J. G. Athey. Washington, DC: Georgetown University Child Development Center, 1989.

Burke, D. S.; Brundage, J. F.; Herbold, J. R.; Berner, W.; Gardner, L. I.; Gunzenhauser, J. D.; Voskovitch, J.; and Redfield, R. "Human Immunodeficiency Virus Infections Among Civilian Applicants for United States Military Service, October 1985 to March 1986: Demographic Factors Associated with Seropositivity." New England Journal of Medicine 317, 3 (July 16, 1987): 131–136.

Centers for Disease Control. "Human Immunodeficiency Virus Infection in the United States: A Review of Current Knowledge." Morbidity and Mortality Weekly Report 36, S-6 (December 18, 1987): 1–48.

Centers for Disease Control. HIV/AIDS Surveillance Report. Atlanta, GA: February 1990.

Chelimsky, E. "The Problem of Runaway and Homeless Youth." Oversight Hearing on Runaway and Homeless Youth Program. U.S. House of Representatives, Subcommittee on Human Resources, Committee on Education and Labor, Washington, DC, 1982.

Deisher, R. W.; Robinson, G.; and Boyer, D. "The Adolescent Female and Male Prostitute." Pediatric Annals 11, 4 (September 1982): 812–825.

Deisher, R. W.; Farrow, J. A.; Hope, K.; and Litchfield, C. "The Pregnant Adolescent Prostitute." American Journal of Diseases of Children 143, 10 (October 1989): 1162–1165.

Essex, D., and Jordan, D. Results to Date: Higher Benefits at Lower Cost. Ventura, CA: The Ventura Model for Mental Health Services, September 1989.

Finkelhor, D.; Hotaling, G.; and Sedlak, A. Missing, Abducted, Runaway, and Thrownaway Children in America. Washington, DC: U.S. Department of Justice, 1990.

Garrison, J. "Services and Treatment Issues: Recommendations of the Work Group." Journal of Adolescent Health Care 10, 35 (May 1989): 48–49.

Government Accounting Office. Homelessness: Homeless and Runaway Youth Receiving Services at Federally Funded Shelters. Washington, DC: Government Accounting Office (GAO/HRD-90-45), 1989.

Gullotta, T. "Runaway; Reality or Myth." Adolescence 13, 52 (Winter 1978): 543–549.

Kelly, J. T. "Trauma: With the Example of San Francisco's Shelter Programs." In Health Care of Homeless People, edited by P. W. Brickner, L. K. Scharer, B. Conanan, A. Elvy, and M. Savarese. New York: Springer, 1985.

Kennedy, J. Covenant House, New York City, NY. Personal communication, 1989.

Liu, K. J.; Darrow, W. W.; and Rutherford, G. W. "A Model-Based Estimate of the Mean Incubation Period for AIDS in Homosexual Men." Science 240, 4857 (June 3, 1988): 1333–1337.

Manov, A., and Lowther, L. "A Health Care Approach for Hard-to-Reach Adolescent Runaways." Nursing Clinics of North America 18, 3 (September 1983): 333–342.

Mott, F. L., and Haurin, R. J. "Linkages Between Sexual Activity and Alcohol and Drug Use Among American Adolescents." Family Planning Perspectives 20, 3 (May–June 1988): 128–136.

National Coalition for the Homeless. America's Nightmare. A Decade of Homelessness in the United States. Washington, DC: National Coalition for the Homeless, 1989.

National Institute on Drug Abuse. Highlights of the 1988 National Household Survey on Drug Abuse. NIDA Capsules, Rockville, MD: NIDA, August 1989.

National Institute on Drug Abuse: "1988 Survey Results from Monitoring the Future: A Continuing Study of the Lifestyles and Values of Youth." Rockville, MD: NIDA (Press Release, February 28, 1989).

Neinstein, L. S., and Stewart, D. C. Adolescent Health Care: A Practical Guide. Baltimore, MD: Urban and Schwarzenberg, 1984.

Nicholas, S. W.; Sondheimer, D. L.; Willoughby, A. D.; Yaffe, S.; and Katz, S. "Human Immunodeficiency Virus Infection in Childhood, Adolescence, and Pregnancy: A Status Report and National Research Agenda." Pediatrics 83, 2 (February 1987): 193–198.

Pires, S. A., and Silber, J. T. On Their Own: Runaway and Homeless Youth and Programs That Serve Them. Washington, DC: Georgetown University Child Development Center, 1991.

Rahdert, E. R. "Treatment Services for Adolescent Drug Abusers: Introduction and Overview." In Adolescent Drug Abuse: Analyses of Treatment Research, edited by E. R. Rahdert and J. Grabowski. NIDA, Research Monograph 77, Rockville, MD: NIDA, 1988.

Robertson, M. "Homeless Youth: An Overview of Recent Literature." Paper delivered at conference on Homeless Children and Youth, Coping with a National Tragedy, Washington, DC, May 1989.

Rotheram-Borus, M. J., and Bradley, J. S. "Evaluation and Triage of Runaways at Risk for Suicide." Unpublished report, Columbia University, Division of Child Psychiatry, 1987.

Rotheram-Borus, M. J.; Koopman, C.; and Bradley, J. S. "Barriers to Successful AIDS Prevention Programs with Runaway Youth." In Troubled Adolescents and HIV Infection, edited by J. O. Woodruff, D. Doherty, and J. G. Athey. Washington, DC: Georgetown University Child Development Center, 1989.

Scanlon, B. Bridge Over Troubled Waters, Boston, MA. Personal Communication, 1989.

Scribner, R.; Cohen, D.; and Dwyer, J. "The Streets of Babylon: Syphilis and Sex for Drugs in Los Angeles County." Paper presented at the American Public Health Association Meeting, Chicago, IL, October 1989.

Seattle Department of Human Resources. Report on Gay and Lesbian Youth in Seattle. Seattle, WA: Commission on Children and Youth, 1988.

Shaffer, D., and Caton, C. L. M. Runaway and Homeless Youth in New York City: A Report to the Ittleson Foundation. New York: Division of Child Psychiatry, New York State Psychiatric Institute and Columbia University College of Physicians and Surgeons, 1984.

Stricof, R. L.; Kennedy, J. T.; Nattell, T. C.; Weisfuse, I. B.; and Novick, L. F. "HIV-Seroprevalence in a Facility for Runaway and Homeless Adolescents." American Journal of Public Health 81 (Supplement) (May 1991): 50–53.

Stroul, B. A., and Friedman, R. M. A System of Care for Severely Emotionally Disturbed Children and Youth. Washington, DC: Georgetown University Child Development Center, 1986.

Trussell, J. Teenage Pregnancy in the U.S. Family Planning Perspectives 20, 6 (November–December 1988): 262–272.

Update. "Case Management." Update—Newsletter of the Research and Training Center for Children's Mental Health 2, 15 (Summer 1986): 10–12.

U.S. Conference of Mayors. A Status Report on Homeless Families in America's Cities. A 29-City Survey. Washington, DC: U.S. Conference of Mayors, 1987.

VanDenBerg, J., and Minton, B. A. "Alaska Native Youth: A New Approach to Services for Emotionally Disturbed Children and Youth." Children Today 16, 5 (September–October 1987): 15–18.

West, M. Kaleidoscope, Chicago, IL. Personal communication, 1989.

Williams, M. L. "High-Risk Drug Use Behaviors and the Risk of AIDS Among a Sample of Adolescent IV Drug Users." Unpublished report under NIDA grant R18DA05156, 1989.

Wright, J. D. "Poverty, Homelessness, Health, Nutrition, and Children." Paper delivered at conference on Homeless Children and Youth. Coping with a National Tragedy, Washington, DC, May 1989.

Yates, G. L.; MacKenzie, R.; Pennbridge, J., and Cohen, E. "A Risk Profile Comparison of Runaway and Non-Runaway Youth." American Journal of Public Health 78, 7 (July 1988): 820–821.

Zelnik, M., and Kanter, J. F. "Sexual Activity, Contraceptive Use and Pregnancy Among Metropolitan-area Teenagers, 1971–1979." Family Planning Perspectives 12, 5 (September–October 1980): 230–237.

STUDY QUESTIONS

1. What kinds of personal circumstances force adolescents into homelessness?
2. What is "survival sex," and how does it differ from rape?
3. How do the sexual behaviors of homeless adolescents place them at particularly high risk of HIV infection?
4. What are the differences in rates of injection drug use between adolescents who live on the streets and those who live at home?
5. What is "coordinated health care," and how can this strategy be used to advantage in meeting the needs of homeless adolescents?
6. How does a "wraparound" program work? In what ways can it be both effective and money-saving?
7. What unique problems do HIV-positive homeless adolescents face that are not shared by other groups affected by the HIV/AIDS epidemic? How does the author suggest we address their needs?

Suggested Additional Readings

Marshall H. Becker and Jill Joseph, "AIDS and Behavioral Change to Reduce Risk: A Review." American Journal of Public Health, vol. 78 (1988):394–410.

Cherrie B. Boyer and Susan M. Kegeles, "AIDS and Risk Prevention Among Adolescents." Social Sciences and Medicine, vol. 33 (1991):11–23.

Susan D. Cochran and Letitia A. Peplau, "Sexual Risk Reduction Behaviors Among Young Heterosexual Adults." *Social Science and Medicine*, vol. 33 (1991):25–36.

Ralph J. DiClemente, editor. *Adolescents and AIDS: A Generation in Jeopardy* (Newbury Park, CA: Sage, 1992).

Ann M. Hardy et al., "The Economic Impact of the First 10,000 Cases of Acquired Immunodeficiency Syndrome in the United States." *Journal of the American Medical Association*, vol. 255 (1986):209–211.

Jeffery A. Kelly et al., "HIV Risk Behavior Reduction Following Intervention with Key Opinion Leaders of Population: An Experimental Analysis." *American Journal of Public Health*, vol. 81, no. 2 (February 1991):168–171.

Linda F. McCaig, Ann M. Hardy, and Deborah M. Winn, "Knowledge About AIDS and HIV in the U.S. Adult Population: Influence of the Local Incidence of AIDS." *American Journal of Public Health*, vol. 81, no. 12 (December 1991):1591–1595.

Rick Petosa and Janet Wessinger, "The AIDS Education Needs of Adolescents: A Theory-Based Approach." *AIDS Education and Prevention,* vol. 2 (1990):127–136.

John R. Quinn, "Distributing Condoms in High School." *America* (November 2, 1992):320.

Beverly Sotille-Malona, "Condoms and AIDS." *America* (November 2, 1992): 317–319.

Rachel L Stricof, James T. Kennedy, and Thomas C. Nattell, "HIV-Seroprevalence in a Facility for Runaway and Homeless Adolescents." *American Journal of Public Health,* vol. 81 (1991):50–53.

Glossary

The following list contains many names and terms that often appear in writings and discussions about HIV/AIDS, including the readings in this book.

Acer, David   the late Florida dentist who is thought by some—without conclusive proof so far—to have intentionally infected a number of his patients with HIV during the early to mid-1980s

ACT UP   AIDS Coalition to Unleash Power; activist organization formed in March 1987 in New York City by Larry Kramer and others dissatisfied with official neglect of people with HIV/AIDS and the need for expanded HIV/AIDS public education and research

acylovir   an antiviral drug used to treat HIV infection

AID   United States Agency for International Development; in the past decade, the agency has contributed to HIV/AIDS education and prevention programs in developing nations

AIDS   Acquired Immune Deficiency Syndrome; replaced GRID as the designation for diminished immune system functioning; the advanced and terminal stage of HIV infection, characterized by a reduced number of T-4 helper cells and the cluster of opportunistic infections

AIDS belt   that portion of the sub-Saharan region in central, southern, and eastern Africa with exceptionally high HIV prevalence rates

AIDS Treatment News   San Francisco publication that grew out of a patient-advocacy network in 1986 and provides updates on available and experimental HIV/AIDS medical therapies

AL-721   experimental Israeli immune-boosting drug barred by the FDA from U.S. distribution

amebiasis   amebic dysentery; an infection of the large intestine characterized by persistent moderate to severe diarrhea and in severe cases by abscesses in the liver and brain

AmFAR   American Foundation for AIDS Research; founded by Mervyn Silverman and Mathilde Krim; major fund-raising agent for HIV/AIDS education, social services, treatment, and research; promotes and sponsors community-based trials of new HIV/AIDS medical therapies

Apuzzio, Virginia M.   director of the National Gay and Lesbian Task Force during the early 1980s; debated gay rights with Jerry Falwell on the *Donahue* show; endorsed Walter Mondale's candidacy for U.S. presidency in 1984

Axelrod, David   New York State Commissioner of Health during the early years of the HIV/AIDS health crisis in the United States; delayed bathhouse closings in New York until 1985

AZT   the abbreviation for azidothymidine, also known as zidovudine

Bergalis, Kimberly   believed to have been infected with HIV by her dentist, Dr. David Acer; died at age 23 in 1991

Brandt, Edward N., Jr.   Assistant Secretary of Health and Human Services, Reagan appointee

Broder, Sam   biomedical researcher; clinical director of the National Cancer Institute's special Task Force on AIDS

Buchanan, Patrick   conservative Republican columnist and Reagan appointee as Director of White House Communications in 1985; promoted the belief that HIV/AIDS is "caused" by homosexuals

Buckley, William F., Jr.   conservative political editorialist who proposed in 1986 that all HIV-seropositive persons be tattooed, on the forearm in the case of injection drug users and on the buttocks in the case of gay men

Burroughs Wellcome   American subsidiary of the British-based Wellcome PLC; pharmaceutical company that developed, patented, and markets AZT

candidiasis   a fungus infection of the oral or vaginal mucous membrane commonly known as thrush or moniliasis; often recurring or chronic and can be sexually transmitted; treated with a range of antifungal drugs

CDC   Centers for Disease Control; Atlanta-based federal agency responsible for monitoring and tracking patterns of infectious disease and other aspects of American public health; CDC staff initially noted the rising incidence of both *Pneumocystis carinii* pneumonia and Kaposi's sarcoma among gay men in 1981, and initiated the epidemiological investigation that alerted the public health community to the impending global health crisis

Cohn, Roy   closeted gay attorney, McCarthyite, Reagan fund-raiser; denied that he was a homosexual or had AIDS in 1986 to *People* magazine; died of AIDS

Compound Q   a cucumber derivative used as an abortifacient in China and reported to have *in vitro* activity against HIV

Compound S   code designator for AZT during laboratory research and development

cryptococcosis   a rare infection caused by inhaling the *cryptococcus neoformans* fungus that develops in soil contaminated by pigeon droppings; generally includes headache, stiffness of the neck, fever, drowsiness, blurred vision, and staggering gait as symptoms; ends in coma and death when not treated

cytomegalovirus   CMV; one of the family of *herpes* viruses; causes infected cells to take on enlarged appearance

Curran, James   director of the Division of HIV/AIDS at the Centers for Disease Control

Dannemeyer, William   California Republican, first elected to the U.S. House of Representatives in 1978; drafted Proposition 102, a proposal for mandatory contact tracing of HIV-infected people, which was defeated by California voters in 1988; led the movement in 1990 to expel Barney Frank from the U.S. House of Representatives for his involvement with a male prostitute

Delphi Projections   "guesstimate" technique developed by the World Health Organization Global Programme on AIDS for estimating maximum and minimum HIV prevalence rates by geographic region and subpopulations

dextran sulfate   an "orphan drug" used in the treatment of AIDS

Dritz, Selma   infectious disease specialist at the San Francisco Health Department who crusaded for public health education that would promote safer sexual practices

ELISA   Enzyme Linked Immunosorbent Assay; confirmatory blood test, developed in 1985, for the presence of HIV antibodies

endemic   refers to a disease that is constantly present in a particular region or specified population

epidemic   refers to a disease that, while ordinarily rare, suddenly spreads rapidly to a large number of people in a community or defined population

Factor VIII   one of several blood protein coagulants derived from multiple (2,000–5,000) blood donations; used to promote blood clotting in hemophiliacs; administered by intravenous injection

Falwell, Jerry   Moral Majority leader who has explained HIV/AIDS as divine retribution against homosexuals for their "war upon nature"

Fauci, Anthony   director of the National Institute of Allergy and Infectious Diseases

FDA   Food and Drug Administration; federal agency that regulates the availability of all drugs in the United States for use in medical therapies

Feinstein, Dianne   former mayor of San Francisco; unsuccessful candidate for Governor of California in 1990

fisting   inserting the hand or fist into the anus of a sex partner

Gallo, Robert   biomedical researcher; credited as the American scientist who discovered HIV, which he named HTLV-III, in 1984

gancyclovir   drug used in the treatment of CMV retinitis

Gay Men's Health Crisis, Inc.   community support organization founded in New York City on January 4, 1982 by Larry Kramer, Edmund White, and others to provide social services to people with HIV/AIDS

Gay Plague/Gay Cancer   terms used during 1981–1982 to describe the epidemic of Kaposi's sarcoma among gay men in the United States, Western Europe, and Australia

Gay-Related Immune Disorder   GRID; term used during 1981–1982 to describe the epidemic of opportunistic infections, particularly PCP, that resulted from an immune disorder of then-unknown cause

giardiasis   a parasitic infection of the small intestine characterized by violent diarrhea, abdominal discomfort, cramps or abdominal swelling, loss of appetite, and nausea

GPA   Global Programme on AIDS; agency within the World Health Organization responsible for monitoring and projecting worldwide HIV/AIDS prevalence, assisting in the development and implementation of in-country education and prevention activities

Harvey Milk Gay Democratic Club   initially organized to support Harvey Milk's candidacy for the San Francisco Board of Supervisors; continues to foster the inclusion of a gay political agenda in San Francisco municipal politics; competes with the Alice B. Toklas Club for gay political hegemony

Heckler, Margaret   Secretary of Health and Human Services, Reagan appointee

Helms, Jesse   North Carolina conservative Republican U.S. Senator who has supported mandatory quarantining of HIV-infected people

hemophilia   an inherited bleeding disorder caused by lack of blood proteins that cause clotting

hepatitis   Types A, B, NON-A/NON-B; blood-transmitted viral infections causing inflammation of the liver

HIV   Human Immunodeficiency Virus; replaced HTLV-III and LAV as the accepted designation for the retrovirus generally believed to cause the immune disorder and cluster of opportunistic infections designated as AIDS; HIV-1 and HIV-2 are variants of the HIV virus

HPA-23   antiviral drug available in France but not the United States during the mid-1980s; Rock Hudson, among others, traveled to France to receive HPA-23 treatments

HTLV-III   Human T-cell LymphoTropic virus; initial designation used by Robert Gallo in 1984 for the virus now named human immunodeficiency virus, HIV

isoprinosine   trade name for the orphan drug inosine pranobex, used to treat brain inflammation resulting from viral infections

Kaposi's sarcoma   malignant skin tumors, generally slow-growing and found almost exclusively in elderly Italian and Jewish men, but highly aggressive in people infected with HIV

Kramer, Larry   playwright and author; gay activist, cofounder of Gay Men's Health Crisis, founder of ACT UP; beginning in 1981, advocated sexual monogamy and led demands of increased public funding for HIV/AIDS research, education, and social services

Krim, Mathilde   AIDS activist; cofounder of American Foundation for AIDS Research

Lancet   British medical journal

LaRouche, Lyndon   conservative Republican California State Representative who drafted the referendum calling for mandatory quarantine of HIV-infected people, which was defeated in 1986

LAV   designation given by Luc Montagnier of the Pasteur Institute for the retrovirus he identified in his laboratory at the Pasteur Institute in 1984 as the cause of AIDS; now designated as HIV

Legionnaire's Disease   a form of pneumonia that caused the death of 29 members of the American Legion who attended a convention in a Philadelphia hotel in 1976; now known to be caused by a bacterium that breeds in warm, moist conditions

Mann, Johnathan   formerly director of the WHO Global Programme on AIDS; since 1991, coordinator of the Global AIDS Policy Coalition

Milk, Harvey   San Francisco City Supervisor who legitimized and formalized gay politics and who was shot and killed by Supervisor Dan White on November 27, 1978

MMWR   *Morbidity and Mortality Weekly Report;* CDC weekly publication circulated among physicians and public health officials that provides routine news, updates, and occasional special reports on health-related matters

Montagnier, Luc   French scientist, director of the Pasteur Institute, who shares credit for the discovery of HIV with American scientist Robert Gallo

Montezuma's revenge   popular designation for the form of amebiasis that U.S. tourists contract in Mexico

New York Native   New York City-based gay publication

NIAID   National Institute of Allergies and Infectious Diseases; sub-unit of NIH

NIH   National Institutes of Health

pandemic   refers to a disease that occurs over a large, rather than limited, geographical area and affects a high proportion of the world population, as opposed to limited and specifiable communities

papovavirus   one of more than 20 large families of viruses; the cause of papovi, or warts

Pasteur Institute   French biomedical research center, equivalent to the U.S. National Institutes of Health

pentamidine isethionate   established antibiotic drug therapy for *Pneumocystis carinii* pneumonia

***Pneumocystis carinii* pneumonia**   PCP or pc pneumonia; a form of pneumonia caused by the *Pneumocystis carinii* protozoan parasite; a major cause of death in people who have AIDS

PWAs   People With AIDS; generally used as a value-free referent alternative to "AIDS victims"

retrovirus   one of more than 20 large families of viruses; any of a family of RNA viruses, including ones causing leukemia, AIDS, and other viral diseases; a virus that modifies the genetic structure of host cells by re-creating itself

ribaviran   drug used in the treatment of respiratory viral conditions

rimming   running the tongue around, or inserting it into, the anus of a sex partner

Sencer, David   New York City Health Commissioner; opposed HIV/AIDS education programs in New York City

shigellosis   an acute intestinal infection caused by shigella bacteria, characterized by diarrhea and abdominal pain, nausea, vomiting, generalized aches, and fever

Silence=Death   ACT UP slogan

Silverman, Mervyn   San Francisco Health Commissioner; cofounder and president of the American Foundation for AIDS Research; supported bathhouse closings and HIV/AIDS education programs

simian   of or pertaining to apes or monkeys

Slim   popular name for HIV/AIDS in those parts of Africa where the wasting away of muscle tissues is one of the presenting symptoms of advanced HIV infection

suramin   a drug licensed to treat sleeping sickness that initially showed *in vivo* anti-HIV activity but proved to have severe side-effects

T-helper cells   CD4+ T-lymphocyte cells; those cells within the human immune system responsible for mobilizing the immune system; the cells which HIV attacks and destroys

Toklas, Alice B.   Gertrude Stein's lifelong companion

Toxic Shock Syndrome   a condition linked to the use of certain brands of tampons, which are no longer marketed in the United States; first recognized in the late 1970s

toxoplasmosis   an infection caused by the protozoan *toxoplasma gondii*, contracted most commonly through eating undercooked pork and lamb; characterized by a feverish illness resembling mononucleosis; in people with an immune system deficiency it can also cause retinitis, enlargement of the liver and spleen, lung and heart damage, and severe encephalitis (brain inflammation)

trimethoprimsulfamethoxazole   antibiotic drug therapy for PCP

Waxman, Henry   Democratic California Congressman; chaired the Congressional Subcommittee on Health and Environment, which investigated AZT pricing

Western Blot test   confirmatory test for HIV antibodies in the blood developed and marketed in 1985

WHO   World Health Organization

Index